James I

JAMES I
Attributed to Jan de Critz (National Maritime Museum, Greenwich)

JAMES I

DAVID MATHEW

EYRE & SPOTTISWOODE

LONDON

First published 1967
© *1967 David Mathew*
Printed in Great Britain for
Eyre & Spottiswoode (Publishers) Ltd.
11 New Fetter Lane, EC4
by Billing & Sons Limited
Guildford and London

for

Sherman and Jeanne Stonor

CONTENTS

CONTENTS

Appendices

ILLUSTRATIONS

ACKNOWLEDGEMENTS

I wish to express my gratitude to the Marquess of Salisbury and to Miss Clare Talbot, the archivist at Hatfield, and to Lord Egremont and Miss D. Beatrice Harris, the secretary at Petworth House, for details of books present in those two libraries in the reign of James I. I am likewise grateful to the Earl of Haddington for an opportunity to examine the volumes that have been at Tyninghame from that same period and to the Marquess of Lothian for showing me the portrait described as that of the Countess of Somerset at Monteviot. I am grateful to Thomas and Georgina Stonor for showing me the Kederminster Library in the parish church at Langley Marish. I have turned to my brother Gervase for his help at every stage.

I have had an opportunity to study the Jacobean portraits in the national collections in England and Scotland and should also like to mention among those in private hands the galleries at Melbourne Hall and Raveningham Hall and Parham. I should explain that I have incorporated in this book three or four brief passages from *The Jacobean Age* and *Scotland under Charles I* and a short description of Francis Bacon from *Sir Tobie Mathew*. It is difficult in going over a subject to find always a different set of words.

This book deals with that early seventeenth-century life in England that I have been considering all through my manhood. I have tried to suggest answers to the various problems. If one can see the men against their period, the judgments may not prove too severe. There have been many writers upon this reign since the days of S. R. Gardiner. I only wish to make my contribution to their joint efforts.

DAVID MATHEW

Stonor Park, *June* 1963

Stonor Park, *July* 1966

James I

INTRODUCTION

At the beginning of the last week of Advent in 1542 King James V of Scotland, the last of the senior old male line of the house of Stewart, died at Falkland Palace. The young king, with death upon him, had ridden in a few days previously; he had wandered almost aimlessly from place to place since the English had defeated his army. Falkland lay in the upland country of central Fife just to the eastward of the Lomond hills. Winter came early there with the December gales that drove down from the coast of Norway.

The queen was at Linlithgow, the most attractive of the royal palaces. She had borne two sons, who died in infancy, and the close of her third pregnancy was drawing near. The dying king awaited the birth of a prince of Scotland and the Isles. The news came to him that the queen had been delivered of a daughter.

The king left two legacies to the Scottish nation. He had built up, beyond the practice of his predecessors, the French alliance. He never went to England and France was the only foreign country that he ever visited; following the French court he went as far south as Lyons. He was first betrothed to Marie de Bourbon, the daughter of the duchess of Vendôme, and then made in succession two French marriages, the first with Madeleine, the child of Francis I, and, on her death, with the widowed duchess of Longueville. The second wife, better known as Marie de Guise-Lorraine, was regent throughout the minority of her child, the Queen of Scots.

It was also her influence that led to the eventual betrothal of the young queen to the French dauphin; she was sent to be brought up at the court of France in 1548 when not quite six years old. It was on the Queen of Scots that this French ancestry and the educational experiences of that foreign court would have impinged; but as a result of her separation from her son, they had little influence on James VI, who succeeded to the Scottish throne in 1567, a year after he was born, when Mary was driven from her throne.

On the other hand the natural sons of James V had a great influence on their young nephew. It seems in general true to say that the relations of James V with the great Scottish families had been poor. It may not be irrelevant that both James V and his father James IV had been accustomed to seek their passing mistresses among these stocks. James V had children by the daughters of lords Elphinstone and Carmichael, by Lady Elizabeth Stewart of Lennox, and by a daughter of Lord Erskine, who afterwards married Sir James Douglas of Lochleven. Three of these children were child-ecclesiastics as James IV's bastards had been before them, the younger generation including the priors of Holyrood and Coldingham and the abbot of Melrose. A fourth became prior of the Charterhouse at Perth. The only daughter was the countess of Argyll. The significant member of this family was the king's second natural son, Lord James, who later became famous as the regent Moray, the first of the four regents who ruled on behalf of the infant James VI after the departure of his mother, the Queen of Scots. To Moray succeeded three others of the great Scottish earls, Lennox and Mar, who lasted a year each, and Morton, who had nine years of rule.

It was in the years that followed the death of James V that the Reformation came to Scotland. There is to my mind a strange and purely accidental resemblance between the situation in Scotland under the regency of the queen dowager and that of France under King Henry II. In both cases there was a Catholic dynasty and episcopate, while among the great nobles of the two kingdoms the Genevan faith began to penetrate like quicksilver. It is worth noting that both the regent Moray and Gaspard de Coligny, to choose the most prominent examples, were converted by argument at a time when Catholicism was in power in both their countries. There were various types of Presbyterian magnate and some, like the regent Morton, had a definite prejudice against the ministers of their new faith. But for the most part they possessed a solid attachment to the Reformed Church of Scotland. There was a positive confidence in the Reformation values in those who ruled or educated King James VI.

In 1542 the close relations between Scotland and France, which would endure for almost another century and would later bring so many Presbyterian ministers and members of the Edinburgh legal stocks into the Huguenot portions of that country and many of the young sons of the Scottish lords into contact with the French capital and court, were already established but naturally at that date they were inevitably Catholic.

David Beaton, cardinal of San Stefano *in Monte Celio* and archbishop of St Andrews, likewise held the diocese of Mirepoix in France; the complex of titles indicates that ancient world. He had succeeded his uncle James Beaton in the archbishopric and his nephew of the same names would become archbishop of Glasgow and die in France in 1603. But Cardinal Beaton had not lasted long. He had been killed at the end of May 1546 in the sea tower at the castle of St Andrews by the master of Rothes.

It is interesting that, while a supporter of the French alliance, he did not favour the Queen of Scots' marriage to the dauphin. It has always seemed to me that neither of the parties who were anxious to marry the young queen to the king of France or to the king of England were acting as Scottish patriots. How could Scotland have then been saved from domination by a foreign power? It was in fact only the early death of Francis II which brought the queen back to her own country.

The most important factor in the reign was Lord Darnley's marriage to the queen. His murder and the queen's flight to England left the prince of Scotland to all intents and purposes an orphan. There then followed the succession of the four regents. Their principal effect on the personal life of James VI was the development of that deep belief in Presbyterian doctrine with which, through his tutors, they inspired him. This was principally the thought-out policy of the earl of Moray. Throughout his life the king was a believer like all the sovereigns of his time, except those kings and queens who had been touched by the spirit of the Renaissance. Further he gained an equally vivid belief in the devil, a fact which deeply harassed his uncourageous mind. When he came to England it was the clear conviction of his Protestant beliefs which so much encouraged the English churchmen.

At this point it is worth attempting to make some reconstruction of the king's relations with his Scottish lords. Scotland was an ancient and indeed an old-fashioned monarchy. There was not that separation between the sovereign and the greater courtiers, which Queen Elizabeth had built up in the southern kingdom. There was not that great gulf which lay between the Tudors and all their subjects. For nine generations the Stewarts had been merely the ruling family among many equals. The young king started a process in the Scottish courts to claim that he was heir-at-law to the countess of Lennox. His relations with the Erskines, the children of the regent Mar, were in some respects fraternal. Later he adopted two successive generations of his cousins, the Stuarts of Aubigny.

B

3

And what went for friendship, also affected enmity. There was in his approach nothing of that royal coldness which led Queen Elizabeth and her father to sacrifice succeeding heads of the house of Howard. In fact King James pursued the Gowries with the enmity of an equal. The other side of the picture is also seen in his kind relations with the earl of Huntly. No Scottish princess of the Stewart line, except his mother, had ever been queen of a foreign country. There was a nexus of blood relationship with the great nobles of his own land.

The king was in no sense a traveller. He never left the British Isles, save for his wedding journey to Norway and Denmark, nor is there any sign that he ever planned or wished to do so. Until he came to England the bulk of the influences from abroad which reached him all came from France. This is seen in the influence of his tutors and in his early attempts at verse, which so much depended on translations from the French, and in the effect upon him of Esmé Stuart of Aubigny. The king admired the French court and way of life, but not the sovereigns of that country. It is worth nothing that, although his mother's first husband had been a Valois prince and his grandfather's first wife a Valois princess, King James himself was not even distantly related to them. Though Henry III of France had the same temperament as he had, the method of his life was quite remote. King James had no sympathy with the Medicean inheritance of that last generation of the Valois house. During his later life Henry IV, that well-informed prince, knew all about him and made fun of him. All this being said, it may seem strange that, when the king came to England, the crown of Spain had such an effect on his imagination.

Various factors had brought him to sympathise with Spain, which was the counter-Reformation monarchy *par excellence*. There was the long course of his thought on kingship; more and more he conceived the royal office as God-given and authoritarian. In the various chapters I have endeavoured to describe the slow evolution of his ideas. There was an element of the *static* in his own conception of monarchy and this chimed with certain attitudes of the Spanish Hapsburgs. There were also restrictions on his knowledge; in effect, in the case of both the kingdoms of France and Spain it all came through ambassadors or through persons whose functions were in part ambassadorial.

In the six years that preceded his mother's death, King James had one guide and two favourites; Aubigny who became the duke of Lennox, James Stewart of Ochiltree and, finally, the master of Gray. The

4

principal problem in Lennox's brief history is the question of his religion. For myself I believe that he had a deep indifference in all questions of denominational belief and was what the French termed a *politique*.

James Stewart is of all those close to King James the man of whom we have least knowledge. He was, perhaps, the first who inspired the king with fear: that emotion which was aroused in him by the earl of Bothwell and in a greater or a lesser degree by all the members of the house of Gowrie. This guide and these favourites are each the subject of a separate chapter. They cover the portion of the reign which ended with the execution of the Queen of Scots. The great gulf between the politics and intrigues of the queen and her son's ideas are then set out.

James VI was an only child, lonely and isolated, buoyed up by his conception of the fact of kingship. It was this, perhaps which separated him from his first favourites, for he let James Stewart and the master of Gray go right out of his life. It may be said that in both these cases there was a failure of loyalty; this was always a defect that the crowned and anointed king would not forgive.

It is one of the difficult aspects of King James's thought that as he came to manhood there were two different forms in which he regarded his religion. On the one hand there was his strongly held belief in the traditional forms of Presbyterian doctrine. He never doubted that it was superior in truth to Romanism. He was a king and did not believe in any case in equality; but it was especially impossible for him to have an equal relationship with a Roman Catholic. To give just one example, his friendship for Huntly did not go so far as to allow him to bring up his son and heir in the old religion. In England, too, except perhaps at the very end of his life when the old tired sovereign fell under the influence of the countess of Buckingham, he was always to act as a proselytising king.

It is his attitude to the devil which is strange to us. He was always conscious of the enmity with which the Powers of Evil bore down upon him. The king was full of fear of the devil and his dark monarchy. For this reason the published work of James I on *Daemonologie* is of real value to an understanding of his fears. As a personal opinion, it seems to me that this has a bearing on his reactions to the earl of Bothwell's warlocks and on his attitude towards the house of Gowrie.

It was in the years following his mother's death that there took place his marriage to the princess of Denmark. King James never showed any interest in women, except as ancillary to the domestic scene; he evinced

5

a mild concern for them in their place as wives or mothers to his own friends. He seems always to have remembered that his consort was of the blood royal of a foreign kingdom. In time his personal contacts with her diminished; he had no respect for the queen's *mind*. In two chapters I deal with the queen's religion in Scotland and in England. This is a subject on which my views have modified over the years. It is still not really clear at which small foreign court she first came into contact with the Roman faith. The chief significance of this question is the effect that it produced on the king's relations with his wife. It is clear that the king was irritated by the political consequences which resulted from the queen's wavering interest in the church of Rome.

It was at the time of his marriage that the king's verse-making ceased, and he only revived this practice on occasions in the last years of his life. He was very young when he first wrote upon this subject and his comments were shrewd and balanced; but in the actual construction of verse he had, in fact, a very slender talent.

The last twelve years of the king's rule in Scotland, before his accession to the English throne, saw the first period of his maturity. There was now nothing complex about his foreign policy; he must just wait with composure for the death of the queen of England. He had made a marriage to which she could raise no technical objection and in 1594 his wife had given birth to a prince of Scotland. Now with the passage of time he was treated with more respect and his love of hunting made him acceptable to his Scottish subjects. He began to appoint his ministers for their utility, quite apart from the question of his liking for them; the first example was the choice of Maitland of Thirlestane as lord chancellor. The chapter on the Octavians describes his fluctuating relations with the various royal officers and his incompetence in money matters is underlined.

The king seems to have aged rapidly and, although only in the late thirties at the end of this period, he had already developed those jocose almost middle-aged friendships with the great courtiers whom he had known since childhood. At this time there was conflict with some of the leaders of the Kirk of Scotland and notably with Andrew Melville. The king's political ideas and his conceptions of the kingship are set out in the chapter on the royal study entitled *Basilikon Doron*.

In August 1600 there took place those events at Gowrie House, which have never been satisfactorily explained and to which it is possible that the key is lost to us. The details and the explanations offered are set out in Chapter 11. It seems likely that the king's life-long fear of the house of Gowrie had a bearing on the catastrophe in which the earl and his brother the master lost their lives.

In 1598 the king had written *The Trew Law of Free Monarchies*. It is of interest to note that it was not in Scotland but in his future kingdom that his work was perused most carefully. It was in the last two years of the queen's reign that the Cecil–Howard correspondence was begun. The correspondence sent by Sir Robert Cecil, with whom was joined Lord Henry Howard, to prepare him for the succession to the English crown is studied in some detail. We must detach ourselves from the practice of the modern world to savour the effect which the high style of compliment used by both these writers produced upon the Scottish king. On March 24, 1603, the queen of England died. The king of Scotland, who was the heir-general of the house of Tudor, succeeded in her place.

It would seem that in Scotland few had read King James's books; but in England the statesmen, the livelier-minded bishops and the judges had made them the object of a painful study. It seems to me that the king had a certain simplicity of character and valued all the praise that came to him. Certainly once he had come to England he liked to write light-hearted letters to the great men of his court and to receive replies well-couched in adulation; it was a style that Sir Walter Raleigh never learned.

The events of the reign in England are described in the degree that they came into King James's life. Thus the Gunpowder plot seems to have remained always in his mind; he reverted to it again and again throughout his years of rule. After all, its discovery was in part due to his sagacity and he could not fail to remember that gunpowder had been used to kill his father. It appears that he judged that the attempt to destroy a mortal king was the extremity of evil. The justices and the counsel in their speeches reflected with accuracy his own opinions on this subject. Among the very few state trials that the king attended was that of Father Garnet and for this reason it is described in detail. The king was there behind the lattice as his counsel knew well while they poured out their compliments.

Parallel with such contacts was the king's work at the conference at Hampton Court, where he first met his English bishops. The question of the king's relations with the different members of the English bench is then examined. Looked at from one angle it may be said that this section of the book deals with the king's reception in his new kingdom by those of his greater subjects who had studied the *Basilikon Doron.*

The English court was much more elaborate than that of Scotland. There was the constant come-and-go of the many on whom in his first years the king conferred the honour of knighthood. There was nothing of that loyal intimacy with which he had been received by his Scottish courtiers. He had placed himself in the hands of Sir Robert Cecil, whom he soon created earl of Salisbury. James I would support him for so long as he proved useful to his royal master. The detail of the chapter on the years of peace suggests the king's multifarious preoccupations and also the limitations of his own experience.

It is to be remembered that on certain questions the views of the king and his great servant were identical. James I was a peace-loving sovereign and Salisbury was by temperament and judgment a peace minister. Both fitted well together in what was in some ways an old-fashioned government. Salisbury well understood the need to keep in good repair his relations with those Scottish lords who were responsible for the administration of the northern kingdom. And while thus maintaining a sound alliance with his Scottish equals, he never in any way interfered with the king's generosity towards his poor compatriots, who had come south with him. It was at this stage of his life that James I displayed his love of *giving.*

Salisbury was also aided by the king's laziness; he often hunted while his ministers were in council. He planned hunting boxes like Ampthill, which would in fact have been a small country palace. The king was not a great huntsman, although he gave up so much time to this pursuit. At this period of his life he would begin the day in his hunting coach, an English innovation. Later he would mount; he loved riding quietly in the open air. He enjoyed staying in great houses and moving from place to place with a fine retinue. He came to know the countryside quite well, although he never penetrated the south-west or crossed the border into Wales.

He had no knowledge of the nascent industry and never himself showed concern for economic matters. He had little contact with the English mercantile world. In later life he welcomed Sir Lionel Cranfield as he hoped that he would relieve him in his necessities. It seems that he never saw that his sale of peerages and also his creation and then sale of baronetcies were bound to curdle his relationship with wealthy men.

In a chapter dealing with Francis Bacon I try to explain how uncongenial Bacon was to the king in spite of the fact that his political ideas were so regalian. They were both learned men; but Bacon was not at ease with the narrow content of the king's learning. The notions of James I were always positive; he had gained the practice of assertion in Scotland long ago. He had no conception of those wide lines of enquiry which were one side of Bacon's thinking, what the nineteenth century Germans called *Verulamisch*. In fact he played but little part in the king's life.

For a quite different reason Lady Arabella Stuart meant little to her sovereign. She was the king's first cousin and until the birth of Prince Henry next in succession to the English but not the Scottish throne. She was on the fringe of the court in England from the king's accession until her imprisonment. But she is an example of someone whom that court could not assimilate. The Puritan strain in her character deprived her of any sympathy from the queen and her ladies, while her sex placed her outside the king's preoccupations. It is difficult to understand what led William Seymour to marry her.

The king's last two favourites were Robert Carr and George Villiers. In both cases James I decided for rather different reasons to leave the imprint of his mind on these disciples. There is much that is not known about Robert Carr (or Kerr) and the history of his contacts with his relations. Almost the whole of Carr's period of influence coincided with the imprisonment and then the death of his mentor, Sir Thomas Overbury. In time this was followed by the trial of Carr and his wife on the charge of poisoning the prisoner. With this was bound up the history of the Suffolk Howards, and of their guide and uncle Lord Henry Howard, now earl of Northampton. As in the other conspiracies and trials there is more than one solution that can be offered.

Before considering the period of the ascendancy of Sir George Villiers, who became the duke of Buckingham, I describe the court masques and plays and the development of those great houses which can fitly be called the Jacobean palaces. And all the time, once Salisbury was dead, there was the oscillating character of the king's foreign policy, that rather strange marriage of the king's only daughter with the Elector Palatine, and then the constant pull of the idea of a Spanish wedding first for Prince Henry and after his death for his brother Prince Charles. It is difficult for us to realise the deep attraction which the count of Gondomar had for the king.

9

James I was very solitary in these Spanish preferences, as he was later in his insistence on the emperor's rights in Bohemia, where his son-in-law proclaimed himself king. There was also the element of Spanish influence in his decision to execute Sir Walter Raleigh. His approaches involved a strange schematic support for the Hapsburg sovereigns. This came from the ideas of the *Basilikon Doron*; to most Englishmen it was incomprehensible.

There is an account of the king's visit to Scotland in 1618. This was the year before the queen's death and the last period of his activity before his health slowly began to fail. This coincided with the real domination of the Villiers family. In time Buckingham became, what Salisbury had never been or wished to be, the actual fount of honour. The nomination to peerages still remained in the hands of the ailing sovereign but increasingly appointments, in particular those of envoys abroad, and the sale of titles became a matter for the favourite. It was, in fact, a great misfortune for the king when his surviving son made up his early quarrel with George Villiers. Henceforward the prince and the favourite between them increasingly excluded King James from final influence. It was they who managed the journey to Madrid and the break with Spain that followed on this. The king could not save Lionel Cranfield, when the favourite had quarrelled with him. James I had displayed an intense interest in his early parliaments, without perhaps fully grasping the English system; but now he was lackadaisical. Perhaps the man nearest to him in these final years was Bishop Williams, who assisted at his death bed. He was like the bishops that he had known in Scotland, very consciously a man of family, and there was something in his broad coarse humour that made the king at home with him.

In domestic matters the king fell under the control of the Villiers family. It marked the change in him that a certain influence was acquired by the unattractive and managing countess of Buckingham. Towards the end he could never exert a separate power or free himself from their society. On this last point there is no evidence that he wished to do so. On March 27, 1625, the king died at Theobalds, the great house where he had been received by Sir Robert Cecil twenty-two years earlier. He had coveted and obtained it and rebuilt it. The house lay on his favourite line of travel, the London to Newmarket road: it has now vanished.

PART ONE

The Reign in Scotland

THE KING'S BACKGROUND

THE prince of Scotland was christened in the last days of Advent 1566. His godparents were the queen of England and the king of France, whose ambassadors presented on their behalf a great golden font and a necklace of pearls and rubies. The duke of Savoy gave a large fan with jewelled feathers. The comte de Brienne, ambassador-extraordinary of France, bore the six-month-old child into the chapel royal at Stirling Castle. The earl of Atholl carried the great sierge of wax and the earl of Eglinton the salt, Lord Ross the basin and laver and Lord Sempill the rood. Archbishop Hamilton performed the christening with Catholic rites. The countess of Argyll acted on behalf of the queen of England. The lords of the Reformed religion stood at the chapel door. The prince's mother was present at the christening, but not his father. Within a year the child would be proclaimed as King James VI of Scotland. It is best to begin this study with an attempt to estimate the character and influence of both his parents.

Henry Stewart, Lord Darnley, better known by this style than as duke of Albany and the titular King Henry, had a short life and one which was eminently miserable. He never lived to inherit property; he was only fifteen at his wife, Mary's, first widowhood; his own marriage lasted only eighteen months and the union ended in his murder. His significance was almost wholly genealogical. He was the queen's first cousin, for his mother Lady Margaret Douglas was half-sister to King James V of Scotland; through his father, that dim character the regent Lennox, he was one of the two claimants to the heirship of the throne of Scotland. The other was the duke of Châtelhèrault. In a period of religious conflict he was, it seems, like his father, wholly without religious beliefs of any kind. He was in no sense a sceptic, only not a thinker. His father Matthew, earl of Lennox, had begun life as a Catholic with an ardent, perhaps partly superstitious, attachment to masses for the dead. He then became a Presbyterian and fled to England, lived as a Protestant under Edward VI, as a Catholic under Mary Tudor, and finally in a kind of snug neutrality under Elizabeth. The prospect of the regency of Scotland brought him back to the Presbyterian church.

Darnley's mother had trained him to attain to the crown matrimonial of Scotland by his marriage with the young queen. Lady Lennox had the ravaging Douglas blood and had given him a chart of his alliances. It must have been a lonely childhood with his parents and his younger brother. No neighbours came to them. His mother was an unprepossessing woman given to playing politics with the Catholic powers. She haunted the Spanish embassy in the early days of Elizabeth I. Not surprisingly she and her husband and her elder son lay to the north of that queen's favour.

Darnley was tall and slender and, apart from other reasons, too immature for Queen Elizabeth. His best surviving portrait is that with his brother, attributed at present to Hans Eworth. They are standing in a long gallery, panelled in light oak, at Temple Newsam; perhaps because the house was new, the background has a suggestion of emptiness. Darnley is only seventeen, but already growing tall with those long slender legs which the Queen of Scots admired. He is dressed wholly in black with a white ruff and white sleeve cuffs. He is holding in his left hand what looks like a pomander box. His hair is described as a sharp yellow, but in this picture it seems darker. He has the gaze of innocence, a virginal look which he would lose.

He came north without any serious financial resources and without a single friend. The arrogance that he soon developed had its roots in the fact that he had never known his equals. He had a good seat on a horse, but otherwise a slender education. He is said to have had accomplished penmanship; the assertion that he translated Valerius Maximus into English has little value.[1] In the early stages of his relationship with the Queen of Scots it was fortunate that he was skilful with the lute. He did not go to any university.

Lord Darnley was just nineteen when he set off for Scotland. He was in fact a cypher, carrying with him only those glorious descents of high Scots blood, which his son later would so prize. The marriage with his nearest relative had been for long a possibility obscured for a time by the abortive negotiations between the Queen of Scots and Don Carlos, the king of Spain's sickly heir; the union seems, however, to have had some six good months, but the marriage tie was then damaged by Darnley's fondness for the bottle and by his infidelity.

[1] It was made by Bishop Montague in his introduction to King James's *Works*, printed in 1616.

The name of David Rizzio would pursue King James VI throughout his life in Scotland. At this time he was in his middle thirties, the son of a musician in the township of Pancalieri in Piedmont, and he had come to Scotland with the Savoyard ambassador. He became bass singer in the queen's private chapel and then secretary for foreign letters, although his French was rather poor. There seems no truth in the rumour that he was the queen's lover, but he was a disturbing political influence for the Scottish lords. Darnley joined with the principal men about the court, who murdered him at supper in the queen's privy chamber. Then he betrayed his allies to the queen, but his own guilt was soon discovered by her. Darnley was nineteen and his life was finished.

He spoke of going abroad, but there was no country that would welcome him. The queen had been six months with child when Rizzio was murdered. Darnley took refuge in the west of Scotland, but was later brought back to Edinburgh so that he might publicly recognize his infant son. He fell ill with what was officially termed smallpox, but may have been venereal. For convalescence, he was taken in a litter, which had been specially fitted up for him,[1] to the deserted house of Kirk o'Fields, near the church of St Mary-in-the-Fields on the outskirts of Edinburgh. In the *salle* there was a small Turkey carpet and a canopy of black velvet over a high chair covered with leather. In the room above stood a great bed of violet velvet with curtains laced with gold and silver and a bedspread of quilted taffeta. There was a *chaise percée* with velvet fittings. He must have thought it was all very French. Three servants slept on a gallery towards the south. When the bell of St Giles' down in the town rang out for two o'clock in the morning of February 10, 1567, a mine was exploded under the house which was totally destroyed. Darnley and his young body-servant were found strangled in a garden some forty yards away. They had probably escaped as soon as they were awakened by the sound of tunnelling. Henry Lord Darnley was only twenty-one and there is not much more to be said about him.

The Queen of Scots is another matter altogether. Agreement is not likely to be found about her life and motives. To me she seems to belong to the small group of the queens of the high Renaissance, with Catherine de Medici and Elizabeth of England. For these minds the movement and control of political factors remained the abiding problem. The personalities with whom they dealt most easily moved within a culti-

[1] The details of the furnishing are printed in Agnes Mure Mackenzie, ed., *Scottish Pageant* (1948), 179.

vated pattern. Religious elements were trimmed into place, a very secondary interest. Such was the standpoint of Catherine de Medici, but many would, for divergent reasons, hold that this did not apply to the two British queens.

By descent Queen Mary came of two contrasted stocks. Her father's line was marked by a sensuality that was quite uncontrolled and her mother's by that character of the princesses of the house of Guise from Lorraine on the German borderlands, a slow-moving brood, withdrawn and a trifle heavy. Her grandmother, the old duchess of Guise who in part brought her up, was French of the royal stock of Bourbon-Vendôme. The Queen of Scots had one step-brother, the duke of Longueville, but he died too young to influence her. All the same her training and upbringing were wholly French. She was destined to be the child bride of the dauphin; but Francis II died in 1560 and left her at eighteen a childless queen.

These years at the Valois court had an effect upon the outlook of the Queen of Scots. Her religious style was that of the French court of the high Renaissance. She was formed before the counter-Reformation. The leading figures of her childhood were the French king's wife Catherine de Medici and his mistress Madame de Valentinois. All this had its effect upon her: she was not exacting in the moral sphere. Her uncles and grand-uncles the cardinals of Guise and of Lorraine held a vast number of abbeys. She came from the old lax Catholic world. She was very calm about the long succession of Italian pontiffs.

There are different angles from which her attachment to Catholic worship can be regarded, but according to her status and the age in which she lived her chapel was a royal appurtenance which it was against her dignity to surrender. Neither the queen, nor her maids of honour, the four Maries, had a shred of fanaticism in their composition. She was easy with the Reformed religion when this could be expressed with any calmness. At the French court she had met its adepts, like the queen of Navarre and the Amirale de Coligny. Among the train of courtiers whom she brought to Scotland was Chatelard, a Huguenot. She was very royal and with this there went a strain of cruelty: she was ready to order the execution of Chatelard and, in another sphere, that of John Gordon the earl of Huntly's younger son. Above all, she possessed, beyond any princess of her time, a sense of theatre.

She was slender as a wand and had, with a lovely voice, the beautiful movements of the court of France. It is said that she was seen at her best when she came back again to her native country wearing her white *deuil*, the half-mourning in memory of her young husband. This threw into relief her fair complexion. She would sit surrounded by her maids in a chestnut velvet dressing gown with silver cords, while the great fires blazed up in the big stone fireplaces at Holyrood.[1] On grand days she would wear her cabochon rubies, the table diamond from the king of France, the verdingale with pearls on either side. In France she had, perhaps, been too tall. Unlike the queen of England she never overdid the jewellery. Was she herself beautiful? No portraits painted during her years in Scotland now survive. The effigies brought out after her death are in some respects repellent. It would seem that she had a clear evanescent attractiveness when she was young.

She was in some ways solitary, as her son would be and for much the same reason. Her whole being was steeped in the French Valois culture. She had a knowledge of Latin and some Italian. With one or two exceptions, this form of culture found no reflection among the Scots lords and their wives. It does not seem unfair to suggest that the queen's approach to the idea of assassination for reasons of state was unlikely to have been different from that traditional among the Guises and the Medici, which had come down unimpeded from the fifteenth century. There is only one thing to be said for that court standpoint: it never permitted murder of the poor. In this matter I do not wish to go too far. I would only state that the idea of a political killing was unlikely to prove abhorrent to the Queen of Scots.

The death of Darnley, not in itself significant, seems to mark the end of the old Scotland which, in foreign affairs, was based on the French alliance between royal houses of the same religion. We now come to the sixteen years when Scotland was ruled by her own great lords, the earl of Bothwell and the four earls who held in turn the regency. One is always conscious of the quasi-ascendancy and ultimately of the rule of the earl of Morton, the chief among Darnley's murderers who fifteen years later was beheaded for that crime. There is something mediaeval in the crudeness of that power exercised under the shadow of retribution. The queen's reign was bleak with Darnley dead.

These points being made, we come to the public actions of the Queen of Scots. She was always in the presence of an unfriendly opinion, a Catholic sovereign returning to her country which had accepted the

---

[1] Cf. *Accounts of the Lord High Treasurer*, 1559–66, for the court furnishings.

Geneva discipline. Her enemies have said that she ordered the murder of her second husband. It does not seem to me to be so; there are many alternatives. Perhaps she knew with her Renaissance mind that something like this was bound to happen. It seems to me that it is her third marriage to the Earl of Bothwell which presents the difficulty. Her admirers, and they are many, accept the statement that she was ravished by Bothwell within two months of Darnley's death. It seems likely she was fascinated by his virility and by his ability to speak in French with her. But when did this fascination first develop?

There does not seem to have been much premeditation, for it was only a year previously that Bothwell had been married at the court to Lady Jean Gordon, Lord Huntly's youngest child. Possibly the happenings at Kirk o'Fields revealed to the queen her loneliness. As soon as she had been "abducted" by Bothwell the countess of Bothwell's marriage was successfully called in question. The earl was then created duke of Orkney and married to the queen according to the Presbyterian formulas by Adam Bothwell, who had formerly been consecrated by Catholic rites as bishop of that island diocese. The marriage lasted just a month. The most favourable comment on Lord Bothwell was made by Sir Francis Walsingham who described him as "a glorious [in the old-fashioned sense of that expression], rash and Hazardous young man". His properties, the title of Lord Admiral, his wardenship of all three marches held in common, his lordship of Liddesdale, his castle of Hermitage, all belonged to an earlier Scotland. From the day she left him, his name seems never to have been mentioned by the Queen of Scots.

The queen's critics draw attention to the casket letters. These are eight in number and were produced at the investigation which took place in England after the queen's flight there. They were the subject of strong controversy in the nineteenth century between those who accepted their authenticity and the queen's defenders, who declared them to be forgeries. They were said to have been found by Morton's agents in a silver box under a bed in Potter Row. According to the same account the lock was prized in the presence of Atholl, Mar, Glencairn, Morton and others. Inside was found the correspondence addressed to Bothwell in the queen's handwriting. They were produced at York in Scots and there has been dispute as to whether they were stated to be originals or translations. The letters are all undated, but the last four were clearly written after Darnley's death. To me these letters seem too clumsy to be forgeries.[1] Surely if one is constructing evidence one would give more point to it? The long second letter is another question; this clearly states the queen's responsibility for Darnley's murder. To my mind this may well have been a fabrication. The labour of subordinates at its construction would seem a small matter if it made sure that the Queen of Scots did not return in freedom to her own country. She was not a woman who forgave her enemies.

Meanwhile, these matters could not affect at once the infant Prince James. He had been taken at birth to Stirling Castle and had been placed under the charge of the earl of Mar. The queen was about to leave her kingdom and the four successive regents, Moray, Lennox, Mar and Morton, were all about him. After Darnley's murder there was no more life in the queen's attempt to reign. There were two small military engagements at Carberry Hill and Langside, mere shadow conflicts in which the queen had no confidence in those who were nominally upon her side. She had deserted Bothwell and had no trust in what the Hamiltons might do to help her. The duke of Châtelhèrault was in France in exile, but his sons rallied to her. They were merely the enemies of her former friends, a cautious, unbalanced, saturnine family. Nevertheless it is only fair to say that after the Bothwell marriage she could hardly inspire her various friends with confidence.

The Queen of Scots had at first renounced her throne, then, after she went to England, had put forth her claims again. She was to live there in captivity for the first twenty years of her son's reign. Henceforward she was only on the periphery of Scottish history.

[1] The most careful discussion of the problem of the Casket letters is that contained in Andrew Lang, *Mystery of Mary Stuart* (1901).

Chapter 2

THE KING'S CHILDHOOD

AMONG the four regents who ruled during the minority of James VI –
the earls of Moray, Lennox, Mar and Morton – it seems a misfortune
that the earl of Moray did not survive to guide his nephew. There was
a strong resemblance, in spite of the very different nature of their
personal lives, in the attitude of the regent Orleans and the earl of
Moray towards their two young charges. At the beginning of his
regency Moray was thirty-six, but old beyond his years. He was
destined always to the second place between his sovereign and the
Scottish nobles. He had the gift of foresight, in the sixteenth-century
meaning of that expression. He was akin by temperament to those
French great nobles who were likewise wedded to Genevan doctrines.
He was strictly moral; a God-fearing Calvinist; his health a little
weak, he was never free from stomach trouble. He was like the great
bâtards of the fifteenth century in France and the Low Countries, who
gave their lives to supporting the stock which fathered them.

Except for the strain of Tudor blood, Moray was completely Scottish.
His mother had been Lady Margaret Erskine, a daughter of the earl
of Mar; this was a matter of some significance when a royal bastard's
standing was determined by his mother's rank. It was characteristic
of the complicated relationship of the great houses that he was a step-
brother to the family of Douglas of Lochleven. He was the nearest male
relative to James VI. As was customary with the royal bastards at this
time he was, with King James's three other sons, destined to the service
of the Church and had received the priorities of St Andrews and
Pittenweems *in commendam* as also the priory of Mâcon in France. He
had turned away later from this way of life and after a betrothal,
which was broken, to the countess of Buchan, he decided to regain his
uncle's appanage as earl of Moray.

It was not for nothing that his companion and adviser, Maitland
of Lethington, should be almost the one Scotsman of his time to be
called Machiavellian in his own country. Moray was probably the
only man in Scotland who had those long cold views which would

have been of value to his young nephew. By temperament and design he stood aloof from the two great state murders of his time. He never failed to understand the crucial significance of Queen Elizabeth and to penetrate her preferences and her designs. His one mistake was to have permitted the Darnley marriage. Like his French prototypes it was his house that he served and not its members. His genuine attachment to the house of Stuart went with a readiness to jettison the Queen of Scots. It was in that sense her misfortune to give birth to a prince of Scotland.

It was natural that his taking over the regency when the rule of Queen Mary ended at Carberry Hill should have meant a complete breach between the earl of Moray and his former mistress. His ideas were strictly practical and he had to bear at times with that sense of the theatrical which both Queen Mary and the queen of England employed in dealing with their friends and servants. He had not time to show his power to rule in Scotland.

He had a slowly forged diplomacy, Gallic in its inspiration. He could checkmate, balance and control his many rivals. He was clear-sighted and lonely without the henchmen and dependants which the other great peers might call upon. His step-brother Lord John Stewart was now dead. His young wife had only two baby daughters. Isolated as he was, it may be considered that he had neutralised the hostility of the great families except the danger from the house of Hamilton. It was his mistake that in his seat of power he was too amenable to his great equals. He was the only one of the four regents who in that position really satisfied the Queen of England. Sir Francis Walsingham would never fail to praise so clear a Protestant. It was in part courtesy towards the southern kingdom that led him to allow the return of the Hamiltons to Scotland. This meant the end of the "good Regent".

The Hamiltons will be considered in more detail when King James's relationships with the next generation are examined. Suffice to say that they had the hostility to the regent which the next heirs to the throne would always manifest. As a family grouping they would prove both weak and implacable. They had a very lax control of their adherents. Their house was at a serious disadvantage. Their leader was the old duke of Châtelhèrault, who had been regent in Queen Mary's childhood. His eldest son, the earl of Arran, had long been a *prétendant* for the queen's hand and was now incurably insane. They had played their hands with unwise caution; they had been stiff with

Queen Mary when Moray had been smooth with her; later they adopted the thankless *rôle* of Protestant Marians. They had been in exile and Moray had permitted their return. In the end it may be said that Scotland was too wild for his careful systems.

Moray's rule lasted just over two years until January 22, 1570, when Bothwellhaugh, a kinsman of the duke's, shot him with his old carbine from behind the curtains of the Hamilton house as he rode through Linlithgow. It was just an ineffectual political assassination; it did the Hamiltons no good. The archbishop, in whose house Bothwellhaugh had been concealed, was hanged and his half-brother the duke of Châtelhèrault retired from public life. After a period of weak health he died at Hamilton Palace four years later.

The next two years were a period of disturbance, which it is hardly accurate to describe as civil war. The Queen of England had pressed for the nomination as regent of the earl of Lennox, Darnley's father. He was nearly half a generation older than Moray and was now fifty-five. If Bothwell belonged to the old Scotland, Matthew, earl of Lennox, was representative of those tangled years when Mary of Guise had ruled in Edinburgh. He was a great lord, who had then given himself to English policies. This was more possible when nationalism had hardly crystallised as far as the ruling families were concerned. Lennox was still almost the bondsman of the Queen of England. He came to Scotland without his wife; she had been retained in England by that queen's wishes. The earl of Lennox was uxorious, but otherwise his character is hardly clear to us. Among the regents he was the closest in relationship to the young king, who was his grandson. He also did the least for him. He had a certain military skill and at least kept alive the fighting. He was killed after a year in some trivial conflict; he had in no sense pacified the country.

His successor, chosen by the Scottish lords, was the young king's guardian, the earl of Mar. During his regency he still retained the guardianship of his child sovereign. He bequeathed to James VI the lifelong friendship of the Erskine family. During his short rule the influence of the earl of Morton was always growing. They had known one another well through all the turmoil of the recent years. Mar acted in harmony with Morton, perhaps because he feared him.

It appears that the regent Mar died from illness and not from poison, but a passage from the *Memoirs* of Sir James Melville gives the rumours of that time.

After this [he writes] the Regent [Mar] went to Edinburgh to convene the Lords of Council, to show them the calamities that our civil wars produced, and to let them see how necessary an agreement would be for the whole country. In the meantime until the appointed council-day, he went to Dalkeith, where he was nobly treated by the Lord of Morton; shortly after which he took a vehement sickness, which caused him to ride suddenly to Stirling, where he died regretted by many. Some of his friends and the vulgar suspected he had gotten wrong at his banquet.[1]

It seems likely that the return of the dying earl of Mar to Stirling Castle was the first time that the events of Scottish history impinged upon the memory of the young sovereign. He had been brought up under a system arranged by the earl of Moray with teachers very carefully selected. The arrangement was to last all his childhood. As a companion he had his guardian's son Lord Erskine, who was only four years his senior. They were educated alone together.

Sir James Melville shows how the different elements in this education struck a contemporary:

Now the young King [he wrote] was brought up in Stirling by Alexander Erskine and my Lady Mar. He had four principal masters, Mr George Buchanan, Mr Peter Young, [and] the Abbots of Cambuskenneth and Dryburgh, descended from the house of Erskine. The Laird of Drumhasel was master of the household. Alexander Erskine was a gallant, well-natured gentleman, loved and honoured by all men for his good qualities and great discretion, noways factious or avaricious, a lover of all honest men, and desired ever to see men of good conversation about the Prince [rather] than his own nearer friends if he found them not so meet.

The Laird of Drumwhasel again was ambitious and greedy, his greatest care was to advance himself and his friends. The two Abbots were wise and modest. My Lady Mar was wise and sharp, and held the King in great awe; and so did Mr George Buchanan.[2]

This wording is a little confusing, but it clearly means that the countess and Mr Buchanan held the king in great awe of them. The next sentence will make this meaning plain.

Mr Peter Young was more gentle, and was loath to offend the King at any time, carrying himself more warily, as a man who had mind of his own weal, by keeping up His Majesty's favour.

Mr George was a stoic philosopher; who looked not far before him: a man

[1] A. Francis Steuart, ed., *Memoirs of Sir James Melville* (1929), 217.
[2] Ibid., 230.

23

of notable endowments for his learning and knowledge in Latin poesy, much honoured in other countries, pleasant in conversation, rehearsing at all occasions moralities short and instructive, whereof he had abundance, inventing where he wanted.

The Erskine abbots mentioned were two laymen, who had been granted the secular privileges and the income attached to two great abbeys. The tutors were very different from one another in both character and reputation. George Buchanan was one of the best-known among learned Scotsmen, an old man with a short temper made more bitter by the gout. He had been born poor at the farm of Mid Leowen in Stirlingshire and was all his life pursued by poverty. He belonged in this respect to the traditions of Erasmus. He was indeed a type of the great poor scholar. All that he obtained was an ill-paid pension out of the revenues of the abbey of Crossraguel and part of this was always held back by the earl of Cassilis. He had travelled much in France in middle life, but had now come to high place. He was a leader of the Presbyterian party. At the same time he held successively the offices of director of chancery and keeper of the privy seal; he was also a member of the Scottish privy council.

In consequence of these employments he was not a resident at Stirling Castle, only a visitor. All the same the king's later comments show that as a boy he was intimidated. Still, the teaching of the classical languages by one who had such standing as a Latinist helped to build up the young king's sense of his unique position. Buchanan had also written the *Historia Scotorum*, the only modern chronicle of his own countrymen. One further point is worth remarking. He had in these years produced the casket letters. His spoken and his written words would show how deeply he detested the Queen of Scots.

Peter Young was very different. His family was connected with the court and he had spent five years at Geneva in his youth; he had been there a pupil of Theodore Bèza. He was always quiet with his young master. He was only thirty-two when he came to Stirling and a well-rewarded career of the second rank stretched out ahead of him. Throughout this book he will reappear holding minor offices. One point should be noticed as Morton's regency got under way. The Erskine family had many links with him; but the attitude of the two tutors was very different. Both men were nominees of the earl of Moray; they had no liking for his harsh successor.

24

Chapter 3

THE ROYAL EDUCATION

THERE was a hot-house quality about King James's education. His course of instruction was given to him fast; by the time he was fourteen his lessons ended. The course had been rather narrow, mainly three languages, Greek and French and Latin, always set within a biblical framework, chiefly the Old Testament. Latin verse was his private recreation. His mother's books, which came to him, provided a set of the works of the French poets. He was from the first always sententious. There was in him a feeling for the family which he had not got. The old countess of Mar, a rather hard old woman and a Catholic, counted for something and the young earl, Jock o'the slaittis, so-called by his royal companion from his unnatural interest in mathematics, for rather more. It was early clear that he extended the sympathy that he felt for his leading courtiers to their wives and children. He liked to find himself embedded in family life.

He set up to be acknowledged as a learned sovereign. More useful than all their teaching was the library, classical, religious and to a lesser extent historical that Buchanan and Young had collected on his behalf. He early acquired a fondness for Calvinistic syllogisms. His whole life, and especially the theories of kingship that he would develop, required a belief in an omnipotent deity. He accepted the religion that was prevalent in the only country that he knew. He had through life that rather limited regard for truth which tended to characterise the sophisticated sovereigns of the later sixteenth century. Some of his writings seem to bear the quality of an exercise. *A Paraphrase upon the Revelation of the Apostle S. John* may serve as an example. It was composed about 1588, although not published until 1616. One wonders whether the king, who so loved all powers and ceremonies, really identified the pope with Antichrist. The conviction that God was his protector went with a sense that the devil was his remorseless enemy. This would show forth in his constant searching out of witches and in the fear that he felt before the earl of Bothwell's necromancy. He had an interest in all the abnormalities of animals; from some aspects he had a ranging mind. This and his great knowledge was the first impression that he made as a young sovereign.

When he grew to manhood he was slender and of the middle height. The weak and spindly legs and his difficulty in pressing food between his narrow jaws were noticed by his later English subjects. In Scotland he was constantly on horseback and he loved the chase, hunting-dogs and horses. In his northern kingdom these were more important than his manners.

His library contained sixty-eight original works in French and only nineteen in English.[1] It was not so much the books themselves as their language which was unusual. The chronicles of Froissart were of course in French, although an English translation by Lord Berners had been printed in 1525; but there were also French versions of Guicciardini and other writers. Among the few English books there was a copy of Ascham's *Scholemaster* given to him by his grandmother, Lady Lennox.

The king's books, and his conversations with visitors and especially with foreign envoys, were of great importance to a sovereign who practically never travelled or met his equals. He only left the British Isles on one occasion to visit the court of Denmark; he had no royal visitors in Scotland. In England certain foreign princes came to him and also the Danish king.

He took pleasure in imparting knowledge, but too much stress should not be laid upon the royal pedagogue. In his maturity he had no feeling for independence of thought like Francis Bacon's; he loved to *mould* and give from his experience. This seems to me to arise from his conception of his great position. He liked to form those who were nearest to him as in the case of the two favourites of his later life, Robert Carr and George Villiers. From the time that he grew up, he had one salient quality, pleasure in giving. A strain of meanness is often allied to majesty; but King James loved to give and go on giving. This went side by side with an absence of a money sense. He was extravagant in his gifts to his subjects. In this respect he was very royal.

His coronation, that ceremony which no one except his mother could impugn, had given him his own high station; he was the anointed king of Scotland. At the same time he was close, as other European sovereigns were not close, to the noble stocks by whom he was surrounded. He was the head of all the families of Stuart or Stewart in

[1] J. Craigie, ed., *The Poems of James VI of Scotland*, Introduction, xvii.

the Scottish peerage. With the exception of the Stewarts of Blantyre and Garlies they could all be linked with him in a chart pedigree.[1] And the house of Stuart was only one among a score of equals.

In one sense the prestige of the Scots monarchy had not recovered from the double failure, first of the old royal house and then of the male line of Robert Bruce. In this connection the tradition of the royal authority was further weakened by the respect with which James VI regarded the legal rights of the high baronage. Thus from 1585 until 1590 the sovereign would be engaged in a suit-at-law to claim the position of heir-general to the earl of Angus. He made this claim, which was ultimately unsuccessful, as the representative of his grandmother Lady Lennox. As soon as he grew up he loved to arrange marriages among the leading families with the intention to assuage the feuds between them. He had a deep desire for peace. As the years went by he gained experience. He learned how he should exercise his God-protected sovereignty.

Throughout his life, from as early as fourteen, the king was basically a convinced doctrinal Presbyterian. His predestinarian Calvinism had a royal setting. In later years he must be described as Anglican; but he never desired to introduce this creed into his native country. I think that it is clear that he considered his differences with the Presbyterian ministers as not doctrinal but as trenching upon the field of politics. Their form of rule was ultimately theocratic and therefore incompatible with his idea of monarchy. His consciousness of his own learning made him ready to argue with ministers, who held the master's degree of Scottish universities. In the long struggle that he was to wage against the retention of political power by the Kirk of Scotland he would be aided by two factors. In the first place the ministers could not forget that he was the only independent Christian sovereign, apart from the king of Navarre, who accepted the Genevan discipline. At the same time King James was by nature conciliatory, at least in appearance. It is, of course, quite clear that had he been more truthful, his course would have been more difficult. He also believed that patience was an element in all wise policy.

He had been called Solomon, the son of David, by the king of Navarre, who was in everything his royal antithesis. However unseemly was this reference to Rizzio, the term Solomon was not without its point. James VI was certainly the first wise king of Scotland and the

[1] Cf. Chart pedigree 1, and David Mathew, *Scotland under Charles I*, 27, n. 3.

genealogy that he had studied as a boy was that of the kings of Israel and Judah. He was attached to the idea of peace and, at least in later life, he saw himself as a peace-making sovereign. In this connection it is worth noting how peaceful his rule had been in both his kingdoms until fairly soon before his death. In his later years in Scotland he pursued the earl of Huntly; but it was only a paper war, there was no conflict.

One element in the king's education had been the development of his interest in the theory of versification and this soon led to a certain pleasure in writing verse. This concern had hardly begun with his first tutors, but those who taught him belonged to the same background, the cadets of landed families who adhered to the Reformed religion and had usually travelled upon the continent. The documents surviving from this period are state papers rather than private writings. We have not sufficient evidence to tell whether there was then at the court of Scotland anything that could be held in structure to resemble the group of the *Pléiades* in France in the early part of the same century.

The one figure who can be held to have had something of the functions of a guide was Alexander Montgomerie, who was later well known as the author of *The Cherrie and the Slae*. In Scotland, as in England, it was at this time the practice that polite verses should pass from hand to hand in manuscript often for many years before they were at last produced for publication. This applies in especial to Montgomerie's work.

If it is felt that the king was helped in his first efforts, it should be remembered that he was only fifteen when he produced his earliest verses and eighteen when, in 1584, he wrote his first treatise, later printed as *The Essays of a Prentice*. In his *Reulis and Cautelis of Scottish Poesie*, apparently written at the same time, the king quoted passages from Montgomerie's poems as indicating different kinds of verse and these included extracts from *The Cherrie and the Slae*.[1]

Montgomerie had been in Morton's service and joined the king's household in 1578, becoming laureate at the court. In that capacity he wrote two pieces, *The Navigatioun* and *A Cartell of three ventrous Knichts*, as pageants for the king's "first and magnificent entry into Edinburgh" in 1579. He seems to have fallen into disgrace and in 1586 obtained permission to travel abroad for five years. There is no

---

[1] Alexander Montgomery, *The cherrie and the slaye. Composed into Scottis meeter*. The first edition was not printed until 1597 and Dempster's Latin version, *Cerasum et Silvestre Prunum*, did not appear until 1631, when both the author and the king were dead.

assurance as to the date of his death. We know from his own poems that he was small of stature. This may have been some recommendation to the king, who soon forgot him.

It is worth noting the influence on the king's own verse of the French books in his library. Those dealing with poetry were few in number, and were surrounded by those on history and by treatises on public affairs and sermons. It was not that these books were necessarily French by origin. Thus in history Froissart and *L'Histoire de Godefroi de Bouillon* and the works of Claude and Guillaume Paradin were outnumbered by French translations from the Italian of Guicciardini, Platina, Rocca and Paolo Giovio. Translations from the German were very rare. Bullinger's *Cent sermons sur l'Apocalypse* is an example. There were works of Calvin and Bodin in the original.

The works on French verse were all by modern writers, but with the exception of Du Bartas they were dead. The work of the last-named, *La Semaine*, had been printed in 1578; the rest were earlier. The volumes were as follows: Du Bellay, *Olive Augmentée* and *La Monomachie*, Marot, *Traductions* and a considerable quantity of Ronsard, *Poémes*, *La Franciade* and *Elégies*, and *Mascarades et Bergerie*.[1] Montgomerie drew most upon Marot and Ronsard; a sonnet written later by the king for Anne of Denmark resembles one of Ronsard's, and an unpublished poem follows fairly closely a sonnet by Melin de Saint Gelais with whom Buchanan was in correspondence. "All the Renaissance poetry", writes Dr Craigie in his introduction to *The Poems of James VI of Scotland*, "produced in Scotland before Drummond of Hawthornden began to write was the work of James's small circle of intimates."[2]

The king was from the first conscious of his classic French inheritance. He makes no reference to Villon, nor to the Scottish poets Dunbar and Henryson. His library did not contain *The Canterbury Tales*, nor does he seem to have known the works of Spenser. The literary contacts with England were very slender. He was to write an epitaph on Sir Philip Sidney and that equivocal figure Henry Constable contributed a sonnet to the preface of the king's *Poetical Exercises*.

The French poet whom the king most favoured was an elder contemporary of his own, Guillaume de Salluste, Sieur du Bartas, a

---

[1] This list and also the preceding titles are printed in Craigie, *The Poems of James VI of Scotland*, *op. cit.*, third series (1955), I, Introduction xvi-xviii.
[2] *Ibid.*, xxiv-xxv.

Gascon Huguenot. King James translated in their entirety both his works *L'Uranie* and *Les Furies*. In his early writing he was curiously exact.

> And soe did Cerberus rage with hiddeous beare
> And all that did Aeneas once befall.[1]

Two quotations from the very lengthy poem described curiously as *The Uranie* will bear out the same impression.

> Whyles in that tongue I gave a lusty glaise
> For to descryve the Troian Kings of old
> And those that Thebes and Maxen's crowns did hole.[2]

> To do lyke Erostrat who brunt the faire
> Ephesian tombes, or him to win a name
> Who built of brasse the crewell Calfe entire.[3]

The king made one venture into nearly contemporary affairs with his poem *Lepanto* celebrating the battle which had been fought in 1571. This was printed in 1590 in *Poeticall Exercises* and a certain robustness of utterance may serve to explain how it was more acceptable in the Scotland of his day than the exercises on classic themes. Much of it was based on Pietro Bizari's *Cyprium Bellum*. A brief quotation will give the poem's idea.

> Which fought was in Lepantoes Gulfe
> Betwixt the baptiz'd race
> And circumcised Turban'd Turkes
> Rencountring in that place.[4]

It was garnished with classical references to the Grecian fleet and Helen's cause. There were also in this poem a *Chorus Venetiae* and a *Chorus Angelorum*.

One must not forget the *Psalmes of His Majestie*, translations of psalms 1–6 and 10–21, which he was working out about this time; but a rather later sonnet, forming a part of a series that he would write upon his marriage, has a reference to the Cheviots which has a special interest for it seems to be the only occasion on which the king refers to Scottish scenery.

---

[1] From Sonnet 9, *The Essays of a Prentise, ibid.*, 15.   [2] *Ibid.*, 19.
[3] This is line 225, *ibid.*, 31.   [4] *Ibid.*, 202.

The Cheviott Hills do with my state agree
In every point excepting onelie one
For on their toppes cloudes are mounted hie
So all my thoughts to skies be higher gone.[1]

These lines, of course, belong to a later period, but it seems best to bring them all together. They give one aspect of his private life as he was growing up to rule in Scotland.

[1] *The Poems of James VI of Scotland*, unpublished and uncollected poems (1958), II, 70.

Chapter 4

ESMÉ STUART

KING JAMES was ten years old. The political scene was dominated by the figure of the earl of Morton, regent and great admiral of Scotland who was just sixty and feeling his advancing years. Life had gone sour on him. He was the last of the grim figures of the house of Douglas and he had none of that kindly feeling which the young king's future favourites would display as they built up the riches for their youthful families. He had himself been the younger brother of the earl of Angus and was now the uncle of the head of that stock, a youngish man, weak and tubercular. His wife was countess of Morton by her own inheritance. She was childless and for long insane; her tainted blood had brought insanity to the children of her sister the duchess of Châtelhèrault. Morton had seven bastards by different mothers.

Throughout life he had fought and fought. There was no concealment of his responsibility for Rizzio's murder, nor of his share in compassing Lord Darnley's death. By this time he had no friends. That sweet-natured usurper the earl of Moray had worked in line with him and was now dead. He had a feeling for the Calvinistic doctrine of election, but the ministers he did not care for; he was not the sort of man to like the clergy. Nor had he the arts to win his strange young sovereign. He had gone free from education as the great earls of Douglas had also gone, and had not the means to teach the questioning boy.[1] As a political Protestant he had no foreign ally save the queen of England. He knew and did not like her. She would never pay her money to help one who could have no other friend.

Morton had early acquired the lord chancellorship and he had held this until the regency had come to him. His own property was not especially extensive. It is noteworthy that his only private interest which is recorded lay in the building of the alleys in the garden at Lochleven.[2] In appearance he was a formidable man, not tall, with little

---

[1] His education was "not so good as was convenient for his birth", Thomas Thomson, ed., *The Historie and Life of King James the Sext*, 182.

[2] *Ibid.*, 165.

grey eyes set close together and a great beard, flaxen with red in it. There is in the National Portrait Gallery of Scotland a picture representing the earl of Morton, which is described as belonging stylistically to Ardel van Bronkhorst. He is painted in a narrow white ruff above the fine rather severe black gown, which was intended to underline his dedicated Calvinism. His short fawn-coloured gloves rest on the green cloth.

In the upper right-hand corner there is a picture representing an imagined castle standing against the blue waters of the Firth of Forth. The castle consists of two great masses connected with the shore by a low arched bridge, the whole construction built in light yellow granite. The sea-line in conjunction with the coast shows that it is placed upon the estuary's southern shore. May he, perhaps, have intended to rebuild the old royal castle of Tantallon?

Morton showed himself a strong ruler, very cool and disillusioned. This was the last great showing of the Douglas blood. It was useless to legitimate any of his bastards. They could not have the lands of Dalkeith and Aberdour, which his wife brought him. There was no saying what would happen when the king came to manhood. Morton was the last of the Scots lords who challenged men to single combat; he challenged Bothwell. And in that case there was a link between them, they had both shared the guilt of Rizzio's death and Darnley's.

The great Scottish earls knew when men were dangerous. There were some whom they would not conspire against or attack, but they felt more at ease when they had fallen. This applied to Morton and to the two earls of Bothwell. In such cases there was a resolute withdrawal from which in later years the house of Gowrie suffered. As a consequence there was no one, save his own nephew, who would come to the earl of Morton's aid. His only friends were the powerless. In his rough youth he had got to know and understand the poor men of the Scottish countryside. He knew them as the later Stewarts never did. It was the regent's final misfortune that the young king was among the men who feared him.

It would seem that King James was a nervous child. After all, throughout his years in Scotland he was never free from the danger of physical assault. It is not known when he began to wear the quilted doublet, which was a guard against a sharp stiletto thrust; it may have been a little after his release by the earl of Gowrie. (It was unfortunate that he did not change this practice when he reached the safe purlieus of the English court.) Capture and murder had been the lot of two or three of the Stewart kings. The opposition to Morton would seem to have been a slow but steady growth in the king's mind; his two tutors were always the regent's enemies.

Bearing a certain resemblance to Morton, and linked with him in the attack on Rizzio, was Lord Ruthven, who was to become the earl of Gowrie. Yet, like all the other peers, he was prepared to let the regent die. He resembled him in that, unlike the younger generation of his own house, he had had no serious education. In time he would have King James in his keeping, but he would have nothing to teach him. In another way the earls of Morton and Gowrie were bound together. They would be the first of the great lords whose lives would be exacted by their youthful sovereign.

Meanwhile there was a certain change. Morton resigned the regency in 1578 into the hands of his young master; but he soon returned as the first of the great peers about the king. There was in some ways an exception in the case of the Mar family; for the rest it seems that to the boy sovereign they were all inimical. Still, Morton left roots and for thirty years, as his reign spread out ahead of him, the young king would be preoccupied with the house of Gowrie. Into his private world there was now to come the profound influence of Esmé Stuart, the Seigneur d'Aubigny.

Stuart's character and intentions have been assessed very differently. His chief importance in the king's life lies in the fact that he was the first to bring him knowledge of the continent in its social context and of the ideas and detail of the Valois court. Buchanan had had some bitter memories, but of the French royal life he was quite ignorant. Besides, Esmé Stuart was in his manner and his outlook wholly French, a Gallic courtier. It would seem that he really came to claim the Lennox inheritance; he was the first cousin of the king's father, Lord Darnley. In my judgment it does not appear that there was any serious political value in his visit; the messages, which he bore from the duke of Guise and the vaguer contacts with the Queen of Scots, these were quite secondary.

The visitor reached Leith as the autumn mists were gathering in the Forth in September 1579. Much criticism of his career by Scottish writers would have been avoided if he had been recognised as a *politique,* one of those whom the French religious conflict had led into

I JAMES VI AND I, AS A CHILD
Attributed to Arnold Bronckhorst (Scottish National Portrait Gallery)

2 MARY QUEEN OF SCOTS,
"EN DEUIL BLANC"
Unknown artist (Scottish National Portrait Gallery)

3 LORD DARNLEY AND
HIS BROTHER
by Hans Eworth (HM the Queen)

indifference. It showed little knowledge of the aristocratic *milieu* of that country to consider him as a scheming Roman Catholic pretending to be a Protestant. He was used to courts and quickly understood the king's true nature; he was very ready to become the king's first convert. Esmé Stuart was now thirty-seven; he had been married for some years to his cousin Catherine de Balsac d'Entragues. They both had descents from noble stocks in Provence and in Lombardy.[1] The relationship that sprang up with the Scottish king was very warm and fresh. That prince was only thirteen. He drank in all that his new cousin could explain to him during those winter months, while the rain was pouring down on Stirling Castle. King James was well aware of his own old kingdom, his Presbyterian tutors had informed him of the genealogy of the kings of Judah. What he learned must have come as a revelation.

He heard, in those tones of respect which Esmé Stuart knew well how to convey, of all the glory of the court of France, the nobles immensely separated from the blood royal, the graded services. The old king had given to Queen Catherine two great pearls shaped like pears. That queen herself had devised the patches of coloured stones and marbles in the frontage of the Tuileries. Paris itself would be brought before him, the hall of the Caryatides in the Louvre, the Centaurs and Neptunes in its decoration, the ceiling of lime and walnut gilt and carved. Outside in the town was the new *Fontaine des Innocents* with the naiads placed between the pilasters.

There were the country palaces, the *château de Madrid* with its enamelled terra cotta, the figure of Vulcan which struck the hours in the great clock at Fontainebleau. And then there were the honourable presents. The duke of Guise had courteously sent over six horses as a gift. It seems likely that King James also learned how differently the rich French lords were housed from his own peers. The new house of the counts of Clermont-Tonnerre at Ancy-le-Franc was now completed; the panels of black marble; the small room with paintings of single flowers; the hall of the Roman emperors. In these conversations the king had painted for him for the first time the graded life of the great monarchies.

King James had given his cousin on his arrival the rich abbey of Arbroath and the custody of Dumbarton Castle. He gave him at once

[1] Cf. Lady Elizabeth Cust's elaborate account of this family, *Some Account of the Stuarts of Aubigny, in France, 1422-1672* (privately printed, 1891).

his own true confidence. And then he rewarded him in the only way he knew with Scottish honours. The earldom of Lennox had been merged in the crown on his grandfather's death. Since that time there had been two grantees, but matters were arranged and Esmé Stuart now received it. Where did the earl of Morton stand in this new picture? It is understandable that he could not prevent Stuart from landing; but it is surprising that he did not hire some patient bravo to strike him down. Perhaps he was too fatigued to try.

Lennox was now the closest to the king and it fell to him to do away with Morton. The other lords were ready by this time for his departure, all save Angus. The actual accusation of Morton's responsibility for Darnley's murder was made before the council in the king's presence by James Stewart, the newly appointed captain of the guard. The former regent was six months in prison and then tried and executed almost immediately at Edinburgh on June 2, 1581. This was just before King James's fifteenth birthday.

His cousin was now all in all to him. He gave him great offices like the lord chancellorship and also minor posts about his person, master of the wardrobe and first gentleman of the royal chamber. Then on the fifth of August of that same year he was created duke of Lennox. Henceforward Esmé Stuart was determined, or so it seems to me, to safeguard for himself and for his heirs his great positions in the northern kingdom. He now asked for admission to the Church of Scotland;[1] there were plans for a French Huguenot minister to come to reside with him and be his chaplain. This decision ran counter to such messages as he had been charged to convey by the duke of Guise and indirectly by the Queen of Scots. Neither of these had had any experience of the young king's informed defence of the Reformed religion. In the light of actual fact such suggestions as the project that the king of Scotland should repair to Spain for education as a Catholic lacked all reality. Comment is not required on such proposals. In one way the duke of Lennox bore resemblance to the great lords among whom he had now come. Like them he fought only for his own hand.

The lords had brought down the late regent and now they were to bring down the regent's successor. Lennox had no close relatives, nor had he yet had time to build himself a personal following. Beside him stood the equivocal figure of James Stewart, who must be examined

---

[1] For the Scottish Presbyterian outlook on the duke of Lennox, cf. David Calderwood, *History of the Kirk of Scotland, passim.*

later. Lennox must have realised clearly his weak position, with no one to defend him but his young sovereign.

The attack was made on August 23, 1582, when King James, separated from the duke, found himself at Perth, a town devoted to the earl of Gowrie. In the operation known as the Raid of Ruthven he was carried off to Gowrie's fortress. This was an action which belonged to the old Scotland. The king's stay at Ruthven Castle lasted ten months until he slipped away to St Andrews on June 27 the next year. He was sixteen when this imprisonment began; it marked a turning point in his whole life.

At first it may seem strange that the earl of Gowrie, by birth a peer of very medium fortune, should have done what no other Scottish lord would ever do, and lay his hands upon an adult sovereign, for this was the king's status once the regency had disappeared. He was in fact a man of mean intelligence. He had received only a year before the earldom of Gowrie and the lands of the dissolved abbey of Scone to support it. He had held the high office of Treasurer of Scotland, which he had gained in the period of the regent Mar. His wife was a legitimated daughter of Henry Stewart Lord Methven and his mother a natural daughter of the earl of Angus. His principal supporters were the lords Angus and Mar. He was just on forty years of age.

The king had had the world before him, he was now enclosed. This was a grave indignity before all Europe and neither Gowrie nor his house would be forgiven. Gowrie, although stupid, was not a cruel man. He and his children had a deep devotion to the Church of Scotland. Lennox was induced to leave the country and the life of James Stewart was carefully spared. Ambassadors appeared quite rapidly from France and England. Sir George Carey and Sir Robert Bowes came to express the queen of England's care for her young cousin. They were to assure Gowrie of her favour once the duke of Lennox was sent away. Two ambassadors came from Paris, M. la Mothe Fénelon and the Marquis de Mayneville. The former spoke of the association of the Queen of Scots with King James upon the throne, but found any such suggestion "coldly digested", as Lennox himself had found. There was a vague proposal for a marriage. The house of Valois was now coming to an end, but the Princess Christine of Lorraine, who was a niece of the king of France, was mentioned. All through this year the king was without a court; he had no proper ministers. His hatred towards the earl of Gowrie grew.

37

The duke of Lennox had gone home by England. He had understandably made a good impression on the queen. A civilised indifference to religious matters was welcome to her. He was only forty-one, but soon to die. Certain facts are undisputed. He was taken ill of fever in Paris in May 1583. There were Catholic priests all around him, but he took the trouble to declare himself a Presbyterian.[1] In my view he was a true *politique*. As he lay dying his mind was clearly bent upon the kingdoms of this world. Without the declaration his son would never be a duke in Scotland. It seems that his Catholic family buried him at Aubigny according to the rites of their own church. The king remained always faithful to this first friendship.

[1] The older view is set out in *DNB* by T. F. Henderson: "In order to lull the Scots into security, he at his death . . . continued to profess himself a convert to the faith which he was doing his utmost to subvert."

Chapter 5

JAMES STEWART

THE next period of King James's life is perhaps of all this run of years the least decipherable: there is so little data about James Stewart, the next favourite, and it is difficult to make out the king's attitude to the last stage of his mother's life and policies. It would in fact seem to be correct to state that his attitude to these policies was pure aversion, but what about his sentiments towards the Queen of Scots?

As time went on the earl of Gowrie showed himself more cordial towards his sovereign, as if cordiality could balance out captivity. Possibly the earl did not see his own way forward. One day in June in the fine weather when movements could easily be made across all Scotland, the king set out for a hunt towards Falkland and, riding on, continued to St Andrews where the northern earls and their followers were assembled. The earl of Gowrie followed him and was well received, being appointed to the king's new privy council. A few months later he was arrested for some real or imagined conspiracy and his friends left the country. The king had spent much time brooding upon the insult to the crown; and the earl of Gowrie was beheaded. The king was seventeen and the only friend of his childhood, the earl of Mar, was now in England.

James Stewart had been among the first to meet his now freed sovereign. It is impossible to obtain a clear impression of his character. There appears to be no portrait of him. The date of his birth is undiscovered and there is nothing positively known about his early life except that he was a younger son of Lord Ochiltree and had seen some service under the prince of Orange in the Low Countries. It may be said that nothing is known of him except the bare bones of his genealogy. Even the house of his stock is vanished. The existing Place of Ochiltree belonged to another family. It is evident that Lord Ochiltree was poor; his name appears obscurely on the Presbyterian side throughout this conflict. His daughter, Lady Ker of Faldonside, had been John Knox's second wife.

James Stewart seems to have been one of those Scotsmen whose sole possession was their pedigree; this was glorious enough. He came in a sense of a great house descended from the bastard but legitimated son of the last duke of Albany of the first royal line. What was the beginning of his relations with his Hamilton cousins? He was already the lover of the young wife of the earl of March. By whom was he made captain of the guard? Esmé Stuart, who selected him when in this post, was in all essentials a French nobleman. It was not within his grasp to understand the honours of Scotland.

More important was the question of Stewart's relationship with the young king. It is possible that the sovereign may have been attracted by his virile strength. And then (for there were two periods of influence) he may have been frightened by his noisy roughness; he lacked physical courage when a boy. Once the king had been relieved of him, he let him go. He never seems to have referred to him again; perhaps he was ashamed of his weakness in their brief contact.

The temporary destruction of the Hamilton power after the death of the duke of Châtelhèrault had been one of the works of the earl of Morton's regency. It may perhaps also be said that Buchanan had insisted with the king on the depravity of the duke and all his family. Stewart, after his share in Morton's fall, had been made tutor to his cousin, the mad young earl of Arran, for the duke's younger sons were at this time exiles in England. James Stewart was sanguine and reckless. He could hardly have thought that the hereditary insanity would wipe out the whole family.[1] In any event during 1581 he had obtained from the crown a grant of the earldom of Arran and the barony of Hamilton in Lanark. In a lucid moment the earl had been persuaded to resign his rights to him. It was true that James Stewart's grandmother had been a half-sister of Châtelhèrault; but he was not her heir male, nor was she herself legitimate. He used an argument familiar in his circle against the legitimacy of the duke of Châtelhèrault.[2]

The point, however, is that even if this argument had been correct

[1] Sir John Scot of Scotstarvet has comments which provide what may be called the folklore of the Hamiltons, "Chatellerault left four sons, James Earl of Arran, John, Claude and David. Three were frantic, as many since of that family have been", *The Staggering State of the Scots Statesmen for one hundred years, viz. from 1550 to 1650*, etc. (Edinburgh, 1754), 86.

[2] The first earl of Arran had by Beatrice, daughter of John Lord Drummond, a natural daughter, Margaret Lady Ochiltree, whose representatives were the master of Ochiltree and his children. Lord Arran married, first, Elizabeth Home, from whom he obtained an annulment, and secondly, Janet Beaton, the mother of the duke of Châtelhèrault. Stewart contended that this annulment was invalid. The situation thus described is set out in *Complete Peerage*, and *Scots Peerage*. *DNB*, in three relevant articles, all contributed by T. F. Henderson, asserts that Arran married Beatrice Drummond.

it would have given the new favourite no right to enter on these great possessions. The usurpation of the Arran earldom was to my mind something that no one could hope to carry through. Its sheer impossibility has not been stressed sufficiently. Esmé Stuart could, perhaps, have stopped the king, but it seems likely that he did not understand the problem. James VI was young. It is worth noting that Stewart was the only favourite whom he abandoned.

The new earl of Arran was given the lord chancellorship and led the king into his first conflict with the Presbyterians. He also encouraged, perhaps over-encouraged, him in his love of hunting. The king's inattention to business is first noticed at this time. Beyond the English frontier Mar, Angus and Glamis waited as also did the Hamiltons. The death of Francis Lord Russell in a border fray brought Arran down. The banished lords came back again to Scotland. In March 1586 he was deprived of the earldom of Arran and left the country. Some years later he returned as Captain Stewart; but the king had forgotten him. He was a sport in the higher world of Scottish politics, the one freebooter. The great earls were much attached to sheer legality.

There was one element that brought together both Esmé Stuart and James Stewart; both of them could in effect have been considered as pseudo-regents. They were not in fact submissive to their youthful sovereign. Even when Arran was brought down, the young king was not yet twenty. The queen of England recognised this situation. These two men were the last ministers in Scotland to whose removal she bent her policies. King James at last acquired his own adult authority and this seems the time to consider his emotional life and also his attitude towards his mother.

There now came into the king's life a courtier, who would remain for some time a constant factor. It is difficult to describe these young men about the king and to differentiate them at all clearly. The master of Gray, who now appears, is particularly elusive. His importance in James's life seems to have rested on a single fact; this was the first friendship with his own sex after he reached maturity.

Patrick, master of Gray, was not more than eight years his sovereign's senior.[1] He was the eldest son of an obscure peer, whose stock had come from England in the fourteenth century. His ancestry was grand;

[1] The date of his birth is not known, but his parents' marriage contract was signed on January 14, 1557.

but he was himself impoverished. His mother was a sister of the earl of Gowrie. On leaving St Andrews University he had gone to England and had had a close association with the duke of Guise and with the Queen of Scots' supporters. Without any justification he had passed as a Catholic overseas, but he sat lightly to religious matters and had no views on politics. He had travelled much in France and his master had sent him into Berri to escort the young duke of Lennox to the Scottish court. He was a tall young man, markedly handsome, relatively gay and burdened by no scruples.

The beginning of this friendship with the master of Gray seems the appropriate point at which to discuss King James's emotional approach. He was wholly polarised to his own sex. He was only thirteen at the arrival of Esmé Stuart and it seems unlikely that he then realised the implications of his warm affections. His cousin must have seen the situation clearly for he was a man of experience, who had just come from the Valois court where Henry III had had his *mignons*.

It was a great advantage for his sovereign that this new favourite was not rapacious; he was at the same time profoundly idle. He was content with his posts as master of the wardrobe and gentleman of the bedchamber. He later became a privy councillor and commendator of Dunfermline; a modest haul. In other respects the master of Gray was, however, a well-bred scoundrel. He became intricately involved in the negotiations concerning the Queen of Scots. He played with the English government; this may have been the reason why he soon lost his sovereign's intimacy.

It is also worth making some attempt to gauge the young king's attitude towards his mother. In the first place he had no memory of the Queen of Scots and that title by itself was quite distasteful. Throughout his short life he had been taught by men who had all told him that his mother had planned his father's death. The situation of King James would have a vague reflection in that of his descendant, George II, during the years when his mother Sophia Dorothea was imprisoned at Schloss Ahlden. The core of the difficulty in James's case lay in the refusal of the Queen of Scots to recognise her son as king. The boy had a very high sense of his regality and of the uniqueness of his own position; the ideas of his mother were from that side disquieting.

It has to be remembered that until the last months of her life the position of Queen Mary was technically strong. The archbishop of Glasgow acted as her ambassador to the court of France living at the

Scots College at Paris in the precincts of Saint-Jean-de-Lateran. He dealt with her domains in Touraine, which she held as queen dowager of France. Through him she made an unsuccessful claim to retain the county of Senlis in an action brought against her by the duchess of Montpensier.[1]

Royal letters,[2] which were never opened during the period of her stay in Sheffield, were sent to her by the duke of Bavaria and by her cousin Louise de Vaudémont, wife of Henry III. Her correspondents humoured her. Thus Catherine de Medici would write: "Madame, my daughter, the King my son is sending the Sieur de la Mothe to the *Prince*, your son."[3] These were the *ménagements* of courtesy. The letters of credence were made out to the king of Scotland.

The young sovereign was further harassed by his real and potential step-fathers. It is surprising to remember that they were so many. The cries which hailed him as the "son of Signior David" must have chilled him at the thought of his mother's imprudence with Rizzio. The name of Bothwell would burden him throughout his reign in Scotland; the dull and heavy duke of Norfolk was a memory of childhood, but the idea of Don John of Austria was much more recent. He was already twelve years old when the plan was adumbrated that that young hero should marry his mother and then set about ruling her kingdoms in her name. In 1584 it was proposed that the Queen of Scots might become the fifth wife of the king of Spain; Philip II as a step-father with the assurance that the queen was not yet past the age of child-bearing. Her son's imagination was exact and cool, even if it sometimes verged on the symbolical. It was burdensome for him to have to realise the figure of the Queen of Scots, which under some aspects had its nightmare elements.

King James was convinced of the sacrosanct character of his kingship, which he felt that no one had the right to take back from him. In their hearts the sovereigns of England and Scotland and their advisers must have hoped that the captive queen would pass away in a decline in her honourable confinement as the earl of Shrewsbury's guest. Of course, from the angle of the Queen of Scots the situation would appear quite differently; but that is outside the scope of the present study.

Throughout these years King James was learning his technique. He

---

[1] Cf. Cal. Scottish Papers (1581-3), VI, 233.
[2] Letters dated December 10, 1582 and October 28, 1582, *ibid.*, 230 and 192.
[3] Letter dated October 29, 1582, *ibid.*, 193.

was fast becoming the young wise sovereign. He had learned from those who had come to him from abroad that there was no one in Scotland who was his equal. His body was insufficient and he used his mind. He had a pride in his mental attributes which never left him. This was a lifelong feature of his character which would remain; it lasted to the time of his old tired wisdom. In his personal relationships he very soon began to show a mastery in all his dealings with his Scottish lords. These were, save for the matter of his mother, the slow beginnings of his happy years.

Proposals began again for his royal marriage. The Princess Christine of Lorraine was now betrothed to the cardinal of Tuscany; but there were other sisters. A daughter and a niece of the duke of Guise were brought in question; but there was something only half-serious in such proposals for these princesses were all Catholics. There was still less meaning in the speculations made on this subject by the Queen of Scots. She went over the Guise and Lorraine names and rejected the archduchesses of Styria as not yet old enough. Curiously enough she also put aside the Tuscan princesses, Romola and Anna;[1] these girls were not closely related to Queen Catherine, but as she sat in her restricted state in her English castles the Medicean memories must have seemed distasteful to her.

Then a suggestion was brought forward that the king should marry the Princess Catherine of Navarre. She was serious and very plain, rather older than he was, a determined Calvinist. And then in 1585 negotiations were begun for the hand of the Princess Anne of Denmark. She was a Lutheran and the match was not favoured in England, where Queen Elizabeth brought forward the king's first cousin, Lady Arabella Stuart, a girl of ten. All the same as the years passed the king's wish for the Danish marriage strengthened. He is never recorded to have had a mistress and in a sense he was detached upon the subject, but a marriage was something that he owed to his royal blood. He envisaged a dynastic marriage to provide the succession to his throne as a move on the chessboard of politics. At longish intervals he would in time produce several children; then willingly abstain from further intercourse. In some ways this would prove difficult for the princess of Denmark; but in that age brides went without expectancy to the royal marriage beds and there was frequently some signal disadvantage.

[1] These were the elder sisters of Marie de Medicis queen of France.

Chapter 6

THE QUEEN OF SCOTS

QUEEN MARY was in a difficult position in which the perils accumulated very slowly. There had been those long quiet years in the earl of Shrewsbury's custody before she had attracted the attention of a younger generation of English Catholics. The arrest of the Babington conspirators, who belonged to this grouping, focused attention on her. There was a feeling immediately reflected in the House of Commons that her continued residence on English soil involved a threat to Queen Elizabeth's life.

It is not easy to determine how early the situation was appreciated correctly by King James: he was only twenty in 1586. The pressures exerted by the government and by parliament upon the queen of England were outside his experience. In Scotland the Babington plot to assassinate Elizabeth I would not seem to have been a serious danger and the situation could surely have been met by the imprisonment of the Queen of Scots in the Tower of London. And then in one matter Queen Elizabeth and King James were in accord: the legal execution of an anointed queen was repugnant to them both. The effort made by Queen Elizabeth to persuade Sir Amyas Paulet, who was her gaoler, to remove the Queen of Scots by poison proved a failure. A court was set up to try the queen at Fotheringhay.

The English government did what was practicable to reconcile the Scottish king to the unreconcilable. The court was adjourned to London before passing sentence and this was not published. The will found at Chartley by which the Queen of Scots bequeathed the crowns of Scotland and England to the king of Spain was brought to the notice of James I. There was a three months' lull and then the royal warrant was conveyed without the queen of England's admitted knowledge to Fotheringhay and the Queen of Scots was executed. As soon as the news reached London Queen Elizabeth declared that this was done against her will and was the result of the action of the privy council working through Davison, the assistant secretary. The queen at once placed him in the Tower and wrote a letter to King James in which she expressed her "extreme dolour" for the "miserable accident" that had befallen.

The actual details as they came through to London must have been painful to the queen of England. "Mr Dean," said Queen Mary upon the scaffold, "I am settled in the ancient Catholic Roman religion, and mind to spend my blood in defence of it."[1] Her rather earlier sentences were very wounding – "And I hope your Mistress, being a maiden Queen, in regard of womanhood will suffer me to have some of my own people about me at my death. You know that I am cousin to your Queen, and descended from the blood of Henry the Seventh, a married Queen of France and the anointed Queen of Scotland." Some months later the queen's body was removed to Peterborough and there received a royal burial exactly as if she had died of sickness in her long exile.

Dr Richard Howland was ordered to preach the funeral sermon. One can imagine that able prelate in his study considering the line he should adopt. He wisely took refuge in theology. These were his words:

Let us give thanks [began the bishop] for the happy dissolution of the high and mighty Princess Mary, late Queen of Scotland and Dowager of France, of whose life and death at this time I have not much to say, because I was not acquainted with the one nor present at the other: I will not enter into judgment further, but because it hath been signified to me that she trusted to be saved by the blood of Christ, we must hope well of her salvation.[2]

An excellent supper had been provided in the bishop's palace for the noble company. The lights flared in the big sconces. The August night closed down upon the Fens.

It is important not to attempt to whitewash the disagreeable aspects of the character whom one is studying. The queen of England had put King James in a position in which he could either accept her statement or publicly throw doubt upon her word. He was no leader of troops, and to take an army into England would be to court disaster. The idea of an alliance with Spain was distasteful to him and would in fact have proved disastrous. As a boy he knew nothing of the crown of Spain; it did not rouse his sympathies. It was only when he was an old wise king that Gondomar would make him think quite differently. He could of course have broken off relations with the English court and have

[1] Printed in Henry Ellis, ed., *Original Letters Illustrative of English History*, II, 113.
[2] Printed in John Nichols, *The Progresses and Public Processions of Queen Elizabeth*, etc. (4 vols., 1788-1821), II, 512.

stayed neutral. But then there was his cousin Arabella Stuart, a girl now twelve years old living in England. Might not the queen of England adopt her and declare her heir to the throne? Unlike the king she was not alien-born.

There was one course of action which would perhaps have been possible. Might King James have suggested to the English queen that his mother as a dowager of France should be transferred to the care of Catherine de Medici? But by this time the last years of the Valois court were running out. There was no armed guard in France that could secure her from a sudden incursion of the duke of Guise and the soldiers of the League. Did this happen she might be transferred to Spanish territory. The king of Spain was slowly assembling the armada. Neither Queen Elizabeth nor her advisers would have dreamed of accepting this proposal. It was one of the defects of the king of Scotland's character that he was in fact over-conscious of the limits of the practicable. It was ever his intention to take no risks, no risks at all. This was the reason for his refusal to break off relations with the queen of England, when his mother had suffered execution.

There were two courses of action which the Queen of Scots might have taken in the years of her imprisonment that could have made her destruction more difficult to accomplish. She could have refrained from any contact with the English plotters and she could have abdicated her claim to the Scottish crown. She was prevented from the first course of action by the nervous energy of her temperament which could not bear inactivity. She was prevented from the second by her pride which was inseparable from her royal courage. She was in a sense born out of her due time like her sister-in-law Marguerite, queen of Navarre. In both cases a clear religious faith went hand in hand with sexual desires which proved tempestuous. Two generations earlier the Roman court would have paid less attention to such vagaries; but the popes of the counter-Reformation were cold at the heart to these princesses.

She had been brought up amid the elegance of the Valois court, which had made her sceptical almost as a young girl. She never had much trust in her own subjects with some good reason. All the family life she had ever known had been given by her uncles and cousins of the Lorraine family; they had certainly conveyed to her their resolution. It seems that she knew in her heart that France must prove the centre of the world. Throughout life she had a desire to exercise that sovereignty which she knew from her earliest childhood was her own possession. Splendour meant nothing to her; sovereignty in the Renaissance sense she always craved. As a sovereign she was apart. A strange absence of compassion was the obverse of her own great courage. Her education had been in France and she had known the northern kingdom during her six years' rule as queen of Scotland. England and English people she did not know except for the rather strange *ménage* of the earl of Shrewsbury and his wife. The high ruins of Wingfield Castle in northern Derbyshire alone survive to show us the sort of England that she knew. Similarly she was just a legend to her English supporters: they never set eyes on her. It may be for all these reasons that she appears to have exaggerated the risks which the queen of England ran. She was over sanguine as to the many chances of her removal. Queen Mary's character and that of her only son were very different. He was worried where she was sceptical and he was fussy where she was diamond-hard.

Looked at psychologically there was more than a generation of time between them. From one angle she was the last fruit of the Valois world; but the Valois were a dying race and she was an old-fashioned queen. In her last years she seems to have had a strong and personal piety based on an increasing consciousness of this world's instability. She was not well-served by those whom she employed; perhaps she expected too little from them. She belonged with every fibre of her being to that high and rather narrow culture which was the last fruit of the French Renaissance world. This was something which the wave of the counter-Reformation would sweep away.

This at any rate is how I see her, though there are clearly several different interpretations of her character. She appears never to have ceased to believe that her son's religion could be changed by a little solid instruction in the right environment. The young king could not fail to be exasperated by this approach. Until he left Scotland James I was never free from the imputations regarding his mother's association with David Rizzio. In his writings and in speech James I would refer to Mary of Guise and to his ancestors the kings of Scotland; but garrulous as he was he seldom referred to his parents once they were dead.

It may be considered that the king's adult reign began when he was twenty. It was from this time that the ascendancy of Chancellor

Maitland can be dated. He was in effect the king's first minister and was in turn succeeded by the group known as the Octavians. This was a form of rule that would continue until James VI received the English crown. It seems that the king chose Sir John Maitland very carefully. After all he was the first of the great officers who had not been in some sense his governor.

Maitland was quite outside the closed circle of the wealthy earldoms and it seems to have been the king's intention that he should remain apart and in his private service. He was at this time just turned forty, a younger brother of Maitland of Lethington, who had been so prominent in Queen Mary's reign and in the years that followed. They came of an ancient stock in the border country, which had long given service to the crown. Both brothers had married into Lord Fleming's family, Lethington's wife being one of the queen's four Maries. Their mother was a Cranstoun of Crosbie; they had kinship among the border lairds. They had been in public life since early manhood and their swift minds would seem to have alarmed the slowly digested thought of the great earls. It is curious that both brothers were at different times compared to Machiavelli. Bannatyne's reference to Lethington is phrased as follows: "About the same tyme [1571] the counsell of Athole held two or thri dayes whare heid of witt Mitchell Wylie with his sore feit was."[1] The following comment, admittedly by the same author, refers to the chancellor many years later. Justice is seen "lamenting that one of Cameleon's clan or of the disciples of Matchiavell had so great a place in the [Scottish] Commonwealth."[2] Nevertheless, it was probably this cool and detached judgment which charmed the king. It was a foretaste and in the Scottish manner of what he was to gain from Robert Cecil.

There was nothing sudden in the sovereign's promotion of Sir John Maitland; like most of his Scottish servants he had known him all his life. He had sat many years in the upper house, at first as lay abbot of Kelso and then for Coldingham. He was already a privy councillor and since 1586 vice chancellor also. He had for some years taken part in feuds, against the regent Morton and later against Arran; his legal education had been in France. A little later in August 1587 the great office of the chancellorship would be conferred upon him. This was practically a perquisite of the higher peerage for, since Cardinal

[1] Richard Bannatyne, *Journal of the Transactions in Scotland*, etc., ed. J. G. Dalyell (Edinburgh, 1806), 37.   [2] *Ibid.*, 349.

Beaton's death, eight earls had held it. In consequence he at once became a target for the opposition. The king, for so young a man, was curiously Olympian throughout the struggle. In this relationship there appears to have been a detached gratitude, but certainly no warmth. The surviving portrait of Chancellor Maitland shows an expanse of face with a great nose and big upturned moustaches. The eyes are careful and considering. The links between the king and chancellor were of the mind. He was the first of the Scottish ministers to treat his master as a wise great sovereign.

Like his brother, Maitland of Lethington, the chancellor was cold at the heart towards religion, in no sense a *politique* but rather veering towards agnosticism. He gained the support of the ministers through the services he rendered them. He had favoured the marriage with Navarre and the princess of Denmark had no use for him from her arrival. Among the great earls, both the king's friends and the king's enemies were hostile to him. It was of real service to his master that he held power during the earl of Bothwell's agitations.

It may be said that these men represented two opposing types, the new minister of the Renaissance state and the noble buccaneer of the old kingdom. The date of birth of the last earl of Bothwell is not known, nor is any portrait of him in existence. His possessions and his archives have all been scattered. His career amounted to very little and it is hard to decipher his character; his chief importance is that for several years he was a nightmare to the king of Scots.

Francis Stewart was the eldest son of Lord John Stewart, prior of Coldingham, the natural son of King James V by Elizabeth, daughter of Lord Carmichael. He was born about 1557, for his first public appearance was in the parliament held at Stirling in 1578, which he attended in his quality as commendator of Kelso. In 1581, after Lord Morton's fall, he was created earl of Bothwell and Lord Hailes, to which titles the office of lord admiral of Scotland was annexed. His uncle the earl of Bothwell had died in prison three years earlier and had been buried in Denmark in the Lutheran church at Faareveile. His father was step-brother to the earl of Moray. In his growing years the king had liked him, but this feeling seems soon to have been replaced by apprehension, for the young earl was wild and unaccountable and irresponsibly courageous. He was married to a fierce woman, at least ten years his senior,[1] Lady Margaret Scott, one of the stock

---

[1] The one certain date is that of the birth of the son by her first marriage, 1565.

IACOBVS · 6 · D · G · R
· SCOTORVM
ÆTA · 29 ·
1595 ·

4 JAMES VI AND I, AS A YOUNG MAN
Unknown artist (Scottish National Portrait Gallery)

5 ANNE OF DENMARK
by Paul van Somer (*HM the Queen*)

of Douglas of Angus and guardian to the boy laird of Buccleugh.

The king had three reasons for his deep hesitations about Lord Bothwell. The young man had approached the Kirk and in his capacity as Moray's nephew had offered them his service. It was feared that he might in time act as an executioner on their behalf. At the same time he had an interest that he never lost in necromancy; he was always communing with his private warlocks. And the king was almost obsessed by the idea of the devil; perhaps his lonely childhood came in here. He knew the enmity that Satan held for his God-guarded realm. And finally it was feared that Bothwell might be aiming at the crown of Scotland. This last point is not as unreasonable as it sounds. Until the birth of the duke of Rothesay in 1594 there was no close heir. His father's bastardy was by a mother of noble blood, nor had that stain prevented the grand master of Aviz from ascending the throne of Portugal.

Bothwell appeared in time to be an actual menace to the king of Scotland, but it was characteristic of the royal weakness at this period that none of the great peers came out against him. He had only one consistent enemy, the Chancellor Maitland. It was on the death of Queen Mary that Bothwell first began to show his independence. He appeared before the king and urged him to lead an army into England to avenge her. This was only the beginning of a long and unaccountable series of adventures. As time went on they played upon the king's weak nerves. The memory of Bothwell's actions sharpened his apprehension: it did much to produce the frame of mind in which the king rode out on his last journey to Gowrie House. This would not be exorcised until he came at length to his southern kingdom. There at last he came to a world which was accountable, where the powerful maintained themselves with a balanced precision and where the accumulation and maintenance of great wealth was the avowed objective.

There was an element of self-destruction in the earl of Bothwell. For five years he kept up a wild activity and it was in winter and in the winter nights that he chose to attack the timid king.

Before the difficulties with Bothwell became acute, James had, however, one quiet winter. On October 22, 1589, accompanied by the chancellor and a large train, he set off for Norway where the princess of Denmark had been driven back on her voyage across to Scotland for her marriage. Negotiations had been going forward for some time and they had involved, as part of the wedding portion, the resignation of the king of Denmark's claims to the sovereignty of the Orkneys and Shetlands.

Anne of Denmark was just about to celebrate her fifteenth birthday. She was slender with a beautiful clear skin and golden hair; she was not to be too tall for him. She had come from a united family and both her brothers would continue to show interest in her throughout her life. They were predominantly a Germanic stock, the royal line came from the house of Oldenburg and the queen had been born a princess of Mecklenburg-Schwerin. Both of the bride's parents were orthodox Lutherans. There was no Calvinism at the Danish court. There were two independent marriage services, the first at Oslo was Presbyterian and the second at Copenhagen was with Lutheran rites. When she came to Scotland she was accompanied by a chaplain of this latter denomination. Her religious outlook appears to have changed (and this will be dealt with later), but even from her first arrival in her husband's kingdom she was not welcome to the church of Scotland.

The fleet carrying the king and queen reached Leith harbour on May Day 1590.

The life of Anne of Denmark was to prove difficult. Her husband went unwillingly to the marriage bed and treated her with kindly courtesy. She knew nothing of the intricacies of Scottish life and never gained such knowledge. She exercised no influence in the kingdom and had her own sphere arranged for her at court. She became attached apparently in a rather superficial fashion to those courtiers who were assigned to her, both men and women. In later life she became attached to her little dogs. In these early years she was in some ways extremely lonely.

Further for nearly four years the purpose of the marriage was not achieved. It was only towards the end of February 1594 that the queen gave birth to a child. It was during these four winters, while the crown was without immediate heirs, that the earl of Bothwell continued his activities. It was not what he did but what he was that so alarmed the shaken king.

Chapter 7

HUNTLY AND BOTHWELL

WITH someone who had been a king from childhood, it is hard to know at which point to begin discussing the characters who influenced him. In Scotland the great earls had always been present to their sovereign. From the time when he had first taken his chair of state at twelve years old, they bowed before him. Still, the knowledge of their attributes and character must have come gradually.

By chance the history of the three great satrapies, those of the Gordons and Campbells, based on the highlands, and that of the house of Hamilton, the heirs to the Scottish throne, did not, with the exception of the first-named, impinge greatly on the polity of James VI. The Campbells were led at this time by the weakest of all the rulers of that resolved dynamic house. Archibald, seventh earl of Argyll, had been under tutors from 1584 until he came of age some twelve years later. It is evident from the *Letters to the Argyll Family* that the king never cared for him.[1] He carried on in a rather flaccid way the traditional policy of his house in harrying Clandonald. In 1618 he rather suddenly became a Catholic and gave up the control of the Campbell interests to his eldest son. It may be said that James VI was the last head of his dynasty who never gave much thought to Campbell power.

The Hamiltons for another reason had relatively little influence at court after the death of the duke of Châtelhèrault in 1575. There had been for some time the natural jealousy between the royal house and its presumptive heirs;[2] but this situation was deeply modified as a result of the duke's marriage with the co-heiress of the elder line of the earls of Morton, which was flawed by hereditary insanity. Her sister, the wife of the regent Morton, was long insane, and it was through the duchess that there came that impassivity and melancholia which settled on the earl of Arran, nominally head of the family until his death in 1608. Among his younger brothers Lord David became frantic and Lord Claud fell into melancholia in his later years. Further the leaders of the

[1] Cf. *Letters to the Argyll Family* (Maitland Club, 1839), Letters of King James to the seventh earl, 29-30 and 33.   [2] Cf. Chart pedigree 3, dealing with the Hamiltons.

family had been for six years exiles in England after the duke's death, and had also been in a carefully muted fashion supporters of the Queen of Scots. There were several reasons why the king was never close to them. He gave them in the course of time the marquessate of Hamilton and the earldom of Abercorn. They did not really count in the development of the king's reign.

It was very different with the earl of Huntly. Together with the earl of Mar, who had been the companion of the royal childhood, and the earl of Haddington, he formed the tiny group of the king's most intimate and faithful friends. This was a friendship which, as far as Huntly was concerned, was truly exacerbating to the Kirk and was the more remarkable in that the earl was so frequently in at least apparent opposition to the sovereign's wishes.

Huntly had inherited his great positions at the age of fourteen, when his father died in 1576.[1] He had received that education at the Valois court which the Scottish king appreciated; he was also within the ranks of royal kinship. The second earl of Huntly had been the son-in-law of James I and had received the grant of the two hereditary sheriffdoms in the north. On his mother's side the present earl was a grandson of the duke of Châtelhèrault. All the same he never had any kindness for the Hamiltons; and was distant with his few equals.

The policies of the earls of Huntly were inevitably polarised towards the Scottish crown, whose holder they tended to look on with a certain jealous intimacy. Their history suggests a desire, which was inevitably ineffectual, to act on Scottish policy. They had not sufficient power to make themselves a force in Scotland's capital. A feeling for Machiavellian principles went very easily with a position of inherent weakness. The possession of almost viceregal power upon the northern borderlands did not provide a sufficient leverage for action upon a national scale.

In considering the earls of Huntly something, too, must be set down to their Seton blood. They were the intimates of kings and in time their victims. And this quality kept them very far away from the interests of their neighbours in Aberdeenshire. In the north country their liking for the court was inexplicable. This is particularly the case in the lives of this Huntly and his eldest son. They had many adherents in the general sense, but very few close relatives.

In all this King James VI counted for very much. He was always closer to Huntly than to any other of his greatest subjects. It seems that

---

[1] Cf. hart pedigree 4, describing the Gordon relationships.

Huntly and his sovereign had the same concepts of monarchy. The earl was essentially a politician, as that term was then used in France in regard to men of his own rank. For his years of education in France at the court of Henry III gave him a detachment in political and religious questions: he never allowed his preferences in such matters to involve him in any serious inconvenience. Thus he disliked the Kirk of Scotland, but he bowed to her requirements. He would never permit the kirkmen, whom he despised, to triumph over him to his material disadvantage.

It was always the king's wish to bring his friends of high rank within his family circle. Thus he arranged the marriages of the two eldest daughters of the late duke of Lennox, Lady Henrietta becoming countess of Huntly and Lady Marie countess of Mar. Looking back on the histories of the European dynasties since the Reformation one frequently discovers a rigid determination on the part of the sovereign to press those of his subjects whom he admitted into intimacy within the confines of his own creed. It is the spirit of the comment of the last Hohenzollern emperor that surely to be a princess of Prussia is worth a little sacrifice of conscience.

But what was the nature of the attachment of the earl of Huntly, the leader of the Catholic earls, to the Roman obedience? He had been brought up a Catholic, as the French court understood that term, and this religion was always at any rate within his background. Far in the future in the summer of 1636, when the king himself was long since dead, the marquess of Huntly, as he had then become, was journeying northwards towards his castle at Strathbogie in "a wand bed within his chariot".[1] He reached Dundee and could go no farther. On his deathbed he declared his attachment to the Catholic faith.

Still it was almost impossible, and the same situation will be found in England, to maintain oneself as a great hereditary office-holder against the full set of the tide. To retain the authority of the house of Gordon, he was prepared to make whatever concessions the king might require of him. Thus he accepted the king's offer that his eldest son Lord Gordon should be brought up at court with the prince of Scotland. Time and again he subscribed the Presbyterian confession of faith. Back in Aberdeenshire many of the leading Gordon lairds had remained Catholic; but this was not practicable for the earl of Huntly. The king was playful with him and sweet tempered; but there was a vein of hardness

[1] John Spalding, *History of the Troubles and Memorable Transactions in Scotland*, ed. John Stuart (Spalding Club, 1850), 74.

in the Stuart character. The king's mind had long been bent upon the religious problem. It appears to me that he did not see why his friends and relatives, who were not his intellectual equals, should disagree with him.

It was through Henrietta Stuart that Catholicism survived among the senior line of the Gordon family. She was very French, a rather formidable woman, deeply devoted to the Society of Jesus. The king, who would deign to argue with her husband, thought meanly of her sex. Huntly, Erroll and Crawford were known as the Catholic earls; but their allegiance to Rome was often shadowy. The survival of Catholicism in Aberdeenshire did not depend on them. So far as the leaders were concerned, it turned upon the marchioness of Huntly.

In some ways Huntly was characteristic of his northern stock. He was a devotee of hunting and built up the hunting lodges across his lands. He was pertinacious in his hereditary feuds and notably in that with the earl of Moray. He battled with the Campbells under their then weak leadership. Perhaps these points have been dealt with in too great detail; but I am anxious to set out such factors as can be gathered before considering the problem of the correspondence with the king of Spain.

From as early as 1588, the year of the Spanish Armada, Huntly had been in regular but secret correspondence with the duke of Parma, who was then viceroy of the Spanish Netherlands. On its discovery he gave up his post as captain of the royal guard and retired to his own country. There had also been a letter to the king of Spain. The general tenor of the correspondence was an encouragement to invade Scotland on behalf of the Catholic cause. The last episode in this series of events was the discovery in the winter of 1592–3 of what is known as the conspiracy of the Spanish Blanks, that is of eight sheets of blank paper two of them signed by Huntly, which it is alleged were on their way to be delivered to Philip II.

What was King James's attitude to these affairs? All that can be said for certain is that it was essential for the king to keep intact his own alliance with the queen of England. At the same time he had a penchant for a masterly inactivity; he was young and long-sighted. But he was in no position to judge the situation in the English Channel, while in these years before the Navarre victory the military strength of Parma's *tercios* appeared compelling. It must have been clear to him that neither Huntly nor the other Catholic earls would rise against him. The warm friendship of Huntly and the king was never clouded. Is it not likely that he permitted this Spanish correspondence as a safeguard for his rights in case England might suffer a military defeat? Huntly could never come to power or indeed live in tranquillity as long as the Kirk of Scotland remained so powerful. The correspondence would serve to indicate the kind of government that might emerge in Scotland if the Spaniards should succeed in defeating England. The letters could hardly have had less importance; they were a dream within a dream.

During these years the king's chief preoccupation was with the earl of Bothwell. There was this distinction between Huntly and Bothwell, that the former was the king's close friend who was being harried by the Kirk, while the latter was his personal enemy, who had proclaimed himself the Kirk's defender. Bothwell's policy seemed to yaw repeatedly, the natural fruit of an unstable mind. He had proclaimed that war should be declared on England to avenge the death of the Queen of Scots; he also pledged himself as the inheritor of the regent Moray's policies. This latter line of thought brought him in contact with the young earl of Moray, who had married the regent's daughter and heir-general, while Bothwell was her cousin and the regent's heir-male. Moray's association with Bothwell would in time prove fatal to him.

Meanwhile, the North Berwick witches had accused Bothwell of consulting them about the date of the king's death and also about methods of achieving this. In June 1591 he was put to the horn and thus became for practical purposes an outlaw until he finally abandoned Scotland. He is a strange wraith-like figure. His home had been the court, where he held the post of admiral. He had hardly lived at all in his great castle at Hermitage, standing high and bare without such amenities as a garden, in the uplands in Liddesdale. Now he could no longer use or derive rents from his own lands, nor from those of the young laird of Buccleugh for whom his wife stood guardian. He had the connection with Moray, already mentioned, and away in the far north there lived his young half-brother the earl of Caithness. His own family had been disrupted; but the great peers had made up their minds that they would not abandon him or, to put it more accurately, that they would take no part in the royal quarrel. To accept any of the Hepburn lands would be to involve themselves in a blood feud. And then Bothwell was a killer: he had stabbed Sir William Stewart of

Monkton in the wynds in Edinburgh and his men had then put him to death at the bottom of a hollow cellar.

Until he was driven from the country Bothwell never gave up the hope that he might see the king and *capture* his favour. I suppose he thought back on those happier times when the king was still a boy. But the king now looked on him as a potential regicide. Bothwell rode here and there on his horse Grey Valentine. For a time he was as close in to Edinburgh as Roslin. Technically his opponent was the chancellor, a "puddock stool of a night", as he called him. This was the sole move that he had made which had, by accident perhaps, a certain shrewdness. Opposition from many quarters was gaining ground against Maitland, whose aloof sovereign did little to support him. In this matter King James was very modern, while Bothwell might have ridden up throughout the Stuart centuries. As for the great Scottish families there was hardly one whose representatives did not feel that if the chancellor's power remained unbroken this would mean the end of their own oligarchy.

At intervals there were three attempts made by Bothwell to surprise the king's person, and it is worth examining them for the effect that they had upon the royal character. The first two attacks were recorded in old age by an eye-witness, Sir James Melville, who was then attached to the court. Except for a natural tendency to overstress his own share in the action or advice his account appears reliable. During the night of December 27, 1591, Lord Bothwell assembled a force of between forty and fifty men. Melville writes:[1]

He [Bothwell] . . . accompanied with James Douglas, sometime Laird of Spot, the Laird of Niddry, Mr John Colvil and some others, entered into the King's palace, late about supper-time, by the passage of an old stable, not without secret intelligence of some about his Majesty. So soon as they were all within the close of the palace, they cried, "Justice, Justice; a Bothwell, a Bothwell"; and had been masters of the whole, were it not that James Douglas of Spot, after that he had taken the keys from the porters, entered within the porter's lodge, to relieve some of his servants, who were kept there in prison . . . where he met with some resistance from the porters, the noise whereof did rise sooner than was the intention of the enterprisers. Which alarmed his Majesty, the Chancellor and others, to shut and fortify their chamber doors, and to make resistance till some relief came from the Canongate, conducted by my brother Sir Andrew Melville of Garvock, master of

[1] Steuart, *Memoirs of Sir James Melville, op. cit.*, 355-6.

his Majesty's household, who knew a secret passage through the abbey church, and entered by the same in armour.

There then follows an account of the murder of John Shaw, master stabler to His Majesty, by the intruders.

The Earl of Bothwell [so the narrative continues] accompanied with Mr John Colvil and others, addressed themselves unto the Queen's chamber-door, where he supposed the King would be found. But the door was defended well by Harry Lindsay of Kinfauns, master of her household. In the meantime his Majesty was conveyed up to that tower above the said chamber, after the door of her Majesty's chamber had been broken with hammers in divers parts, and that Mr John Colvill had caused bring fire to burn it.[1]

The next passage is an eye-witness's account.

At their first entry within the palace, I was sitting at supper with my Lord Duke of Lennox, who incontinently took his sword, and pressed forth; but he had no company, and the place already was full of enemies. We were compelled to fortify the doors and stairs, with tables, forms and stools, and be spectators of that strange hurly-burly for the space of an hour, beholding with torchlight forth of the Duke's gallery their reeling, their rumbling with halberds, the clacking of their culverins and pistols, the dunting of mells and hammers, and their crying for justice. . . . So soon as my Lord Duke saw a company of friends within the close, he went forth to pursue the Earl of Bothwell and his company; but the night was dark, and they took them speedily to their horses, and escaped.[2]

A curious point is that there were numerous rumours and warnings of these attacks, the second of which took place some six months later. On this occasion the earl of Bothwell and his company were seen upon the heights of the Lomonds making eastwards. He arrived before Falkland Palace between one and two in the morning of June 28, 1592. It had been easy riding through the summer night. The force dismounted and set up their petards to break down the gates and doors. The king was alerted and took refuge in the Tower. This was a less serious attack and Bothwell drew off at about seven in the morning. In this connection Melville has an interesting note.[3] "The said Earl and his company retired and fled, none pursuing them: whereas a few might easily have overtaken, and overthrown them." The Scottish lords in general considered the king's misfortunes with a singular passivity. The palace lay almost in open country, so the king left for the town of Burntisland

[1] *Memoirs of Sir James Melville*, 356.   [2] *Ibid.*, 356-7.   [3] *Ibid.*, 366.

and crossed the Forth next day to take up residence again at Holyrood.

On August 9 following there was a rumour of another attack to be made on the king when at Dalkeith.[1] On this occasion the laird of Logie, a gentleman-in-waiting, confessed that it had been arranged that the back gate would be opened for Bothwell's men and that they should come in through the yard and find the king.

It is noticeable that as the attempts went on they diminished in their gravity. Nearly a year elapsed before the final meeting which took place at Holyrood on July 24, 1593, between eight and nine in the morning.[2] Bothwell was accompanied by between 200 and 300 men, who remained outside the palace. He was let in by the back gate by the countess of Atholl, who led him to the royal bedchamber where the king was dressing. The earl and Mr John Colvill fell upon their knees and placed their swords upon the ground. Most humbly they craved pardon and mercy. Several lords were party to this last attempt including the duke of Lennox, the earl of Atholl and Lord Ochiltree. Meanwhile the people of Edinburgh had passed down the hill to Holyrood in arms. The king spoke to Bothwell with caution and policy rather than sincerity. He had been very frightened. The threat was over. It was the greatest folly to enter King James's presence carrying a naked sword.

This was the earl of Bothwell's last adventure, but before describing his further movements it is best to examine the murder of the earl of Moray, which took place on February 7, 1592, towards the end of the winter which had seen Bothwell's Christmas attack. The murder presents an unsolved problem in regard to the measure of the king's responsibility.

One can still trace the site in the demesne lands of Donibristle on the north shore of the Firth of Forth. On the south side of the old road which leads from Inverkeithing to Aberdour there stands the great eighteenth century grey stone entrance put up by the later earls of Moray. The ground plan of the original house, the Place of Donibristle, is rather small. In 1592 it was the residence of Lady Doune, the earl's mother.

The young earl of Moray was well favoured and very tall,[3] a favourite at the queen's court and with the Edinburgh populace. He had had

---

[1] Cf. David Moysie, *Memoirs of the Affairs of Scotland*, ed. James Dennistoun (Bannatyne Club, 1830), 95.   [2] *Ibid.*, 103.

[3] A report made to the English government in 1582 describes him as "a yonge man of xvii yeres of age; of a very tall stature, but lyttle proof", *Bannatyne Club Misc.* I, 57. A return of 1586 gives his age as 24, *Cal. S. P. Scottish* (1586-8), 226. Since his marriage took place in 1581, the latter date appears more likely to be correct.

a fortunate life for when still a youth and without resources he had been granted by King James, then at the council chamber and nominally in charge, the guardianship of the two daughters of the regent Moray. He had himself married the elder child and had thus obtained the regent's properties. He had recently arrived at Donibristle at the request of the king, conveyed to him by Lord Ochiltree, the head of his father's house. He had lately lost his wife, and his five young children with his sister were all then at Donibristle, where they had probably been placed in his mother's care. It is clear that the king feared that his cousin Bothwell would take refuge with him at Darnaway, his northern home.

His wife had brought with her as her dowry both her great landed inheritance and a fierce long-standing feud with the earls of Huntly. From the early fifteenth century the Gordons had endeavoured to obtain the earldom of Moray from the Dunbars and eventually the grandfather of the present earl of Huntly had obtained a grant of it from the queen regent. This a few years later he had been compelled to surrender and the earldom had been granted to the future regent.

In the fighting on his borders the new earl of Moray had taken part with the Grants and with other enemies to the Gordon power. Lady Doune was a Campbell of Argyll, another hostile element. There was also a blood-feud with some of the lesser Gordon stocks following upon the death of Gordon of Cluny at the hands of Moray's men. It seems to me improbable that the king adverted to these facts when he gave Huntly a warrant to pursue Bothwell and his supporters.

We have no evidence as to what the king thought of the earl of Moray. There is no authority for the statement in the traditional ballad that the queen was fond of him, and the king did not usually take to those who were much esteemed by the Kirk. Moray came from a background which was deeply Protestant. The warmth of the citizens of Edinburgh towards him was not appealing. Further, it may have seemed that there was something sinister in any one who was a heart-friend of the earl of Bothwell.

The earl of Huntly was at court when Moray came to Donibristle. Accompanied by his supporters he left on the pretence of going to Leith to watch the races. Instead he made for Queensferry and on reaching the northern shore made arrangements to stop the ferry service. It was after nightfall when he arrived at the Place of Donibristle with a large company and summoned Moray to come with him in custody to the king. The women and children left the house, but the men refused. The house was set on fire and the sheriff of Moray was killed in the doorway. Moray was late in attempting to escape. He had risen and armed himself and the silk plumes of his helmet were caught by the flames. He rushed down to the water's edge, but the flames enabled him to be followed in the darkness. He was killed in a cave beside the shore.

When the news reached the king his first effort was to prevent further conflict. The royal officers took charge of the stables which contained the horses of Ochiltree's troop and checked Douglas's movement to bring in his men from Aberdour. He was determined to avoid an open conflict between his lords. He also succeeded in capturing Gordon of Gight and his servant, who had both taken part in the actual killing. They were brought to Edinburgh and executed. So far, so good. But towards Huntly himself he showed a strange passivity. He granted him an interview at Linlithgow and placed him in ward for a time in Blackness Castle. It has been suggested that the king inspired Huntly to make a murderous attack on Moray; but this has been merely hazarded and does not fit in with the king's character. Huntly was forced to admit that he was in charge of the operation, but he always asserted that he merely intended to take Moray a prisoner by virtue of his warrant. The blood-feud of some Gordons against Moray had caused his death, and Gight had been executed. Whether this was accurate or not it seems likely that the king believed it. The English agent, hardly a neutral observer, wrote that Huntly had struck Moray the last blow in the face with his dagger, but the question remains as to whether this was true. There was no trial and as a result no evidence of those who had been between the Place of Donibristle and the shore on that dark night.

One result of this murder was to bring Ochiltree over to the group supporting Bothwell. This was remarkable for there was a blood-feud between them since the murder of Sir William Stewart of Monkton. One should not be too schematic, however, in approaching the Scottish blood-feuds; there were other matters which might intervene. Re-examining this period has led me to revise my attitude on the relations between King James and the Stuart (or Stewart) family. I no longer think that it can be maintained that the king had a special feeling for all those who shared his name and blood. Ochiltree, Sir William Stewart and their brother James Stewart, sometime earl of Arran, and their cousin the earl of Moray, to give one example, were all descended by a legitimated line from the second duke of Albany of the first creation. The king had no especial feeling for them, that he alone retained for his Stuart cousins of the Lennox line. The years that were now opening were a solitary period for James VI. There was always a certain solitude in the adult life of an anointed king.

A characteristic of this time was the increasing tension between the king and the Kirk. Those whom the Kirk favoured had indeed proved unfortunate. Bothwell had proved a broken reed and Moray had been murdered. They were suspicious of the royal favour shown to Huntly, their enemy. Then there came from the king's point of view an easing of the situation, for on February 19, 1593, at Stirling Castle the queen gave birth to a prince. There was at last a clear heir to the Scottish throne.

Throughout the reign of Queen Mary and until his death in 1575 this place had been filled by the duke of Châtelhèrault. He had been a solid pursy man, a little lacking in will-power, but with, in general, a sufficient capacity for managing the affairs of his great house. Since he died the situation had altered greatly for his eldest son, the earl of Arran, was a lunatic. If the throne had become vacant should his brother Lord John Hamilton rule as regent in his name? Would such an arrangement be accepted by the great Scots lords? As a further point the position was affected by the complicated marriages of the duke of Châtelhèrault's father. Should this in fact exclude the Hamiltons, the heirs would be the representatives of Elizabeth countess of Lennox, Princess Mary's daughter. It was all confusing. Further, the Scottish and English crowns would not remain joined unless King James had children. Should the king die childless Lady Arabella Stuart would inherit the English, but not the Scottish, throne. Now with the birth of the prince of Scotland such speculations vanished, nor was there need to fear such claimants as the earl of Bothwell. For the first time King James could know security.

There still remained the problem of the future of the earl of Huntly, and here again the king's solution seems to bear the pattern of his thought. Huntly himself would wish for a royal pardon and thereafter freedom. The Kirk was aiming at his destruction and the rooting out of all the Gordon power. The other great lords showed the customary indifference to the fate of their rich neighbour. He had of course a form of alliance with Lord Erroll and more clearly than that a bond with the earl of Crawford's brother Lord Spynie in return for Huntly's rights in

63

the lands of the bishopric of Moray.[1] But the king, among the circle of his advisers, was almost alone in wishing to preserve Huntly in his power, but on conditions.

Bothwell, who had been in the north of Scotland and then in England, had now returned and joined forces with Huntly with whom he had very long connections. In the autumn of 1594 the king moved up to Aberdeenshire, accompanied by leaders of the Kirk. Huntly had considerable forces, but he was wisely not prepared to commit them against a basically friendly sovereign. Under pressure from Andrew Melville, the Presbyterian leader, the king ordered Strathbogie Castle to be blown up with gunpowder. Huntly was offered a full pardon if he would deliver up Bothwell to justice, but this he refused. Still, this aspect of the problem was soon solved. Bothwell fled north to his stepbrother in Caithness. Until the following April he remained in hiding there. Then he took ship for France and never came back again to his own country. He lived abroad in Catholic Europe, in France and Spain. One wonders how he lived, perhaps at times he practised astrology. References to him are very rare; he died in poverty in Naples in 1624, the year before his master.

Meanwhile, if Huntly would not fight and wished to avoid capture, he had no alternative but to go abroad. Accompanied by Erroll, he sailed from Aberdeen on March 19, 1595. Chancellor Maitland, who had accompanied the king on his northern journey, died at Thirlestane on October 3, of the same year. In 1596 the two earls secretly returned to Scotland. In 1597 they made their formal submission to the Kirk at Aberdeen; this was the king's condition, that they should definitely accept the Reformed religion. At the parliament held in 1598 they were restored to their estates and in 1599, on the occasion of the christening of the king's daughter Princess Margaret, the senior of them was created marquess of Huntly. James VI and his persevering supporter were thus rewarded; the king appreciated an obedient friendship.

[1] The bond was signed at Edinburgh on December 18, 1590, and is printed in *Spalding Club Miscellany*, IV, 244.

Chapter 8

THE OCTAVIANS

THE king seems to have gained a new confidence from the scattering of his enemies and the rescue of his friend. He has been accused of ingratitude towards Chancellor Maitland and it is clear that he did not consider it his duty to protect his servant from the latter's enemies. In addition there was it seems to me a touch of the pedagogue about Lord Maitland of Thirlestane. He had his policy which he offered to the king with much respect; he was, as an example, very ready to conciliate the Presbyterian leaders. The chancellor had no friends, although he had some temporary alliances. As a consequence there were few to whom he could speak his mind or who could speak theirs to him. As he grew older he became more authoritative. No one liked the velvet glove better than King James, but he preferred it without the iron fist in it. One consequence of the Maitland régime was that the king waited four years before he made another chancellor.

In fact his next ministers, the group known as the Octavians, were appointed almost by chance. They were for the most part royal officers, who had put order into the queen's finances and were brought over to take sole charge of the king's arrangements. They had been known to their master throughout his lifetime and were, certainly in a financial sense, the ablest group among his courtiers. There were no feuds among them and they showed a tranquil goodwill to one another. Although some of them were trained in the law, their origins were predominantly aristocratic. Those lords of session, who were to become a *noblesse de la robe* and a special element in the Scottish social system, belonged to the next century. Three of the seniors of this grouping were already turned forty.[1] Walter Stewart, prior of Blantyre, came of a junior branch of the Stewarts of Garlies, and had been brought up in childhood with the king. There was also Sir Peter Young of Easter Seaton, who had been one of the king's two tutors. He was turned fifty, and two others who had not been in the queen's service were added, Sir David Carnegie of

---

[1] Lord Menmuir was born in 1552, Lord Balmerino in 1553? and Sir Alexander Seton in 1555?

Colluthie and Sir John Spens, Lord Curriehill, one of the judges. In age these were also seniors. The leading members were lords Menmuir, Balmerino and Drumcairn and Sir Alexander Seton. The total number was therefore eight, hence the Octavians.

In some respects this was for the king an ideal arrangement. No appeal was to be allowed from their decisions in the financial field. To a great extent this served to free the king. In general he did not allow himself to be too close to them; he was their sovereign. And as an episode in later years was to show, their service to the king was much more real to them than were their links with one another. Long after this time in 1608 Lord Balmerino fell into disfavour for one of his actions as a royal officer. He had been Drumcairn's school fellow and they had been in the king's service together for many years. "I do not doubt," wrote Drumcairn on this occasion,[1] "but some men will presse to bring me in suspicion in respect of my friendship with my Lord Balmerino. But I thank God I can discerne that it holds no greater propoertion with that superlative duty which I owe to so great a king, so gracious a master, and so bountiful a benefactor, not as a mote to a mountain or a midge to an elephant." This somehow seems to me to sum up the spirit of the Octavians.

It is only fair to state that Drumcairn was at the time lord advocate, but it is the hyperbole at the end of the second sentence which is significant. Among the Octavians, it was Drumcairn alone who gained the king's close friendship. Thomas Hamilton, who came from a stock distantly related to the great family of that name, would have several titles – Lord Drumcairn, Lord Binning, earl of Melrose and finally earl of Haddington. He was a most able lawyer and a great and calm accumulator and manipulator of landed property, for the most part formerly ecclesiastical estates. He had close ties with the Edinburgh merchant grouping. His mother had been a Heriot and he was first cousin to George Heriot, "His Majesty's Jeweller" and the founder of Heriot's hospital.

He had had that education in France which the king so valued and he read with ease both French and Italian. There were other sides to his character which proved attractive. He was nothing of a soldier, nor was he a great lord with his armed retainers. On the contrary he was the nearest that one could come in Scotland to a smooth working courtier.

[1] Letter to Sir Alexander Hay dated December 27, 1608, printed in Sir William Fraser, *Memorials of the Earls of Haddington* (1889), II, 215-16.

He slowly built up a great Scottish fortune. The details of the silver plate that he would leave at his death, the canopies, the carpets and the tapestries, mostly scenes from the Old Testament, indicate perhaps the most lavish furnishings of the Scotland of his day. With all this he was a man of learning and it was one of the king's most appealing qualities that he gave his sober favour to learned men. In the great house at Tyninghame, where he moved in his old age when the king was dead, there still remains a portion of his library. He had such English law books as Dyer's *Collected Cases* and the *Commentaries and Reports* by Edmund Plowden. There was a translation of Matthieu's *History of Lewis the Eleventh*, Ariosto's *Il Furioso*, Machiavelli's *Historie Fiorentini* and Bernard de Girard's *L'Histoire de France*. The memorandum books at Tyninghame contain the notes that he made on Seneca, and on the antiquaries Stow and Camden, on the Essays of Montaigne, the works of D'Aubigné, De Thou's *History* and Bodin's *La République*. There is understandably an analysis of the writings of Sir Edward Coke.

King James always showed Haddington quite special favour and a real confidence. He valued his quickness of mind and his adaptability. It was encouraging that he could read both French and Italian. At the beginning of his life in politics he lived in a house in the Cowgate, while the king was at Holyrood. The royal comment made many years later on the marriage of Haddington's heir to the youngest daughter of the house of Mar throws light on all the parties. "The Lord haud a grup o' me. If Tam o'the Cowgate's son marry Jock o'Slaittis' dochter what's to come o' me." The king was always faithful to his old Scots friendships.

The mention of the earl of Mar brings back one of the king's preoccupations during these years, the welfare of the children of the duke of Lennox. The elder brother, the second duke, had been brought over from France way back in 1584, when he was just ten years of age. He was placed in all his father's honours and was named joint lieutenant of Scotland for six months when the king went overseas to claim the hand of Anne of Denmark. It was stated by Calderwood that he was recognised as next in succession to the Scottish crown;[1] but this appears impossible. It would depend on the exclusion of the whole Hamilton family; nor was the duke the heir-general of John, first earl of Lennox, through whose marriage the claim would be derived. He was, however, certainly heir-male to the as yet childless king in regard to the Lennox branch of the house of Stuart.

[1] Calderwood, *History of the Kirk of Scotland*, IV, 621.

Ludovic, duke of Lennox, was unmarried during these years for he had been only fifteen when he lost his child-bride Sophia Ruthven. The Van Somer portrait painted in his later days gives him a Scottish look and a far-off resemblance to the king. There are few letters and little opportunity to decipher his character. He seems to have had a French courtesy from his early upbringing and was complaisant. He at once accepted the king's religion. He was cheerful and, in his youth, even a trifle wild. James VI was happy to play the sovereign and the elder brother to all his family. One sister was marchioness of Huntly, the other, since 1592, countess of Mar. There was a younger brother, the Sieur d'Aubigny. The king was always fond of a mitigated form of family life.

With his detachment towards the Octavians the king showed a measure of favour towards their opponents, the so-called Cubiculars, a party composed of those ambitious courtiers who had been omitted when the body of Octavians was first formed. It is worth noting that the two men to whom beyond others King James would entrust the ruling of Scotland during his London years, one, Seton, later earl of Dunfermline, was an Octavian and the other, Home, later earl of Dunbar, was a Cubicular.

It was one of Seton's assets that his family had been for generations hereditary courtiers; it was, however, a drawback that they had been faithful to the Queen of Scots. It was difficult for King James to understand any one living so near the court who failed to recognise his crowned and anointed king. The prior of Pluscardine, as Alexander Seton was known in youth, had studied as a boy at the Roman college and had delivered an oration before Gregory XIII. When he returned to Scotland he abandoned such ideas[1] and became in name at least an adherent of the king's religion. He was at this time president of the court of Sessions and later received marks of royal favour. Eventually he would be chancellor. These posts he earned by his ability; but neither he nor his brother George Lord Seton ever seems to have penetrated to the king's inner circle. It may have been difficult for the sovereign to feel

---

[1] His three wives were Presbyterians and his children educated in that religion. Cf. a letter dated September 30, 1605, from Fr James Seton to Fr C. Aquaviva, general of the Society of Jesus. "He [Alexander Seton] publicly professes the state religion . . . and goes occasionally, though rarely, to the sermons, sometimes to their heretical communion. He has also subscribed their confession of faith. Two or three times a year he comes to Catholic confession and communion with his mother, brother, sister and nephews, who are better Catholics than himself." W. Forbes-Leith, S.J., ed., *Narratives of Scottish Catholics* (1885) 279.

at ease with those who had supported his mother's religion and his mother's claims.

The future minister among the Cubiculars was Sir George Home. He was in the time of the Octavians a gentleman of the bedchamber and master of the royal wardrobe; he was one of the organisers of the opposition. Later he would become earl of Dunbar and the king's chief adviser on Scottish matters.

After this brief account of sections of the courtiers, we can consider for a moment the court itself. Perhaps from motives of economy, and in this matter the appointment of the Octavians was a symptom, James VI appears to have made few alterations in his palaces in Scotland. They were in any case inherited in a rather shabby state. The various regents had no reason to spend money on them while the king was a boy in Stirling Castle. The Queen of Scots had little time to think about their structure in her unquiet reign and while she was in France they were for the most part untenanted. Most of the modern alterations dated from the time of James V, the king's grandfather. This is notably the case at the palaces of Falkland and Linlithgow. The chapel at Falkland was in particular both simple and old-fashioned, the screens were of oak beneath a plain oak ceiling. And there was apparently a royal pew in the same material with arcading and pilasters.[1] It seems that some of the furnishings at Holyrood were even earlier. Thus the red and blue hangings in the dining room and the canopy of state went back to the time of James V,[2] while the tapestries of the history of Troy in the great chamber, the tapestries of that siege in the king's hall and the series about Hercules in the king's chamber had all been hanging since that reign.

The performance of the masque seems to have been introduced at court after the marriage with Anne of Denmark. The younger courtiers took part in processions on one occasion as knights of Malta and on another as Moorish nobles. I suggest tentatively that this was the old kind of masque, which went back to the entertainments in the Hotel de Berri and to that disaster, recorded by Froissart, when the son of the count of Foix was burned to death.

There is one element in the decoration of Holyrood which should be recorded. On the oak ceiling of the audience chamber there was displayed the arms of the king's grandmother, Marie de Guise-Lorraine.

---

[1] Cf. the volume of the Royal Commission on *The Counties of Fife, Kinross and Clackmannan*, 139. [2] Cf. the volume of the Royal Commission on *The City of Edinburgh*, 144.

These included "1st, barry of eight, argent and gules, for Hungary; 2nd, azure, the fleur-de-lys of France ancient, or, for Anjou-Sicily; 3rd, argent, a cross-crosslet or, for Jerusalem; 4th, or, four pallets gules, for Aragon."[1] These armorial bearings were something which the king did not share with his Scottish cousins. Except for certain German dukes whom he addressed in Latin, the king wrote his letters in French to foreign princes. When writing in this language it was his custom to transmute Holyrood into "Sainte Croix". Snow fell early on the palace of Holyrood. The king never forgot the links he held with the great monarchies of southern Europe.

We must now consider King James's relationship with the Kirk of Scotland. If this had been a history of the reign the question of the Presbyterian kirk would have been treated long ago, but as it is a biography of a sovereign it has seemed best to leave an examination of this question until it came up when the king was already adult. It has been made clear that James VI was throughout his boyhood a convinced sincere believer in Presbyterian doctrine. He had been surely too young to understand the periods of difficulty between the government and the Kirk which had arisen through the ignorance of the first duke of Lennox or the malice of James Stuart, earl of Arran. In some respects King James was from the Presbyterian point of view a perfect ruler and had it not been for the theocratic outlook of the leading ministers the relationship would have been entirely peaceful. This theocratic approach derived directly from Geneva, although in that city there was no hereditary prince. In France the situation was very different. It is true that the queen of Navarre in her own states had had a relationship with the Calvinist ministers which was both close and had some element of dependence. But the king of Navarre her son was very different. In only one corner of France in the little sovereign principality of Sedan, which was ruled by the duke of Bouillon, was the Scottish situation to some extent reflected. In the Low Countries neither the prince of Orange nor his successor Maurice of Nassau was close to the church Establishment, while for various reasons the Scottish position was not found in the few Calvinist states within the empire.

A number of causes had created the special outlook of the Scottish ministers. In the first place they included among their leaders a number of men belonging to the lesser baronage and this gave them confidence. Further the ministers had originally belonged to a great political party

[1] *The City of Edinburgh*, 151.

which had included the majority of the Scottish earls. Finally they had an avowed and understandable suspicion of the "papist" influences to which the young king gave such unaccountable support.

Now the peers, belonging to the second generation of the Reformed faith, had for the most part lost their earlier fervour. It was left to the Kirk alone to check the king's proclivities. James VI was patient and, in his early years, magnanimous. He was, moreover, linked with many of the leading ministers by his own deep respect for learning. In the lowlands of Scotland he was always close at hand and he had seen what the ministers had done for the study of Greek in the universities. Thus even Andrew Melville, who can be considered as the leader of the opposition, had in the past owed much to him.

Melville was now fifty-one years old and had known the king since he was first presented to him at Stirling Castle in 1574 on his return from several years in France and in Geneva. It was a royal nomination which had transferred him from his post as principal of Glasgow University to the same office at St Mary's in the university of St Andrews. His establishment of the chairs for Greek and for philosophy and theology on the Genevan model and everything that he did for studies in the kingdom was welcome to his sovereign. He had been on several occasions moderator of the general assembly of the church of Scotland.

Melville had surveyed the king's friendship with Huntly and did not like it. This was natural, for behind Huntly in his own family and in his clan there was a strong element of "popery". Now, encouraged by the Cubicular faction, he made an attack on the Octavians. He accused Lord Drumcairn, Sir Alexander Seton and Lord Balmerino of being "papists". In the case of Balmerino there is very little evidence, perhaps the charge had some foundation. It is not wise to be too sceptical. Drumcairn had studied in Paris under his Catholic uncle. Whatever had been his opinions at that time there had never afterwards been a hint of any departure from a strongly royalist Presbyterianism. The case of Sir Alexander Seton was rather different for he had certainly at one time been a Catholic, but it seems to me that this religious outlook had later vanished. The letter from Father Seton, quoted earlier, sounds confusing. How could Alexander Seton have received the Catholic sacraments, while he remained a member of the church of Scotland? Still, the Kirk was justified in her suspicions. Both these statesmen were regalians, that is to say whole-hearted supporters of the rights and power of the Scottish monarchy.

71

It was burdensome to the king that it was his more intimate friends who were subjected to this clerical inquisition, and all the more so because his own faith in Presbyterian doctrine was so clear. It was he himself who had been responsible for the submission of the earls of Huntly and Erroll to the Kirk and he had secured the Presbyterian upbringing of their heirs Lord Gordon and Lord Hay. He was always seeking for converts from Rome, as witness his cousin Lady Mar.

As a result of or at least concurrently with this intervention the grouping of the Octavians was abandoned; but the more important effect was the king's determination to check the power of the Kirk. This campaign, which lasted for the remaining years of his reign before the death of Queen Elizabeth, was carried on with skill and confidence. The king showed himself both douce and crafty. The Kirk had small power to reward and her influence in the king's circle was now slight. It is also clear that it was a campaign without danger; it did not call upon the king's small stock of physical courage.

The action which set off this movement was the appearance of Andrew Melville and a group of ministers at Falkland Palace. The speech made on that occasion is well known, but it should be remembered in considering it again that the word "silly" then employed indicated feeble or ignorant rather than its modern meaning. "Howbeit the King", so runs the account, "used his authority in most crabbed and choleric manner, yet Mr Andrew [Melville] bore him down, calling the King but God's silly vassal; and, taking him by the sleeve, says this in effect: Sir, you are brought in extreme danger both of your life and Crown, and with you the country and Kirk of Christ is like to wreck."

The next event delivered the ministers into the hands of their cautious sovereign. David Black, minister of St Andrews, in a violent sermon described all kings as devil's bairns and also declared that Queen Elizabeth was an atheist. The queen of England had often toyed with the Presbyterian opposition towards whom Walsingham, among her advisers, had always shown much sympathy. Now was the time when the king could move against his enemies, with the queen's full support. This coincided with an attempt of the other courtiers to get rid of the Octavians. It was explained to the four ministers in Edinburgh that the king's advisers were determined on their ruin. On December 17, 1596, there took place a little riot, which has become known as the "corslet tumult". On that day the pulpits began to sound against the government. At the end of the sermon at St Giles, there was a shout of "Save yourselves. Armour, armour, bills and axes." The king was in the Tolbooth with the lords of session. A mob pressed on the doors crying "Bring forth the wicked Haman". This was an evil moment for the king's proud servants. The disturbance was soon quelled without any difficulty by the provost and craftsmen. There is a statement by Baillie, who was perhaps hardly an impartial witness. "No tumult in the world was ever more harmless in the effects, nor more innocent in the causes, if you consider all those who did openly act therein."[1] The king went down the hill to Holyrood.

The next day he rode quietly to Linlithgow accompanied by all his courtiers. The seat of justice was transferred from Edinburgh to this small county town. The council described the riot as an act of treason and the Edinburgh ministers took flight. A fine of twenty thousand marks was levied on the city. It must have been a happiness for the king to have had all the arguments upon his side.

From this time forward the king began to make headway against the Kirk particularly in regard to the Presbyterian theories of the place of the kingship in the nation. The king took up the question of making bishops with a view to checking the rights of ministers to speak on questions of policy in the name of the Church of God. Their egalitarian theories were obnoxious to him. Certainly not now, nor even later did the king display much interest in the Anglican view of episcopal succession. What he needed in effect was a small body, chosen by himself, who would act as royal officers.

The idea of an episcopate in the Reformed Church had flickered on throughout the reign; it did not start with him. When he was a boy there had been the "tulchan" bishops and then the appointments dating from the Lennox-Arran period. There is little sign that the king had much regard for them. The leading figure had been Patrick Adamson, who had held the archbishopric of St Andrews in the king's boyhood from 1576 until he was cast out by Melville's fierce attacks on him. In 1591 he made the following confession[2] a short while before his death. It is the third paragraph that is significant. "I gloried in my riches and great living, and now I am so poore that I have no meanes to intertaine my selfe; I gloried in my eloquence, and now few can understand what I speake; I gloried in the favour of my Prince, and now he loveth any of the dogges of his kennell better nor me." The fact appears to be that

---

[1] Robert Baillie, *An Historicall Vindication of the Government of the Church of Scotland*, etc. (2 pts, 1646), 70, 71.   [2] John Row, *Historie of the Kirk of Scotland*, pt I, 35-6.

King James had little personal interest in his Scottish bishops. They had to be chosen from among the Presbyterian ministers, a class from whom he had become alienated increasingly. He had, it seems, one object in all these questions, to free the crown.

By an act of 1592 the king retained the right to call and to decide the place of meetings of the general assemblies. For some years he carefully abstained from calling meetings in the Lothians and in the west of Scotland. In 1597 there were gatherings at Perth and at Dundee and three years later another at Montrose. These were in the relatively calmer areas. He obtained a council of ministers as his advisers and laboured with them. Finally "the Trojan Horse, the Episcopacy was brought in busked and covered with caveats, that the danger and deformity might not be seen".[1] The appointments of three bishops, Lindsay to Ross, Gladstanes to Caithness and Sutherland, and Blackburn to Moray, were made in 1602. These had no unfettered diocesan authority. He had worked very slowly. It is now time to consider other aspects of the king's character.

[1] Calderwood, *History of the Kirk of Scotland*, VII, 20.

Chapter 9

DAEMONOLOGIE

THE DEVIL was inside North Berwick kirk. He had a tall black hat on his head above his dark face. He was sitting in the pulpit. He was clad in a black gown and he had need of these accoutrements for he was cold as ice and his body "hard like iron as they thought who handled him".[1] His face was terrible; his nose like the beak of an eagle; great burning eyes. He was surrounded by lighted candles and he spoke with a low voice.

He had been invited to the kirk by the earl of Bothwell's private warlock. Many witches came together to this coven. They were led by Geilles Duncan playing a Jew's trump to which they sang these words.

> Commer goe ye before, Commer goe ye,
> Gif ye will not goe before, commer let me.[2]

Thus it was all set out and there was much in these recitals to disturb the king, who was always conscious of the prince of Darkness. In this instance those present at the coven had related what the devil had said sitting in the pulpit. He had been asked why he had not succeeded in his various efforts to harm the king. "*Il est un homme de Dieu.* Certainly he is a man of God and does no wrong wittingly, but he is inclined to all godliness, justice and virtue." It seems that King James savoured this tribute from his great enemy. His duty to extirpate all witches was a burden on his conscience. It is clear that he maintained a clear belief in these phenomena.

In these days it is the witches who gain our sympathy. Often they lived for years giving herbalist remedies with some use of white magic before grave trouble came to them. Those about Edinburgh, who were involved in the North Berwick and other manifestations, seem for the most part to have come from the deeply Presbyterian lower middle class. Two of them were of superior education, Euphemia Macalzean, who

---

[1] Steuart, *Memoirs of Sir James Melville*, 353.

[2] Cf. *Newes from Scotland, declaring the damnable life and death of Dr Vian a notable Sorcerer*, printed 1591, ed. G. B. Harrison, from Bodleian Douce MSS, F. 210, p. 14.

was the only child of the judge Lord Cliftonhall, and Barbara Napier.[1] The differing shades of religious mania have their place here. Some of these women appear to have possessed a long-established conviction of their own reprobation. As they went forward, sometimes throwing themselves towards their own destruction, the Edinburgh witches came upon the king's strange interest. It is related that "these confessions made the King in a wonderful admiration and [he] sent for ye said Geillis Duncan, who upon the Trump did playe the dance before the Kings Majestie, who in respect of the strangeness of these matters tooke great delight to bee present at their examinations."[2] Thus the Lothian witches spiralled forward, dazzled by the earnest questions from their sovereign and his private colloquies. It is a repellent story. The best that can be said is that their strangling was not deeply painful; they were dead before the burning.

It is worth noting that the type of witchcraft which was associated with the countryside appears to have aroused but little interest in King James's mind. Such rites as those which involved filling a white pitcher with lax water from a south-running well[3] went with agricultural customs which were remote from him. The king was in no sense a countryman; the country was a region in which to pursue his hunting.

One would wish to curb a tendency towards the fanciful, but it sometimes seems to me that King James's concern with the devil was part of the interest which he showed in the Dark monarchy, an interest that was always lapped in fear. He would perhaps see the prince of Darkness as another kind of ruler who would exercise his sway over the king of Scotland's subjects. Whatever was the mixture of his motives he settled down to write for his own people his little treatise on *Daemonologie*.

This was a slender volume in three books printed at Edinburgh in 1597 by the king's printer, Robert Waldegrave. Philomanthes and Epistemon reason the matter, the second speaker who had the king's own voice gives all the arguments. They begin by basing themselves soundly on the scriptures and the king draws attention to a number of those who spoke with the devil's voice, beginning with the Pythoness with Saul and ending up with Simon Magus. He warned his reader

---

[1] She was burned for killing the earl of Angus with her spells. Cf., for a discussion of witchcraft in the Lothians a little later, Mathew, *Scotland under Charles I*, 55-8, and *Register of the Privy Council of Scotland*, II, Introduction, xlii.

[2] *Newes from Scotland, op. cit.,* 14.

[3] *Register of the Privy Council of Scotland*, V, 565-6.

seriously to have no dealings with the Evil One lest he be carried from the earth.

And this farre onelie I Touche, that when the conjured Spirit appeares, which will not be while after manie circumstances, long praiers, and much muttering and murmuring of the conjurers; like a Papist priest, dispatching a hunting Masse: how sone I say, he appears, if they have missed one iote of all their rites; or if any of their feete once slyd over the circle through terror of his fearful apparition, he payes himself at that time in his owne hande, of that due debt which they ought [owe] him; and other-wise would have delayed longer to have payed him; I meane he carries them with him bodie and soul.[1]

On the other hand the early effects might be tolerable enough.

To the most curious sorte, in the formes he will oblish [oblige] himself, to enter in a dead bodie, and there out to give such answers, of the event of battles, of matters concerning the estate of commonwelths, and such like oether great questions: yea, to some he will be a continuall attender, in the form of a Page.[2]

His other services were well set out.

These formes, wherein Sataan oblishes [obliges] himselfe to the greatest of the Magicians, are wounderfull curious; so are the effects correspondent unto the same: For he will oblish [oblige] himselfe to teach them artes and sciences, which he may easelie doe, being so learned a knave as he is: To carrie them news from anie parte of the worlde, which the agilities of a Spirite may easelie perform: to reveale to them the secretes of anie persons, so being they bee once spoken. . . . Such-like, he will guard his schollers with faire armies of horse-men and footemen in appearance, castles and fortes: Which all are but impressiones in the aire, easelie gathered by a Spirite, drawing so neare to that substance himselfe.[3]

In the first book he has set out with great care the limit of the services that the devil can offer.

This little book, somewhat didactic and very earnest, keeps almost too strictly to the point at issue; but it does quite casually give an insight into King James's approach to denominational religion. One reference to the papists has been given already, but in the course of this small tract there are some others. The king speaks, for instance, of the impossibility of the devil contracting a solid body into a tiny space. "I thinke", he writes, "that this is contrarie to the qualitie of a natural

[1] *Daemonologie*, 18.   [2] *Ibid.*, 20.   [3] *Ibid.*, 21.

bodie, and so like to the little transubtantiat god in the Papistes Masse, that I never can believe it."[1]

There are certain severe references to the state of Catholicism in the Middle Ages. "For as we know, moe [more] Ghostes and spirites were seene, nor tongue can tell, in the time of blinde Papistrie in these [northern] countries."[2] The king accepted no belief in fairies. "To speake of the many vaine trattles founded upon that illusion. How there was a King and Queen of Phairie . . . was one of the sortes . . . that was rifest in the times of Papistrie."[3] There was yet another reference to "the times of Papistrie and blindness".[4]

These phrases are very telling. They show that into the beginnings of middle life the king had accepted each aspect of the Presbyterian teaching. Yet even from this early days there was a tendency to show favour to the Catholic earls. He also had, what all the monarchs of his century with the possible exception of Henry IV of France shared with him, a desire for religious uniformity among his subjects. As the years went by his views would moderate until eventually he was much less opposed to the church of Rome than were the members of the English House of Commons. In a sense it seems to have been his worldliness that gained on him, that sense of the comity of the great monarchies. In his later years he would regard with favour the projects for introducing Catholic princesses of Spain, France or Savoy into his family. His attitude to the papacy would also change, bearing in mind that the pope was a temporal sovereign. Later he felt that as a western king there were possible developments in which he might support the western patriarch. "And," he would come to write, "for his temporal principality over the Signory of Rome, I do not quarrel [with] it either."[5] All the same it was the monarchical and not the dogmatic conceptions of the Tridentine world which would in time appeal to him. The comments in *Daemonologie* exhibit the simpler approaches of the Scottish sovereign.

In the second book the king touches upon sorcery and witchcraft. He makes it clear that it is always in solitude that Satan approaches those whom he wishes to make his adepts.

He finde[s] the time proper to discover himself unto them. At which time, either upon their walking solitarie in the fieldes, or else lying pansing in their bed; but alwaies without the company of any other, he either by a voyce or in likeness of a man inquires of them, what troubles them; and promiseth

[1] *Daemonologie*, 40.   [2] *Ibid.*, 54.   [3] *Ibid.*, 74.   [4] *Ibid.*, 65.   [5] *A Premonition.*

them a suddaine and certaine waie of remedie, upon condition on the other parte, that they follow his advise; and do such thinges as he will require of them.[1]

This is succeeded by a detailed account of the devil's practice of marking witches in a secret place.[2] And the reader is assured that he is still "the same Devil and as craftie nowe as he was then".[3]

King James believed that Satan might carry witches through the air on their way to the covens where they adored him.

One way [he wrote] is natural, which is natural riding, going or sayling, at what houre their Master comes and advertises them. And this way may be easilie beleved: an other way is some-what more strange, and yet is it possible to be true: which is by being carryed by the force of the Spirite which is their conducter, either above the earth or above the sea swiftlie, to the place where they are to meet: which I am perswaded to be likewaies possible.[4]

The king pointed out that water would refuse to receive witches, nor were their eyes able to shed tears "albeit the women kinde especially be able other-waies to shed tears at every light occasion when they will, yea, although it were dissemblingly like the Crocodiles." At one stage Philomanthes makes an interjection.[5] "I pray you to interrupt . . . one worde, which yee have put mee in memorie of by speaking of women. What can be the cause that there are twentie women given to that craft, where ther is one man?" To this Epistemon made reply. "The reason is easie, for as that sexe is frailer than man is, so is it easier to be intrapped in these grosse snares of the Devil, as was over well proved to be true by the Serpent's deceiving of Eva at the beginning, which makes him the homelier with that sexe since then." After discussing the devil's use of human semen, Philomanthes puts this question.[6] "But what is the cause that this kinde of abuse is thought to be most common in such wilde partes of the world, as Lapland and Finland, or in the north iles of Orknay and Shetland?" The reply is quite explicit. "Because where the Devil findes greatest ignorance and barbarities, there assayles he grosseliest, as I gave you the reason wherefore there was more witches of women kinde nor men." The king shows here that lack of esteem for the female sex which always marked him.

The last words of this treatise have their significance. "The consummation of the worlde, and our deliverance drawing near, makes Sathan

---

[1] *Daemonologie*, 32. [2] *Ibid.*, 33. [3] *Ibid.*, 37. [4] *Ibid.*, 38.
[5] *Ibid.*, 43. [6] *Ibid.*, 69.

to rage the more in his instruments, knowing his kingdome to be so neare an ende."[1] But the king's true outlook is revealed in an earlier passage. "For where God beginnes justlie to strike by his lawful Lieutennentes, it is not in the Devil's power to defraude or bereave him of the office or effect of his powerfull and revenging Scepter."[2] The king knew well that he was God's lieutenant.

At the same time this book reveals that King James had no belief in astrology, which had still its numerous adepts throughout Europe. The subject was wholly alien to his rational and Presbyterian standpoint. "One word onely", he declared with lucid firmness, "I will answer to them [the Astrologers], & that in the Scriptures (which must be an infallible ground to all true Christians) : that in the Prophet Jeremie it is plainelie forbidden, to beleeve or hearken unto them that prophecies & fore-speakes by the course of the Planets & Starres."[3] He based himself with orthodoxy upon the Scriptures. There were many upon the continent who did not. Albrecht Wenzel Eusebius von Wallenstein, the great general of that Thirty Years War during which King James was to die, is an example. In the midst of his tortuous negotiations he would call in his astrologers to learn what the stars foretold for him. It is important not to overstress these points which separate men most from the understanding of our own days. Both demonology and astrology are disciplines which are alien to us now. They made no difference to their adherents' judgment of other issues.

As the years went by the personal devil seems to have counted for less in the king's judgments. It was a conception which belonged essentially to his northern kingdom and was bound up with the less sophisticated world of the earl of Bothwell. It is difficult for us to disentangle the motives that lay behind the actions of that strange man. The same difficulty in another form lies behind the happenings of what is generally known as the rising of the Catholic earls. In this case it turns upon their areas of knowledge. What exactly did Spain mean to them? And how did they consider that their own fortunes could be assisted by King Philip's victory? A further question as to what was King James's attitude towards this project has already been examined.

[1] *Daemonologie*, 81. [2] *Ibid.*, 51. [3] *Ibid.*, 14.

Chapter 10

BASILIKON DORON

THE *Basilikon Doron* is sometimes misunderstood because it is not appreciated that it was written while King James was ruling in his Scottish kingdom. It is this that gives the survey its importance. It was composed while the king was still surrounded by his relatively small court in Scotland. Except for the ambassadors who had come to the Scottish court, he had at that time met no foreigners except on his brief visit to the king of Denmark. As far as the book is concerned he was clearly pleased with his sage observations. He began by a private printing of seven copies by Waldegrave, his Edinburgh printer, in 1599 and followed this up four years later by a public edition from the same press. Further it was reprinted in the folio collection of the king's *Works* in 1616 and 1620. It is worth examining with care.

As long as he was in Scotland King James was the chief author at his own court. It would be different when he came to England where he would find great polymaths like Sir Francis Bacon and Sir Walter Raleigh. In spite of all their sugared courtesies he does not seem to have been at ease at any time with either of them. To find out the reason why, it is only necessary to study the *Basilikon Doron*.

This book carries as its sub-title the words "Or His Majesties instructions to his dearest sonne Henry the Prince". The argument is headed by one of the king's own sonnets. A brief quotation will give an impression of the introduction addressed to his eldest son. "Charging you in the presence of God, and by the fatherly authoritie I have over you, that yee keepe it ever with you, as carefully as Alexander did the *Iliads* of Homer. Ye will finde it a just and impartiall counsellor."[1]

The introduction to the "charitable reader" contains a graceful reference to the queen of England.

But notwithstanding, since there is a lawfull Queene, who hath so long with so great wisdome and felicitie governed her kingdomes, as (I must in trewe sinceritie confesse) the like hath not been read or heard of, either in our time,

---

[1] C. H. McIlwain, ed., *The Political Works of James I*, 4.

or since the dayes of the Romane Emperour Augustus; it could no wayes become me, farre inferiour to her in knowledge and experience, to be a busie-body in other princes matters, and to fish in other folkes waters, as the proverbe is.[1]

The first book deals with "A King's Christian duetie towards God". The position is set out very clearly.[2]

Therfore (my Sonne) first of all things, learne to know and love God, whom-to ye have a double obligation; first, for that he made you a man; and next, for that he made you a little God to sit on his Throne, and rule over other men. Remember that this glistering worldie glorie of Kings, is given them by God, to teach them . . . so to glister and shine before their people, in all workes of sanctification and righteousnesse, that their persons as bright lampes of godlinesse and vertue, may, going in and out before their people, give light to all their steps.

The same line of thought continues and at length the rewards of a virtuous sovereign are set forth. "For a good King . . . eternal felicitie in heaven."

The king now comes to more mundane considerations and has a comment upon the use of parliaments.[3]

Onely remember that as Parliaments have bene ordained for making of Lawes, so ye abuse not their institution in holding them for any mens particulars. For as a Parliament is the honourablest and highest judgement in the land (as being the Kings head Court) if it be well used, which is making of good Lawes in it; so is it the injustest Judgement-seat that may be being abused to men's particulars. . . . And therefore hold no Parliaments, but for necessities of new Lawes, which would be but seldome.

The king, it seems, was thinking of the use of parliaments for bringing forfeiture upon particular nobles; he had had enough of this.

And when yee have? [he continued] by the severities of Justice once setled your countries, and made them know that ye can strike, then may ye there-after all the daies of your life mixe Justice with Mercie, punishing or sparing, as ye shall finde the crime to have bene wilfully or rashly committed, and according to the by-past behaviour of the committer. . . . But in this, my over-deare bought experience may serve you for a sufficient lesson. For I confesse, where I thought (by being gracious at the beginning) to win all mens hearts to a loving and willing obedience, I by the contrary found, the disorder of the countrie, and the losse of my thankes to be all my reward.[4]

---

[1] *The Political Works of James I*, 11.   [2] *Ibid.*, 12.   [3] *Ibid.*, 19.   [4] *Ibid.*, 20.

He next comes to a list of crimes which should be considered carefully.

But as this severe Justice of yours upon all offences would bee but for a time, (as I have alreadie said) so is there some horrible crimes that yee are bound in conscience never to forgive: such as Witch-craft, wilfull murther, Incest (especiallie within the degrees of consanguinitie), Sodomie, poisoning, and false witness. As for offences against your owne person and authoritie, since the fault concerneth your selfe, I remit to your owne choise to punish or pardon therein, as your heart serveth you, and according to the circumstances of the turne, and the qualitie of the committer.[1]

That witchcraft should be placed ahead of wilful murder is in keeping with all that we know of the king's character. The word that makes me pause is sodomy. Little is known of the king's private life in 1599. It seems likely enough that he was then without a favourite. The king was fond of tumbling with his young men; perhaps he held that he did not complete the act which merited the severest penalties.

There then come certain phrases which throw light on King James's outlook on his own relations.

Wherefore destroy men innocent young sucking Wolves and Foxes, but for the hatred they beare to their race? And why wil a coult of a Courser of Naples, give a greater price in a market, than an Asse-colt, but for love of the race? . . . And for conclusion of this point, I may also alledge my own experience. For besides the judgments of God, that with my eyes I have seene fall upon all them that were chiefe traitours to my parents, I may justly affirme, I never found yet a constant biding by me in all my straites, by any that were of perfite age in my parents dayes, but onely by such as constantly bode by them; I meane specially by them that served the Queene my mother.[2]

There was also a reference to James V. "Have the King my grandfathers example before your eyes, who by his adulterie bred the wracke of his lawful daughter and heire; in begetting that bastard [the earl of Moray], who unnaturally rebelled, and procured the ruine of his own Soverane and sister. And what good her posteritie hath gotten sensyne, of some of that unlawfull generation, Bothwell his treacherous attempts can beare witnesse."[3]

He would return to his son's power of judging. "Remember when ye sit in judgement, that the Throne ye sit on is God's, as Moyses saith, and sway neither to the right hand nor to the left; either loving the rich, or

[1] *The Political Works of James I*, 20-1.   [2] *Ibid.*, 21.   [3] *Ibid.*, 36.

pittying the poore. Justice should be blinde and friendlesse."[1] Again the king went back to his own childhood.

Some fierie spirited men in the [Presbyterian] ministrie got such a guiding of the people at that time of confusion, as finding the gust of government sweete, they begouth to fantasie to themselves a Democraticke forme of Government: and having (by the iniquitie of time) beene overwell baited upon the wracke, first of my Grandmother, and next of mine owne mother, and after usurping the libertie of the time in my long minoritie, setled themselves to fass upon that imagined Democracie, as they fed themselves with the hope to become *Tribuni Plebis*: and so in a popular government by leading the people by the nose, to beare the sway of all the rule.[2]

He soon returned to this same subject. "I protest before the great God, and since I am here as upon my Testament, it is no place for me to lie in, that ye shall never finde with anie Hie-land or Border theeves greater ingratitude, and more lies and vile perjuries, than with these phanatique spirits. And suffer not the principals of them to brooke your land, if ye like to sit at rest; except yee would keepe them for trying your patience, as Socrates did an evill wife."[3]

After certain comments on the feuds of the nobility, he set down some often-quoted sentences.

But the greatest hindrance to the execution of our Lawes in this countrie, are these heritable Sherifdomes and Regalities, which being in the hands of the great men do wracke the whole countrie. For which I know no present remedie, but by taking the sharper account of them in their offices; using all punishment against the slouthfull, that the Law will permit: and ever as they vaike [become vacant] for any offences committed by them, dispone them never heritably againe.[4]

There is then the comment on the merchants. "They transport from us things necessarie; bringing backe sometimes unnecessary things, and at other times nothing at all. They buy for us the worst wares, and sell them at the dearest prices."[5] The final comment deals with the artisans. "And the Craftsmen thinke, we should be content their worke, how bad and deare soever it be: and if they in any thing be controlled, up goeth the blew-blanket."[6] The king recommended the English practice of bringing in from abroad numbers of foreign artisans and craftsmen.[7]

[1] *The Political Works of James I*, 22.   [2] *Ibid.*, 23.   [3] *Ibid.*, 24.   [4] *Ibid.*, 26.   [5] *Ibid.*, 26.
[6] *Ibid.*, 25-6.   [7] Cf., for the settlement of French and Dutch subjects for the purposes of trade at a rather later date, *Register of Burgesses of the Burgh of Aberdeen, 1631-1700* (Miscellany of the New Spalding Club), I.

In the third book dealing with "a King's behaviour in indifferent things" there are reflections of the simple customs of the Scottish court.

Let your table be honourably served; but serve your appetite with few dishes, as yong Cyrus did: which both is wholesommest and freest from the vice of delicacie. . . . And use most to eate of reasonablie-grosse and common-meates; as well for making your bodie strong and durable for travell at all occasions. . . . In the forme of your meate-eating bee neither uncivill, like a grosse cynicke; nor affectatlie mignarre, like a daintie dame, but eate in a manlie, round and honest fashion.[1]

This brought back the food stuffs of the earl of Mar at Stirling Castle; it was a contrast to the queen of England's more dainty meats. "Let all your food bee simple, without composition or sauces; which are more like medecines than meate."[2]

Especially in his last years in Scotland King James was ridden by suspicions and this is reflected in the present comments.

Let not your Chamber be throng and common in the time of your rest, as well for comelinesse as for eschewing of carrying reports out of the same. Let them that have the credits to serve in your Chamber be trustie and secret; for a King will have need to use secrecie in many things; but behave your selfe so in your greatest secretes as ye neede not bee ashamed, suppose they were call proclaimed at the Mercate Cross. . . . Take no heede to any of your dreames.[3]

The prince was in his clothes to be strictly moderate, not clad "over lightly like a Candie soldier or a vaine young Courtier."[4]

Then the king came once more to a subject which was always with him. "Let your selfe and all your Court weare no ordinarie armour with your cloathes, but such as is knightly and honourable; I meane rapier-swordes and daggers. . . . And therefore bannish not onely from your Court, all traiterous offensive weapons, forbidden by the Lawes, as guns and such like (whereof I spake alreadie)[5] but also all traiterous defensive armes, as secrets, plate-sleeves, and such like unseene arm-our."[6] He went on for some sentences arguing against these practices and then concluded. "For answere against these arguments, I know none but the old Scots fashion; which if it be wrong, is no more to be allowed for ancientnesse, than the old Masse is, which also our fore-fathers used."

[1] McIlwain, *The Political Works of James I*, 44.   [2] *Ibid.*, 44.   [3] *Ibid.*, 44-5.   [4] *Ibid.*, 45.
[5] Cf. "And for your easier abolishing of them, put sharpelie to execution my lawes made against Gunnes and traiterous Pistolets" *ibid.*, 25.   [6] *Ibid.*, 46.

The king warned him to be plain in his language and to avoid "pen and inke-horne termes".[1] He was not to act "unsetledly, with an uncouth morgue, like a new-comeover Cavalier".[2] At an earlier stage he had commended certain books to the young prince.

I would have you [he explained] to be well versed in authentick histories, and in the Chronicles of all nations, but specially in our owne histories the example whereof most neerely concernes you. I meane not such infamous invectives as Buchanans or Knoxes Chronicles. . . . And among all prophane histories I must not omit most specially to recommend unto you the Commentaries of Caesar; both for the sweete flowing of the stile, as also for the worthinesse of the matter it selfe. For I have ever beene of that opinion, that of all the Ethnick Emperors, or great Captaines that ever were, he hath farthest excelled both in his practise and in his precepts in martiall affaires.[3]

King James was a peaceful sovereign. He had only one foreigner upon his frontier and he knew well that he had not the strength ever to engage the queen of England's forces. "I graunte," he said, and there seems something perfunctory about his words, "it is meete yee have some entrance, specially in the Mathematickes; for the knowledge of the arte militarie, in situation of campes, ordering of battels, making fortifications, placing of batteries, or such like."[4] There is here a curious sentence. "And so," he is found exclaiming, "where ye finde a notable injurie, spare not to give course to the torrents of your wrath."[5] He ends up with a quotation from Proverbs, 20, *The wrath of a King is like to the roaring of a Lyon.* This must have been how he pictured himself in his imagination for in fact his voice was weak and though sometimes he brought men down he did this silently. He had two deeply attractive qualities which throughout the *Basilikon Doron* he does not mention . . . He was gentle and very generous.

There are a few other comments which throw some light upon King James's private life.

It becommeth a Prince best of any man to be a faire and good horse-man. . . . I debarre all rough and violent exercises, as the footeball; meeter for laming than making able the users thereof: as likewise such tumbling trickes as only serve for Comoedians and Balladines, to win their bread with . . . . I cannot omit heere the hunting, namely with running hounds; which is the most honourable and noblest sorte thereof: for it is a theevish forme of hunting to shoote with gunnes and bowes.[6]

[1] *The Political Works of James I,* 46.   [2] *Ibid.,* 47.   [3] *Ibid.,* 40.   [4] *Ibid.,* 40.
[5] *Ibid.,* 41.   [6] *Ibid.,* 48-50.

And then there is a comment on the prince's life indoors. "Ye may lawfully play at the cardes or tables. For as to dicing, I thinke it becommeth best deboshed souldiers to play at, on the head of their drums, being onely ruled by hazard and subject to knavish cogging. And as for the chesse, I thinke it over fond, because it is over-wise and Philosophicke a folly."[1] Thus the young prince might amuse himself in the future at Holyrood or Falkland or Linlithgow when it was "foul and stormie weather".

What can we say of the *Basilikon Doron*? It is marked throughout by a certain *naïveté* and seems very genuine. The queen of England had had a cool judgment of the merits and the needs of a Protestantism considered as essentially political. The king's interests on the other hand were theological at a low level of intensity. He was a Protestant royalist and this must have given comfort to the bishops and to all the aspiring English churchmen as they read these writings. It was a change from the old queen who had so much preferred her military servitors. King James never feared longwindedness and was much at home when settling down to state the obvious. It is to be noted that he paid lip service to the poor. What the courtiers thought of the *Basilikon Doron* they did not say. It has no references to France and only one to Spain, a comment on the discipline of Spanish infantry.

A certain turmoil seems reflected in this book; there are so many references to arms and guns. One can see how fear might well expel the royal gentleness, when the hostile forces pressed against the king's fine theory. He could not have been unconscious of his great burdens. The king at one point was explaining how in certain families sickness of the mind tended "to infect in the seede". He added a note to the 1616 edition, "Witnesse the experience of the late House of Gowrie". The king's ideas, as expressed in *Basilikon Doron*, do indeed throw a certain light on that conspiracy.[2]

[1] *The Political Works of James I*, 49.   [2] *Ibid.*, 31 *n.*

87

Chapter 11

THE HOUSE OF GOWRIE

It was the early morning of Tuesday August 4, 1600, and with the short nights of that high latitude the sun was already rising beyond the open lands of the Carse of Gowrie when at four o'clock Alexander Ruthven, accompanied by his brother's chamberlain and one other servant, set out from Gowrie House to ride to Falkland Palace where the king was staying. For some years now the house of Gowrie had lived in peace. Their head was by inheritance provost of Perth, they had great influence in their home city. In 1586 by the royal favour their rights had been restored to them. Except for the married daughters they were a united family.[1] The thirteen children of the first earl of Gowrie had been brought up at Perth by the widowed countess, who was by birth a Stewart of Methven. They were now all alive except the eldest son, James, earl of Gowrie, who had died aged thirteen, and the third daughter, Sophia, who had not long survived her marriage to the duke of Lennox. The two surviving elder sons, the young earl and his brother Alexander, were living together, both unmarried, at Gowrie House, the two youngest sons were both at school in Edinburgh. The countess of Gowrie was staying at this time at Dirleton in the Lothians. It is worth noting that both the heads of the family were very young. Gowrie was twenty-two and his next brother twenty. The earl had returned this year from studying at Padua; he had stayed on his way home with Theodore Bèza in Geneva, he had also visited the English court. The Ruthvens were among the first of the Scottish families to accept the Geneva discipline; they had never faltered.

There were certain connections with the royal stock. Dorothea countess of Gowrie was the daughter, legitimated *per subsequentem matrimonium*, of Lord Methven.[2] Her father had been married earlier to the queen of Scotland, while her father-in-law Lord Ruthven had claimed to avenge the honour of his cousin Darnley when he killed Rizzio. This

---

[1] Cf. Chart pedigree 6 for the house of Gowrie.

[2] In an attempt to suggest a Ruthven claim to the English throne it has been suggested that Lady Gowrie was the daughter of the master of Methven, who was killed at Pinkie. But it is now clear that the master of Methven was not the son of Queen Margaret (Tudor), but of his father's earlier marriage.

relationship had come through Ruthven's marriage to a natural daughter of the earl of Angus. These points are merely mentioned to be dismissed. They played no part in bringing about the Gowrie catastrophe. Only two members of the family were attached to the royal court, Alexander Ruthven known as the Master of Gowrie until his elder brother should bear a son, and his unmarried sister Lady Barbara. Both were attached to the queen's household.

The master's wait outside Falkland Palace that August morning is the most fitting moment for us to consider the two main theories which have been brought forward to explain what is known as the Gowrie conspiracy. They must be examined here because they are the only two explanations which involve the element of premeditation. The first, which the king supported, was that this was a plot by the Ruthven family against their sovereign. The second theory was that this was a manoeuvre by which the king intended to extirpate the house of Gowrie.

The second theory has the support of Mr W. N. Roughead;[1] but in view of King James's character it appears quite unconvincing. It would involve a murderous action by a sovereign who loved legality. That the king should have ridden alone to do this deed would have needed an element of foolhardy courage which runs counter to all that we know of his life of fears. The first theory was ultimately put forward by the king on his own behalf. The reasons which make it appear impossible will be brought forward as the events are described.

These are the two theories which involve plotting; if neither of them is correct and if no variant of either appears practicable it follows that when the king accepted the invitation of the master of Gowrie to ride to Perth they were both of them unaware of the destruction that would overtake the Ruthven family. On this reading of the events the account generally given of the happenings before the king reached Gowrie House can be accepted.

Shortly after the king came out of Falkland Palace and before he could mount he was approached by the master. Genuflecting he begged a private word and the two men walked up and down, the courtiers standing at a little distance. These included the duke of Lennox and the earl of Mar, the brothers James and Thomas Erskine, John Ramsay and Sir Hugh Herries with John Murray carrying the king's hawk.

[1] The period of most active discussion was at the close of the last century. Andrew Lang, *James VI and the Gowrie Conspiracy*, was printed in 1902, and W. N. Roughead, *The Riddle of the Ruthvens and other Studies*, in 1919. A more recent analysis of these events by W. F. Arbuckle appears in *Scottish Historical Review*, xxxvi.

It should be mentioned at this point that the earl of Gowrie owed a very large sum of money, about £80,000, to the crown dating from the period when his father had held the office of lord treasurer of Scotland.

The story put forward by the master of Gowrie has often been regarded as incredible, but there are some elements in the exchanges which sound convincing. The master explained that on the previous evening he had found a man in the fields near Perth carrying under his cloak a pot filled with gold coins. He had seized the man and his burden. They were both safely secured either in or near to Gowrie House. He begged the king to come at once. The earl of Gowrie was at church and they could finish their matter privately. King James argued that the gold could not belong to the crown as treasure trove since it was not buried in the earth. The master replied that it was the man's intention so to bury it. The king answered that the question should be left to the magistrates of Perth. The master said that if either the magistrates or his brother the earl had to do with the pot of gold there would not be much left for His Majesty. The king was attracted by the idea of foreign coinage; it caused his mind to speculate. Meanwhile the lords were waiting and the king gave orders to begin the buck hunt. They all set off and the master followed them.

During the hunt the master had been pressing his sovereign and when the kill was made at about eleven in the morning the king decided to go forward and investigate. The master had urged him to come privately or at any rate with only "two or three of his owne meane servantes". At every point the king must have had in mind the reputation of the house of Gowrie. He would not stay for the "curry of the deer", but before leaving he called Lennox aside and told him that he was going to Perth to get a hoard of treasure. The duke replied that the whole story sounded most unlikely. The courtiers sent for their swords and for fresh horses and followed the master and the king as they rode together to the north-westward along the roads between the little hills of Fife until they crossed the border into Perthshire.[1]

Whatever they had in mind there were only these two young men, the master and his brother, to deal with their wise king, who had all the knowledge of his fifteen years of rule in Scotland. It should be stressed at this point that the king had a deep and fearful interest in any witchcraft. It was held that the grandfather of his hosts, the old Lord Ruthven who had killed Rizzio in Queen Mary's presence, had communed

[1] The actual route cannot be traced for there is no evidence where the kill took place.

with spirits. Near Perth the master rode on to warn his brother of the party that was approching. Lord Gowrie crossed the Tay and explained to the king that he had not been expecting so large a company. Whatever arrangements had been made to receive the king must now be changed if a private conversation was to be secured with him.

Old Gowrie House was pulled down in 1807, but it is a simple matter to reconstruct it. The building was in grey stone, tall and also long with its back against the river. It faced the Speygate and also the privy gardens. The main block had been standing for some eighty years. The king was kept waiting in a room on the ground floor where he was served alone out of respect. The dinner was a little time in coming. His gentlemen went to dine in the great hall. The meal consisted of a moorfowl, a shoulder of mutton, a chicken, strawberries. The earl had been going in and out and when the dinner had been finished the master told the king that the time had come for their private talk. The master suggested that the king should send the earl away. The king, rallying the earl on his gloom, sent him off to drink a royal toast with the courtiers in the great hall. The king rose and told the master to bring Sir Thomas Erskine. It appears that this request was neglected. They then went out of the room together, passing through the end of the hall where the gentlemen were at dinner, up a great staircase, down a corridor. They came at last into a large room in which was a door leading into a small turret chamber. We have now reached the centre of the mystery.

The events just described, in so far as they concern the king, rest only on his own authority[1] for neither the master nor the earl of Gowrie lived to substantiate them. There seems nothing intrinsically improbable. The king stated in addition that as they went through the house the master kept locking doors behind them. This may be doubted.

To return to what is in no dispute. After their dinner, which began later than the king's, the courtiers went out into the gardens, which lay beyond the house towards the town. They ate cherries, waiting till the king should be ready to depart. Alone among the courtiers the young John Ramsay was separate from the rest. He had taken charge of the king's hawk, so that Murray might dine unhampered, and had been taken by one of Gowrie's household to see the great gallery.

During the period that the king and the master of Gowrie remained together in the turret chamber, there was one other event outside that is

---

[1] In addition to the king's account, there is a consecutive description of these events in Calderwood, *History of the Kirk of Scotland*.

recorded. It is alleged that as the courtiers waited, presumably with some impatience, in the garden a gentleman of Lord Gowrie's called to them that the king had already mounted and ridden away. This was apparently taken up by the earl himself. It is possible, but it does not seem to me of much importance. There would be no one of the courtiers to support the cause of either the earl of Gowrie or his brother when both were dead.

At this point, when the courtiers were some still in the garden and others in the street, the king was heard calling from one of the high rooms within the house. The duke of Lennox called to the earl of Mar. "That is the King's voice, be he where he will." They turned and at the window of the turret chamber they saw the king. He was red and hatless with one hand up to his cheek and mouth. He called out to them. "I am murdered. Treason. My Lord Mar, help, help." With these words the king ensured the death of Gowrie and of his younger brother.

Once these words were spoken, the events went forward in a progression which can be seen as inevitable. To recall them briefly, John Ramsay was the first to reach the scene running up the turnpike stair. The master was, apparently and very naturally, endeavouring to prevent the king from shouting. But this was unsuccessful for the king cried out "Fy, strike him high because he has a chayne doublet upon him." Ramsay let go his hawk, the king standing on the leash. Ramsay struck the master with his dagger and he fell down upon the stairway. Sir Hugh Herries and Sir Thomas Erskine, with one of his servants, ran up the stair. Herries thrust at the body of the wounded master, who cried out "Alas, I had no wyte [blame] of it" and died. Gowrie ran up the staircase and was killed by Ramsay. The latter was only a boy of twenty; it was a battle of the young.

There was a confused *émeute*; some townsmen, loyal to the Ruthven family, shouted against the king, "Come down, come down, thou son of Seigneur Davie". The great town bell was tolling and the bailie and his force came down the slope to relieve their sovereign. The sky was overcast and at about eight in the evening King James and the royal party rode back again to Falkland through drifting rain.

The king was always sensitive about the acceptance of his royal word and he had shouted "Treason". The destruction of the Ruthvens and all their name was thus inevitable. It was a modern earldom and the family had no cadets of consequence. The late earl had certain sisters married to peers and one of them was to be the mother of the great marquess of Montrose. There was no reaction. The brothers-in-law admitted that they had been unlucky in the marriages which they had arranged. The Ruthven properties were divided up. Sir Thomas Erskine obtained the lands round Dirleton on which his later earldom of Kellie would be based. John Ramsay received a knighthood. He went forward and the king later created him earl of Hodderness in England. He also received the right on every anniversary of this happy deliverance to bear the sword of state before the king.

It was decided that the Ruthvens had determined to kidnap their sovereign, to transfer him to Robert Logan's fortalice, Fast Castle in Berwickshire, and thence to England. It was never indicated what Queen Elizabeth would do with this royal guest. Certain letters from Logan dealing with the alleged project were discovered later, but have been dismissed as forgeries. If the Ruthvens had wished to rule Scotland through him, how could they have kept him prisoner with their weak power? The king at one time seems to have thought that they wished to kill him, but in that case why take him to their own castle? It would have been much wiser to have hired some gallant bravo.

Three theories have been brought forward as to what transpired in the turret room while the king and the master were alone there. The version of the English ambassador Sir William Bowes is characteristic of his goodwill towards the Ruthven family.[1] He believed that the king being alone with the young master, "a learned, sweet and artless young gentleman", had called his father a traitor "whereas the young man showed a grieved and expostulatory countenance. The King seeing himself alone and without a weapon, cried 'Treason, Treason'." In regard to this account it can be said that it hardly seems sufficient.

An opinion among the people, whose mind always leans to heterosexual subjects, ran to the effect that the king had noticed at Falkland when the young master was lying on the grass a blue ribbon that the queen had given him. The earl of Moray, too, a few years earlier had been thought of by the people as the queen's lover. There seems no reason to credit this idea. A more plausible suggestion was put forward by the editor of the *Complete Peerage*.[2] The king, whose liking for his own sex was well known, was held to have made a pass at his companion on which the master had drawn his weapon. This suggestion may have been in accord with the king's temperament, but this was not the way in which he ever acted.

[1] Cf. Cal. State Papers, Scotland.   [2] *Complete Peerage*, VI, 41-2.

I have omitted the king's account of his conversations in the turret chamber. They explain that the master tried to bind him but give no reasons. I have also not mentioned the alleged presence of a man in armour, so accoutred to take a Highlandman, who is said to have been in the turret with the other two. After some days the earl of Gowrie's chamberlain came forward and stated that he had fulfilled this role. It is not impossible; but it sounds unlikely.

Before leaving this subject I should like to put forward my own suggestion. I just indicate what may perhaps have happened. The Ruthvens owed the king the sum of £80,000, which was a crippling burden on their estates. It is assumed that the brothers may have decided to appeal to the king, whose generosity about money was proverbial. The pot of gold in fact existed and the master planned to hand it over and on the kindly feelings thus set up to plead for the remission of the debt. The master was to carry out the interview for he was in closer contact with the king and it was easier to ask on his brother's behalf than on his own. It was essential that the king should be seen in private.

Meanwhile the king approached the meeting with very different feelings. It was a case of the royal courage being pursued by human fear. As he rode alone with the master his dread of the Gowrie family grew upon him. On his arrival at Gowrie House he was treated with respect, but kept apart. His meal was served in solitude, save for the two young Ruthvens; he was taken up alone to the turret chamber. He had a horror of naked steel and here he was alone with the master, who represented an ancient enmity. The story of the pot of gold, about which the master continued speaking, would seem to him increasingly a thin invention. Then he decided to move towards the window and to call to his followers to break off this interview that was alarming him. But the master understood what might happen if his royal guest should cry for help. In trying to stop this he seized him, but his touch set off the royal imagination which was at fever-point. The window was opened and he shouted "Treason".

On this assumption the question of the earl's debts was never raised. If this was so it was unfortunate for it might have served to calm the royal visitor. It may be that the king convinced himself that murder was intended, we cannot tell. Perhaps as he rode home it became clear to him that he had been the victim of an attempted regicide. It seems very likely that we shall never know what happened in the turret room in Gowrie House.

94

Chapter 12

THE TWO AMBASSADORS

DURING almost the whole of the reign of Elizabeth I, from the time of his proclamation as king of Scotland in 1567, James VI was the inevitable successor to the English throne. For the first nineteen years of his reign in Scotland his claim would have been challenged by his mother the imprisoned Queen of Scots. There was, however, no time at which the fugitive queen, with the charges of murdering her husband hanging over her, would have been acceptable to the ruling classes in Elizabethan England. The only other persons whose claims might have been brought forward were, like King James himself, descendants of the two sisters of Henry VIII. James VI, who was the representative of the elder sister, had a clear claim. After the king and his children stood his first cousin the Lady Arabella Stuart. It has to be noted that the representatives of the younger sister Mary, the wife of Charles Brandon, duke of Suffolk, had been placed by the will of Henry VIII before the Scottish royal family on the grounds of the latter's foreign birth. They were represented at this time by Edward Seymour, Lord Beauchamp. There was, however, a certain doubt about his father's marriage with Lady Catherine Grey. He was a nonentity, married to the daughter of a Dorset squire. His name was not brought forward. After him came the three infant daughters of Ferdinando Stanley, earl of Derby. None of these names was in fact considered for the king of Scotland's claim was so impregnable.

The senior line of the Courtenays was now extinct, but the old earl of Huntingdon represented as heir-general the duke of Clarence, who had been brother to Edward IV. Abroad in certain Catholic circles the infanta Isabella Clara Eugenia, the elder daughter of Philip II, was sometimes mentioned. These never received any serious consideration. King James VI already possessed a long experience and his accession would mean the union with England of the Scottish kingdom.

These factors had always been appreciated by Lord Burghley and his second son. The father had guided English policy through all the upheavals of the queen's reign; his son was concerned with the later and more peaceful period. Those years in which King James's accession was approaching came under the scrutiny of Sir Robert Cecil. It is worth pausing for a moment to give an impression of him. He was in the first place essentially a peace-time minister and in this his wishes were in accord with those of the king of Scotland. In temperament he was profoundly withdrawn, remote and unemotional. He would lay men aside, but he never quarrelled. He had no need to. He had always been delicate with those long slender hands, a little man just five feet three and apparently a hunchback, though this is not revealed in his few portraits.

He was solitary, a widower with two small children from several years before the king's accession. He seems to have had no favourite, male or female. His purely private correspondence seems to have disappeared, but on the other hand no gossip has survived about him. According to the traditions of the time he was a true statesman; he had no friendships. His life was bound up with the service of the English monarchy. At the same time he had an appreciation for those great men who managed their affairs successfully in the tricky weather of the later Elizabethan polity. He was cool and not given to encroachment on another's sphere or properties. He had a deep mundane respect for great possessions.

His father Lord Burghley had had antiquarian tastes. Sir Robert Cecil, on the other hand, lived in the present. He was not a hard man and he saw the advantages of giving pleasure. He was too busy with the affairs of the kingdom to be a patron of art or letters. He thought much and read but seldom. He was not the creator of his own fortune; he took what came to him. His gift was for accretion. Hatfield and its gardens are his true monument. It was a difficulty for Sir Robert Cecil that he had come to the highest power too young. He had been a marked man almost from his boyhood. He never had and he never seems to have wished to have an equal partner. It was a supreme good fortune for King James to have so great a minister to bend before him.

It was in perfect accordance with Cecil's character that his sober judgment could not approve the hot-headed emotions of the earl of Essex. There was at the turn of the century the possibility that the obvious successor to the crown might choose not Cecil, but what we can loosely and inaccurately call some other government. The earl of Essex was at this time in secret communication with King James and the men whom he was likely to select, Southampton and Anthony and Francis Bacon, would none of them satisfy Cecil's requirements. He needed for the high offices of the future court quiet prudent men of great inheritance. He would himself supply the working brain.

When the earl of Essex was destroyed as the inevitable consequence of what is called the Essex rising, Sir Robert Cecil took careful stock of the position. The queen had still two years to live and in this twilight of the great reign Cecil at last approached his future sovereign. In doing this he decided to take Lord Henry Howard as his companion. The man whom he now chose was an elderly and penurious nobleman, who had never had success with Queen Elizabeth. He was without charm and his style was accurately described by the king of Scotland as producing "Asiatic and endless volumes". He could in no sense be Cecil's rival. At the same time he was the careful mentor of the Howard grouping whom Sir Robert had decided to cultivate and to advance in the new reign. It was lucky that both he and his future master much disliked a fiery energy. Always excepting Lord Henry, there was something a little sluggish now about the Howard grouping. This family, under the earl of Salisbury, as Cecil would become, was a dominant feature in the kingdom until it was dispersed in the days of the full favour of the duke of Buckingham.

Lord Henry was the man of character in all this grouping. With one exception the other members of the Howard family were at this time of small importance. The dukedom of Norfolk was attainted and the earldom of Arundel not yet restored. A fourteen-year old boy was heir to both. Lord Henry's nephews were Lord William and Lord Thomas Howard, the latter a naval commander in the late wars. There remained his cousin the earl of Nottingham, who had defeated the Armada as Howard of Effingham. He held the great post of lord admiral. He was separated from the other Howards in that his mother was a Welshwoman, a Gamage from Coity in Glamorgan, and his daughters were married into landed stocks with strong naval affiliations. He had nothing to do with the Catholic or half-Catholic preferences which marked to some extent the elder line. He was a rather grand dull fellow; when he came as an ambassador the Spaniards liked him. In later life he developed a great pride and just a touch of avarice. As an old man his mind decayed a little and he found it difficult to manage his own finances. As opposed to the senior Howards, he had from the first his own links with Sir Robert Cecil.

Lord Henry was a man of sixty, small and trim, a skilful Latinist. His life throughout had been unfortunate. His father, the earl of

Surrey, had been executed by Henry VIII, when his younger son was seven years of age. And then for the next six years the children had been under the care of the duchess of Richmond, the first Lutheran in the Howard family, and under the tuition of John Foxe, the author of *The Book of Martyrs*.[1] The tutor had made a life-long Protestant of the elder brother Thomas, duke of Norfolk, and of the elder sister Jane, who became countess of Westmorland. Perhaps in the case of Lord Henry his robust style broke against a sceptical intelligence. Throughout his life he always was to regard the Hot Gospellers with exacerbation.

It can be said that Lord Henry was to have no career throughout the long Elizabethan reign. He had been educated at Cambridge at the queen's charges, but nothing came of this. The period had been starred with disasters to his own family, the execution of his brother the duke of Norfolk and later the imprisonment and death of his nephew, Philip earl of Arundel. In consequence Lord Henry had gained no resources; he had no income except a pension.

His life had varied between the time that he passed in the first house, the Tudor building, at Audley End, the inheritance of his brother's second wife, looking after the late duke's orphaned children, and the long years in different lodgings. He never married. The historians of the last century always spoke of him with harshness. He has been accused of the murder of Sir Thomas Overbury, but, as I hope to show, this is "not proven". S. R. Gardiner called him a Catholic and even the leader of the Catholic party. As a consequence he is charged with pro-Catholic duplicity. This does not seem to me to account at all for his true attitude towards religion. To make the clear-cut division into Catholic or Protestant inevitable appears, except sometimes in a political sense, unrealistic.

It may be said with probability that nothing was so actual to Lord Henry as the reconstruction of the fortunes of the house of Howard. He was not a traveller for he had not the money. He made one journey to Paris; but the statement in Lloyd's *Worthies* that he had been to Italy and Rome is not convincing.[2] He seems to have had a certain preference for the Erastian atmosphere of the Catholic monarchies. He had been "reconciled" to Rome for a short time in middle life. This was before the war with Spain; in those years he haunted the Spanish embassy. Soon after he recommended his nephew to conform. It was his weakness

---

[1] John Foxe, *Actes and monuments*, 1563.   [2] Lloyd, *Worthies*, I, 67.

that he was given too much to flattery. Still, he understood most clearly that nothing was so important to King James as an acceptance of his religious postulates. Howard himself had some tincture of learning. This made it more agreeable that he should bow to his wise sovereign. On one matter Lord Henry felt very strongly. He had a sharp dislike for the Society of Jesus. There was therefore no insincerity in the part that he later took in the trial of Father Garnet. He disapproved of the busy way that the Jesuits moved about among the richer members of the country gentry. As far as Father Garnet was concerned, it was a satisfaction to destroy him.

I am not suggesting that Lord Henry was a kind man. He had been battered by fortune far too much for that. The sovereign and the sovereign alone could rebuild for him his just position. If the reading of his character here described should be in any way approximately correct, it justifies Sir Robert Cecil. He was accurate in believing that Lord Henry Howard would not fail the general purposes of English government.

The death of the earl of Essex, the gradual weakening of the queen's health and the consequent unlikelihood that there would be any further changes in the government during what remained of the long reign were the principal reasons for the initiation of Sir Robert Cecil's correspondence with his future sovereign. The actual occasion was an attack upon Cecil in the course of Essex's trial.

During the trial the earl had declared that he had been told that Sir Robert Cecil had said to one of his fellow councillors that the title of the infanta to the inheritance of the English crown was as good as that of any other person. Cecil had at once challenged this and called upon Essex to name the councillor to whom he was alleged to have so spoken. Essex turned to Southampton, who was likewise a prisoner, and declared that he had also heard these words. After some hesitation Southampton had named Sir William Knollys, the comptroller of the household, who was at that time at the court. Sir William was fetched and the lord steward asked him whether Mr Secretary had used any such expressions in his hearing or to his knowledge. Sir William then replied, "I never heard him speak any words to that effect."

This claim to the throne was based on the fact that Philip II, who in the course of his reign had inherited the position of heir-general to the royal lines of Aragon, Castile and Portugal, represented in that capacity both Philippa, queen of Portugal and Catherine, queen of

H   99

Castile, the two half-sisters who were daughters of John of Gaunt, duke of Lancaster, who had died just two hundred years before. Still neither of these princesses was heir-general to the duke of Lancaster whose representation lay among the descendants of his son Henry IV; nor was the position of heir-general to the house of Plantagenet to be found among these lines. That heirship, on which had turned the claims of the house of York, remained with the descendants of Lionel of Antwerp, duke of Clarence, John of Gaunt's elder brother. Further, any claim to which Philip II might have been entitled would pass to his only son Philip III. As against her step-brother the Infanta Isabella Clara Eugenia was without rights. In 1594 this claim had been put forward by Father Parsons in *A conference about the next succession to the Crowne of England* printed at St Omer under the name of R. Doleman. The argument was not assisted by the addition of "a new & perfect arbor of genealogie".

It is of course true that had Sir Robert Cecil supported such pretensions he would have been at once disgraced both with Queen Elizabeth and King James. Only those who wished for that result could have thought of bringing the story forward. There were also arguments about Cecil receiving a Spanish pension. This in the years after the death of Philip II in 1598 is not impossible. When peace was at length arranged Spanish pensions were accepted by most of the leaders at the English court, and it is clear that Cecil was essentially a peace minister. The only result of Essex's accusation was to provide a new substantial reason for leading Cecil to begin a correspondence with the king of Scots.

In the course of March 1601, when the trial was over and Essex had been executed, a Scottish embassy headed by the earl of Mar, who was accompanied by Edward Bruce, the lay abbot of Kinloss, came into London. Mar was great master of the household and governor of Edinburgh Castle. He was among the closest of the royal familiars and for long years he had roused his master's quick suspicions. The king had recently arranged a second marriage for him with his own cousin, Lady Marie Stuart. Bruce, a man of about fifty, was a Scottish judge, who had been in England on an earlier mission.

At their first meeting, which took place at the office of the duchy of Lancaster in the Strand, it was arranged that Sir Robert Cecil should enter into a correspondence with the Scottish sovereign. It is not yet clear how the letters were conveyed. David Foulis, who came with Mar and Bruce as their secretary and was sent regularly to London to receive allowances paid by Queen Elizabeth to the king, may have transmitted them. It has also been suggested that James Hamilton, later Viscount Clandeboye, who was then living in Dublin as King James's private representative may have received them; but in that case it is not clear how they were forwarded from Dublin to Edinburgh. They were for the most part sealed by minor officials of the Scottish court, Edward Bruce and David Foulis, who have already been mentioned, Sir Thomas Erskine and Patrick Young. Their passage was not known either to the governor of Berwick or to the English ambassador in Scotland.

Certain numerals were set aside to represent the different parties, but the only ones surviving are those which were actually in use. Sir Robert Cecil and Lord Henry Howard, who was already in correspondence with the king, were numbers 10 and 3 respectively.[1] The earl of Northumberland and Lord Cobham were represented by 0 and 7 and Sir Walter Raleigh apparently by 2; the king and queen by 30 and 24. One, number 40, has not yet been detected. This figure represented some influential colleague of Robert Cecil's. It is found directly only in one letter,[2] with a side reference in another. To my mind it was probably Thomas Sackville, Lord Buckhurst, later earl of Dorset. He was an old man and had been the object of accusations, as surely groundless as those against Cecil, of Spanish sympathies. The reasons for this early selection of Raleigh, Northumberland and Cobham as the subjects of this correspondence will be considered later. In any case, except for a single reference to Raleigh, they do not find a place in Cecil's letters. It is Lord Henry who expatiates upon this subject. Sir Robert Cecil's object in writing was to soothe a prince, whose character he had estimated quite exactly.

Lord Henry's role in this correspondence was a combination of praise of the future king and a warning as to certain enemies. Cecil's part was very different. He wanted to write to the king, but not to hear from him since James was an unsuspecting letter writer. Cecil was most anxious that his own letters should not fall into the hands of the queen of England, but each was so couched that did this happen his impregnable loyalty to her was manifest. The real object of his letters was to gain the king. He attempted and successfully to manage himself every

---

[1] The numbers are printed in John Bruce, ed., *Correspondence of King James VI of Scotland with Sir Robert Cecil and Others in England* (Camden Society, 1861), Introduction, xxxv, xxxvi.
[2] *Ibid.*, 15-16, 35.

element in the succession. He had laboured carefully and prudently at the assessment of King James's character. Not until the time of Sir Robert Walpole would the crown have another minister who worked so hard.

Cecil's letters were filled with a subtle recognition of the recipient's unique position. They were garnished with occasional references to the Old Testament and with that savour of Latinity that the king loved. They could not have been written by any of the courtiers of his northern kingdom. The letters are for the most part undated, but they have been numbered and preserved in a definite order. The earliest of this series now surviving is endorsed in the handwriting of Sir Robert Cecil. "1600, 30 (The K.) first letter to 10 (Secretary)." With his reply Sir Robert had moved into that high style, which he always retained throughout this correspondence.

Although it has pleased you to let me read in royal characters, what the constitution of your mind is towards me, what you esteem my disposition towards you, and upon what arguments both your favour and opinion are and shall be grounded, yet can I not deny my mind that justice which it exacteth from me, to be heard speak as much (with his proper organ) as hath been already reported by other means. A desire derived from no exception to the least article of their relations (of whose integrity and wisdom your Majesties letters have yielded so clear demonstration), but only as a motive from those reverend respects of mine which live in doubt how silence would be censured to such a summons. In which consideration I have resolved in this form to return my humble thanks . . . because you promise hereafter in all accusations to deal with me as God did with Adam, *Ubi est?*[1]

Further in the same letter there comes his famous parallel with the glass of time.

For, though it is true that natural cares and providence might have importuned me long since, to seek some honest means to dissolve those hard obstructions which other men's practice had bred within your heart, yet had I still determined constantly to have run out the glass of time, rather than by the least circumstance of my actions to give any ground for insidious spirits to suspect that I would vary from the former compass of a sole dependency, by which I have only steered my courses.[2]

Cecil then went on to explain that the opposition to Essex had been forced upon him. "For who knows not that have lived in Israel, that such were the mutual affections in our tender years, and so many re-

[1] Letter No. 1, *ibid.*, 3-4.   [2] Same letter, *ibid.*, 4.

ciprocal benefits interchanged in our growing fortunes. . . . From myself and my friend 3 (Lord Henry Howard) you shall not be cumbered with other petition. . . . We do neither presume to indent with you for future favours, nor present reservedness because we think it not ingenious to recommend to Honour itself the things which Honour requireth; with which conclusion I humbly kiss your royal hands."[1]

With his next letter the secretary's confidence in himself had gained a trifle. "When I beheld", he began, "this second letter of yours, so full of wisdom, greatness and moderation, it gave my mind a double consolation, first, because I found you vouchsafed to dispense with my borrowed hand, which brought you no coloured merchandise, next, because it showed plainly that whensoever men of honesty shall deal with your Majesty that they do still *in portu navigare*."[2] The general tone of the letter, for all its praise-laden phrases, urges the king to prudence and towards the end there are these sentences. "I have little more to say, besides that comfort I take to see the mind which I do reverence so well tempered, but that when all the roots and fractions of numbers shall be searched by the greatest mathematics you will find that this is only the golden number which will show you *veram Galaxiam*, for all other plots are dreams."[3]

The fourth letter contains this courteous protest. "Beseeching your Majesty to believe that I am so far, and will be, from any remissness to advertise you as if there should happen in one night an universal deluge of all the posts of England, I would make the only son of my body serve as a postillion, to carry my packet, before the least hair of your head should miscarry which you could not spare."[4] The extract from the fifth letter is an assessment of the royal qualities, a subject on which the king would often meditate, but which had not hitherto been put in words to him. "It is the property of the creator to accept the labours of men according to his knowledge of their desire without measure of their ability. Of this divine quality, if ever man's eyes beheld on earth a lively image, the same appeareth in your person."[5] He then goes on to explain the delay and the defects of his reply. "For itself, in that (being admitted an immediate messenger to so complete a Prince) it delivereth not all which it hath in charge, a fault surely unpardonable, if any paper or any words could contain it, but your Majesty's exquisite judgment cannot but know, that that which I can tender you, must be finite, imper-

---

[1] Same letter, *ibid.*, 6. [2] Second letter, *ibid.*, 12. [3] Same letter, *ibid.*, 14.
[4] Fourth letter, *ibid.*, 22. [5] Fifth letter, *ibid.*, 27.

fect and of small value, though the duty, the affection and zealous thankfulness of my heart be like your favours, infinite, perfect and matchless." These letters make it clear why James I would always retain Cecil in his high posts.

It is worth noting that this correspondence also includes a statement by Cecil of his own religious faith as well as a comment upon Lord Henry's outlook. "What can give more rest to an honest man", he began, "than to foresee the continued blessing of living under a religious Prince; and for myself I will beseech you to know by this that I am in hope to concur with Jerome, in this particular, that *in qua fide puer natus sum, in eadem senex moriar*, so have I been bred, so baptised, instructed and lived."[1] In a later note he wrote of "your fidel 3 (Lord Henry Howard) ... whom though I cannot make either puritan or protestant, yet must I protest him to all men to be *et virum et civem bonum*, and towards your Majesty my life should be pledge, if it were needful to you, that he hath ever ready his gauntlet of defiance against Pope and Cardinals in your quarrel."[2]

This is the point at which to set down the gradually increasing warmth of the king of Scotland towards the queen's great minister. "If at my first dealing with you by my late ambassadors, I had not been settled in that assurance that the party I dealt with was wise, and that my favour was to be grounded upon a fixed star, and not a mobile or wavering planet, I could not have thought myself fully secure of a thankful meeting. . . . I am no usurper; it is for them to play the Absalom."[3] The sovereign's goodwill mounted constantly. "My dearest 10", he wrote, "I am ashamed . . . that your travails of so great worth and inestimable value should be repaid with so poor a recompense, but the best excuse is that these papers are but witnesses of that treasure of gratitude which by your good deserts is daily nourished in my heart."[4] The final passage is all that a future minister could desire. "Thus may you see my dearest 10, how my love to you hath bred my plainness, for friendship without freedom is nothing but a fountain of affected compliments."[5] King James had made his choice; his course was set and it would never change.

It was to Sir Robert Cecil's credit that he so early grasped the king of Scotland's attitude to his royal status. This was in sharp contrast with the approach of Queen Elizabeth. The latter sovereign had a high and

Sixth letter, *ibid.*, 33.　　[2] Same letter, *ibid.*, 35-6.　　[3] *Ibid.*, 9 and 10.
[4] *Ibid.*, 26.　　[5] *Ibid.*, 32.

mannered presentation of her role as queen of England. She used the phrases which would be expected from King Henry's child. She had no especial interests in foreign monarchs. She was without either liking or respect for the king of Spain, her former brother-in-law. She seems to have despised the last sad scions of the house of Valois. King James was very different. He felt that an aura surrounded the crowned heads of Europe. A sense of the glory of kingship bound him to the king of France and Navarre and to the king of Spain. It was his sense of identity with the others of his high estate that was one of the principal factors in his wish for peace, and Cecil was well qualified to serve a *Rex Pacificus*.

It was natural that in his correspondence Sir Robert Cecil should indicate the strength of the opposition against which he strove successfully. It is noteworthy that the only opponent whom he mentions by name should be Sir Walter Raleigh. It was, so Sir Robert explained, his practice "to cast a stone into the mouth of these gaping crabs" else "they would not stick to confess daily how contrary it is to their nature to resolve to be under your sovereignty; though they confess (Raleigh especially) that (*rebus sic stantibus*) natural policy forces them to keep on foot such a trade against the great day of mart."[1] He made it clear that Sir Walter was "a person whom most religious men do hold Anathema".[2]

From the detail given in this chapter the course of the new reign could be foreseen.

[1] *Correspondence of King James VI*, 18.   [2] *Ibid.*, 19.

Chapter 13

THE LAST OF SCOTLAND

THE queen of England lay dying and King James prepared to leave his northern kingdom. How far were the king and queen ready to rule in their new sphere? It seems that King James had a conception of Reformation unity; he was quite prepared to undertake the headship of the Church of England. The queen was, however, in religious matters a liability. At about the end of the century there appears to have taken place a change in the queen of Scotland's religious outlook. Since her influence in politics was so small, very little comment was aroused. No references appear in the correspondence of the English ambassadors and thus no rumour seems to have reached the queen of England.

After the Catholic earls had been defeated, a deputation was sent by the Kirk "to speak and deal with her (the Queen) touching her religion, her manners, for favouring and acting towards the enemies of the Truth – namely the Earl of Huntly; her speaking contemptuously and reproachfully of the ministry as also her not repairing to the word and sacraments".[1] She had, for some years after her marriage, attended, in company with her few Danish retainers, the Lutheran services said for her by the minister, who had come from Denmark as her chaplain. In course of time this minister became a Presbyterian and the queen removed him from his post at court. The matter was complicated because there was a clause in the marriage treaty[2] securing her the right to Lutheran worship.

It appears that it was the earl of Huntly who induced her to discuss religious questions with Father Robert Abercrombie, an elderly Scottish Jesuit. The only description of this visit is contained in a letter written by Father Abercrombie to the prior of the Scottish monastery at Ratisbon in 1608. At this date he was seventy-four and his memory, perhaps, on some facts hazy. The most interesting point in the letter is the reference to the queen's early life. This section runs as follows.

---

[1] Calderwood, V, 459.
[2] Cf. J. T. Gibson Craig, ed., *Papers Relative to the Marriage of James the Sixth* (Bannatyne Club (1828)), 37.

It recurred to her (the Queen) how, being in Germany while she was very young, and resident for her education in the house of a certain great princess, who was a Catholic, she had seen a priest who daily celebrated Mass; the memory of whom and the love of the princess (who, if I be not mistaken, was the grand-daughter of Charles the Fifth), suggested to her that she should embrace that religion.[1]

The question that remains open is the identity of this princess.

Looked at from one angle it might seem that the Princess Anne had been sent to the court of her cousin Christine, dowager duchess of Lorraine and by birth a princess of Denmark. She lived on the marches of Germany and was a niece of Charles V. For myself I do not see the reason for so long a journey. It appears to be more likely that she stayed at the court of the dowager margravine of Baden Rodemachern, by birth Princess Cecilia of Sweden; during her widowhood, this was probably in the north. She was a convert to the Catholic Church and her sister was married to the Princess Anne's uncle. This seems much more within her family circle.

The queen was reconciled to the Church of Rome and on nine occasions during her reign in Scotland she had Communion brought to her. It appears that in England priests came to her more rarely; she was visited at Denmark House and Oatlands and she once received Communion at the Spanish Embassy. It seems that her few Catholic friends were Scots. Lady Jane Drummond, her chief favourite among her younger ladies at the English court, is described as a Catholic; but I can find no evidence to support this. The queen's Catholic interests may have existed at a rather superficial level and she had reason to know that they irked the king. She had rather a lymphatic character and lacked tenacity.

The change of religion in fact foreshadowed a carefully masked separation, which lasted until Anne of Denmark's death. She had proved her usefulness and had brought James I a daughter and two sons, two other daughters and a son had died in early childhood. Her last child was conceived in 1604; henceforward she and her husband lived their lives separately. It is noteworthy that none of her children were entrusted to her for their education. The king greatly prized his judgment and in the queen's judgment he placed no value. Notably she had shown imprudence in the question of her religion.

At the same time one should not overstress the religious question;

---

[1] William Forbes-Leith, *Narratives of Scottish Catholics*, I, 63-5.

there were other angles. Their relations fluctuated and were, in some respects, more cordial after the separation. The king never failed to build up her position and to treat her as a queen, who was herself the king of Denmark's daughter. It was only that in Scotland they had had one court, while in England in effect they had two separate ones.

The attitude with which King James would approach the English constitution can be seen in *The Trew Law of Free Monarchies*, the shortest of all his treatises, which he wrote in 1598, five years before he was called to the English throne. According to Professor McIlwain[1] this "is not only the first but the most comprehensive of all his political writings. The stubbornness, with which, throughout all the vicissitudes of his later struggles with the English Parliament, James held to all points of the doctrine there laid down explains much." It would be of interest to know what was the circulation of this tract in the early years of the king's rule in England. From 1616 it had its established place in the edition of King James's works which Bishop Montague then produced. "I have chosen", explained the royal author, "to set downe in this short treatise, the trew grounds of the mutual dewtie and allegeance betwixt a free and absolute Monarche and his people."[2]

"Kings", he wrote and this is a recurrent thought, "are called Gods by the propheticall King David,[3] because they sit upon God his Throne in the earth, and have the count of their administration to give unto Him."[4] He stresses that persecution does not justify rebellion. "And although there was never a more monstrous persecutor and tyrant nor Achab was: yet all the rebellion that Elias ever raised him was to flie to the wilderness: where for fault of sustentation he was fed with the Corbies."[5]

He then gave an interesting view of the beginnings of the Scottish kingdom.

For as our Chronicles beare witnesse, this Ile, and especially our (Scottish) part of it, being scantily inhabited, but by very few, and they as barbarous and scant of civilitie, as number, there comes our first King Fergus, with a great number with him, out of Ireland, which was long inhabited before us, and making himself master of the countrey, by his owne friendship, and force, as well of the Irelandmen that came with him, hee made himselfe King and Lord, as well of the whole landes, as of the whole inhabitantes within the same.[6]

[1] C. H. McIlwain, *The Political Works of James I*, Introduction, xxxvii.
[2] *Ibid.*, 54. [3] Cf. *Psalm* 82.6. [4] McIlwain, *The Political Works of James I*, 54-5.
[5] *Ibid.*, 60. [6] *Ibid.*, 62.

These long sentences are difficult to read; but the gist of the position is set out in the paragraphs that follow.

The King therefore in Scotland was before any estates or rankes of men within the same, before any Parliaments were holden, or lawes made: and by them was the land distributed (which at the first was whole theirs) states erected and discerned, and formes of government devised and established . . . The King is *Dominus omnium bonorum* . . . who according to good services done unto him, chaungeth their holdings from tacke to few, from ward to blanch, erecteth new baronies, and uniteth olde, without advice or authoritie of either Parliament or any other subaltern judiciall seate.[1]

Although they came down from a hoary past, there was something of the seventeenth century in these statements. They were of that same schematic order which Hobbes would reveal in his *Leviathan*. On the other hand it seems that to King James Fergus of Dalriada was as actual as the kings of Israel and Judah. James Ussher was a young man in these days and history was foreshortened. All happenings had occurred within the years of Dr Ussher's brief chronology.

The king came back once more to the dangers of rebellion.

It is easie [he wrote] to be understood, what allegeance & obedience his lieges owe unto him; I meane alwaies of such free monarchies as our king is, and not of elective kings, and much lesse of such sorts of governors, as the dukes of Venice are, whose Aristocratick and limited government, is nothing like to free Monarchies; although the malice of some writers hath not been ashamed to misknow any difference to be betwixt them.[2]

Before concluding he returned again to the relations of king and Parliament.

We daily see that in the Parliament (which is nothing else but the head court of the King and his vassals) the laws are not craved by his subjects, and only made by him at their rogation and with their advice: for albeit the King make daily statutes and ordinances, enjoyning such paines thereto as hee thinkes meet, without any advice of Parliament or estates.[3]

In this description of parliament as "the head court of the King and his vassals" we find again reflected those feudal concepts, which were still so powerful in the old Scotland. The king's chief problem on the civil side was still how to deal with the most powerful among the Scottish lords. They might be dealt with as members of the privy council or as lords of parliament.

[1] *The Political Works of James I*, 62.　　[2] *Ibid.*, 64.　　[3] *Ibid.*, 62.

The long conflict with the general assembly of the Kirk was in no sense a struggle against parliament. The Convention of the Royal Burghs, which undertook for the main group of towns so many of the parliamentary functions, was wholly tame. The parliament itself had not the strength or the regularity of meeting or the assured attendance of its members to enable it to measure up in any way against the sovereign. It is strange that the king's authoritarian doctrine was manufactured at a time before he knew the great authoritarian monarchies. It was only in England that he came in contact with the constitution of Castile.

Similarly the king had no knowledge in those days of the supporters of the authoritarian states of Europe, save only for the memory of Esmé Stuart. The king's personal relations with his cousins of the house of Lorraine would only develop after he reached London. In these last years in Scotland his connections lay rather with the eastern states and monarchies. Thus at the christening of his elder son there had been present, besides the earl of Sussex, ambassador extraordinary from England, the envoys from Denmark, from the estates of Holland and Zealand, from the queen's cousins the Brunswick dukes and the city of Magdeburg. It was King James's accession to the English throne which would bring him into contact with the actual structure of the Spanish monarchy.

A bulk of foreign imports came through the Scottish staple at Campveere in Zealand. In the kirks along the border there were bells cast at Jan Burgherhous's foundry in Middelburg.[1] The withdrawing-room at Craigievar was panelled in Memel pine.

The queen of England died just before the break of dawn at Richmond Palace on March 24, 1603. As soon as he heard the news from Sir Robert Carey the king decided to go to London. He had no reason to suppose that he would be unwelcome. Bishop Goodman later wrote that "there was a general report throughout the whole kingdom (of England) what a good King he was, that he was the King of poor men, and would hear any man in a just cause. . . . Then for the Queen she was ever hard of access and grew to be very covertous in her old days."[2] On Sunday April 3 King James appeared in public at St Giles's and bade his people farewell after the sermon. Two days later he began his

---

[1] For example, at Melrose, Maxton and Ancrum, cf. *An inventory of the Ancient and Historical Monuments of Roxburghshire*, I, 42.

[2] Godfrey Goodman, *The Court of King James the First* (2 vols, 1839), I, 96-7.

journey south. He was moving slowly because he did not want to enter his new capital until his predecessor had been buried.

He was going through that lowland countryside to which he was all his life accustomed, past the apple trees and gardens, with the east wind coming in across the Firth in the still sharp April weather. In the Lothians clumps of trees, ash, elm and sycamore, were planted around the small lairds' houses to give them shelter. There were already the growing trees and the herb and flower plots in the garden at Chapel of Wemyss. On the hills there strayed the sheep, which were the wealth of Scotland. The situation has been well analysed by a modern historian. "Commerce and industry played but a small part in Scottish economy, the towns were centres of small exchange and opened up some opportunities for foreign trading, but they were of little importance compared to the great rural interests of the whole country. The agricultural interests of the towns were large: in wealth and population the towns were behind the country."[1] And this had helped to keep up unimpaired the feudal elements of the Scottish State.

The king rode southward to take up his new inheritance.

[1] Douglas Nobbs, *England and Scotland 1560-1707*, 26-7.

PART TWO

The Reign in England

Chapter I

THE KING'S ENTRY

KING JAMES rode at a leisurely pace through his new kingdom. He came in by Berwick and was met at the entrance to each shire by the lord lieutenant or the sheriff, and by the justices of the peace and leading gentry. These accompanied him from the northern to the southern end of the county where they were relieved by the same officials from the next shire. At Durham the king heard a sermon from the bishop of that place and at York minster another from the bishop of Limerick. As he went southward he emptied the gaols except for those charged with treason, murder and "papistrie".

He knighted Robert Dudley, mayor of Newcastle, at Gateside close by that town. On one occasion he stayed at a hostelry, the *Bear* at Doncaster. Arrangements were made for days of hunting in the course of his journey. On Easter Sunday he was at Burghley House and the bishop of Lincoln came to preach before him in the chapel there. The king spent three days at Burghley and then moved on to Apthorpe where he dined with Sir Anthony Mildmay and then spent the night at Hinchingbrook. On the following Sunday he reached Standon in Hertfordshire and the bishop of London came to the edge of his diocese to preach for him. At Brockesbourne the next day he was met by Lord Keeper Ellesmere, by Dorset, the lord treasurer, and Howard of Effingham, the lord admiral. The king then rode four miles to meet Sir Robert Cecil at Theobalds.

His practice of conferring knighthoods began at Grimston Hall and grew in profusion as he moved southwards. It was natural that these knighthoods should be conferred for the most part on gentlemen of the counties through which he passed. There were some exceptions, Sir Roger and Sir Thomas Aston from Cheshire and Sir Walter Cope from Oxfordshire. There were no knighthoods conferred at this time on gentlemen from Lancashire and the north-western counties, nor were any of the East Anglian gentry honoured. At Theobalds Sir William Killigrew from Cornwall was knighted and after the king reached London Sir John Sydenham of Somerset and Sir Thomas Arundell of the Cornish

I

branch of his family; these were the only examples from the west of England.

Among those knighted, either on the journey or after the king had reached his capital were Sir William Petre, Sir Roger Dallison, Sir James Harington, Sir John Byron, Sir Gamaliel Capel, Sir Henry Boteler, Sir William Feilding, Sir Eusebius Isham, Sir John Leventhorpe, Sir William Caryll, Sir Richard Tichbourne, Sir Thomas Wenman, Sir Robert Cotton, Sir Richard Blount of Mapledurham, Sir Francis Carew and Sir John Fortescue. The official world was represented by Sir Julius Caesar, Sir Thomas Lake and Sir Edward Coke. There was the great figure of Sir Francis Bacon and two men who would come upon misfortune, Sir Everard Digby and Sir Gervase Elwes. It was in fact an impression of the future court in miniature.

There also came to the king the letters of congratulation from his foreign relatives and from the crowns of Europe. It is worth setting out the list in full[1] for it indicates the names of those European princes who knew or wished to know him. It should be noted that the Emperor Rudolf was of unsound mind and that the king of Spain was still at war with England. Letters came from the king and queen of France and from the archdukes in the low countries. There were very few from Germany, only from the Elector Palatine, from John George, margrave of Brandenburg[2] and from Frederick, duke of Wurttemberg. There were no letters from the Danish royal family or from their German relatives; but it is possible that these had been sent to the queen instead. There was only one letter from an Italian ruling prince, from the duke of Savoy.

An interesting list is that of those sent in by his relatives, the Lorraine family. These include among the writers, Henri Duke of Bar, the eldest son of the duke of Lorraine, Catherine the elder duchess of Guise, her son and brother-in-law the dukes of Guise and Mayenne, and two other ladies of this stock, the duchesses of Florence[3] and Cleves. Apart from the relatives on the Danish side these letters indicate the range of princes who might be visitors at the king's new court. To give an instance, Frederick, duke of Wurttemberg and Teck, count of Montbéliard arrived to receive the honour of the Garter. He was accom-

---

[1] This list is printed in John Nicholl, *Progresses . . . of James I*, I, 51, from Harleian MSS 1760.

[2] This is presumably John George, duke of Jägerndorf, fourth son of the elector of Brandenburg and son-in-law of duke Frederick I of Wurttemberg.

[3] The correct description would have been grand duchess of Tuscany. The three ladies mentioned wrote in their own hands.

panied by his five young sons and their tutor and also by the grand master and marshal of his own court. Throughout the reign there was always this tendency for visits from the continent. The Prince de Joinville and the Duc de Bouillon came from the eastern borderlands of France.

The new knights, who might or might not appear in the court circle, have been mentioned and also the occasional royal visitor. There remain the great peers, who had formed the background to the personal life of Queen Elizabeth. It may be noted that there are very few references to the people. The late queen had had the talent to convey her personality to the crowds who lined the roads; she was also notable for her broad comments. The new king had neither the personality nor that ability. His kindness went as far as those with whom he had some personal contact. With his outdoor servants especially he was generous in gifts and pensions, to his huntsmen and the keepers of his hunting lodges. He never had the arts to win the crowd. His ideas of finance were nebulous; he could not understand the grip of poverty on the working classes. He only saw the needs of his spendthrift companions, and this he did his earnest best to rectify.

When we begin to examine the detailed way of life which King James found on entering his new kingdom, we are immediately impressed by the riches of the Elizabethan world. There was a difference both in elaboration and in scale from anything that had belonged to preceding generations and this had come about from the peaceful prosperity of the first twenty-five years of the queen's reign. The great houses were by now much bigger; Bramshill, perhaps, the perfect Jacobean house, so grand and stately; but Burghley near Stamford is representative of the Elizabethan mansion on the largest scale. As opposed to the small cabinets of the royal palaces which date from King Henry's reign there is a range of large apartments of equal height on the ground floor and on the floor above it. The walls were covered by hangings and by great full-length portraits. Pictures of these proportions had not yet come to Scotland.

Perhaps the best idea that we can form of the contents of a great Jacobean house is that provided by a study of the inventory of household furniture at Kenilworth Castle taken in 1583. It has certain aspects which give it a greater value than more recent lists, in particular its completeness and the measurements which it records. The actual date of its compilation was not so very far away especially when it is remembered that the Spanish war was soon to interrupt the import of luxuries from the Spanish Netherlands and from Venice.

At that time the great earl of Leicester, who had once been proposed as a husband for the Queen of Scots, was growing old. The days of his lavish entertainments belonged to the years of his widowerhood, which were behind him. Some of the furnishings were destined for Leicester House and some for Wanstead; they were at this time all in store.[1]

There were no uncovered wall spaces at Kenilworth. There were sixteen pieces of gilt leather hangings and six which told the story of Naaman the Assyrian. Eleven pieces of fine tapestry of Forrest work had come from Grafton in 1579 and a set of eight with deep hangings had been purchased from the Lady Lennox. There were one hundred and sixty-five pieces of hangings. The chairs were still perhaps a little rudimentary save those for the earl and his chief guests. His own chair was lined with crimson velvet, the seat and back embroidered with R.L. on cloth of gold. The frame was covered with velvet, edged with gold lace and studded with gilt nails. The chairs for the lower portions of the hall were all lined with peach cloth.

It is worth examining the carpeting in some detail for this was novel. Among the many items mentioned was a carpet of crimson velvet for a window. It is hard to discover what is here meant, presumably the covering for a window seat. There were various other carpets of the same material and colour, possibly these were used for staircases. There was also a carpet of needlework "of sundried coloured crewell and silke, the grounde sadde greene".[2] This, perhaps, alone recalled the carpets in the northern kingdom.

In general the expenditure was very lavish. It was no longer a question of occasional expensive rugs scattered upon the shining boards. It is not surprising that the Persian carpets were still comparatively rare. In the store at Kenilworth there was only one, "a Persian carpet like Turkey worke, the ground red". On the other hand the Turkey carpets were not only numerous but very large. "A great Turkey carpet, the grounde blew with a lyst of yellow at each end" was ten yards in length and four in breadth. There was also one of medium size in orient colours, and there were also twenty-six small Turkey carpets.

There were thirty-five cloth carpets, but these were put to very varied uses. Among them were six window carpets of blue cloth fringed

---

[1] Inventory of household furniture at Kenilworth Castle in 1583, Cal. De L'Isle and Dudley MSS, I, 278-98.   [2] *Ibid.*, 289.

with blue silk on one side and embroidered with black velvet. There were also carpets of green and blue cloth for lining cupboards. It will be seen that the term was then used loosely. There were curtains, then still in some sense a novelty. They numbered only twenty-one in all, of crimson and green taffeta and striped and blue bridges (Bruges) satin.

The great bed was of the older fashion. It is described as "a faire, riche, new, standing square bedstead of walnutte and painted over with crimson and silvered with roses". There were four bears with ragged staffs all silvered standing upon the corner posts. The tester, ceeler and double vallance were of crimson velvet richly embroidered with cinque-foils of cloth of silver. There were also nine bedsteads of walnut tree and a great spruce wainscot bedstead, gilt and carved, bought of the Lady Lennox. There was a Venice bed, and two others folded up into red leather cases.

It is needless to catalogue the canopies in various stuffs, in green and yellow changeable taffeta, and purple lawn and "sarcenett". In these domestic matters it is the quantities that are significant. There were one hundred and sixteen feather beds and seventy pillows. There were further pillows and pillow-frames of varying quality. In addition there were noted thirty-three-and-a-half pairs of fine Holland sheets, seventeen pairs of Holland and fifty-five of coarse Holland, adjusted to the ranking of the guests and their servants.

After this domestic furnishing we now come to the contents of the public rooms. These were high and could now take the new great pictures. There were two portraits of my lord (of Leicester) in whole proportion, the one in armour and the other in russet satin and "welted" velvet. Among the many pictures those of the duke of Feria and Sir Walter Mildmay are noted as being "in whole proportion". These would foreshadow the normal full-length, such as Daniel Mytens painted.

In this connection it may be mentioned that portraits of this period sometimes begin to give more detail of domestic interiors. Thus the same elaborate carpet is depicted in the two independent portraits of the third earl of Dorset and Sir Edward Sackville by this painter. This may help us towards the furnishing of Knole. This careful patterning is in contrast with the dark and rather crude carpet in the Mytens portrait of Frances Countess of Thanet now at Parham and with the oaten-coloured squares on which the Leventhorpe family stands in the picture now at Melbourne Hall.

Compared to the admirable detail so far provided the inventory at Kenilworth seems rather sparse when its deals with the contents not included in the castle's fittings. There were models of five of the seven planets, painted and placed in frames. There was a little folding table of ebony garnished with white bone and covered with verses written in gilded lettering. An instrument of organs and virginals covered with crimson velvet and embroidered lace stood beside a desk inset with the same coloured leather. Beside it in a gilded leather case lined with green cotton stood an ebony chessboard with thirty-two crystal chessmen in a silver setting.

The only books mentioned are a Bible and psalter and service books, each bound in red leather gilt. There was a jewel case bound in the same material and colour and covered with fustian of Naples. With this there stood four flat Venetian chests of walnut tree, three Flanders chests and another lined with black fustian of Naples. Finally there were five close stools of black quilted velvet with pewter pans. This was the standing gear of a great house.

Parallel with this, we can consider the books that were in the possession of the most lettered of the English peers at the date of the king's accession. It would seem that the finest private library of which a catalogue[1] has been preserved was that of the ninth earl of Northumberland. It appears to have been collected in the twenty years preceding the queen's death; its beginnings may perhaps be traced to the young peer's rather limited foreign tour, to the Low Countries, France and northern Italy, which was all that that disturbed time then permitted. There does not seem evidence that any of the books had once belonged to Northumberland's father or uncle, the eighth or seventh earl.

It appears that Northumberland did not read German and none of the books is in that language, although some Latin works were printed within the frontiers of the empire. His acquaintance with both French and Italian was fairly widely reflected in his own circle. It is worth noting how many of his books were printed in Venice or in the Swiss republic. The classical texts in his library are not unexpected except in the relative completeness of their range; Aeschylus, Archimedes, Ausonius, Boethius, Cicero, Euclid, Euripides, Herodotus, Livy, Lucian, Lucretius, Ovid, Pindar, Plato, Pliny, Plotinus, Plutarch and Xenophon.[2]

[1] I must express my gratitude for permission to use the MS. catalogue of the books at Petworth House compiled by Mr G. D. Batho.

[2] Northumberland went on purchasing classics in later life, an *Iliad* in 1611 and a Virgil from Basle two years later.

There were two editions of Terence from Venice and Nuremberg respectively and a copy of *Oracula Sybillina* in Greek and Latin.

This is an interesting list and, except that it omits most of the Roman histories,[1] it might be found as the genesis of those libraries of largely unopened books which would be placed for three centuries in the great English country house. It may be noted that Northumberland was never at the university; there was already forming that *corpus* of erudition which would make the background for the cultivated English nobleman.

Northumberland's library also contained numerous works dealing with Aristotle, some French and Italian translations and various sixteenth-century commentaries, but no Aquinas. This was a concentration of interest which would not endure. In general modern books tended to have an Italian *provenance*, Machiavelli, Guicciardini (Lorenzo and not Francesco), Giordano Bruno and Torquato Tasso. Together with these went Baronius and Theodore Bèza and the *Commentaries* of Blaise de Montluc. There were also books coming from an earlier period, Rabelais, Erasmus and Ulrich von Hutten, and the *Opera Omnia* of Sir Thomas More, printed at Louvain in 1566. There was one volume of Linacre from a Leipzig edition of 1580. It will be seen that Northumberland was accustomed to make purchases upon the continent.

His library contains some books in Spanish. Obregon's *Confutacion del Alcoran* is an example. One wonders if he knew that language, and how he learned it and why? There is a certain haphazard element in the collection, which includes some sheets of genealogical data relating to the families of the counts of Nassau, the arms tricked out in colour and a carefully coloured map labelled "Lotheringia". There were two volumes dealing with royal genealogy, Cesare Campana's *Arbori delle famiglie regali di Spagna* and Paradin's *Alliances genealogiques des Rois . . . de Gaule*.

A recent purchase had been Tycho Brahe's *Astronomiae mechanica* in the Nuremberg edition of 1602. A few years later he would add Kepler's *Astronomia Nova* obtained from Prague. A more specialised interest was Northumberland's concern for modern architecture, both civil and military. He began with an old book, Albrecht Durer's *De urbibus, arcibus, castellisque condendis*, and assembled Vitruvius, Philibert de

---

[1] It appears that in 1604 he received a presentation copy of Sir Clement Edmondes's *Observations upon . . . Caesar's Commentaries* (1600). The edition of the *Commentaries* in the library is of a later date. In 1609 a compendium was purchased entitled *Historiae Romanae scriptores Latini veteres*.

l'Orme, Palladio and Sebastian Serlio. He had Giacomo Barozzi de Vignola's *Le Cinque Ordine*, Simon Stevin's *Castramétation*, and two editions of Jacques Perret's *Architecture et perspective: des fortifications et artifices*, the one printed at Paris and the other at Frankfurt. The library had also other specialised sections; that relating to discovery will be considered later.

This was, as far as internal furnishing was concerned, what the new king would find in England. As far as the library was under consideration, it was not at all what he would wish to find. The intimate study of war was repugnant to him and in Northumberland's library there was almost no theology. It was true that this collection did contain three volumes of a *Biblia Sacra*, but the rest were missing. There was a further reason why he would have little contact with its owner. The earl of Northumberland, like his younger contemporary the earl of Arundel, was of a temperament rarely if ever found in Scotland. Both peers had a cold pride which would keep them aloof from the king's advances. Neither would be amenable to the rough and playful friendship which was what their sovereign had to offer.

In general, one of the purposes of the construction of the great Jacobean mansions was to house the king. It was envisaged that the sovereign would be accompanied by his great officers of state. He could hold court in the long galleries. This was something that he had never had in Scotland. There the actual size of the big houses was very different. In Scotland large mansions were not yet built that were utterly indefensible. Until 1603 there were always stirs along the English border and in the north-east there was the chance of highland raids. Thus the great galleries in English houses, like those at Hatfield and Blickling, were impossible in the north. They were in fact the English equivalent, bearing in mind the rain-laden climate, to the great galleries with porticoes opening to the south which would arise in Lombardy and the Venetian plain. Nor was this a novelty in England as witness the long gallery in the Henrican house at Sutton Place.

The construction of the great house came before that of the avenues and formal gardens. In such matters it is of value to be exact. Salisbury was in advance of his time in the care which he gave to the elaborate waterworks at Theobalds and later to the careful laying out of the Hatfield gardens, many of whose plants came from the Spanish Netherlands, now at peace. A difficulty of the time was caused by the rarity of the use of ornamental iron work. Thus a great entrance like the worked stone piers, which supported the gateway to Hampstead Marshall, belonged to a later generation. The iron gates of Cowdray House in Sussex, with fixed side panels,[1] may have owed their existence to the proximity of the Wealden forges.

Still, this is not the place to do more than indicate the type of building which would arise to house the vast Elizabethan impedimenta, which had come down to this Age of Peace, the tall pictures and the beds and the great carpets. The contrast with Scotland was one that within twenty years would fade away. The king on "his towardly riding horse" had entered into a great rich country.

[1] Cf. J. Starkie Gardiner, *English Ironwork*, 22-3.

Chapter 2

CHURCH AND STATE

On January 14, 1604, there opened at Hampton Court the conference which goes by its name. The king had settled down at this old-fashioned palace, which lay fourteen miles west of London across the fields on the north bank of the river, well away from the unhealthy vapours of the capital, where the plague was raging. It was a mass of brick buildings dating, for the most part, from Wolsey's time; it had all the air of the great cardinal. Towards the end of the late queen's reign a privy garden had been laid out with two new fountains.

The conference was held in a withdrawing room within the privy chamber and was attended on the first day by the royal advisers, the Archbishop of Canterbury and eight members of the episcopate, Bancroft of London, Mathew of Durham, Bilson of Winchester, Babington of Worcester, Watson of Chichester, Robinson of Carlisle and Dove of Peterborough. Among the four Welsh bishops only one was present, Rudd of St David's. There were also present five deans, the most notable being Lancelot Andrewes of Westminster. These contributed little to the discussions. All the lords of the privy council were entitled to be present as spectators.

The great value of this conference for any biography of James I lies in the revelation of the king's mind. It is also evident that the sovereign was at his most natural and quite relaxed. After a rather slow beginning of his opening speech,[1] he was soon going forward very briskly.

For blessed be God's gracious goodness, who hath brought me into the promised Land, where religion is purely professed, where I sit amongst grave, learned and reverend men, not as before, elsewhere, a king without state, without honour, without order, where beardless boys would brave us to the face . . . Our purpose therefore is, like a good physician, to examine and try the complaints, and fully to remove the occasions thereof, if scandalous; cure them, if dangerous; and take knowledge of them, if frivolous, there by to cast a sop into Cerberus's mouth, that he bark no more.

The king then explained that he needed to be satisfied about the use

[1] Account printed in *State Trials*, II, 71-2.

of confirmation, absolution and private baptism in the Church of England. Two brief notes of the exchanges on part of this discussion will give the atmosphere that prevailed on this first day:

Abp of Canterbury. As for the point of Absolution (wherein Your Majesty desires satisfaction) it is clear from all abuse or superstition, as it is used in our Church of England, as will appear on reading both of the Confession and Absolution following it, in the beginning of the Communion book. [Here the King perused both and returned.]
His Majesty. I like, and approve them, finding it to be very true what you say.
Bp of London. It becometh us to deal plainly with your Majesty. There is also in the book a more particular and personal Absolution in the Visitation of the Sick. Not only the confessions of Augusta (Augsburg), Boheme and Saxony, retain and allow it, but Mr Calvin doth also approve both such a general, and such a private (for so he terms it) Confession and Absolution.
His Majesty. I exceedingly well approve it, being an Apostolical and Godly Ordinance, given in the name of Christ to one that deserveth it, upon the clearing of his conscience.[1]

The king sat in his furs in the cold weather as the fire roared up the great chimneys of Hampton Court. He could speak with freedom to men of learning. At last he found the bending hierarchies.

Two days later on Monday, January 16, they met again in the same place. On this occasion Prince Henry, then nine years old, sat on a stool beside his father. Some privy councillors exercised their right of attendance and the four carefully chosen members of the Puritan party were now brought in. On the day of the previous meeting they had been kept waiting in another room. Certain deans were added to the conference and also Patrick Galloway, the minister of Perth in Scotland.

These two final meetings, for they concluded on the Tuesday evening, dealt for the most part with the objections brought forward by Dr Reynolds, who was the spokesman for the moderate Puritans. Occasional contributions were made by Lord Cecil and a single utterance was made by the lord chancellor, the lord treasurer and Lord Henry Howard and by an intervener who is described as a "nameless Lord".[2] The Puritan requests concerned matters which had been long discussed, the abandonment of the Cross in baptism, the discarding of the surplice and the need for an abundance of "preaching ministers".

The king's comments at this meeting tend to show the working of his mind. One of his first interventions contained a celebrated sentence.

[1] *State Trials*, II, 75.   [2] *Ibid.*, II, 86.

"I approve," he explained, "the calling and use of bishops in the Church, and it is my aphorism, 'No Bishop, No King'."[1] On the need for a Catechism he made two points. "First, that curious and deep questions be avoided in the fundamental instructions of a people, secondly, that there should not be so general a departure from the Papists, that every thing should be accounted an error wherein we agree with them."[2] Then there came his two accounts of the Church of Scotland as he saw her.

Why then [said the king as the discussion went slowly through the third day] I will tell you a tale; after that the religion restored by King Edward the sixth, was soon overthrown by Queen Mary here in England, we in Scotland felt the effect of it. For thereupon Mr Knox wrote to the Queen Regent (a virtuous and moderate lady) telling her that she was the supreme head of the Church; and charged her, as she would answer it at God's tribunal, to take care of Christ his Evangel, in suppressing the Popish prelates, who withstood the same; but how long trow you did this continue? Even till by her authority, the Popish bishops were repressed, and Knox, with his adherents being brought in, made strong enough. . . . How they used the poor lady my mother is not unknown, and how they dealt with me in my minority.[3]

At another time he amplified his own position. "If you aim at a Scottish Presbytery, it agreeth as well with monarchy, as God with the devil. Then Jack, and Tom, and Will, and Dick shall meet and censure me and my council. Therefore I reiterate my former speech, *Le Roy s'avisera*."[4]

The king was in his element as he set forth his learned observations; the texts of Scripture flowed from him. He was still a youngish man, just thirty-seven, and the bishops around him were much his seniors. In no other setting did his wisdom receive such great appreciation. "I protest," Bishop Bancroft had said during this conference, "my heart melteth with joy, that Almighty God, of his singular mercy, hath given us such a King as, since Christ's time, the like hath not been."[5] To hear these words there was present one minister of the Church of Scotland.

The matter of a new translation of the Scriptures had been first raised by Dr Reynolds. The king had accepted the project eagerly.

Profess [he explained] I could never yet see a Bible well-translated in English; but I think, that of all, that of Geneva is the worst. I wish some special pains were taken for an uniform translation; which should be done by the best learned in both Universities, then reviewed by the bishops, presented to

[1] *State Trials*, II, 77.   [2] *Ibid.*, II, 79.   [3] *Ibid.*, II, 83.   [4] *Ibid.*, II, 83.   [5] *Ibid.*, II, 87.

the privy council, lastly ratified by royal authority, to be read in the whole church, and no other.

At this point Bishop Bancroft had commented that it was fitting that marginal notes should not be added.

That caveat [replied the king] is well put in, for in the Geneva translation, some notes are partial, untrue, seditious, and savouring of traitorous conceits: As, when from Exodus i, 19. Disobedience to Kings is allowed in a marginal note. And 2 Chron. xv, 16, King Asa (is) taxed in the note for only deposing his mother for idolatry, and not killing her. To conclude this point, let errors, in matters of faith, be amended, and indifferent things be interpreted, and a gloss added unto them.[1]

Thus was the new translation set on foot.

It should be explained that, apart from Mr Patrick Galloway, the prelates at this conference had a common background. They had for the most part held office in one or other of the universities, even the four Puritans included two heads of houses; Dr Reynolds, President of Corpus, and Mr Chaderton, Master of Emmanuel. The later Elizabethan episcopate has sometimes been aspersed unfairly; it was in fact a self-perpetuating body chosen to a great extent from and by the heads of houses. The holders of the greater deaneries had their own share and there was also the influence of the existing bishops. All the same the new sovereign's interest was grateful to them.

Elizabeth and Catherine de Medici as Renaissance queens had but little concern for bishops, who seemed a relic of the Middle Ages, although both rulers preferred that they should technically be celibate. Queen Elizabeth's interest in the Reformation was at heart political. The bishops must have been encouraged now to find a scripturally minded sovereign. It is not by any means so certain that this liking was returned by the new king. It was indeed a relief to be free from the Scottish ministers; but the king remained at heart a regal Calvinist. The sacerdotal element which was to mark the relationship of Charles I with Archbishop Laud was not so much repellent to King James as wholly alien. It was only in the later years of his reign in England that he would find the two prelates, Archbishop Abbot and Bishop Williams, with whom he would be intimate.

Meanwhile the system of promotion mainly from among the heads of houses went forward tranquilly. The old archbishop had set his

[1] State Trials, II, 80.

heart upon the succession of Bishop Bancroft to the primatial see. It was an idea established in his mind in the old queen's days and the new king consented. Dr Whitgift fell ill towards the end of this same winter, catching cold in his barge while travelling upstream from Lambeth Palace to visit Bishop Bancroft at Fulham. He died on February 29, 1604, and the bishop of London was promoted in his place. King James did not have real intimacy with either of his first two primates. It may have been, perhaps, that he required an informality which they could not give him.

It is worth noting that all the archbishops of Canterbury (although not the archbishops of York) in the first half of the seventeenth century were unmarried. This situation had arisen purely by accident; but it had certain consequences. There was, perhaps, a closer relationship between Whitgift and Bancroft than was likely to have developed if either of them had been preoccupied with family ties. This was likewise the only period in her history when the Anglican episcopate has been disturbed by that fierce strife of the celibate which has been said to characterise certain epochs of the history of the Church of Rome.

The king would probably have appreciated an interest in secular learning and in sport. In his heart, as is shown in his dealings with the Church of Scotland, James I thought of his bishops as superintendents; he had no feeling for the episcopal caste which was beginning. Above all he loved to teach, but the bishops whom he found when he came to England were, most of them, some twenty years his senior. They were, however, a most suitable appanage to the English court.

The question of the king's attitude towards Lancelot Andrewes has been often canvassed. In the first year of Archbishop Bancroft's rule at Canterbury the king advanced the dean of Westminister to the see of Chichester. He had long been *episcopabile* and had refused both the dioceses of Salisbury and Ely in the old queen's reign because this would have involved acceptance of the alienation to the crown of some episcopal lands. At that time he had been Master of Pembroke Hall. Andrewes had begun among the followers of the more Puritan wing of the Church of England, his first patrons were the earl of Huntingdon and Sir Francis Walsingham; but he had now moved to a High Church position with which King James was not at ease. The sovereign combined a sense of his own divinely given authority with a deep and genial belief in the subordinate rights of all his subjects. This last was masked by the cheerful kindness of his approach to each associate. He could not accept the claims of a High Church prelate; nor did he take readily to an ascetic.

At the same time he was prepared to promote Dr Andrewes first to Chichester and then to Winchester and finally to Ely. The position of Lord Almoner had been held by Anthony Watson, his predecessor in the see of Chichester. He thus reached the royal palace almost accidentally. Both as dean and as bishop Lancelot Andrewes was useful to the king in his translation of the Bible and in his controversy with Cardinal Bellarmine. It seems to me, however, that in the personal side of the reign he never counted. Canterbury, once Bancroft had departed, was reserved for a very different figure.

Two other prelates belonged to Bishop Andrewes's school of thought, Richard Neile, who succeeded him in the deanery of Westminster, and John Buckeridge, who was at that time president of St John's College, Oxford. The latter became bishop of Rochester and the former, bishop of Lichfield, Lincoln and Durham. All these promotions were effected in the course of King James's reign.[1] It cannot be said that both remained aloof from the sovereign for Neile belonged to a type which the king appreciated, the bishop who has a cheerful temperament and is a friend to every prosperous man. He was also not an intellectual, nor had he the academic manner of the university office-holders. But Neile was important for the men he bred and fostered, the High Church ultra-royalists of the next reign. In all the early part of his career Laud was rustled along by these two prelates, at St John's by Dr Buckeridge and then later on by Bishop Neile. It was natural that a prince with King James's royal tranquillity would not take to a man with Dr Laud's censorious mind.

The king was not attracted by either the doctrine or the symbolism. He was unfamiliar with the high port of the contemporary episcopate upon the continent. Its reflection in the canopy and vallance of crimson and violet paned damask above the bishop's seat in Dr Andrewes's chapel did not appeal to him. He was also concerned in theological disputes in the Dutch Netherlands. These three bishops would all in time be termed Arminians. This was not a school of thought which the king liked.

---

[1] Under Charles I Dr Neile was further promoted to the archbishopric of York and Dr Buckeridge to the bishopric of Ely.

Chapter 3

THE HOUSE OF COMMONS

KING JAMES, during his years in Scotland, had followed with care the foreign policy of the sister kingdom and the shifting influence of his cousin's leading courtiers. It seems that he had given but little thought to the constitution. As a consequence he altogether failed to understand the composition of the House of Commons or to appreciate its power. By conferring a peerage on Sir Robert Cecil he removed from the lower house the secretary of state, who had in effect managed the royal policy there. He was therefore left in his first parliament without a representative, for the solitary privy councillor who had a seat was the insignificant Sir John Herbert. The powers of parliament had increased during the last seventy years. The queen's dexterity had made things difficult for her successor.

It is worth examining with some care the membership of the lower house. To obtain a seat was not an objective sought for among the great body of the country gentry; the summit of their ambition was quite naturally the post of sheriff in their own county. It was for this annual office that the senior lines of the leading families strove together. The duties were carried out within the borders of their native county; unlike the membership of the House of Commons no establishment in London was involved and no prolonged absence from their estates. In consequence the county seats were held for the most part by representatives of a few already wealthy families.

The members of this category may be divided into those who were open to a certain extent to the royal wishes and those who were by habit somewhat hostile to the court. It does not appear that the king realised that there was no way by which he could reduce the opposition of a wealthy and independent squire like Sir John Eliot of Port Eliot. The king's mind was fixed on the Roman Catholics; it does not seem that he realised that there were Protestants who did not like his kind of monarchy. He did not understand that in England there were laymen who had something of the outlook of the Scottish ministers.

It appears that very little trouble had been taken by Cecil in making

preparations for the summoning of this parliament. It may have been
difficult to launch a campaign for developing a governmental party
among the members when the king seemed unaware of any need for
such an action. The secretary of state was, moreover, and this was
natural, much more concerned in building up a Cecilian group among
the privy councillors than in any operations in the House of Commons.
There was further a possible difficulty in regard to the management of
the lower house. There was one experienced member of the ruling caste
whose work could have been of value to the king in the House of Commons, for Sir Francis Bacon was, with all his talents, a perfect royalist.
He was Cecil's first cousin and the secretary of state was well aware that
he could not afford to entrust such power to him. There were many able
lawyers in the House of Commons placed there by friends or patrons in
the small borough constituencies. The king had still to begin his long
and difficult course with the English judiciary.

In the House the mercantile grouping was still in embryo; they were
found as members for some seaport towns, Dartmouth is an example.
In the more substantial towns which had two burgesses, one might have
some connection with local trade. The great London merchant dynasties
were only in process of formation; a seat in parliament did not yet seem
to them to be of value. The poorer group among the members were
usually men without an independent income who held office in the
households of the greater peers and had been preferred by their masters
to small boroughs in which the peer might hold the stewardship. Such
men had no direct connection with the court save through their masters, to whom they were useful in different ways. Not one of them had
any political future. As ever many members did not speak; attention
was concentrated on the vocal minority. It is important that one should
not exaggerate the effect of the apparent abstention of the crown from
exercising its influence in this first election.

It is difficult to envisage a House of Commons which had no concern
with the day-to-day administration of the state. The average member
was very far removed from the privy councillors among whom the ad-
ministrators would be chosen. In consequence they were not in touch,
except in a broad way, with any trends. They reflected the majority
ideas of the prosperous classes in town and country upon foreign policy.
This involved a strong wish to come to the aid of Protestants abroad
and in this context it meant support for Calvinists, for the Huguenots
in France, for the Dutch and for the Genevan princes in western Ger-

many. The Lutheran world was hardly within their picture. This outlook was a fixed standpoint; throughout the reign it never varied.

In the sphere of religion there was a Puritan element, very strong in the city of London. It was bound up with the opposition and had come down, as in the case of Walsingham's relatives the Wentworths of Livingstone Lovell, from the last parliaments of the old queen's reign. The Jacobean court was anathema to such Puritans. As a factor such men grew in strength and separateness until after the sailing of the *Mayflower*. They pored over their rare books and drew strength from the Bible and historical knowledge from the *Book of Martyrs*. They had a fierce fixed belief in the Pure Evangel and saw with reprobation the devil and his Roman fortresses. It is difficult for us now to envisage this position, just as the old Tridentine Church is far away. Beside them was the now established Low Church squirearchy. One factor arose from this combination. It was not possible to remit the laws against the English Roman Catholics.

The power by which the House of Commons clogged the king's intentions was the right to vote supplies. He was dealing with large groups of men he did not know and could not influence. In his first kingdom there had been something personal about the rule of the young king. Here he was speaking to those who heard, but did not heed him. The king's opening speech to his first English parliament began as follows. "It did no sooner please God to lighten his hand and relent of the violence of his devouring angel against the poor people of this City, but as soon did I resolve to call this Parliament." Having made the religious reference to the plague, he went on to express gratitude for the welcome he had received on coming to this country.

Or shall it ever be blotted out of my mind how at my first entry into this kingdom the people of all sorts rode and ran, nay rather flew to meet me, their eyes flaming nothing but sparkles of affection; their mouths and tongues uttering nothing but sounds of joy; their hands, feet and all the rest of their members in their gestures discovering a passionate longing and earnestness to meet and embrace their new sovereign? . . . the first, then, of those blessings which God hath, jointly with my power, sent unto you is outward peace.[1]

The Puritans sat glumly with their hats upon their heads.

He spoke about the union of England and Scotland which was without appeal for them. The old queen's approach had been truly regal;

[1] Delivered on March 19, 1604, printed in J. R. Tanner, *Constitutional Documents of the Reign of James I* (Cambridge, 1930), 24.

they did not at all accept these Scottish familiarities. To men who set a value on their purse the king's scheme would seem a costly project. "What God hath conjoined then," said the king, "let no man separate, I am the husband and the whole isle is my wife; I am the head and it is my body; I am the shepherd and it is my flock."[1] He returned to the same subject on the adjournment of this house some three years later.

Can you imagine I will respect the lesser and neglect the greater? . . . . You know that I am careful to preserve the woods and game through all England, nay through all the Isles: yet none of you doubts I would be more offended with any disorder in the forest of Waltham (in Essex) for stealing of a deer there, which lieth as it were under my nose and in a manner joineth with my garden, than with cutting of timber or stealing of a deer in any forest of the north parts of Yorkshire or the Bishopric.[2]

These words, the cheery homely tones, fell on deaf ears.

This parliament continued almost until the death of the earl of Salisbury, as Sir Robert Cecil had then become. In the early years affairs proceeded with tranquillity for the king did not seem conscious of his need of money. And this was as well for whatever they might grant with a war in prospect, the house had no desire to provide finances for a court at peace.

At the very beginning of parliament there developed the celebrated matter known as Goodwin's case. This was a disputed election for the county member for Buckinghamshire. On the proposal of Lord Chancellor Ellesmere orders had been issued for the return of all election results to the court of Chancery. In accordance with this arrangement that court declared this election void on the ground that Goodwin was an outlaw.[3] In consequence the seat was given to the other candidate Sir John Fortescue, an aged and wealthy squire, who had held the office of chancellor of the exchequer. The case has not been studied in depth and there is very little known about Sir Francis Goodwin.

The House of Commons took the view that the determination of elections lay in their hands. They summoned Goodwin to the bar and, after hearing his side of the question, ordered him to take his seat. The matter was raised with the commons by a request for information from

[1] *Constitutional Documents of the Reign of James I*, 26.
[2] Delivered on March 31, 1607, *ibid.*, 37.
[3] Sir Francis Goodwin of Upper Winchendon, a brother-in-law of Lord Grey de Wilton, returned to a seat in parliament after this *débâcle*, a shadowy figure. Cf. A note in Brunton and Pennington, *Members of the Long Parliament*, 190-1.

the House of Lords. When it was made clear that the king had interested himself in this affair, the lower house agreed to have a conference.

At this meeting the king explained the situation as he saw it, stating tranquilly that he had no purpose to impeach their privilege, but that since they derived all matters of privilege from himself and by his grant, he expected that they should not be turned against him. The house replied with caution. Making Bacon the spokesman of their committee, they explained that hitherto they had always decided cases of disputed election. The king accepted this contention, but asked the commons to issue a writ for a new election. This was the easier to manage since there were no deep personal interests involved. Goodwin was an outlaw and his rival, who belonged to Sir Adrian Fortescue's family, had submerged Catholic sympathies and founded the well-known recusant stock, the Fortescues of Salden Hill.[1] He also had associations that the king did not care for with Lord Cobham and Sir Walter Raleigh.

[1] On April 9, 1628, Dame Grace Fortesque, after the death of Sir Francis, devised Salden to Lords Shrewsbury and Savage, Mr Talbot, Sir John Curson and Mr Lane and became a recusant convict, Cal. S.P. Dom. 1627-8, 68.

Chapter 4

SIR WALTER RALEIGH

AT the very beginning of the reign there were discovered two small conspiracies, which are only of concern to us because the second brought about the fall of Sir Walter Raleigh. The first of these was an abortive plot whose intentions it is at this date hardly possible to decipher. In fact no convincing explanation may ever be forthcoming.[1]

Both conspiracies, however, display that full paraphernalia of a state trial whose elaborate defence of the king's position must have been a surprise and surely a deeply encouraging surprise to King James of Scotland. It is for this reason that Sir Walter Raleigh's trial at Winchester is reported in some detail. There the king could consider the actions of his leading privy councillors and the great judges; there were so many lions beneath his throne.

The two conspiracies with which the new reign opened, the Main plot and the Bye, are of small interest. They have complexity, but no depth. In a certain way they hardly had existence, in the sense that no plot reached its conclusion, perhaps they were not intended to. Their real interest for this period centres in the light that they throw on the character of Sir Walter Raleigh.

Raleigh may have been at certain times dishonourable, but his mind was lucid. There had to be a serious reason behind all his actions. At the time that these events open he was just past fifty years of age and had been dismissed from all his offices. He had lost, naturally, the captaincy of the king's guard and also, understandably, Durham House in the Strand, which he was instructed after nearly twenty years to restore to the bishop. The other royal acts were rather questionable. The removal of the monopoly of sweet wines, the loss of the governorship of Jersey and, perhaps most of all, the taking away of his great post of lord warden of the Stannaries had left him bare. Looking back it seems imprudent. Raleigh belonged essentially to the war-like period of the Elizabethan age. He had that swagger, which, when displayed by a

---

[1] The period of S. R. Gardiner was the heyday of concern for these complexities. In the last three-quarters of a century the interest of historians has turned to broader channels.

man of middle age, was quite repugnant to the Scottish sovereign. He commanded no alliance. It might have been wiser to leave him his large employments in the west of England, which he could have carried on far from the court. At any rate he was now in a position where a desperate throw may well have had an attraction to his bold mind.

The Bye plot can be soon dismissed. The originator, Mr William Watson, was a secular priest, who was out of his mind. He had built himself up into a form of self-chosen leadership of the secular clergy against the Jesuits and had gone to Scotland as soon as King James had succeeded. He seems to have believed that the king had given him personal assurances of better treatment for the Catholics, which were reflected in his first actions in not levying the recusancy fines. But while the king was in Scotland there were two factors of which he was unaware. The recusancy fines in fact provided a method of rewarding his followers which he had not envisaged; nor did Scotland possess a House of Commons. The lower house in England had a firm attachment to the maintenance of all the penal laws. This is supposed to account for Watson's conspiracy. All that is known of him is that he was in the early forties and had come from County Durham, "a very short man, very purblind and looketh asquint". This character envisaged himself as capturing the king and then emerging as lord chancellor of England. He had four companions, one of whom was a priest named Clarke, a very simple fellow, and the others laymen; Sir Griffin Markham was more personable than his priest companions, "a large broad face, black complexion . . . big nose and one of his hands maimed by a hurt in his arm received by shot of bullet".[1] He was related to Babington and more distantly to Vaux of Harrowden. He was a convert swordsman and had fought under Essex. In fact he might have been a gunpowder plotter. Presumably it was Markham who made contact with the men of rank, George Brooke and Lord Grey de Wilton. They were arrested before they had come together. How far were the two last-named really guilty? The two priests and Brooke were executed.

It is a relief to turn to the Main plot, not that it was much more tangible; but at least there is a reasonable motive for bringing it about. In fact in my view it was cooked up, so that it could be offered to the king.

It would appear that Sir Walter Raleigh was shocked by the abruptness of his own downfall. My suggestion is as follows. He was a solitary

[1] Cal. Salisbury MSS, XV, 193.

and friendless man as far as his equals were concerned. His few real supporters were not at court, men like Lawrence Kemeys and other partners in his sea ventures. He had in recent years been pestered by Lord Cobham, a man whom he despised, with offers of intimacy. Cobham is described as a "very passionate man";[1] he was also tactless and pursued by fears, the typical example of a weakling at the tough Elizabethan court. He had lost his influence with Salisbury, whose wife had been his sister. He had married the wealthy countess of Kildare, but this marriage was childless and now disintegrating. He had had handed down from his father the post of warden of the Cinque Ports, and he also had inherited Cobham Hall, which he was completing. He was one of those who was quite certain that he had no future as long as Sir Robert Cecil held the keys.

It is not clear who first had the idea that Cobham should make contact with Count d'Aremberg, the ambassador of the sovereigns of the Spanish Netherlands. Large sums were to be paid out in pensions and a Spanish force was to land in Britain. After the murder of the "King and his cubs", the Lady Arabella Stuart would mount the throne. She was to marry according to the advice of Catholic kings. It should be pointed out that if all the "cubs" were in fact killed, she would be by law the heiress to the English crown. It is my suggestion that when everything had been tied up neatly, Raleigh would have handed over Cobham to the government. Surely such an action would content the king and Raleigh would be restored to partial favour.

It may be thought that this is going too far, but let us now examine the only possible alternative. Raleigh's own outlook was glorious and Elizabethan. He had fought the Spaniards, he neither liked nor respected them. He had the ordinary west country gentleman's hearty dislike for the Church of Rome. Is it possible that he could have changed so suddenly in these essentials? Could he have embarked on a conspiracy where his only fellow-worker was poor Lord Cobham? His sense of self-interest was especially well nourished. That he could really have engaged in such a plot strikes me as incredible.

At the same time his talent had always been for open enmity. He could not manage this slow and secret winding up of his companion. One morning when he was walking on the terrace of Windsor Castle, for he had not abandoned following the court, he received instructions to attend a meeting of the council. Evidence against Lord Cobham

[1] Raleigh at his trial. "He is as passionate a man as lives", *State Trials*, II 12.

had been discovered and he was asked as the friend of that isolated peer to help the government. The time had already passed in the development of the situation, as I see it, when Raleigh could make use of the discovery for his own benefit. Under this new light he was soon inevitably involved not in the manufacture of a plot but in abetting a conspiracy. He was then arrested and conveyed for trial to Winchester; the plague in London ruled out the prosecution of the case in the capital. The king soon moved south-westward and throughout the trial remained in the pleasaunces at Wilton.

It seems probable that Salisbury, who knew so much, saw what had happened. The trial of the conspirators in the Bye plot had taken place in Winchester on November 15, 1603, and was just concluded. All, with the exception of Sir Edward Parham, had been condemned. It was at this first trial that the nomenclature of the two plots was established. The phrases were attributed to Lord Cobham. He is said to have termed the conspiracy in which his brother George Brooke was engaged as the Bye, while "Walter Raleigh and I are chanced at the Main".[1]

The actual commissioners foreshadowed those engaged in later trials, the earls of Suffolk, Devon and Salisbury, Lord Henry Howard soon to be earl of Northampton, Lord Wotton, Sir John Stanhope and certain judges. The attorney general, Sir Edward Coke, began with a detailed account of the Bye plot concluding with these words, "so you see these Treasons were like Sampson's foxes, which were joined in their tails, though their heads were severed".[2] This new trial had begun as soon as the Bye plot proceedings were completed. Raleigh stated, for he was most able on his own behalf, "Your words cannot condemn me, my innocency is my defence". At this the attorney general said: "Nay, I will prove all: thou art a monster; thou hast an English face, but a Spanish heart. Now you must have Money: Aremberg was no sooner in England (I charge thee Raleigh) but though incidedst Cobham to go unto him and to deal with him for Money, to bestow on discontented persons to raise Rebellion in this kingdom."[3]

Throughout Raleigh demanded to be confronted with his accuser; but all that he could get were Cobham's confessions. The authorities were in this matter shrewd to deny him. Raleigh had loomed over that unfortunate man, who was now deeply frightened of him. Sir Walter's words reveal the nature of their association.

I never [he said] came to Lord Cobham's, but about matter of his profit;

[1] *State Trials*, II, 63.   [2] *Ibid.*, II, 6.   [3] *Ibid.*, II, 7, 8,

as the ordering of his house, paying of his servants' board wages etc. I had of his, when I was examined £4000 worth of jewels for a purchase; a pearl of £3000 and a ring of £400. If he had had a fancy to run away, he would not have left so much to have purchased a lease in fee-farm. I saw him buy £300 worth of books to send to his library at Canterbury.[1]

Raleigh was asked about the plan for Lord Cobham, "a man bred in England with no experience (of travel)", to visit the archdukes at Brussels and the king of Spain. "If I had been the Plotter," he exclaimed, "would not I have given Cobham some arguments, whereby to persuade the King of Spain and answer his objections? I knew Westmoreland and Bothwell, men of other understandings than Cobham, were ready to beg their bread."[2] The answer, as in the case of other conspiracies, was probably that Cobham was never intended to go to Madrid at all. He would be trussed up and handed over to the government before that voyage took place.

It was said that Raleigh trusted that he could not be condemned on the evidence of a single witness. In this connection the attorney general gave his view of the position. "*Scientia sceleris est mera ignorantia.* You have read the letter of the law, but understand it not. Here was your anchorhold, and your rendezvous: you trust to Cobham, either Cobham must accuse you, or nobody; if he did, then it would not hurt you, because he is but one Witness; if he did not, then you are safe."[3] To which Raleigh at once replied: "If ever I read a word of the law or statutes before I was prisoner in the Tower, God confound me."[4] Later they came again to the expression "destroying the King and his cubs". This led to a further exchange. Raleigh began,

Oh barbarous. If they, like unnatural villains, should use those words, shall I be charged with them? I will not hear it; I was never any Plotter with them against my country, I was never false to the crown of England. I have spent 4000 pounds of my own against the Spanish Faction, for the good of my country. Do you bring the words of these hellish spiders, Clark, Watson, and others, against me?[5]

To which the attorney general replied: "Though hast a Spanish heart, and thyself art a Spider of Hell; for thou confessest the King to be a most sweet and gracious prince, and yet thou hast conspired against him."[6] And, to my mind, these words of Raleigh's were absolutely true.

---

[1] *State Trials*, II, 12. [2] *Ibid.*, II, 13. [3] *Ibid.*, II, 16. [4] *Ibid.*, II, 16.
[5] *Ibid.*, II, 19, 20. [6] *Ibid.*, II, 20.

He was never false to the crown of England. One man had just complaint against him, foolish Lord Cobham.

The case was drawing towards its close and they came to the question of a letter sent by Lord Cobham to Lady Arabella Stuart. She was in court beside the lord admiral (Nottingham) who now declared, "The lady doth here protest upon her salvation that she never dealt in any of these things and so she willed me to tell the court."[1] The verdict of guilty was brought in.

The king at Wilton considered the evidence and all these verdicts. He was conscious that the decision as to carrying out the sentences in these state trials belonged to him alone. He sent a reprieve, which reached them on the scaffold, in favour of Lord Cobham, Lord Grey de Wilton and Sir Griffin Markham. A few days later Sir Walter Raleigh's reprieve also reached him. The king seems to have shown a wise valuation of the evidence in all these cases. Sir Walter and the others were brought back to London. He was treated with the utmost courtesy that a gentleman, who was not a peer, could then expect. He was given a set of rooms on the top floor of the Bloody Tower. His wife and his young son joined him there. He was allowed a couple of servants to wait upon him. There he would remain, a factor in the situation, for the first two-thirds of the reign. Some words that Raleigh used at the very end of the trial are worth quoting here for they forecast the future. "Presumption must proceed from precedent or subsequent facts. I have spent 40,000 crowns against the Spaniards. I had not purchased 40 pounds a year. If I had died in Guiana I would not have left 300 marks a year to my wife and son. I that have always condemned the Spanish Faction...."[2]

[1] *State Trials*, II, 23.   [2] *Ibid.*, II, 25.

Chapter 5

THE GUNPOWDER PLOT

IT is perhaps best to begin a consideration of the Gunpowder plot by printing King James's own account of the affair. He was always long-winded and in this case sententious.

While [began this royal account] this land and whole monarchy flourished in a most happy and plentiful peace, as well at home as abroad, sustained and conducted by these two main pillars of all good government, piety and justice, no foreign grudge, nor inward whispering of discontentment any way appearing: the King being upon his return from his hunting exercise at Royston, upon occasion of the drawing near of the parliament-time, which had been twice prorogued already partly in regard of the season of the year, and partly of the term: as the winds are ever stillest immediately before a storm . . . so, at that time of greatest calm, did this secretly hatched thunder begin to cast forth the first flashes, and flaming lightnings of the approaching tempest. For, the Saturday of the week immediately preceding the King's return, which was upon a Thursday, being but ten days before the Parliament, the Lord Monteagle, son and heir to Lord Morley, being in his own lodgings ready to go to supper, at seven of the clock at night, one of his footmen, whom he had sent on an errand over the street, was met by a man of a reasonable tall personage, who delivered him a Letter, charging him to put it in my lord his master's hands.[1]

The king then goes on to describe Lord Monteagle's perplexity in studying this paper, which was without date or superscription and in an unknown hand "somewhat unlegible". After a short time

notwithstanding the lateness and darkness of the night in that season of the year, he presently repaired to His Majesty's palace at Whitehall, and there delivered the same to the Earl of Salisbury, His Majesty's principal secretary. Whereupon the said Earl of Salisbury having read the Letter and heard the manner of the coming of it to his hands, did greatly encourage and commend my Lord for his discretion, telling him plainly that . . . this accident put him in mind of divers advertisements he had received from beyond the seas, wherewith he had acquainted, as well the King himself as divers of his

[1] Reprinted from the collection of King James's *Works*, in *State Trials*, II, 195-8.

privy counsellors, concerning some business the Papists were in, both at home and abroad, making preparations for some combination amongst them against this Parliament-time.

The next day the letter was delivered to the king in the gallery at Whitehall. The principal sentences ran as follows.

Out of the love I bear to some of your friends, I have a care of your preservation, therefore I would advise you, as you tender your life, to devise some excuse, to shift off your attendance at this Parliament. For God and men have contrived to punish the wickedness of this time. . . . For though there is no appearance of any stir, yet I say they shall receive a terrible blow this Parliament, and yet they shall not see who hurts them.

The king soon penetrated to the true meaning. It became clear to him that there could be no destruction with "the authors thereof unseen, except only if it was by a blowing up of powder which might be performed by one base knave in a dark corner".

Thus the king was to be destroyed in parliament by a papist conspiracy. Gunpowder had already scarred the royal imagination. This was the method used against his father. He must often have had in mind that February night in Edinburgh with the cold wind blowing in across the Forth, while the walls beneath the gallery at Kirk o'Fields began to waver and the townsmen waked uneasily with the great noise of the explosion. There must have been some who knew that gunpowder was what the king most feared.

After he had perused the letter, the earl of Salisbury at once consulted with the earl of Suffolk, who held the chamberlainship of the royal household, and then with three further privy councillors, the lord admiral and the earls of Worcester and Northampton. It is said in one account that they had been dining together.

It was soon discovered that Mrs Bright, a tenant of Mr Whynniard, one of the minor court officials, had sub-let her cellar under the Parliament House to Thomas Percy, a confidential agent of the earl of Northumberland. This gentleman had also bought her stock of coal. At eleven o'clock on the night preceding the opening of parliament Sir Thomas Knyvet, in his joint capacity as a gentleman of the privy chamber and a justice of the peace for Westminster, entered the cellar where he found Guy Fawkes standing guard over the coals which were heaped above a thousand billets of wood and five hundred faggots. These lay on bars of iron, intended to increase the force of the explosion and underneath them thirty-six barrels of gunpowder.

It is worth pausing for a moment to consider the position of the five councillors with whom the prosecution was now to rest. For Salisbury the matter was quite simple. From whatever angle the affair could be regarded, he had saved his sovereign. Nottingham, the lord admiral, and his cousin Suffolk had neither links nor sympathy with the Catholic minority of the population. It was a testimony to Salisbury's sense of tactics that the house of Howard, so very much blamed in previous reigns, could now emerge in the forefront of the new king's saviours. There remained Northampton and Worcester, the two men in this grouping who have often been described as Catholics. Northampton's position has been discussed. He was, as I see it, a politician; the English crown was all in all to him. He was in fact a regalian. Moreover, he was a member of the Howard phalanx; he had a distaste for foreign ecclesiastics in all their forms and a true detestation for the Society of Jesus.

Worcester was, compared to the Howard phalanx, a minor figure. But as he was to be about the court throughout the reign, it is best to consider him at his first entrance. He was the head of the Somersets descended from a natural son of the last duke of that name, who had married the heiress of the Herberts, earls of Pembroke of the first creation. His great properties lay in Monmouthshire around Raglan and included the former possessions of Tintern Abbey. He had been at court since boyhood, a quiet consistent supporter of the Cecils, father and son. He had succeeded as fourth earl in 1589 and was just turned fifty. He was a superb horseman and an expert tilter and was at this time Master of the Horse.

It is alleged that Queen Elizabeth had said of him that "he reconciled what she believed impossible, a stiff Papist with a loyal subject".[1] This, however, is not exact. His life reflected that of his father who had been conservative in religious questions; but it is clear that he appreciated that a great house should move with the times. He appointed a Welsh Protestant tutor for his sons and attended Protestant sermons from time to him in his capacity of lord lieutenant.[2] It was in keeping with this line that he had married a sister of the Puritan earl of Hunt-

[1] This story cannot be traced back further than 1670 when it appeared in Lloyd's *State Worthies*, 582.
[2] These facts were established by Professor A. H. Dodd. Cf. "The Pattern of Politics in Stuart World", *Transactions of the Society of Cymmrodorion* (1948), 17.

ingdon.[1] But then the Jesuits had entered into his family circle. They converted first his wife and then his daughters. Fairly recently his eldest son had been reconciled after making the grand tour. The only later sentiment that Worcester evinced, as far as religious matters were concerned, was a certain bitterness against the Society of Jesus.

On the morning of November 5 as far as the councillors associated with this case were concerned, with the exception of the earl of Salisbury, the situation appeared as follows. Guy Fawkes, thoroughly exhausted, had passed the night with his boots on, maintaining a strict silence, a Roman pose "like Mutius Scaevola".[2] The discovery of Thomas Percy's hiring of the cellar had thrown suspicion on the earl of Northumberland, with whom he lived when in London at Sion House. Francis Tresham had left that morning for Rushton, his house in Northamptonshire.

Lord Monteagle, son and heir to Lord Morley, remains throughout a rather shadowy figure. He was just thirty years of age and somewhat extravagant. There have been discussions about his religion. He had recently written to the king announcing his intention to become a Protestant, but there is little evidence that he ever had believed in Roman doctrines. It is nevertheless true that he had an intimate knowledge of that communion in its ramifying branches among the richer squires of the south Midlands. It would seem that that group of families was something that he had always known and was quite ready to get away from.

He was the child of parents, one long dead and the other somewhat alienated, who belonged to two very different families. His father's stock, the Parkers, were wealthy gentry in East Anglia, who had acquired by inheritance the ancient Morley barony. They had two main houses, Great Hallingbury Hall in Essex and Old Morley Hall, together with the ancestral manor of Hallingbury Morley. They had been a court family under Henry VIII and had suffered one disaster. Lord Morley's great-aunt Jane, viscountess Rochford, had been mistress of the maids to Queen Catherine Howard and had been executed with her. Lord Monteagle's father Lord Morley, an elderly subdued Anglican, would survive until 1618; he would have to wait for his inheritance. His mother was of quite a different background, the daughter and

---

[1] Nevertheless, the religious ancestry was mixed, for the countess of Worcester was the daughter of Catherine (Pole), countess of Huntingdon, niece of the cardinal.

[2] The king's account, printed in *State Trials*, II, 201.

heiress of the last Stanley Lord Monteagle, a junior branch of the earl of Derby's family. She had died while her son was quite a little boy and had left him Hornby Castle on the borders of Lancashire and Yorkshire and two manors in the Pennine moorland country of the latter county.

Monteagle had married Elizabeth Tresham when he was seventeen. He was thereafter much at Rushton. This was one of the good marriages that old Sir Thomas Tresham procured for his daughters. Monteagle thus obtained the Tresham house at Hoxton "in a little orchard and less garden",[1] where he was staying when he received the Letter. It is a misfortune that Sir Thomas Tresham, who paints his relatives by marriage without flattery, has left us no account of Lord Monteagle. His political career had been discouraging. He had been a close supporter of the earl of Essex, whom he had accompanied to Ireland. He was present at the siege of Essex House and had been sent to the Tower and only released on the payment of £8,000.

Attention was at once focused on Francis Tresham, Monteagle's brother-in-law, who was the most recently joined of the conspirators. He was at this time thirty-eight and already middle-aged by the standards of his day. In his youth he had been "a wylde and unstayed man", constantly involved in money troubles. Like Monteagle, he had frequented Essex House. His health was already poor; it appears that he was tubercular. His father Sir Thomas Tresham had died on September 11, 1605, and the plot was revealed to him on October 24. His recently gained inheritance would have been useful.

It has been suggested that Tresham wrote the celebrated letter. It is also supposed that he discussed this document with Lord Monteagle before delivering it. It is said that Monteagle seldom used his house in Hoxton and that on this occasion he came up suddenly and ordered dinner. It is noted that Monteagle gave the letter, as soon as he received it, to Thomas Warde, a gentleman in his service. Warde in fact informed one of the conspirators, who therefore scattered.

The question arises as to who wrote the letter. In fact it could have been written by anyone who knew of the conspiracy and wished to bring it to an end and realised that Monteagle would prove to be a useful channel. It is not necessary that the writer of the letter should have been known to the recipient. It has been suggested that at this time both Monteagle and Tresham were already employed in government service. It is of course possible, but there seems to be no reason to

[1] This description is found among the Cal. Clarke Thornhill MSS, p. 65.

assume this.[1] To my mind it is to quite another quarter that we should turn to trace the information collected by the earl of Salisbury. It would seem that in both the development and the unravelling of this conspiracy there are traces of what would be called a fine Italian hand. It is now time to consider the situation in the country.

In the very centre of Northamptonshire, a few miles from the town of Kettering and within an easy ride of Rushton, lay Harrowden Hall, which since the first coming of Campion in the summer of 1580 had been a regular centre for the Jesuits. It was at that time a modern house, since disappeared. As a resort of Jesuits it was of course well known to the government, but on the other hand it was realised in the same quarter that Lord Vaux of Harrowden, Sir Thomas Tresham and Mr Talbot, whose name will recur in this account, were all wholeheartedly opposed to the Spanish cause. For two generations the owners of this house had taken little part in domestic politics and, what was remarkable for members of the wealthy gentry, they had obtained no monastic land. The third Lord Vaux of Harrowden, who lost his intellectuals before his fairly early death in 1595, was described by his brother-in-law Sir Thomas Tresham in these forthright terms. He had just come up to London "raggedly suited and clothed unfittedest to give attendance of royal presence . . . moneyless and creditless, the unfortunatest peer of parliament that ever was".[2]

In the autumn of 1605 it was a house of women, Mrs George Vaux and her husband's step-sisters,[3] Mistress Anne Vaux and Mrs Brooksby. Mrs Vaux's five children were all quite young and her eldest son Lord Vaux was just fourteen. But the main interest of the house at this time lay in the fact that it was among the places of refuge of Father Henry Garnet, superior of the Society of Jesus. Mistress Anne Vaux had for some years given herself to the work of a lay missionary. "The vestments and altar furniture," we are told by Father John Gerard, "were both plentiful and costly . . . some were embroidered with gold and pearls and figures by well-skilled hands. There were six massive candlesticks upon the altar, lamps hanging by silver chains and a silver crucifix."[4] The cruets, basin for the *lavabo*, the bell and thurible were all of silver.

[1] Tresham died in prison on December 22, 1605.

[2] Letter of Sir Thomas Tresham, Cal. Clarke Thornhill MSS, p. 65.

[3] William, third Lord Vaux of Harrowden married, first, Elizabeth Beaumont of Grace Dieu and left issue Anne and Eleanor, wife of Edward Brooksby. He married, secondly, Mary Tresham of Rushton and had a son, George, who predeceased him.

[4] Rev. Philip Caraman, S.J., trans., *John Gerard, The Autobiography of an Elizabethan* (1951), 195.

There was a crucifix of gold for greater festivals. This was very like the Jesuit set-up in Ethiopia. They used contemporary material, in this case the product of the gold and silver mines in Spanish America, to do honour to the King of Glory.

One can understand how this would have appealed to the conventional, rather urban mind of Father Garnet. It will be noted that all this gear was movable; it could be stowed away in the hiding places constructed for it. There was a small wing of three storeys, just lately built to accommodate the priests close to the old chapel. "We could pass out into the private garden," wrote Father Gerard, "and thence through the broad walks into the fields, and there mount our horses to go wherever we wanted."[1] Still, it should be remembered that Father Gerard was an outdoor type, the son of a northern squire, a very different sort of man from Father Garnet.

On the day after his arrest Guy Fawkes was taken to the Tower and racked, after which he gave a full list of the conspirators. There were few names that would have seemed remarkable to the councillors or really unexpected; there are perhaps two exceptions, Sir Everard Digby of Gayhurst in Buckinghamshire and Ambrose Rookwood of Coldham Hall in Suffolk. They were different from other plotters in the future of their families. Ambrose Rookwood's son Robert was knighted in the last year of James I. Sir Everard's son, who was a little younger, would be the celebrated Sir Kenelm Digby. These two wealthy squires were not related to any other of the conspirators and were recruited late to help the plotters with Digby's funds and Rookwood's stable. Many of the others were soldiers of fortune, survivors of the Essex conspiracy. One of the problems of this Gunpowder plot is that the government already knew so much about the leading plotters.

The Essex conspiracy falls outside the subject of this study, but it was memorable as the last example in action of the old mediaeval hierarchic grouping, a gathering based to a great extent on Wales, but also calling to its aid the type of the unattached impoverished gentleman, usually discontented, who had little to offer beside his sword. Among those deeply involved was Robert Catesby, who is known as the leader of the Gunpowder plot. Associated with him were Thomas Percy and three of the lesser plotters.[2] Francis Tresham and Monteagle were associated with the same affair at a different, a more moneyed level. The chief vic-

---

[1] *John Gerard, The Autobiography of an Elizabethan*, 160-1.
[2] Thomas Winter and John and Christopher Wright.

tim of the Essex conspiracy was intended to be Sir Robert Cecil. King James might view that *émeute* very calmly. It was not easy for his minister to do the same.

Much has been said of Catesby's charm. It is difficult to detect that now. He was a tall man verging on middle age. He is represented in one of the high-crowned hats of his period with a full beard and long moustachios. He certainly had a masculine character and that swordsman's piety which was found among the officers of the League and of the Spanish *Tercios*. He had a clear ascendancy over his unintellectual young companions and the older men were mostly of his kidney. He was a first cousin to that very different character, Francis Tresham.[1]

Among the last to be initiated was Catesby's body servant Thomas Bates. He was the pathetic member of this conspiracy. In the portraits his young clean-shaven face has a look of great simplicity. He had obviously shown some interest in all this rolling about of barrels of gunpowder. Catesby called him in to his lodging at Puddle Wharf and revealed the matter to him. There was no way in which he could have saved his life, unless he had immediately betrayed his master.

It appeared that the plan had been for Fawkes to light a slow match and then make his way downstream to Wapping, where a hoy was waiting to take him to Gravelines. The others who were in town were to ride to Dunsmoor Heath, where Digby had assembled a hunting party of the Catholic gentry. Warned by Ward, they left London a little early; but none of the guests would take part in a rising and when they called on John Talbot of Grafton, the second heir to the earldom of Shrewsbury and the father-in-law of Robert Winter, they were driven from his door. The plan is said to have been to carry off the king's daughter, the Princess Elizabeth, and declare her queen on the assumption that the two sons of James I would have perished with him in the explosion or in its aftermath. All this part of the plan seems to me very weak and in fact rather difficult to credit. How for instance were they to form a government in the young girl's name? Where were the responsible ministers to be obtained?

After the failure at Dunsmoor Heath, Catesby and his companions went on by Huddington and Hewell Grange, where they collected some armour in Lord Windsor's absence. At ten o'clock in the evening of

---

[1] He was also a second cousin to Robert Winter of Huddington and his brother Thomas. Again, John Grant had married their sister Dorothy Winter; Thomas Percy had married the sister of John Wright of Plowland in Yorkshire and his brother Christopher, who brought in his friend Robert Keyes.

November 7 they arrived and established themselves at Holbeach House. On the following day the sheriff of Worcestershire and his force attacked them. Catesby and Percy and the two Wrights were killed before Holbeach was taken. The others were made prisoner, Digby being captured at a little distance.

The question at once arose as to whether there was any knowledge of the plot among the Catholic peers. Viscount Montagu, a wealthy young man, who had married Lady Jane Sackville, Lord Treasurer Dorset's daughter, had employed Guy Fawkes for a few months as a footman at Cowdray in Sussex at the time of his marriage. Lord Mordaunt had among his great household at Drayton Hall in Northamptonshire retained Mr and Mrs Keyes, the latter as a governess to his daughters. Lord Stourton was suspected as a brother-in-law of Francis Tresham. All three were arrested for a while. This covers the whole episode of the plot, except in so far as it concerned the Society of Jesus.

The question arises as to how much was known to government. My own impression is that the earl of Salisbury was familiar with the whole project from the beginning. He and his father had long conceived it to be their duty to protect the person of their sovereign. His methods were not very different from those traditionally associated with counter-espionage. It was bound up with the perfection of his information as to all the happenings in the state. But if Salisbury really had this knowledged, the next point is who was his agent?

It is likely to have been someone who was in the plot from the beginning and also did not live to face his trial. Tresham, who died soon after capture, would appear to have joined the plot too late to influence events. It is my suggestion that the earl of Salisbury's agent was probably Thomas Percy. In that case the secretary of state could have watched over the events from their quiet origin. Each step which led to the involvement of Northumberland would have been clear to him. Few Englishmen could appreciate as well as Salisbury the effect of the threat of gunpowder upon the new king's mind. He could have watched over the idea of the explosion and he had a clear impression of where the thirty-six barrels of gunpowder could best be obtained.

In this connection it may be noted that the trial itself was curious. There were the criminals but no accomplices, not even unconscious ones. No evidence was presented as to where the gunpowder was obtained. Did it come from the Low Countries and in that case how did it escape the customs? Was it obtained from some military depôt in England such as the Tower of London? The more that one considers the details of the conspiracy as presented to us, the more does it become a surface story lacking in depth. The reading of the situation here presented would also serve to explain why the aims of the conspiracy appear so vague. The future after the meeting on Dunsmoor Heath would have been left sketchy just because there would in fact have been no future.

Finally a serious step would have been taken towards disembarrassing the English scene of the activities of the Jesuits. It is possible that this picture may be in some respects inaccurate; but it is unlikely that we shall ever know for certain. The earl of Salisbury was a secret man. On such a subject he would have left no papers, nor would he have communicated such private projects to his fellow-councillors or to his king.

Chapter 6

FATHER GARNET'S TRIAL

A FEW days before the discovery of the Gunpowder plot Father Garnet, accompanied by Anne Vaux, had ridden into Warwickshire to keep
the feast of All Saints at Coughton Court, the main house of the Throckmortons. The then head of the family John Throckmorton was an
elderly man, who leaves rather a feint impression. His two younger
step-sisters Lady Tresham and Lady Catesby were mothers of the conspirators of these names. It appears that Mr Throckmorton was absent
from his house throughout the duration of Father Garnet's visit. There
were a number of Catholics gathered at Coughton including Lady
Digby, Sir Everard's young wife. As soon as the news of the conspiracy
was made public, Father Garnet wrote a letter to Lord Salisbury carefully concealing his address but expressing his ignorance of the whole
affair. Soon warrants were out for the arrest of Father Garnet and two
of his subjects, Fathers Gerard and Tesimond, who made their way out
of the country. It seems that as superior Father Garnet did not feel entitled to go abroad.

He was, however, invited by Father Oldcorne, who had worked for
some years in these midland counties, to come to his own headquarters
at Hindlip Hall, which lay some fifteen miles to the westward. He rode
across on December 10. This large new house had the most elaborate
series of hiding places in the country. It stood on high ground and it was
easy to detect very early any group of horsemen who might approach.
The estate belonged to John Habington, whose family had recently
settled in Worcestershire. He had been imprisoned in connection with
the Babington plot, which had led to the execution of his elder brother.
He was now more or less confined to his own county and gave himself to
antiquarian studies. He had married fairly recently a sister of Lord
Monteagle and his eldest son William Habington, later the author of
the *Queen of Arragon*, had been born on that remembered date November 5, 1605.

Mr Habington was devoted throughout his life to the Society; years
later he would send his son to the Jesuit college at St Omer. Father

Garnet must have felt very much at home at Hindlip. By origin he came from the rising middle class, the son of a schoolmaster in Nottingham, had gone to Winchester as a scholar and had then come up to London as a corrector in the press to Tottel, the celebrated law printer. Later he had been professor of Hebrew at the Roman college.[1] He was in no sense of the word an outdoor man. A placard issued with a view to his arrest gives an impression of his appearance. "Henry Garnet *alias* Walley *alias* Darcey *alias* Farmer. Of a middling stature, full-faced, fat of body, of complexion fair: his forehead high on each side, with a little thin hair coming down upon the midst of the fore part of his head: the hair of his head and beard grizzled; of age between fifty and three score [he was in fact fifty]: his beard on his cheeks cut close, on his chin but thin and somewhat short: his gait upright and comely for a fat man."

Father Edward Oldcorne came from a similar background, but lacked Father Garnet's elaborate education. The son of a bricklayer in York, he went overseas to study for the secular priesthood and joined the Society aged twenty-six in 1587. He was a priest of austere life constantly wearing a hair-shirt. Since 1589 he had been working in Warwickshire and Worcestershire, mainly based upon Hindlip; it had been a long period without disturbance. Tranquillity had also been the note of Father Garnet's life. He is described by his adherents as kind and gentle; much had been done on his behalf. Thus Anne Vaux had taken a house near London for him, White Webbs at Enfield. He had been for eighteen years Superior, based apparently on Baddesley Clinton and other country houses. It is probable that he was to some extent moulded by this life surrounded by the sober and wealthy families whose members (especially the women) had almost a hero-worship for this quiet, approachable and learned priest. It was a very different life from that of Campion and Southwell with their relatively constant movement and final swift catastrophe.

It is worth considering Father Garnet's qualifications for the post of Superior. He had had a period in Rome and not only wrote Italian, but also had absorbed the atmosphere of the Roman College. These qualities were ancillary; but the next it seems to me was crucial. He was above all swift and unquestioning in his obedience. This last to my mind was probably decisive. He would never fail to carry out at once the

[1] There is a detailed modern biography by the Rev. Philip Caraman, S.J., *Henry Garnet and the Gunpowder Plot* (1964).

instructions and suggestions that he received from Father Claudius Acquaviva, the General, or from Father Robert Parsons, who was, to use a modern expression, his English assistant.

It was Father Garnet's misfortune that he had so many links with different plotters. He, perhaps, hardly realised the dangerous character of members of the group among whom he moved so peacefully. He had a certain gentleness and a form of simplicity. He saw these raffish swordsmen in their domestic life as sons and brothers.

The actual occasion of his arrest was the statement of Humphrey Littleton of the Holbeach family that Father Garnet, as well as Father Oldcorne, was now at Hindlip. It was at this point that King James intervened. He had not shown interest in the despatch of the ordinary conspirators. He seems to have been keen to watch the display of intellect, once they had netted the famous Jesuit. He had always had an ambivalent attitude towards the Society of Jesus, which was heightened once Cardinal Bellarmine, S.J., had come into the lists against him. This makes sense of the king's personal instructions that Father Garnet should be treated courteously on his journey south to prison. The priests together with two lay brothers, Ralph Ashby and Nicholas Owen, were arrested at Hindlip by Sir Henry Bromley of Holt Castle.

From this point the events developed as they had been planned, Father Garnet was taken to Worcester in Sir Henry's coach. He was then kept in his captor's house for several days and rode under guard to London on a good horse. On St Valentine's Day he was lodged in the Tower. He was given the better style of accommodation and was allowed with every meal a draught of excellent claret; from his own purse he purchased sack. At a later stage he obtained some new glasses in a black leather case. A black skull cap was procured for his bald head. Considered in this way, it is a pathetic story. The king was determined to keep the great Jesuit in good shape. He liked an intellectual exercise. The trial was clearly meant to be the earl of Salisbury's *chef d'oeuvre*.

The actual trial began in the Guildhall on March 28, 1606. The prisoner had previously been subjected to twenty-two examinations. The commissioners present were first the lord mayor, Sir Leonard Holyday, for this trial was in the city, and with him the earls of Nottingham, Suffolk, Worcester, Northampton and Salisbury, the Lord Chief Justice of England, the Chief Baron of the Exchequer and one of the Justices of the King's Bench. Among the visitors present were Lady Arabella Stuart and the countess of Suffolk. Behind a lattice, specially constructed, sat the king. It will be observed that the prosecuting counsel were well aware of the king's presence.

It was of course wholly unwarranted to accuse Father Garnet of being an originator of the conspiracy; but the aim was to remove the Jesuits root and branch. Lord Salisbury must have felt that England had suffered from them long enough. Sir John Croke opening the case declared that Henry Garnet, of the profession of the Jesuits, otherwise Wally, otherwise Darcy, otherwise Roberts, otherwise Farmer, otherwise Philips (for by all those names he called himself) stood indicted of the most barbarous and damnable treasons, the like whereof was never heard of. He made it clear that the prisoner was adorned by God and nature with many gifts and graces, if the Grace of God had been joined with them. He explained that this Garnet together with Catesby, lately slain in open rebellion, and with Oswald Tesimond a Jesuit, otherwise Oswald Greenwell, had conspired "as a false traitor against the most mighty and most renowned king our sovereign lord King James . . . to destroy and kill the King, and the noble Prince Henry his eldest son: such a King and such a prince, such a son of such a father, whose virtues are rather with amazed silence to be wondered at, than able by any speech to be expressed."[1] The discourse wound on as the king sat in deep contentment on his soft cushion. And always the speech returned upon these loyal right-minded sentiments. Sir John Croke felt himself compelled to mention "that religious observation so religiously observed by his religious majesty, wishing it were engraven in letters of gold in the hearts of all his people; the more hellish the imagination, the more divine the preservation".[2] After this the charge was soon completed. Garnet pleaded not guilty and what was termed "a very discreet and substantial"[3] jury was sworn at the bar for his trial.

The attorney general, the celebrated Sir Edward Coke, took over after the close of what he called this "succinct opening".

For [he explained] the principal person offending, here at the bar, he is as you have heard a man of many names, Garnet, Wally, Darcy, Roberts, Farmer, Philips: and surely I have not commonly known and observed a true man, that hath had so many false appellations: he is by country an Englishman, by birth a gentleman, by education a scholar . . . He hath many gifts and endowments of nature, by art learned, a good linguist, and by profession a Jesuit and a superior.[4]

---

[1] *State Trials*, II, 218. [2] *Ibid.*, II, 219. [3] *Ibid.*, II, 219. [4] *Ibid.*, II, 233-4.

Thus Father Garnet was built up so that his defeat would have the more effect in this arena.

The attorney general went through[1] all the events of the late reign dealing with the Church of Rome beginning with "the bull of *Impius Pius Quintus* in the eleventh year of the Queen"[2] until the time of Powder-Treason. He had reached the present day and then there came again the grateful phrases. "For the persons offended they were these: I. The King of whom I have spoken often, but never enough: a king of high and most ancient noble descent, as hath been briefly declared; and in himself full of all imperial virtues, religious, justice, clemency, learning, wisdom and memory."[3] Sir Edward was now going through the list of proposed victims. "The noble Prince. . . . Never prince, true heir-apparent to the imperial crown, had such a father, nor ever king had such a son." These words must have been warming to the royal heart.

The list of those to be affected by the plot was now unfolding. "Then the whole royal issue, the council, the nobility, the clergy . . . and especially the city of London that is famous for her riches, most famous for her people, having about five hundred thousand souls within her and her liberties, most famous for her fidelity, and more than most famous of all the cities in the world for her true religion."[4] The king sat on. This was all very different from his Scottish kingdom.

A little later Father Garnet was permitted to begin to speak. He gave a rather detailed explanation of equivocation.[5] "So then no man may equivocate when he ought to tell the truth, otherwise he may." He asserted that the doctrine of the power of the Pope in deposing princes was by all other Catholic princes tolerated without grievance; that for his own part he always made a difference "betwixt the condition and state of our own King and others, who have some time been Catholic did or shall afterwards fall back." He was confused as to his sending letters and admitted that he had received some moneys to maintain the title of the king of Spain.

Soon after this two witnesses were called who had listened behind the door to talks that Fathers Garnet and Oldcorne had had together through the kind permission of a turnkey. Garnet admitted that Greenwell (Tesimond) had told him in confession the various details of the plot which he had learned from Catesby, who had requested that this should be repeated to Father Garnet under the seal. He mentioned that

---

[1] *State Trials*, II, 222. [2] 35 Pius V. [3] *State Trials*, II, 226. [4] *Ibid.*, II, 236.
[5] *Ibid.*, II, 239-40.

he had some vague knowledge *in confuso* from Mr Catesby. "I was very much distempered and could never sleep quietly afterwards, but sometimes prayed to God that it should not take effect."[1]

The attorney general drew to a close and the earl of Northampton took his place. It was an interminable speech. "Yet as the case stands now in this Trial, Mr Garnet, between my dear sovereign, *ex cujus spiritu*, as one said of Alexander, *nos omnes spiritum ducimus*; and you who were so well content to let the course of conspiracy run forward to the stopping of his breath . . . between his honour and your error, his just proceedings and your painted shews. . . . As though you, Mr Garnet, being then *Magister in Israel* and *Rector Chori*, could or would be ignorant of their prefixed end."[2] Northampton then referred to the great lieger Jesuits of the Low Countries and Spain, Father Baldwin and Father Cresswell. He knew that the king sitting there thought much about the devil and then he spoke to rouse his interest. "The Dragon's ambition," he explained, "extended no further than the sweeping away with his tail of the third part of the Stars: but now the plot of him (Garnet) and his disciples, was to sweep away the Sun, the Moon and Stars, both out of star chamber and parliament, that no light be given in this kingdom to the best labourers."[3] At an earlier point he had spoken in sorrow of the spiritual state of the Jesuit superior. "We must believe that all this while you were in charity, because all this while (which it grieves me to remember) you were not afraid to communicate."[4] He accused Garnet of "dissembling, as about the place of your rendezvous, which was the Lapwing's Nest".[5] It is clear that Father Garnet must by this time have been exhausted.

The earl of Salisbury now brought up a reference to Father Tesimond. It is probable that Tesimond had been a *mauvais sujet*. There is some reason to suppose that this "brown-bearded, long-visaged man, with his lean face and red complexion and his nose somewhat sharp at the end" had not been on the best of terms with his superior. But the *State Trials* must be used with caution. They were after all printed for the prosecution and at that date there was not the same care in reporting the words of the defence. It appears to me that at this point the printed text of Garnet's reply is quite corrupt. In any case the wording did not affect his guilt or innocence.

Then the earl of Salisbury made his last address to him. "Mr Garnet," he said, "is it not a lamentable thing, that if the Pope or Claudius

[1] *State Trials*, II, 242. [2] *Ibid.*, II, 247. [3] *Ibid.*, II, 254. [4] *Ibid.*, II, 251. [5] *Ibid.*, II, 248.

Aquaviva or yourself command poor Catholicks anything, that they must obey you, although it be to endanger, both body and soul? And if you maintain such doctrine among you, how can the King be safe?"[1] Raising his voice Garnet said very passionately, "My Lord, I would to God I had never known of the Powder-Treason." This is in essence the end of the trial scene.

The earl of Northampton had produced a lengthy document. He was not able to read it all so that he afterwards enlarged and amplified it and then delivered it to the bookseller. In this he cast his mind upon the papacy. He had little care for Rome where the Jesuits were so powerful. One example will give the tone of this long document. "Thus Alexander VI and his darling Borgia, the only monster of that age, were poisoned by error of the cupboard-keeper, out of the bottles that were kept in store, and by Caesar's own appointment against supper, for the destruction of certain Cardinals. And thus it happens many times; God's justice far surmounting men's capacity."[2] He was never very successful as a flatterer for he was burdened by his sense of high descent. But like every flatterer, it was when he was bitter that he touched sincerity.

Father Garnet went back to his airy cell. There was still a cordiality of treatment and it seems that he thought until the last that the Spanish ambassador would secure a pardon for him. He was hanged on May 3, 1606. The king's instructions saved him from the barbarities.

It seems likely that when this news and the sheets from the London booksellers reached Father Parsons in the Roman College that he approved of Father Garnet's conduct. After all he had sent the bulls and had instructed Garnet in his Spanish contacts. He would have applauded that he had discussed equivocation and had refused to answer when questioned as to his action if papal forces were launched against England.

The ultimate judgment upon Father Garnet depends upon one's view of Father Parsons, who was his master. It seems that Henry Garnet had a strong sense of duty and of pastoral care; he had, as has been said, a rare obedience; he followed the elder priest implicitly. To my mind Father Parsons was a man of great cunning, a quality more valued then than now. He was also denationalised, out of touch with England and narrow in his ideas. Of course another judgment of Father Parsons is quite possible, although I do not myself subscribe to it. In that case one would take another view of Father Garnet. It is a difficult stratum to understand where religion interpenetrated with the High Baroque; the mingling of Church and State in the Mediterranean world of 1600.

There are two further points that should be made and about these we can be refreshingly confident. Father Oldcorne was taken back to Worcestershire and was hanged, drawn and quartered at Redhill outside the county town. He had had no connection with the conspiracy and was only captured because he had agreed to shelter his superior. Nicholas Owen died in the Tower, when Garnet was a prisoner. He was a very small man and lame and suffered from a rupture. He was apparently originally a builder and had had a hard life for twenty years riding round with the Jesuits as their servant and constructing the secret hiding places. The most difficult labour was the penetration and replacement of the stone walling. He had to work without help, the plan only known to the master of each house. It appears that most of the network of hiding places had been either made by Owen himsel or in certain cases from his designs. He died as the result of torture without speaking. The only point he would admit was that he was Father Garnet's servant. The figure of Nicholas Owen is more easily grasped with sympathy in these days for it requires no understanding of Jacobean politics. His was a very simple steadfast fidelity. Still, unlike Father Garnet, he did not come into the king's life.

King James was very severe against witches because he believed that his enemy the devil had entered into them. He probably had little knowledge of the priests who suffered in his reign. Salisbury had his own approach to his new sovereign and it is unlikely that these unpleasant subjects were ever mentioned. Of course the king was well aware of the fines for recusancy; but then he had to satisfy his needy courtiers. I do not think that it is special pleading to suggest that King James was easily bored by domestic detail. In one sense he was a very lazy man. His interests were concerned with his court life and in his kindness to those who formed his court. It must be admitted that by giving all the allusions to the sovereign in this case there has been an element of disproportion; but this is a biography of James I and I am anxious to draw attention to the clouds of incense as the censers swung before the king continually. James I was interested in kingship in all its manifestations; he thought in terms of ambassadors and kings and princes.

Chapter 7

THE YEARS OF PEACE

THE earl of Salisbury sat at Theobalds near Royston, two hours' ride
northward from the capital. The spring sunshine fell upon the Fountain Court and on the golden vanes that swung in the forepaws of the
gold lions that stood upon the turrets on the long façade. This was the
second and more sophisticated of the great houses that Lord Treasurer
Burghley had constructed; it had come appropriately to his second son.

It was now Easter 1606. The long trouble of the Gunpowder plot was
all behind him, and the realm at peace. Salisbury was essentially, to
use a modern term, a peace minister and served a sovereign who had
always considered himself to be by destiny a peace maker. That master
had seemed for the moment to have grown away from the need of a
young favourite. In some respects Philip Herbert, Lord Pembroke's
second son, had filled that place during the king's first years in England.
He had become a gentleman of the bedchamber and earl of Montgomery; he had married Lady Susan Vere, Salisbury's niece; in politics
he was quite negligible. The king contented his chief peers with earldoms. There was no one ripe to move against the secretary of state.

After all there were reasons which kept the Howards loyal to him.
Northampton had only got to see what had happened to Northumberland. It was not that the king was against him, for he had given him the
old royal palace of Sion to be his London residence. Still he, a Protestant, had found himself entangled; the actual charge had been bound
up with admitting Thomas Percy to the gentleman pensioners without
tendering him the oath of supremacy. Now he was in the Tower of London with Sir Walter Raleigh and, as far as the earl of Salisbury was concerned, they would both stay there, like flies in amber. It was his custom
to make few moves; he never released men or killed them without good
reason. In fact it is quite clear that, if he had survived, Raleigh would
not have been released. He would have died of old age within that
citadel. Peace settled down upon the Tower of London.

In fact for the next few years the two chief prisoners within the
Tower, although confined, took their part in the ebb and flow of life

in the great capital. This was in part because neither of them had offended the king himself. It seems that in keeping them in captivity he had followed the advice of his wise minister.

From his surviving household papers we can follow the details of the captivity of the ninth earl of Northumberland. He had first acquired for himself a suite of rooms and then some space to keep his privacy. The Bowling Alley garden in the Tower was hired for his own use.[1] He had a still house built for the distillation of medicines and spirit.[2] He made arrangements for his retainers. Thus he installed a housekeeper at Brick House on Tower Hill,[3] which he had rented to accommodate his servants who came in to wait on him. He also hired a stable in Milford Lane[4] for keeping horses for his servants' use and for his own riding in Coldharbour Court within the Tower. His receiver paid to the lieutenant of the Tower £100 a year[5] to compensate him for the fact that he did not feed the earl; this was done by his own servants. Boats for his laundry and other needs were constantly coming to the Water Gate. Mr (later Sir John) Hippisley acted as treasurer for all the expenses that he incurred in residence. Lady Northumberland and her husband were uncongenial, but his heir and the young children were with him constantly. These were also the easy years in the Tower for Sir Walter Raleigh. There were learned visitors to help him with his *History of the World*. Northumberland kept a certain entertainment for men of rank. As the reign went on Raleigh was visited by the Prince of Wales.

The magnates who survived from the Elizabethan world were perfectly at ease with the earl of Salisbury. Lord Treasurer Dorset, who kept his great office, lived at the palace of Knole, which he had just finished building. He made Salisbury the overseer of his will; he was always close to him. Lord Chancellor Ellesmere, who lasted longer, was at his large new house at Harefield in Middlesex, since disappeared. Both peers were busy founding a noble family, gathering in that wealth which would lie at the core of the future dukedoms of Dorset and Bridgwater. This was a time of quiet accretion for the very wealthy. But from these great households there would also come the working ministers of the later part of the reign of James I, from Northumberland's Sir Dudley Carleton, from Dorset's Archbishop Abbot and from Ellesmere's Lord Keeper Williams. There were in these years no sudden

---

[1] G. R. Batho, ed., *The Household Papers of Henry Earl of Northumberland* (Camden, third series), xciii, p. 94. [2] *Ibid.*, 90. This building was demolished in 1609. [3] *Ibid.*, 161, 162. [4] *Ibid.*, 90. [5] *Ibid.*, 89.

changes. As far as the aristocracy and the greater gentry were concerned, this was to some extent the overspill of the Elizabethan certainties.

Salisbury's father, Lord Burghley, had been a *novus homo*. He never was at ease with the great peers; he paid too much attention to them; he busied himself with little pedigrees set down on scraps of paper showing relationships. His first house at Burghley in its grey Elizabethan stone with its high turrets and long vaulted staircases was set down uncompromisingly in the fields to the south of Stamford. He seldom went there.

The whole of Robert Cecil's life was very different. Like William Pitt the younger, he had always been in office. There were few things that he did not know about the state of England. He was very kind to those who would not like to try a fall with him. He stood there, as he is shown in the portrait by Jan de Critz, his long and delicate white fingers playing with the jewel hung round his neck by a thin chain. The king, in spite of all his cheerful mockery, knew that he was fortunate. And yet this mockery must have been quite hard to bear. A few extracts from Salisbury's correspondence show how he entered into his sovereign's style of writing. High and detached, it seems that the actual words he used meant little to him.

Salisbury, of course, kept on friendly terms with the great Scottish office holders. Their letters would seem to suggest that they trusted one another from the beginning; in reality it is likely that both sides early knew that their opposite numbers were irremovable. Thus, quite soon, the earl of Mar is found writing to the English statesman: "Albeit there be no great matter wherewith I can acquaint your Lordship, I have written this short letter to present my affectionate duty to you. We are here (at Hinchinbrooke) continually busied either at hunting or examining of witches, and although I like the first better than the last, yet I must confess both uncertain sports."[1] It is clear that the English and Scottish lords were at one in deprecating their master's taste for testing witchcraft. It was not that they had any sympathy for the witches, but they seem to have felt that it was not a suitable subject for the exercise of the royal mind.

Salisbury would also tune his correspondence with his sovereign so that the same jests were reflected in his letters to those Scottish lords who were close to him. A letter to Sir Thomas Lake bears this out. The

[1] Letter dated January 26, 1605, Cal. Salisbury MSS, xiii, 37.

secretary had known Lake all his life for he had been amanuensis to Sir Francis Walsingham. At the beginning of the reign the king had given him the secretariate for Latin letters. He was an adaptable man in early middle life, now always friendly to the Scottish courtiers. After expressing a hope that the king's health was better, Salisbury continued, "his monkey loves him not better than his 'little beagle', nor his great Commissioner in Scotland (the Earl of Dunbar) than his 'little secretary' ".[1] This was only two months after the king had granted to the earl of Dunbar the sum of over £3,000 secured upon the tithes of the see of Lincoln.[2]

It is, perhaps, as well to examine the nature of the letters between Salisbury and the king. "My Lord", wrote the secretary to Sir Thomas Erskine who had recently become Lord Dirleton, "being newly come home from a long and late session in Parliament, and being close by my chimney's end, a proper place for beagles, I was in dispute whether I should trouble His Majesty with this day's journal."[3] The letter was now well under way, and he remembered to quote a statement that he had made that afternoon in the upper house. "I daily discerned," Salisbury had told the peers, "how great an advantage we had that lived at the feet of Gamaliel in respect of others more removed." It was a sound rule never to forget to tell the king when one had praised him.

Salisbury and the great lords by whom he was surrounded all shared an old Elizabethan wisdom. It was a small price to pay for their position to put up with their Scottish master's verbal pranks. At an unknown date, but apparently in this same year, the king sent to Salisbury a paper headed "a cartel or challenge to a trinity of knaves".[4] It was written when the sovereign was about to remove to Greenwich Palace.

If I find not at my coming that the big chamberlain have ordered well all my lodging, that the little saucy constable have made the house sweet and built a coke pit and that the fast walking keeper of the park have the park in good order and the does all in fawn, although he have never been a good breeder himself, then shall I at my return finding these things out of order make the fat chamberlain to puff, the little cankered beagle to whine and the tall black and cat-faced keeper to glower, as Sir Roger Aston said.

[1] Letter dated April 15, 1607, Cal. S.P.Dom., 1603-10, 355.
[2] Grant dated February 4, 1607, ibid., 347.
[3] Letter dated February 6, 1606, Cecil MSS.
[4] Cal. Salisbury MSS, xvii, 120-1.

SERO SED SERIO

6 EARL OF SALISBURY
Attributed to Jan de Critz (National Portrait Galley)

7 SIR WALTER RALEIGH AND HIS SON
Unknown artist (National Portrait Gallery)

While these jests were being made about the chief officials within that royal palace which Henry VIII had named Placentia, letters of a different character lay upon the secretary's desk. Among them was a petition[1] for the paving of the main streets of Greenwich. The ways were described as loathsome, dangerous and infectious. The square church tower was rent from the top to the bottom; the steeple was ruinous and expected to fall.

At about the same time the king sent another letter to the secretary by the hands of Lord Montgomery.

My little beagle, although I have been out of privy intelligence with you since my last parting, for having been kept ever so busy with hunting of witches, prophets, puritans, dead cats and hares, yet will I not suffer this bearer your fellow secretary to go unaccompanied with this present; who should have carried the witches with him as you desired, had it not been that he rides post and witches ride never post but to the devil. He hath conjured all the devils here with his *Welsh* tongue, for the devil himself I trow dare not speak Welsh. Haste him back I pray you . . . if your niece (Lady Montgomery) be angry with me for his short abode at this time, tell her I shall make her satisfaction at my return with a tribute of kisses, but this must be kept counsel of both from the bearer and my wife.[2]

This letter was endorsed by its recipient "His Majesty". It had two seals united by a golden thread.

The council knew well what gave pleasure to their master. If one letter is presented in some detail it will give the drift of what the king required.

What kind of gratitude is it possible for us to represent unto your Majesty, who . . . so favourably approve our proceedings in Council, which (when they be good) are but slender streams derived from the fountain of your own wise directions. And if your Majesty may repute it for the least point of happiness to be served by us, how much more may we account ourselves thrice happy to be guided and governed by such a King, from whom not only we receive a kind of influence to the enabling of our advice and counsels, but (if it were possible) all the kings of the earth might be glad as from the Oracle to take instructions from the King of Great Britanye.[3]

They then go on to deal with the prosecution of Bywater, "a seditious sectary". Towards the end of the letter there is this sentence. "As the characters of your own hand in your Majesty's letter are most evident

---

[1] Cal. Salisbury MSS, xvii, 183.   [2] *Ibid.*, 121-2.   [3] *Ibid.*, 122-3.

testimonies of your grace to us, and of your justice and virtue they have left deep impressions of joy and admiration in our hearts."

The king in this part of his reign was often all day at the hunt, whilst his ministers were labouring. Two letters bear upon this matter, both coming from the time when he was using Oatlands as his hunting lodge. On the first occasion the king had spent seven hours in toiling after a stag which he had lost. He had an early supper and retired to rest. There ensconced in his wide bed he enquired from his lord-in-waiting whether the secretary was still hard at work. "I told him," wrote Lord Stanhope, "that no day escaped. He enquired what money [had] been made. I said it was the greatest care how it might be well raised, and that both by leases and upon the arrearages of recusants' debts there was and would be good sums come in. He seemed best pleased therewith."[1] The second letter was sent to Salisbury by Sir Roger Aston. "I acquainted his Majesty with your letter, which came to me this day. He being at the hunting came not home till after six. He took your careful letter very kindly, and bade me give you thanks; and being at this present at his supper, drank to you, and bade me tell you that the pains you took in his service to make him to live was the best plaster could be ministered to his sore side."[2] He means, explained Sir Roger, "on Monday to take a revenge of the stag that this day has defied him and all his hounds". Before he mounted, the king would sit in his hunting coach, an English innovation which would carry him through the easy glades. He was not a great huntsman; he loved riding quietly in the open air. It must have been a joy for him to hear the praises of that wisdom which he knew so well that he alone possessed. And then Salisbury, always sensitive to the needs of his royal master, would pay tribute to the king's "heroicall spirit".[3]

There was often some unexpected reference in the king's letters as in his comment on a certain Frenchman "whereupon he may add a book to the bibliotheque of his countryman Rabelais".[4] Salisbury at this time was always sending fruit from Theobalds, cherries, grapes, apricots and peaches; the last did not arrive at court in good condition. At his own great house he was still building. "Your pool," wrote Sir Fulke Greville after he had made an examination, "I have surveyed with the best discretion I have, and methinks the five islands, as they are, show pleasantly one in proportion to another. Notwithstanding, if they were taken out your judgment is true, that you should have the

[1] Cal. Salisbury MSS, xvii, 287.   [2] *Ibid.*, 572.   [3] *Ibid.*, 461.   [4] *Ibid.*, 457.

more water; but because it is so well already I dare not counsel a change. The banks that be all along under the water were in my poor opinion much more necessary to be removed."[1] He then gave his opinion as to the windows beside the leaded terrace. "The alteration in your lodgings is passing good and will amend them both for sight and use exceedingly." Towards the end of a longish letter Sir Fulke mentions that Salisbury's stags come on apace. This may have been one of the reasons why the king in time should yearn for Theobalds.

Salisbury offered his support, which was with justice so greatly valued, to the men of high position by whom he was surrounded. It may be said, leaving aside certain elements of the Howard alliance, that he made no man's fortune. He accepted all those whom the king might honour. He was, perhaps, too secret to have close dependants. Although he received reports from the English ambassadors abroad, there is little evidence that he had himself a foreign policy. At heart he was quite deeply insular. He was not interested in foreign rulers or in their envoys. His close knowledge of the domestic field in his own country showed that she needed peace. He never cared for an adventurous policy; his temperament was unsympathetic to all adventurers. One cannot forget that, besides his infirmities, he was almost a dwarf.

There was much in his outlook that was *terre-à-terre*. His father had been beguiled into building up a great Welsh pedigree and had accepted his descent from the Cecils or Syssilts of Alt-yr-Ynis, a manor farm in Monmouthshire within the hills.[2] Salisbury's reactions to these conjectures is crystal clear. In 1605 a stranger named William George had written to him. "For your pedigree out of Wales, I cannot find Bleddyn's[3] coat impaled, the ancientest of the five Princes of Wales. His name died in Elizabeth, your father's great grandmother. I have found his coat in the house of Thomas Prichard, a gentleman in Glamorganshire."[4] On this letter there is a note in Salisbury's hand. "I desire none of these vain toys, nor to hear of such absurdities."

In his dealings with the Scots the secretary was always tranquil. With the great lords he was friendly while, as for the lesser men, it had been evident that they in their measure would make their spoil. This was one of the consequences of a Scottish sovereign. It was part of the reason for the success of both Lord Burghley and his second son that they never interfered in the bounty of their respective masters. Other minis-

---

[1] Cal. Salisbury MSS, xvii, 215.   [2] Cf. *ibid.*, xi, 413.
[3] Bleddyn ap Cynfyn (d 1075).   [4] Letter calendared 1605, Salisbury MSS, xvii, 595.

ters both before and after, like Wolsey, Cromwell and Buckingham, made men seek for place at court through them. Burghley and Salisbury left the monarch free.

This practice was the more important because King James much liked spontaneous giving; every gift must be his own. By nature he was complaisant to all about him. It was not always a question of demand; he seems to have liked to provide immediate happiness to his companions. This delight in smiling faces was a royal trait too rare among the English sovereigns. There would, of course, be certain difficulties, but very muted and low-voiced, when he gave English properties to his northern followers. For example he gave the goods of Sir George Rodney of Stoke Rodney, who had been forfeited for suicide, to Sir John Ramsay and Sir James Sandilands[1] and these men later partitioned this estate with James Hamilton, their fellow-countryman. Sir William Anstruther received a moiety of all the goods in the possession of Sir Everard Digby and seven others.[2] The grants of recusants' lands to Scots were fairly numerous.[3]

It was natural that the king should not grasp the attitude of Englishmen of position towards the more impoverished of his fellow Scots. Thus in the second year of his reign he is found writing to Grey, lord Chandos that he understands that his daughter has incurred his displeasure by marrying Sir John Kennedy. He begs that he will deal kindly with Sir John as he had a great regard for him.[4] Still, he did not only favour Scots; he had a feeling for the family and for long established service. Thus Robert Graham, the rider of the royal hunting horses, was granted the keepership for life of the king's house at Royston.

It was a part of Salisbury's responsibilities to provide the king with suitable accommodation. It is not surprising that the new sovereign did not care for London, "that great wen". His mind turned to hunting in the home counties and he planned to build a lodge at Ampthill in Bedfordshire. There is a clear account of what he had in mind in a letter from the earl of Dorset, a copy of which was sent to Theobalds.

I have received [began the letter] signification of his Majesty's express pleasure for the building of a fit and convenient house upon the ruins of Ampthill

---

[1] Grant dated February 20, 1604, Cal. S.P. Dom., 1603–10, 79.

[2] Grant dated January 25, 1607, ibid., 346.

[3] Among the beneficiaries, mostly drawn from those with minor posts about the king or queen, were Sir James Sempill, Sir James Douglas, John Elphinstone, John Auchmuty and Archibald Napier. Cf. ibid., 356, 181, 408 and 415.

[4] Letter dated February 19, 1604, ibid., 79.

in which he may be lodged, though not in state, yet sufficient to serve for the enjoying of his pleasures of hunting and hawking by the attendance of all necessary officers. . . . Therein also place must be provided for the Queen and the noble Prince, if haply it shall please his Majesty to desire their coming while he is there, not lodgings of state but lodgings of necessity. And because it may be that some occasion may require the attendance of some of his Council upon his Majesty there, I wish also that some convenient rooms for half a dozen Privy Councillors, besides the Lord Chamberlain, the Treasurer, the Controller, Master of the Horse and Principal Secretary be likewise appointed, such as are of necessity, not any of pleasure.[1]

He explained that the surveyor should not only examine "the stately place" where the old ruins of Ampthill remain, but also any other place which might be fitter and more convenient in respect of water. He should likewise examine under the direction of His Majesty's woodward on this side Trent all the royal forests within thirty miles of Ampthill, also any special timber in private woods within that radius. He was also to inform himself of the fittest place from which water could be drawn to serve the house and estimate the cost of the lead piping.

In September of the same year (1605) a plan for the house was produced which contained presence chambers for the king and queen, a gallery for each of the sovereigns and a closet for the queen.[2] These plans, which were in fact for a small palace, did not progress beyond the drawing board. The king was restless. Ampthill was, however, one of the royal parks and placed under the charge of Sir Thomas Erskine. In 1620 three small lodges were ordered to be built for the king's hunting, in Waltham Forest and at Nonesuch Park and Ampthill.[3] From King James's later years there is a single letter[4] dated from the Little Lodge at Ampthill. In 1610 there was a plan for renting from Sir Christopher Hatton the mansion and park of Holdenby in Northamptonshire as a seat for the youthful duke of York.[5]

The earl of Salisbury had a sensitive knowledge of his royal master's moods and fancies and it cannot have been altogether a surprise when in 1607 the king asked him for Theobalds, giving the royal manor of Hatfield and the old house there in exchange. There is a letter from Salisbury to Sir Thomas Lake upon this subject. He explained that he had been to take a last look at Theobalds before it passed into his

[1] Letter dated August 3, 1605, Cal. Salisbury MSS, xvii, 349.   [2] *Ibid.*, 444.
[3] Cal. S.P. Dom., 1619–23, 150.   [4] Dated July 21, 1621, *ibid.*, 278.
[5] Cal. S.P. Dom., 1603–10, 451 and 453.

sovereign's hands. The earls of Northampton, Suffolk and Worcester had met him at Hatfield to discuss the fittest site for his new mansion.[1]

The next years saw the gradual achievement of the design and the construction of Hatfield House. His personal situation was in good trim and it was aided by the fact that Salisbury really did share with the king an appreciation for the more civilised forms of the latter's humour. "At one thing ye will smile," wrote the king to his minister "He (Hay) advised me not to see the bear's skin before he was slain."[2] All was well for Salisbury in these peaceful years – Robert Carr had not yet come to court and George Villiers was still a boy. It could not be foreseen that the king's affection would soon be concentrated successively on these young men.

The examination of the Hatfield papers of this period makes it clear how prudently the secretary had built up his position, with a calm that would not betray him into anger and a political tolerance instinct with courtesy. Perhaps it is not unfair to attribute to him that gift for the appropriate which makes men successful, but not loved. There was something alarming in his self-command and in that clear vision with which he swept the nearer landscape. Yet it was this efficiency that secured Salisbury in his power which was aided by the royal lethargy and only menaced in a slight degree by the slow ebbing of King James's gratitude.

In the handling of the general matters which came before him, Salisbury displayed a competence and a quiet shrewd resolution. Balanced and calm, his methods do not appear to indicate any very definite preoccupation with colonisation or on the other hand with the administration of justice, with piracy or crime or local law. His decisions bear the mark of a subdued efficiency which was only saved from grimness by his strange pacific courtesy.

Despatches from the ambassadors abroad arrived incessantly, but they always dealt with politics and there was only an intermittent correspondence with Sir Thomas Glover "at the Vines of Pera". In connection with the agency at Constantinople it is worth mentioning that explicit details of commercial traffic appear infrequently among Lord Salisbury's papers. The agents would correspond with London merchants about "what sorts of stones will sell best (in Pera)" and "the valewe of pearle and unicornes horne, currall and ruffe amber";[3] but

---

[1] Letter dated April 15, 1607, ibid., 354.
[2] Letter of the king, undated, Cecil MSS, vol. 154, f. 147.
[3] Cf. Sir William Foster, ed., *Correspondence of John Sanderson* (Hakluyt Society, 1930), 128.

these were matters for the Turkey Company and just over the horizon of Salisbury's responsibility.

In the mass of papers one fact emerges clearly. It was a great part of Lord Salisbury's duty to protect the person of his sovereign. While his secretaries would scrutinise the postal endorsements of the letters from Dover and the north to test the efficiency of the service, the entry and departure of suspected persons was the secretary's personal responsibility. Details of doubtful characters crossing the English Channel were brought before him by Sir Thomas Fane, who combined the offices of deputy warden of the Cinque ports and lieutenant of Dover. For years now the minister had been familiar with all the regulations governing entry to the kingdom: the control exercised by the deputy warden over the owners of the passage boats; the respective functions of the searchers of the customs and the clerk of the passage; the time taken by the messengers in foul or fair weather on the ride between the capital and Dover harbour.

Salisbury's mind seems to have worked rapidly when he was dealing with these personal problems. He appears to have been what we should now term a great Home Secretary. When concerned with financial questions he seems to have accepted current practice. Thus the drafting of the patent for white mulberry trees and the renewal of Sir Michael Stanhope's grant for the importation of Spanish hat wools went forward normally.[1] There was here, to his mind, no need for innovation.

The type of entrenched political influence built up by the first minister was for practicable purposes impregnable, but there is little doubt that his personal relations with the king were very gradually less cordial. It was not easy for an exhausted statesman to play the "little beagle", and to maintain the appearances of spontaneity. And then in the last three years there had been the question of young Robert Carr, who had come from Scotland in Lord Hay's service in the early portion of the reign. His influence will be examined later and as long as Salisbury lived it could hardly be said to be political. It was the intimate relationship with the king that this young Scotsman was undermining. The only change in the great offices of state about this time had been the transfer of the lord treasurer's staff which Salisbury had inherited when the earl of Dorset died in 1608. He was still only in middle life, but his

---

[1] Letter from Sir Michael Stanhope to the earl of Salisbury, dated May 31, 1606. For the mulberry patent, cf. Cecil MSS, vol. 193, f. 28.

health was a doubtful factor and he seems to have felt the need of that retirement which he was in no position to achieve.

Hatfield was now at last completed, the palace of a great officer of state and in no sense a place for quiet withdrawal as it stood high and spreading and magnificent, right in the track of all King James's movements. The building was finished and all was hoisted into place. It was eighteen months since "the content of thirty marble stones provided at Carera in the Prince of Masse his country, and transported into Leghorn and shipped for England" had been landed and erected in position. The fireplaces were masked by those great chimney-pieces which are rightly described with such pomp in the detailed accounts at Hatfield House. "One chimney-piece," so runs the note of the expenses, "with fower dorrick columns upon two pedestals with two wide panels between supporting a vase with a frieze and swelling panels under it."

It is in this strain that the accounts for the expenditure in 1611 are all conceived; painting the timber work of the great stairs; working the naked boys and lions standing upon those stairs: gilding the great pendants from the ceiling; completing the frieze in gold and walnut-tree colour. It does not sound restful for a tired man. Down in the west country lay Cranborne Manor, his small, lovely and secluded house. But there was no possibility of retirement. During the opening part of the seventeenth century some men were thrust out from their court preferment; the others stayed on in their great offices until they dropped.

Although his health was breaking, his days were still bound up with every detail of the new Hatfield House. The glass of the chapel windows were now in place with the intertwining legends like *Dauid Goliam superat*. The designs were realistic with troops marching like the army of the prince of Parma. The young David held aloft the Giant's head transfixed on a broad sword while the sunlight filtered through the forest of spears. On the right Naaman the Syrian stood dignified and composed in the blue water, as the biblical scenes unfolded themselves in an incontestable rotation.

From beyond the chapel there stretched the new long gallery with its conscious vista. The pictures in the house were in position as was the mosaic with its conventionalised likeness of Lord Salisbury sent from Venice by Sir Henry Wotton. A small portrait represented that wife whom Salisbury had lost, Frances Cecil, with the great pearl guard above her hair and the powdered silver on grey satin. Her triangular face, remote and unaustere, looked pale and satisfied and Elizabethan.

Out through the high windows, and in contrast to the oak and the new bright golden paint, lay the garden with its terraces and parterres and the mown green walks and the borders set with pinks. There was the new vineyard and the nectarines and plum trees. There would soon be so much more when the lavish planning had matured; the four hundred sycamores from the Low Countries; the tulip bulbs from Leyden; the rose trees; the melon plants, the Flemish cherries. Hatfield roofed and glazed lay spread across the still unfinished landscape. In the east garden the men were colouring the rocks in the great cistern.

It seems that the lord treasurer only spent eight nights in his new palace.

Chapter 8

LORD VERULAM

THE end was not entirely unexpected. Sir Theodore Turquet de Mayerne, the court physician, had declared that the lord treasurer was quite worn out. In the spring of 1612 dropsy was gaining on him and in April he set off for the Bath in his Emden coach with the white horses. His only son and his daughter Lady Cumberland went with him. They were accompanied by his chaplain, Mr Bowle, a sign of the serious view that he took of his condition.[1] The cure was unsuccessful and he set off homewards with the same party. They were joined *en route* by his chief Scottish friend, Lord Hay. From Lady Stapleton's manor at Laycock he was moved to Marlborough and there in the parsonage house the great earl of Salisbury died on May 24, "the Sabbaoth day".

They were approaching the mid-point of King James's reign in England and this date had importance for he would never again have a sole chief minister. The great office of lord treasurer was passed to the earl of Suffolk. There was speculation as to the post of secretary, and this, perhaps, is the point at which to consider the career of Francis Bacon.

Lord Salisbury had been content that the king should grant to all his other subjects everything save power; this he retained. And it was only after power that Bacon hungered. Then Bacon, like his master, was detached about the House of Commons, nor was there in either kingdom a more perfect royalist.

There are certain points that are still in doubt in Francis Bacon's career, but it is evident that his rise was blocked as long as his cousin Robert Cecil lived. By birth he was the younger son of the second marriage of Sir Nicholas Bacon, who had been Queen Elizabeth's first lord keeper. His father had been a *novus homo*, rare amongst the great figures of the Elizabethan court, the son of the sheep reeve of the abbey of Bury St Edmunds. Francis Bacon was almost entirely without known relatives, a genuine solitary. He had quarrelled with his step-brothers

[1] Cf. MS. observations of the Rev. John Bowle on the earl of Salisbury's sickness, *Desiderata Curiosa*, 206.

Sir Nicholas and Sir Nathaniel about his father's inheritance. His brother Antony, to whom he was attached, was dead. Apart from the Hobys, he had only a single cousin, Robert, earl of Salisbury. His aims were high and conventional; from an early age he wished to be lord chancellor.

It is necessary here to go back a little. From the age of twenty-three he had always been a member of the House of Commons. Ten years later he applied for the solicitor-generalship and was refused. The next year he applied for the higher post of attorney general and was again rejected; his uncle Lord Burghley was opposed to his promotion in both cases. The post of solicitor general became vacant again. In this case Burghley supported him, but the queen refused. He then attached himself to Essex, but eventually took part as one of the queen's counsel at his trial. The succeeding years were calmer but most deeply disappointing. At the king's accession he had sent him a letter which was delivered by Tobie Mathew, and he had been among the many to receive the honour of knighthood. In 1606 he applied again for the post of attorney general and, when that was filled, for the lower office. Finally in 1607 the post of solicitor general came to him. All this shows how hard it was for Sir Francis Bacon to obtain official place. At the time Lord Salisbury died Sir Francis was already fifty-one and still unsatisfied. For it was not legal office he really wanted so much as political power. He had immense and hard-won knowledge; he would lay his cornucopia before the king.

The impression that one receives is that Sir Francis was better at talking than at listening. It does not seem that he appreciated how much the king prized his own knowledge and how different this was from his own. King James's erudition had come from his Scottish teachers. It included the classic languages with an accomplished use of Latin, a perfect knowledge of the history of the Old Testament, a good impression of many facets of the subjects of theological debate and a sense of history. The whole was illuminated by his common sense. There was only one field in which King James and his subject had both long speculated, the powers and indeed the mechanism of the royal kingship. The relations of the two men can be explained in a single sentence. This contact by itself was not sufficient.

The king was homely, but few thinkers less homely than Francis Bacon have ever lived. He was not a great traveller; for four years as a boy he had been based on Sir Amyas Paulet's embassy in Paris. But he accepted all phenomena for his enquiry. While James I had learned only too much about the kings of Judah, Bacon took the Roman emperors for his smooth province. It is to Bacon that is due the phrase[1] that Gibbon has made famous. "Which felicity of times doth best appear in the age which passed from the death of Domitian the emperor until the reign of Commodus." To me it seems that these sage reflections do not marry with King James's humours. Besides, Bacon's mind was above all wide-ranging. In a few lines on a single experiment he turns from the properties of the water of the Euxine Sea as it reaches the haven of Constantinople to the oyster pits at Colchester.[2] There is a reference to the Sargasso Sea. "And they report", he writes, "there is in some of the Indian seas a swimming plant, which they call *Salgazus*, spreading over the seas in such sort as one would think it were a meadow."[3] There was his essay on the colours of good and evil; his probing the making of gold; his high experiments. These were matters which would be appreciated by Charles II alone of all the royal Stuarts. It would seem that the king of England of his time was alarmed by all this knowledge. There was no place in Bacon's life for jocularity; the king could not play and jest with him as he played and jested with the sharp Erskines and the unintellectual members of the house of Howard.

At different times Sir Francis Bacon jotted down a collection of apophthegms old and new. There were rather over three hundred and fifty of these sayings and seven relate to James I. Two of these are worth recalling. "His Majesty . . . having made unto his Parliament an excellent and large declaration, concluded thus: 'I have now given you a clear mirrour of my mind; use it therefor like a mirrour, and take heed how you let it fall, or how you soil it with your breath.' "[4] And again he repeats a pregnant saying, this time in answer to a book of the cardinal of Evreux, who had in a grave argument of divinity sprinkled many witty ornaments of poesy and humanity, "that these flowers were like blue, and yellow, and red flowers in the corn, which make a pleasant shew to those that look on, but they hurt the corn".[5] This shows what Bacon liked, but these mannered phrases were hardly characteristic of the sovereign at his ease.

Francis Bacon meant much to King James's reign. In both cases their experience of life was almost entirely insular, but Bacon had none of

[1] Francis Bacon, viscount St Albans, *Of the Advancement of Learning* (1605), I, 26.
[2] Bacon, *Natural History* (Historia naturalis, etc., 1622), Century VIII.
[3] *Ibid.*, Century VII.　　[4] Bacon (Apophthegmes new and old, 1625), *Apophthegm*, No. 3.
[5] *Ibid.*, *Apophthegm*, No. 7.

his master's feeling for the great monarchies, he had a deep contentment with the realm of England. He always stood forth as a defender of Reformation values, but the whole tenor of his life would seem to show that what he defended was Protestantism considered as a political situation and not in any sense as a doctrinal faith. He was without interest in and rather repelled by Catholicism, but his opposition to Catholics as such was the result of their hostility to the Elizabethan settlement. Bacon's own career was founded on the Elizabethan scheme, which he seems always to have conceived as entirely political.

He appears to have considered the nascent Puritans as a valuable element in a state which would maintain itself in isolation from the Catholic monarchies. It was characteristic of Bacon's temperament that he never reacted against any form of thought or belief; on the contrary he strove to disentangle in each person and idea some elements which would prove of utility to the state.

An element in Bacon's isolation arose from the fact that he must always be the prince's sole adviser. His ideas did not marry with those of his contemporaries. The written word had power with him and alone fully clothed his thought. It seems clear that Bacon saw into men's characters, but could not foresee their actions. He was sharp and perceptive with regard to enmity within his own closed circles, but he did not note the cooling of those who might have been his friends. It was his misfortune that there were so many points which linked him with King James, if only he could have got near enough. He was, for instance, wholly alien to that martial temperament with which the king was not at ease. With all his plumed words, he was by nature both cool and unemotional. With this there went one of his many Renaissance legacies: he was perfectly uncensorious. His dislikes were not suffused by any prejudices based upon moral grounds.

The real barrier to the relationship of James I and Francis Bacon was the result of the latter's clear knowledge of each aspect of the king's affections. King James liked to surround his majesty with a kind of homely and innocent confusion. But out at Gorhambury, reposing in the clement weather on a marble seat above the hornbeam avenue, holding his high-crowned silvered bonnet in his hand, sat Bacon, now Lord Verulam, who knew it all. It was not in him to criticise another's pleasures.

There are elements of unfairness in the way that the charge of flattery is presented. The rich phrasing was in general reserved for the throne and for those whom the sovereign deigned to honour. Much must be allowed for the conventions of that century. The language of compliment was universal and a letter was not considered well constructed unless it was both formalised and deferential. With Bacon it was not the style but the content, and very often the implied content, that marked him off from other men. The Machiavellian precepts were shared by Francis Bacon with many of his contemporaries; it was as a clear-cut royalist in doctrine and in conviction that he stands alone. He placed certain unique values in the juxtaposition of the crown of England and the English commonwealth. He matured early and throughout his life would offer to his sovereigns advice and admonition, praise and service.

There was in Bacon no tendency to any reckless political action. The supreme governor of Bacon's actions was wisdom as a Renaissance statesman would have interpreted that term. He certainly possessed one central weakness: it was not in accordance with the sweep of his large mind to enquire into the attitude towards himself of those who chanced to fall beneath his sliding observation.

His spirit of magnificence, the very conscious magnanimity and that high learning, which he wore with as little concealment as a diamond, were not qualities calculated to ease his personal relations with his colleagues. In the long series of his letters there is no touch of the ordinary and he never possessed that gift of being commonplace which was so essential for the reassurance of his equals in high politics. That lack of intimacy, which is so marked a feature of all his correspondence that has a direct political bearing, was the cause rather than the effect of his protracted disappointments. He extended to all men that mixture of irony and didactic metaphor which was only relished by his private friends. Above all he never made explicit compacts.

That his learning should be a separating factor was very natural.[1] The very name of Verulamius seems to preclude the possibility of patient and unrequited labour. As a figure of the end of the high Renaissance he was incapable of curbing his display. The new generation, the men who would be mature in the next reign, was to be in its wide acceptances theological; but Bacon's mind was freed from the element of devotion. In addition it was inevitable that the fierce and the unsophisticated should alike repel him and that in consequence he could never really gain the king's young friends, not even Villiers.

[1] Cf. The chapter by Dr Rudolf Metz, *Seventeenth Century Studies presented to Sir Herbert Grierson* (1937).

The reasons which have been given may be sufficient to explain his solitude, but they do not cover his disaster when he was deprived of the lord chancellorship for taking bribes. The explanation now put forward seems to me to cover the possible circumstances of the case. There was an uncoordinated air about many of his actions; for instance his marriage in 1606 with Alderman Barnham's younger child. His wife's relations, the great silkmen and drapers, did not appeal to him. His sister-in-law was married to the disreputable Lord Castlehaven. There is no reason to suppose that Bacon was suited to marital domesticity. In the whole matter there was insufficient care. And this applies likewise to the question of gifts from suitors when he had reached the Bench. He did not pay some cunning fellow to take his bribes for him. He thought too little. He did not consider the strange nature of the perpetual litigant to whom litigation was another form of the urge to gamble. He took, it seems quite heedlessly, the gold coins in the worked silk purse which Lady Wharton handed him. He gave judgment without regard to such gifts of any kind. His mind was given to his large endeavours and especially to the *Novum Organum*, that effort "to bring in estimation Philosophy or Universality, name and thing". These points are the possible beginnings of an explanation.

He was in some ways truly isolated, the one solitary figure of the Jacobean world. There are some comments by Aubrey which bite into the memory. "Mr Thomas Hobbes," Aubrey relates in a familiar passage, "was beloved by his lordship, who was wont to have him walke with him in his delicate groves, when he did meditate: and when a notion darted into his minde, Mr Hobbes was presently to write it downe."[1] Before him was "the stately walke of trees",[2] planted with elm and hornbeam and Spanish ash, that led to his small country house at Gorhambury where stood his statues of the Claudian emperors.

At every meal Bacon is said to have strewed his table with sweet herbs and flowers, and had "musique in the next room when he meditated" and as he sat designing the islands in his garden with their tritons and the musk roses. He gave his thought to marble statuary. At several good views he planned for the erection of elegant summer houses well built of Roman architecture.[3] He found it difficult to bear the smell of neat's-leather; he disliked the small beer in Gray's Inn Hall; he was lavish and magnificent.

He always maintained a marked aloofness, a concentration, according

---

[1] John Aubrey, *Brief Lives*, I, 70. [2] *Ibid.*, 79. [3] *Ibid.*, 83.

to report, on his ganymedes[1] and favourites and a perpetual readiness to enter into such large discourses as that on "the benefit of irrigation ... because of the nitre in the air and the universall spirit of the world". There is no reference to Lady Verulam. If only he could have shed his learning, he would have been a great support to the Scottish king.

[1] According to Aubrey, *Brief Lives*, 71.

8 FRANCIS BACON, VISCOUNT ST ALBAN
Studio of Paul van Somer (National Portrait Gallery)

9 GEORGE VILLIERS, IST DUKE OF BUCKINGHAM
Unknown artist (National Portrait Gallery)

Chapter 9

LADY ARABELLA

THERE have been various comments on Lady Arabella Stuart earlier in this book, but it has seemed best to wait to assess her significance, if that is not too elaborate a word, until we reached the crisis in her affairs. But the expression "crisis" seems too serious for her sad *dénouement*. Her life was guided and dominated by members of her own sex; it can be expressed in terms of the influence on her of the two countesses of Shrewsbury, her grandmother and her aunt. Queen Elizabeth had seldom seen her and had not liked what she had heard about her. As a young woman she was infinitely biddable.

Until King James had children, she was the second heir to the English crown but not to Scotland. She was that sovereign's closest relative. They were both the only children of two brothers; but it was not until he came as king to England that she first met him. She had inherited nothing from her father, the young earl of Lennox. There was no substance in her claim to be countess *suo jure* and Queen Elizabeth had reabsorbed the Lennox lands in England.

It is worth examining carefully Lady Arabella's attitude towards religion. This is because there was only one party who could have used her, the disillusioned Catholic plotters. Her grandmother Elizabeth, countess of Shrewsbury, was in these matters a true regalian. She had been born in 1518 and was always faithful to whatever might be the royal religion. Her private friendships, which were few, included the Grey family. She had made her second marriage from the marquess of Dorset's house at Bradgate. Her fourth husband, the earl of Shrewsbury, had been custodian of Mary Queen of Scots from 1569 until 1584 and during this time Lady Shrewsbury had married her daughter Elizabeth Cavendish to Charles Stuart, earl of Lennox, who was a consumptive just nineteen years of age. He is the little boy in a black cassock standing beside his elder brother Darnley in the bare upper hall at Temple Newsam in the Eworth portrait. He only lived to father a single child, the Lady Arabella.

Although there was more forethought shown in the planning of great

N

marriages in the Elizabethan age than in any other period, there is no reason to suppose that either then or at any other time did Lady Shrewsbury think of a royal succession. The young bridegroom was dying and had he left a son the boy could eventually have been shipped back to Scotland. In that event he might have gained in time that Lennox dukedom which was granted in fact to Esmé Stuart d'Aubigny. As there was only a girl Lady Shrewsbury took one precaution: she assured herself about the child's religion.

The Catholic influences came in from two directions. The earls of Shrewsbury were a great post-Catholic family. Until the death of Francis, the fifth earl, in 1560, they had been the leaders of the old religion in Derbyshire and in the southern part of the West Riding. Their cadet branches still remained faithful, but the sixth earl had gone with the times. There were still Catholics among his entourage, however. Anthony Babington, who came from a quasi-Catholic background, had been one of the pages at Sheffield Castle.

There was another Catholic in the wife of the seventh earl of Shrewsbury. She came from the centre of that Cavendish stock to whose advancement their mother was devoted. Elizabeth Lady Shrewsbury was in fact the matriarch of the two lines of dukes of Devonshire and Newcastle. She built the first, the Elizabethan, house at Chatsworth. Mary Cavendish, countess of Shrewsbury, her daughter who was married to her step-son, appears to have been the only convert to the Church of Rome in her family's long history. She would be one of those who urged her niece into her last adventures. Lady Arabella was all her life almost a Puritan.

At the time of the king's accession she was twenty-eight years of age and still unmarried. The only serious project in her earlier years was that she should marry the duke of Lennox, the eldest son of Esmé Stuart d'Aubigny. This had fallen through owing to the queen of England's opposition. King James gave her precedence above the countesses, but provided no income beyond a pension. It was this that made her constant and rather disagreeable search for monopolies so very necessary. These were obtainable from the royal court. It seems that the king and his advisers were convinced that Lady Arabella would live and die a virgin princess. This would certainly have been a great convenience.

She was something of a blue-stocking and a great reader. She had a form of Protestant pietism, not then found among the young great ladies of King James's court. It is worth quoting a comment sent back to Venice by the ambassador of that republic in 1607.[1] He begins by stating that she was "not very beautiful". This, for the period, is a strong expression. Then comes the praise. She was "highly accomplished, of most refined manners. She speaks fluently Latin, Italian, French and Spanish, she reads Greek and Hebrew and is always studying". The following sentence relates to the possibility of a dowry. "She is not very rich." In the next year she suffered from smallpox. She was now established at her own house in Blackfriars precinct. Why should she not have gone on thus quietly until she died?

Two factors were of importance to her. First, the old countess of Shrewsbury died in the cold winter of 1608 and left her very little; second, it seems that she could not get on terms with the king and queen. The latter was too light-minded for her husband's studious cousin, while the king was not attracted to the female sex.

It is easy to understand how the Seymour family came to appeal to her. Her grandmother had been a friend of Lady Catherine Grey, who had married long ago the old and still surviving earl of Hertford. It is also true that in certain ways Lady Arabella's life recalls that of the much more vital character Lady Jane Grey, the nine days' queen. It seems possible, as is suggested by her recent biographer,[2] that in imagination she modelled herself upon this prototype; such a theory accounts for the fixation with which she followed the Seymour family.

She had begun to think of a Seymour marriage in the old queen's day when the boy that she had fixed upon, Edward Seymour, who was Lord Hertford's heir and grandson, was only fifteen. He was married later to Lady Anne Sackville, but died childless before his grandfather. His younger brother William first met Lady Arabella in 1609, when he was twenty-one. He thought her "a lady of great means"; he had always a vein of simplicity in his character. Lady Arabella's intentions, granted her very limited knowledge of the world, seem sufficiently clear. William Seymour is impossible to make out. It may be easier to penetrate the situation if we examine how it is likely to have been viewed by the earl of Hertford, a sober peer, freed from the fantasies of the young people.

A man of diminutive stature and yielding disposition, Hertford was the elder son of the second marriage[3] of Protector Somerset. His own

---

[1] Cal. S.P. Venetian, X, 514.   [2] Cf. P. M. Handover, *Arbella Stuart* (1957), 166.

[3] The descendants of his first marriage, which had been annulled, the Seymours of Berry Pomeroy, were at this time debarred from the succession, although they were allowed to inherit the dukedom in 1750.

secret marriage to Lady Catherine Grey and his later efforts to get this marriage recognised cost him the royal favour throughout the late queen's reign. He had now come into a certain tolerance. He had received the lord lieutenancy of Wiltshire and had been sent in 1605 as ambassador extraordinary to the Spanish Netherlands; he had entertained the king at Tottenham Park. The proposed marriage of his grandson with Lady Arabella threatened all this careful establishment of royal goodwill. The bride was thirteen years older than his grandson; she was in the strict sense a royal ward and was almost without property. Her pension was terminable and her licence to nominate sellers of wine in Ireland revocable at will. She had no land, and just a certain supply of jewellery. But what use was a fleur de lys set with diamonds as a marriage jointure? There was also always the fact that his grandson would inherit a parliamentary title to the crown, which gave the Seymours preference to the Stuarts. This by itself was alone sufficient to prohibit such a union without the king's express permission.

No such permission was sought or given and Lady Arabella and Mr Seymour were married by Anglican rites in lodgings at Greenwich in the night of June 22, 1610. The only persons of standing connected with this affair were Mary, countess of Shrewsbury, and a Mr Rodney. Lady Shrewsbury was an increasingly bellicose Catholic, but apparently unconnected with her co-religionists. After seventeen days of married life William Seymour was haled before the council and imprisoned in the Tower, while Lady Arabella was placed in the charge of Sir Thomas Parry. Lady Shrewsbury was later also placed in the Tower. The earls of Hertford and Shrewsbury at once declared their horror of the intended marriage; they both disowned the two young people.

It was to be expected that Lady Arabella and Mr Seymour should attempt to escape together. They had ample opportunity to communicate with one another. On June 3, 1611, Lady Arabella escaped from her easy confinement and, assisted by her former servants, made her way down river to Leigh, where a French ship was waiting for them both. Seymour was late so that they were compelled to set sail without him. The ship was overtaken in Calais Road by Sir William Monson in the *Adventure*, a royal vessel. Lady Arabella was brought back to England and placed in the Tower.

She was lodged on the upper floor of the Bell Tower in the same room where fifty years earlier Lady Catherine Grey had given birth to Lord Beauchamp, who became her father-in-law. She had a four-poster bed, and hangings and a carpet were sent in for her. As time went on her mind became unhinged and she purchased four new gowns, one costing £1,500, to be worn when Princess Elizabeth was married. It seems that she was later moved to the lieutenant's lodging, which had quite naturally the best accommodation within the Tower. She died there on September 25, 1615. Her life had been a very sad adventure.

William Seymour, after missing the ship in which Lady Arabella sailed, found a collier which was ready to take him to Ostend. He went on to Bruges, where he heard of his wife's recapture. He is a curious example of a man of birth whose early life is almost unknown, while his later years are fully documented. It is only known that he spent two years at Oxford at Magdalen College and gained a love of study which, together with a certain lack of energy, were permanent features of his character.

It must be admitted that the comments now to be made are speculation. We know so very little of the youth of that young man, who was to become in later years the grave and royalist marquess of Hertford. His motives in his marriage can be only guessed. He may have been moved by some chivalrous and non-sexual love for the plain and wide-eyed woman, so much his senior. He may have been driven to protect her from the world which neither knew.

During his time of exile we come upon a fact, which is in some way unexpected. It has in recent years been discovered that he was received into the Church of Rome at St Omer.[1] Motives of conversion lay frequently upon a purely worldly plane, as in the case of those young German officers, cadets of Lutheran princely stocks, in the emperor's service for whom this opened the gateway to high promotion and made the social life so much more agreeable. It must have been a relief for this young man with small knowledge of French to find this house of Englishmen. Possibly Seymour thought that conversion might well make the bread of exile less unpalatable. But whatever notions he may have had, these were soon swept away by his wife's death.

As soon as he learned that he was free, he made approaches to the king and received permission to return to England. He returned to his own country on February 10, 1616, and never again left it. In 1618 his elder brother died and he became Lord Beauchamp. In the same year he married Lady Frances Devereux, a younger sister of the earl of Essex. His subsequent opinions owed much to his new brother-in-

---

[1] Cf. *Biographical Studies*, I, 117.

law. Three years later he succeeded his grandfather as earl of Hertford inheriting those large estates in Wiltshire, including Savernake Forest, which had come down from the Protector.

After his return he remained for all his life a steady Anglican, a little wary of the bishops. He was governor to the son of Charles I, the Prince of Wales. It was in connection with these later actions that he received this encomium from Lord Clarendon. "The Marquess of Hertford was a man of great honour, great interest in fortune and estate, and of an universal esteem over the kingdom."[1] He survived the Restoration and received the revived dukedom of Somerset. He lies in the family tomb at Bedwyn Magna beneath a ducal coronet and with his Garter.

Lady Arabella was not buried in the Tower of London. She was found a place beside the Queen of Scots. Old Lady Shrewsbury made a mistake in arranging for her conception.

[1] Clarendon, *History of the Rebellion* (1706), I, 425.

Chapter 10

ROMAN CONTROVERSY

THE effects of the Gunpowder plot upon the imagination of King James were deep and lasting. At the opening of parliament, which followed the detection of that conspiracy, the king expressed himself upon this subject.

And now [he began] I must crave a little pardon of you that since Kings are in the word of God itselfe called Gods, as being his lieutenants and vice-gerents on earth, and so adorned and furnished with some sparkles of the Divinitie; to compare some of the workes of God the great King, towards the whole and generall world, to some of his workes towardes mee, and the Little world of my Dominions, compassed and severed by the sea from the rest of the earth.[1]

In analysing the conspiracy he gave in tedious detail a description of all the sections of the leaders in the state who would have perished.

And then consider therewithall the cruell forme of that practise: for by three different sorts in generall may mankinde be put to death. The first, by other men and reasonable creatures, which is the least cruell. . . . And the second way more cruell than that is by Animal and unreasonable creatures. . . . But yet with them both resistance may availe, and also some pitie may be had, as was in the Lions, in whose denne Daniel was throwne; or that thankefull Lion that had the Romane in his mercy. But the third, which is most cruel and unmercifull of all, is the destruction by insensible and inanimate things, and amongst them all the most cruell are the two elements of water and fire; and of these two the fire most raging and mercilesse.[2]

The same theme is found in other of his books and speeches. "What monstrous, rare, nay never-heard of Treacherous attempt was plotted within these few yeeres here in England, for the destruction of Mee, my Bed-fellow, and our posteritie, the whole house of Parliament, and a great number of good subjects of all sorts and degrees",[3] so starts off the *Triplici Nodo, Triplex Cuneus*, one of King James's later works of controversy.

---

[1] McIlwain, *The Political Works of James I,* 281. [2] *Ibid.,* 282. [3] *Ibid.,* 71.

This was a memory which the king could not escape and it was never far away in all his writings. It had also inspired the oath of allegiance, which Archbishop Bancroft worded for him in 1606. This document, which was intended to produce a division among English Catholics, would have had more effect if it had been confined to a denial of the Pope's right to depose the king or "to authorise any forreigne Prince to invade or annoy him". The later portion of the oath, however, contained these further sentences. "And I doe further sweare that I doe from my heart abhorre, detest and abjure as impious and hereticall, this damnable doctrine and position, that Princes which be excommunicated or deprived by the Pope may be deposed or murdered by their subjects." It would seem that it was the words "impious", "hereticall" and "damnable" which made it unacceptable to so many. George Blackwell, a secular priest who had held since the later years of Queen Elizabeth the title of archpriest from the Holy See, was induced in prison to accept the oath and was removed from office the next year by Pope Paul V. The oath is only mentioned because so much of the controversy centred around it.

Indeed the king was convinced and remained so all his life that every sovereign in Europe would be moved by this detestable conspiracy aimed against him. It is worth noting, in considering his fellow-sovereigns, that he knew more about their titles than their personalities. The emperor Rudolf II, who reigned from 1576 until 1612, was in many respects a shadowy figure. It is unlikely that King James ever grasped him. In his *Premonition* sent out in 1609 the king begins with an address "To the most sacred and invincible Prince, Rodolphe the Second, by God's Clemencie Elect Emperour of the Romanes; King of Germanie, Hungarie, Boheme etc etc." Nor did he realise that in all these communications no prince of the Roman obedience could accept incivilities to the Pope.

A Premonition ranks among King James's later works and Cardinal Bellarmine had for some time entered into the field against him before it was composed; but it should be studied in some detail for it gives the closest view of the judgments on doctrinal questions formed by the king. It is interesting, also, because the tone changes as the narrative moves forward.

I am [he begins] such a Catholike Christian, as beleeveth the three Creeds; that of the Apostles, that of the Councell of Nice, and that of Athanasius; the two latter being paraphrases to the former. And I beleeve them in that sense, as the ancient Fathers and Counsels that made them did understand them: to which three Creeds all the Ministers of England doe subscribe at their ordination. And I also acknowledge for Orthodoxe all those other formes of Creedes that either were devised by Councels or particular Fathers against such particular heresies as most reigned in their times. I reverence and admit the foure first generall Councels as Catholicque and Orthodoxe: and the said foure generall Councels are acknowledged by our Acts of Parliament, and received for Orthodoxe by our Church.[1]

After comments on the Fathers and the Scriptures, the king describes his doctrine on the position of the Virgin Mary.

And first for the blessed Virgin Marie, I yeeld her that which the Angel Gabriel pronounced of her, and which in her Canticle she prophecied of herselfe: that is, That she is blessed amongst women, and That all generations shall call her blessed. I reverence her as the Mother of Christ, whom of our Saviour tooke his flesh, and so the Mother of God, since the Divinitie and Humanitie of Christ are inseparable. And I freely confesse that she is in glory both above angels and men, her owne Sonne (that is both God and man) only excepted.[2]

As regards to prayers to the saints the king enquires:

What warrant have we to have recourse unto these *Dij Penates* or *Tutelares,* these Courtiers of God, I know not. . . . It satisfieth mee to pray to God through Christ as I am commanded, which I am sure must be the safest way; and I am sure that the safest way is the best way in points of salvation. . . .[3] As for Purgatorie and all the trash (Jubilees, Indulgences, satisfactions for the dead &c) depending thereupon, it is not worth the talking of; Bellarmine cannot finde any ground for it in all the Scriptures. Only I would pray him to tell me, if that faire greene meadowe that is in Purgatorie have a brooke running thorow it, that in case I come there I may have hawking upon it. But as for me; I am sure there is a Heaven and a Hell, *praemium & poena*, for the Elect and reprobate. How many other roomes there be, I am not on God his Counsell.[4]

There now comes his famous passage.

Of Bishops and Church Hierarchie I very well allow (as I said before) and likewise of ranks and degrees amongst Bishops. Patriarches (I know) were in the time of the Primitive Church, and I likewise reverence that institution for order sake: and amongst them was a contention for the first place. And for my selfe (if that were yet the question) I would with all my heart give

---

[1] *The Political Works of James I,* 122.   [2] *Ibid.,* 123.   [3] *Ibid.,* 124.   [4] *Ibid.,* 125.

my consent that the Bishop of Rome should have the first seate: I being a westerne King would goe with the Patriarch of the West. And for his temporall Principalitie over the Signiory of Rome, I doe not quarrel it neither.[1]

There is a reference to Rome, that queen of cities.

So far the *Premonition* was in general a calm appraisal of an Anglican position likely to be received with a reasonable sympathy by Catholic princes. While always retaining his Predestinarian standpoint, the king's references to Marian doctrine and his comments on the Pope's position have reflections of what would be a Laudian attitude. There is here that remarkable naturalness which is a feature of his writings. He complains to the princes of his own originally pseudonymous pamphlets and books being answered by the chaplain of a cardinal. He refers to the line of common men who were Bellarmine's ancestors and makes clear his view that the princes of the Church were merely the parish priests and deacons of the Roman city.[2]

In the later sections of the *Premonition* the king's mood changes as a result of his preoccupation with the idea of Antichrist. He first tells of "a Beast with seven heads and tenne hornes, like a Leopard, as well for the colour because it was full of spots . . . as also using a bastard forme of government, in shew spirituall but indeed temporall over the Kings of the earth; like the Leopard that is a bastard beast betwixt a Lion and a Parde: having feete like a Beare, to signifie his great strength, and the mouth of a Lion, to shew his ravenous and cruell disposition."[3] Another aspect of the theme of Antichrist soon follows.

And the merchants of the earth, and all shipmasters, and traffickers upon the Sea shall lament the fall of that great Citie, which never had a fellow, for the losse of their riches and traffique, which they enjoyed by her meanes. There (were) . . . all sorts of rich wares, whereof that great Citie was the Staple: for indeed she hath a necessary use for all such rich and glorious wares, as well for ornaments to her Churches and princely Prelates, as for garments and ornaments to her woodden Saints.[4]

There is an account of Antichrist upon the seven hills.

The question arises as to whether King James believed all this that he was saying. At times it seems that what the king is writing is a painted show, an exercise. It appears that he is determined to repay the Pope for his discourtesy. The following passage seems to support this view that I advance.

[1] *The Political Works of James I*, 126–7.   [2] Cf. *Ibid.*, 151.   [3] *Ibid.*, 143.   [4] *Ibid.*, 148.

Thus hath the Cardinals shameless wresting of those two places of Scripture, *Pasce oves meas*, and *Tibi dabo claves*, for prooving of the Pope's supreame Temporall authoritie over Princes; animated mee to proove the Pope to be the AntiChrist out of this foresaid booke of Scripture; so to paye him in his owne money againe. And this opinion no Pope cane ever make me to recant; except they first renounce any further medling with Princes, in any thing belonging to their Temporall Jurisdiction.[1]

Nevertheless it was a strange book to send forth to the Catholic princes. It can be understood that when these beautifully bound volumes were presented by the English ambassadors to the rulers of these kingdoms and republics, which were in communion with the Holy See, they were received with some embarrassment.

Almost the last of King James's important writings was that set forth after a speech made in Paris on January 15, 1615. In this work he had the English ecclesiastics to help him and the passages selected for quotation each deal with one of the king's own favourite themes and naturally include the powder-miners.

The nature of the royal controversy is perhaps best seen in *A Remonstrance for the Rights of Kings, and the Independance of their Crownes*, which was provoked by an Oration of Cardinal Du Perron. Some passages will give the king's effect.

From whence [he asks] did the last civill warres, wherein a world of blood was not more profusely than prodigiously and unnaturally spilt, and wherein the parricide of King Henrie III was impiously and abominably committed; from whence did those bloodie warres proceed, but from the deposing of the said King by the head of the Church? Were they not Prelats, Curats and Confessours; were they not Ecclesiasticks, who partly by seditious preachments, and partly by secret confession, powred many a jarre of oyle upon this flame? Was not he that killed the forenamed King, was not he one of the Clergie? Was not Guignard a Jesuite? Was not John Chastel brought up in the same schoole? Did not Rauaillac that monster of men, upon interrogatories made at his examination; among the rest, by whom he had beene so diabolically tempted and stirred up to his most execrable attempt and act of extreme horror: did not he referre his examiners to the Sermons made the Lent next before, where they might be satisfied concerning the causes of his abominable undertaking and execution? Are not Bellarmine, Eudaemonoiohannes, Suarez, Becanus, Mariana, with such other monsters, who teach the doctrine of parricides, uphold the craft of Janus-like Equivocations in Courts of Justice, and in secret confessions; are they not all Clerics?[2]

[1] *The Political Works of James I*, 149.   [2] *Ibid.*, 176-7.

After a litttle space the king returned once more to his favourite topic.

Hath not Faux by name, a confederate of the same damned crew; hath not he stoutly stood to the gunners part, which then he was to act in that most doleful Tragedie, with asseveration of a conscience well assured and setled, touching the lawfulnesse of his enterprise? Did he not yield this reason? to wit, because he had bin armed with instruction of musket proofe in the case, before he made passage over from the Low Countries.[1]

In the many mediaeval examples of the disputes between the popes and sovereign princes one seems to detect the work of King James's Anglican advisers; but there is on occasion certain phrasings which seem to bear the stamp of the king's mind. "Most notable is the example of Philip the faire, and hits the bird in the right eye"[2] appears to be a case in point.

There is then an excursus on the Crusades.

Then, to be short, his most bountifull Holiness (see the Bull of Innoc. 3) gave to any of the riffe-raffe-rank, that would undertake this expedition into the Holy Land, a free and full pardon for all his sinnes, besides a degree of glory above the vulgar in the Celestial Paradise. Military virtue, I confesse, is commendable and honourable; provided it bee employed for justice, and that generous noblenesse of valiant spirits bee not under a colour and shadow of piety, fetcht over with some casts and devises of Italian cunning.[3]

From time to time he would turn to the Scriptures. "Item, Jesus Christ not onely commaunded Peter to *feed his lambs*; but said also to Peter, *Arise, kill and eat*: the pleasant glosse, the rare invention of the Lord Cardinal Baronius."[4]

His mind went back again to the misconduct of his Catholic subjects.

All which notwithstanding, I deale with such Romane-Catholikes by the rules and wayes of Princely clemencie; their heinous and pernicious error, in effect no lesse than the capitall crime of high treason, I use to call some disease or distemper of the mind. Last of all, I beleeve my said brother of France will set downe in his tables, as in record, how little hee standeth ingaged to the Lord Cardinall (of Evreux) in this behalfe. For those of the reformed Religion professe and proclaime, that next under God, they owe their preservation and safetie to the wisdome and benignity of their Kings.[5]

King James's thought went to the reigning pontiff.

---

[1] *The Political Works of James I*, 177.   [2] *Ibid.*, 196.   [3] *Ibid.*, 229.   [4] *Ibid.*, 230.   [5] *Ibid.*, 232.

Wherefore did hee suffer Garnet and Oldcorne my powder-miners, both by bookes and pictures vendible under his nose in Rome, to be inrowled in the Canon of holy Martyrs? And when he saw two great Kings murdered one after another, wherefore by some publike declaration did not his Holinesse testifie to all Christendome, his inward sense and trew apprehension of so great misfortune, as all Europe had cause to lament on the behalfe of France.[1]

He looked with horror on the position of a king cast out by his subjects from his kingdom.

What fowle [he wrote] is more beautifull than the peacocke? Let her be plumed and bereft of her feathers; what owle, what jacke-daw more ridiculous, more without all pleasant fashion? The homely sowter, the infamous catchpol, the base tincker, the rude artificer, the pack-horse porter, then living In Rome with libertie, when Valentinian was detain'd captive by Saporas the Persian King, was more happie than that Romane Emperour.[2]

The king was approaching his conclusion and he went back once more to the old subject.

A King shall be better entreated and more mildly dealth withall . . . if at a siege of some city hee be blowne up with a myne, than by a myne made, and a traine of gunpowder laid under his Palace of Parliament house in time of peace. . . . . But Mariana likes better, to have a Tyrant poysoned by his chaire, or by his apparell and robes, after the example of the Mauritanian King. . . . O hel-hounds, O diabolical wretches, O infernal monsters! Did they onely suspect and imagine, that either in Kings there is any remainder of Kingly courage, or in their subjects any sparke left of ancient libertie. . . . How long then, how long shall Kings rule whom the Lord hath called his Anointed, Kings the breathing Images of God upon earth. . . How long the Majestie of God in their person and Royal Maiestie, to be so notoriously vilified, so dishonourably trampled under foot?[3]

[1] *The Political Works of James I*, 247.   [2] *Ibid.*, 249.   [3] *Ibid.*, 248.

Chapter 11

THE PALATINE MARRIAGE

I⊤ was natural that King James with his high sense of the royal status should throughout his reign give thought to the marriages of his children, the princes and the princess of Great Britain. Owing to the early death of the two younger princesses King James had been left with an only daughter. The Princess Elizabeth had been brought up since she came to England by Lord Harington of Exton and his wife, for the most part at the latter's inheritance, Combe Abbey outside Coventry. When the princess came to London in 1608 they were in charge of her household and remained in that office until her marriage. Their only son was Prince Henry's chosen friend. The Haringtons were closely related to the Sidneys and belonged to the group of inner families in the second half of the old queen's reign. They were extravagant and as a stock soon vanished. Nothing now remains save the front wall of their Elizabethan house lost in a thicket in Exton Park. Both Haringtons held to that broad Elizabethan Protestantism, which the princess, with her brother Prince Henry, alone reflected among the Stuart family.

She was brought up with Lady Harington's niece Anne Dudley, who accompanied her to Germany on her marriage. Anne Dudley herself soon married the marshal of the Palatinate and died in giving birth to her only child, the duke of Schomberg.

The first offer for the princess's hand, from the young Gustavus Adolphus, king of Sweden, was rejected through the opposition of Queen Anne. The second was a long and rather languid negotiation put forward by the duke of Savoy on behalf of his son and heir the prince of Piedmont. Charles Emmanuel was at this time in the pro-French stage of his political career and Salisbury was inclined to recommend the king to listen to him. Finally there emerged the Elector Palatine; but while this proposition was in progress a formal offer came of the hand of the king of Spain. Philip III had recently become a widower and Queen Anne favoured this idea. It came, however, in the last months of Salisbury's life and through his influence it was set aside.

There are reasons why we should examine the Palatine marriage, which took place early in 1613, with some care. The consequences of this alliance formed the background to King James's foreign policy for all the later period of his reign. The proposer and the settings of the proposal were both French, that world of high French Calvinism with which the king had been familiar from his childhood. The actual proposal was first made to the English ambassador in Paris by the bridegroom's uncle, the duke of Bouillon, who held the sovereign principality of Sedan on the north-eastern frontier of France. The Huguenot dukes of the old house of La Marck had sometimes irritated King James in Scotland by the protection that they offered to Scottish ministers at their university.[1] The duke of the new family, the first of the house of La Tour d'Auvergne, had been more courteous. At this time he was asking King James whether he would allow Andrew Melville to accept a chair of biblical theology.

The duke of Bouillon was conscious of his status as a sovereign prince and he was also bitterly jealous of the confidence King Henry had accorded to Maximilien de Béthune, Baron de Rosny, whom he created duke of Sully. He therefore cannot be considered as at all times faithful to the French royal policy. Nevertheless he was a pivotal force in that three-cornered union of French and Dutch and German Calvinists. He had himself married Elizabeth the second daughter of William prince of Orange by his Bourbon wife. Her elder sister Louisa Juliana was the widowed mother of the young Elector Palatine.

The marriage which he proposed to King James would also require the consent of the Stadtholder Maurice of Nassau, who was one of his nephew's guardians. The connections with France were very close. John Casimir of Pfalz-Neustadt, who had dominated the Palatinate's policy in earlier years, had fought beside Henry IV against the house of Guise. The family were tied by their religion to the French language, through Calvin and his works and through French-speaking Geneva. French was in use at the court to which Princess Elizabeth was destined. All her life her letters back to England were strewn with French phrases, *Voix de Chapitre* for instance. Did she know German?

Heidelberg had reflections of both France and the Low Countries. The young elector had been brought up with a liking for Italian façades; Inigo Jones's architecture would have met with his approval.

[1] Cf. a comment in connection with the life of Robert Boyd of Trochrig. "And I observe at this time that most of the professors, in the accademies at Saumure, Montalban, Sedan and Lescar, were Scotsmen", Rev. Robert Wodrow, *Collections upon the Lives of the Reformers and most eminent Ministers of the Church of Scotland* (Maitland Club, 1844), II, 27.

The old castle at Heidelberg had been refaced during his father's brief adult reign. It had received a new frontage in the Italo-Flemish style. The Frederick Palace was a new construction and the Italian garden, which was now in process of creation, was to be the first in Germany. All these factors could be grasped quite easily. But did the king really understand the formidable problems which faced the house of Wittelsbach?

The great house of Wittelsbach had been divided since the early part of the thirteenth century into two main lines, the elder holding the position of Elector Palatine and the younger that of duke of Bavaria. Marriages between the branches had once been common, but none had taken place since the Reformation. The position had been complicated as a result of the war of succession between the Palatinate and Bavaria, which had followed the death of the duke of Landshut in 1503. His lands had been divided, Landshut going to the duke of Bavaria and the complex of his northern lands to the Elector Palatine. The latter area was known henceforward as the Upper Palatinate.

The gains from the Landshut war were again divided among the branches of the Palatine family, the northern section going to the count Palatine or *Pfalz Graf* of Sulzbach and the southern to the Neuburg house. The balance stayed with the Elector Palatine.

The chief portion of the Elector Palatine's dominions, the Rhenish or Lower Palatinate, consisted of good agricultural and vineyard country lying for the most part to the west of Heidelberg and stretching southward past the County Palatine of Zweibrücken (or Deux Ponts) until it reached the frontiers of Lorraine.

This was the main territory, but the gains from the Landshut war lay far away, nearly a hundred miles to the eastward along those elm-lined roads which crossed Franconia. It was a compact land in what has now long been known as North Bavaria. It was centred upon but did not rule the town of Regensburg. On the east there lay the upland country which marked the borders of the kingdom of Bohemia, while to the south there stood the forces of Duke Maximilian of Bavaria eager to regain his lost possessions. Dividing the two portions of the Elector Palatine's sovereignty there lay the Brandenburg margraviate of Ansbach, the county of Hohenlohe and the southern lands of the spiritual electorate of Mainz. From a military point of view the Upper Palatinate was almost indefensible.

It seems most unlikely that the English king appreciated these elements in the situation. They would have mattered less had the Palatinate been a peaceful state; but the Elector Palatine was the hereditary chief of the Evangelical Union, that body of Calvinist German princes through whom France had long channelled her aggressive influence. Just as the France of Henry of Navarre understood and worked upon the German Calvinists, so also they were relatively remote from the Lutheran princes, who had a certain traditional bond of sympathy with the old Hapsburg dynasty.

Before his daughter's marriage King James gave his signature to the Evangelical Alliance, but his alliances were all for peace. He was a peace-maker. Still, a chief factor in the situation was the duke of Bavaria's unappeased desire for the Upper Palatinate. This was the more dangerous because although the general policy of France was anti-imperialist, it always contained a pro-Bavarian element.

King James was more concerned with the actual details of the wedding than with these remote effects and consequences. He would be compelled in the future to consider the geographical situation of the two Palatinates. The form of the elector's Protestantism left him quite tranquil. The deep Calvinism riled the queen, but this clear Protestantism gave contentment to the opposition and also to all that privileged world which in its heart preferred an anti-Spanish policy.

This may have been the reason why the king made this marriage the greatest, as it was certainly the most popular, celebration of his reign. The warrant to the Great Wardrobe on the occasion of the marriage preparations gives the impression of lavish uncontrolled expenditure illuminated by an interest in a neat invention. From the white baize "masking sutes" and Orpheus in "his antique coate armour" and Entheus and Prometheus in their robes and mantles, making their entrances from behind the holland curtains, attention was drawn to the stars, "which moved in an exceeding strange and delightful manner". "I suppose," runs a contemporary account, "fewe haue ever seene more neat artifice than Master Inningoe Jones shewed in continuing their Motion, who in all the rest of the workmanship which belong's to the whole invention shewed extraordinarie industrie and skill." It is worth recording something of the detail.[1]

In the bride chamber in the court of St James's there were hangings embroidered with Venetian gold twist and gold chain lace, and coloured Naples silk, and yellow Spanish curtains of the same material.

[1] All these details are from B.M. Add. MS. 5751, printed in *Archaeologia*, XXVI, 380–91.

There was a careful choice in the great procession, the Florence cloth of silver for the bride-maidens, the pages with gold-edged roses on their shoulders and doublets of cloth of gold and tawny hose, and the ladies with their farthingales of taffeta and damask "with wire and silke to them". An exact precedence is reflected in the material and its ornament, the fine black cloth for teachers and the French grey for footmen, the black wrought velvet for the queen's physician, the livery cloaks of incarnadine French plush, the outfits of sarcenet for the coachmen and the black Perpetuana "for a madman's sute". Mr Inigo Jones walked in a retired position in a broad cloth gown "with furr of budge".

The crown jewels were brought forth for this occasion, "the faire great pearle pendante called the Bretherin, the Portugall Dyamond and the great table diamond sett in gould called the Mirror of France".[1] This was what the king most liked, the display of his majesty. He moved forward, amid the jewellery and the new-fashioned ropes of pearls, with the light falling on his black velvet hatband on which shone twenty-five diamonds set in the Spanish manner in buttons of gold. King James was the last English sovereign to love such a riot, a legacy from the Elizabethans. He moved on contented and insolvent, the ideal royal patron for Ben Jonson.

The Elector Palatine and his wife were seventeen; they were children in a world which he, at least, probably never really understood. He was youthful and uxorious, not a good combination. It is curious that he was known in England as the Prince Palatine and commonly as the Palsgrave from the German *PfalzGraf*. He was not referred to as the Elector. It may have been that this last title implied in England some inferiority in the sense that he was an elector of some other sovereign. In this connection it is worth noting that the Spanish ambassador was prevented from attending the wedding by indisposition. There was no ambassador in London from the Roman emperor.

The marriage procession went slowly down to Rochester where the royal couple stayed at the castle which, with the title, had lately been conferred on Robert Carr. That favourite was now at his brief untroubled apogee. The king and queen took their farewell at Rochester and the procession wound on through Kent to the Isle of Thanet.

---

[1] A detailed inventory of that section of the royal jewels which were in constant use in 1623 and noting such matters as which of the diamond hatbands had been Prince Henry's is printed in *Archaeologia*, XXI, 151-4.

When they reached Margate, they were delayed by April storms in the English Channel.

The *Royal Prince* was lying in the Downs. The flag of the lord admiral was broken, for the earl of Nottingham himself was to escort the royal couple to Flushing where they would meet the Nassau princes. The ship was the larger of the two first-rates added to the navy in King James's reign. Her designer Phineas Pett well understood exactly what his master wanted. Her gilded lanterns stood high above her tall stern gallery with its tiers of scroll work. There were twenty-four round ports each worked with a lion in gold paint on wood. There was one other vessel like her, the *Sovereign of the Seas,* built in the next reign by the same designer. She had been built as a symbol of royal sea-power conceived at peace. The king of Denmark on his visit had been brought down river to Greenwich to see the *Royal Prince.* The other naval vessels were suitable to convey the king's ambassadors to foreign ports; she bore away his only daughter. King James had a feeling for things Venetian. She had something of the value in the state which the Bucentaur held for the Doge of Venice.

The king was solitary with Prince Henry dead. The two Palatinates were far away; they would come back to him. The royal party returned to London. The king still had his favourite. He could give himself to the fashioning of Robert Carr.

Chapter 12

ROBERT CARR

THE last thirteen years of the reign, the period that followed the death of the earl of Salisbury, are marked by the influence of two successive favourites, the earl of Somerset and the duke of Buckingham. They were very different figures. George Villiers, duke of Buckingham, was one of the great favourites in European history. Considering the time at which he lived almost everything is known about him, his ancestry and the character of his relations, the degree of his knowledge, his tastes and preferences. He has left a mass of correspondence; there is an extensive iconography. With Robert Carr the situation is quite different. The date of his birth is unknown, his early life is difficult to plot. What the king seems to have seen was a hitherto unknown young man whom he could mould. He spoke with a Scottish accent and knew French. He made a disastrous marriage which, within two years, swept him out of public life. In consequence, so far as his career is concerned, the chief point is that from a personal point of view we can know so very little.

In the course of 1607, on a date which is unknown, Robert Carr was thrown from his horse in the tiltyard at Whitehall when about to present to the king the shield and device of Sir James Hay his master. The king was struck by his long yellow hair. He lay on the ground with a broken leg. He was taken into the palace and the king, visiting him, soon determined to fashion and to educate this Scottish youth. There is an account of Robert Carr by Arthur Wilson, who was then at court. "For his person he was rather well-compacted than tall, his features and favour comely and handsome, rather than beautiful, the hair of his head flaxen, that of his face (for he already carried a *pic devant*) tinctured with yellow of the Sycambrian colour."

There was another way in which Robert Carr was a great contrast to George Villiers: he never did anything for his own relations. He was born Robert Kerr, a spelling he soon changed, one of the sons of the second marriage of the head of the Ferniehurst branch of that great Border family. He seems to have lost contact both with his elder step-brother, who became Lord Jedburgh, and with his step-sister who was married to the old earl of Haddington. There is a reference in his days of power to his first cousin Walter Scott, who was serving in the Netherlands against the Spaniards, but the latter did not receive the earldom of Buccleugh until Carr had fallen. The Kerrs were a family much given to subdividing their estates, but Robert Carr was only a small child at his father's death. This may perhaps serve as an explanation for what seems to have been a breach with his own stock. Whatever the reason for his lack of contact with the Kerrs, the new favourite never inherited and never held an acre of land in his native Scotland.

He was in fact, as his new spelling of his surname indicates, an Anglicised Scotsman following the course of action of Sir James Hay, who had employed him. There was, perhaps, some connection with the greater man for Robert Carr was doubly related to the Hays of Yester. His training at court, in so far as he had ever had any, had come from Sir James Hay, who had been with the king since he had left his northern kingdom. Even at this date Hay, who had received various grants and whose marriage with Honora Denny had been arranged by his royal master, held no higher position than that of gentleman of the bedchamber. He had served with the Scots archers at the court of Paris and had the most delightful and winning manners. He charmed the king and pacified the English courtiers. He showed a tranquil goodwill to the new favourite; it was in another quarter that Sir Robert Carr, as he had now become, would find his friends.

He had, it is true, one companion whose influence with him was overriding. This man was Thomas Overbury for whom he soon secured a knighthood and a place in the bedchamber. Overbury's name would stay with him for ever, since it would bring about his own disaster. They had met years before when Thomas Overbury, accompanied by his father's chief clerk (with £60 between them), had gone north to Edinburgh. He belonged to the minor gentry and was one of the younger sons of the recorder of Gloucester. He had been born at the house of his maternal grandfather at Compton Scorfae in the parish of Ilmington in Warwickshire and was twenty-six when his friend had caught the king's attention. He was witty, overbearingly conceited and desperately poor. He had literary ambitions and his own ties with Alsatia. He had no friends of consequence and saw little of his family. In the time of his misfortune they were confused by the great men he moved among. His brother-in-law Lidcott visited his corpse. When his catastrophe was all over and Carr, now earl of Somerset, was on trial, Sir Francis Bacon made no attempt to gild Sir Thomas Overbury's reputation. "But the truth was," he declared, "Overbury, who (to speak plainly) had little that was solid for religion, or moral virtue, but was wholly possessed with ambition and vain-glory. . . . Overbury was naught and corrupt."[1] He had got into the high court circle in which he was not at home and he was penniless.

There were three stages in Sir Robert Carr's brief years of favour. At first, when the king began instructing him, Salisbury still lived and the new favourite was unconnected with the government. These were the years when he obtained the great estate of Sherborne which had belonged to Sir Walter Raleigh. Then Salisbury died and the king formed the notion of using Carr as secretary of state, of training him and moulding him. This was the period when Overbury had had his quick ambitions; the idea of Sir Henry Neville in the government appealed to him. Very soon the third stage opened in which the favourite allied himself with the house of Howard.

By 1611, four years after the beginning of his rise, Sir Robert Carr's position was established. By this time he was Viscount Rochester with a royal grant of the castle there. He had received the office of keeper of the Palace of Westminster. In this year he was created a Knight of the Garter and was made a privy councillor. Except for the Garter, it was not a very remarkable list; but it was one of Carr's characteristics that he asked little for himself. It appears to have been in the following year, but the evidence is very uncertain on this point, that the earls of Suffolk and Northampton offered their powerful friendship to the young man. It cannot have been an easy association since the ordinary politician, and that expression can cover both these peers, loses what liveliness he ever had as old age approaches. It must have been in fact a grim alliance. It was also clear that neither nobleman had any use for the services of Sir Thomas Overbury. This was a strictly business association which also had the effect of increasing the areas of hostility by which the young Lord Rochester was surrounded. He was not supported by his Scottish relatives, nor by any Scottish faction. At the court in general the emotion that his rise aroused was jealousy, and now he was in close association with this great and singularly friendless house. For a time all went well upon the surface. The courtiers were soon accustomed to approach Lord Rochester through Sir Thomas Over-

[1] *State Trials*, II, 974.

bury. There were rumours that the king had planned a great marriage for his favourite with Lady Anne Clifford, the only child and heiress of the late earl of Cumberland. And then he fell in love with Lady Essex.

The ordeal of a great trial was to bear down upon the life of Frances, countess of Essex, and as a result we can still plot the course of her life with an exactness which in a sense resembles that of Roger Tichborne two and a half centuries later. It is also difficult to write about her for she has been so much studied; one has no opportunity to leave the trodden snow. She was born in 1591, one of thirteen children and among these the second daughter of Thomas Howard, earl of Suffolk by his second marriage with Katharine Knyvet, a Wiltshire heiress. Her father has already been described and her mother was an avaricious woman of easy morals, her face marred by smallpox. Lady Suffolk appears to have derived much of her approach from her mother, who belonged to a family of great Wiltshire clothiers, the Stumpes of Malmesbury.

Lady Frances seems to have had a rather lonely childhood and at the age of fourteen in the winter after the Gunpowder plot she was married with great ceremony at court to the earl of Essex. This was one of those marriages by which the king hoped to fortify and reconcile his southern families. It was a policy that he had long pursued in his northern kingdom. The Devereux properties, the valuable estate of Chartley in Staffordshire and the extensive Welsh lands of rather poor quality in Pembrokeshire, were in the hands of the crown at the king's accession. They were at once assigned to the young earl, whose dignities were restored to him. After the marriage ceremony the youthful husband left for the Low Countries. It seems that it was during his years of campaigning in the Netherlands that he adopted Puritan opinions; these were quite alien to the tradition of the Devereux. It was in 1610, when his wife was just nineteen, that he came home.

In the same year Prince Henry was given his separate household at St James's Palace and created Prince of Wales. He was now sixteen (and died of typhoid two years later). All the gossips about the court say that he was attracted to Lady Essex. During that century it was not the practice for married ladies of position to surrender their reputations to a royal prince without an establishment as *maîtresse-en-titre*. Apart from the fact that the king found unregulated unions of this character quite repellent, the prince was much too young. He was after all just a boy, but nevertheless a jealous boy, when it became clear that his father's favourite was now in love with the court lady whom he admired.

It was now decided by her family that Lady Essex should sue for an annulment of her marriage on the grounds that her husband was unable to consummate it. In the action that now ensued a clear light is thrown upon her movements. It is evident that she and her husband very seldom paid visits except to those who belonged within a very close-knit family circle. It was their practice to drive straight from London to Chartley stopping the night at one of the inns on the great highway. In the capital they stayed together in various houses, at Salisbury House in the Strand and at Durham House and at Lady Walsingham's lodgings in the tiltyard. They stayed with Lady Essex's brother-in-law at Caversham, with the countess of Leicester at Drayton in Warwickshire, and of course with her parents at Audley End. Lady Leicester and Lady Walsingham were Essex's two grandmothers. There is only one house in the list where I have not detected the relationship, the Lady Corbett's.

Further it is worth noting that they seem to have avoided wholly the Catholic relations on either side. The names of the old countess of Arundel and Lord William Howard, who were aunt and uncle to Lady Essex, do not appear; nor does that of Essex's mother, the countess of Clanricarde. She lived at Summer Hill near Tonbridge with her second husband; she had, however, become a Catholic.

Among the visitors they received at Chartley was the Bishop of Lichfield and Coventry, whose wife was related to them through the Stumpes. Essex, who was by nature reserved and withdrawn, had one friend, the earl of Southampton, who looked after him for his father's sake. It was always said that Lady Essex was very beautiful; but it appears doubtful if there is a surviving authentic portrait. The three-quarter-length at Welbeck in the style of Isaac Oliver is described as Frances Countess of Essex, but this attribution does not seem likely.[1] There is a miniature in the National Portrait Gallery. There were not many portrait painters working in the few years of her brief apogee.

[1] This portrait may represent Frances Countess of Essex, her mother-in-law. There is a portrait described as the countess of Somerset at Monteviot which may have been presented in the days of her power to the earl of Roxburgh, who certainly received the portrait of John Donne. The lady in this picture is represented with a half-smile, the light brown hair frizzed, the eyebrows above the grey eyes plucked. The colour of her dress is a clear red sown with black flakes and with a falling band of gold and black. Above the white ruff is an arrangement in fine lace around and above her head. She has a single coral ear-ring and, remarkably, she wears no jewels.

She came forth to the court from an isolated childhood and it seems that she had that beauty suited to the great masques which were then in fashion. In spite of all her brothers and sisters she appears to have been alone except for her "sweet Turner", a companion of a rather ill-defined status with whom she had formed an intimacy. Lady Frances Howard was not an intellectual, but a firm-minded, rather headstrong girl addicted to astrology. Religion in the sense of orthodox Christianity she never knew. It is not surprising that her father could not convey to her that Erastianism in an Elizabethan mould which was all that he ever held by. Mrs Turner had put her in touch with Dr Simon Forman. Until his death she put her trust in his magic philtres. It must be stressed that Dr Forman was not a poisoner; if he had been he would have been hanged long before.

The relations with Rochester are not yet clear. It seems that he was soon in love with her and love letters were composed by Overbury for his patron to copy out. For her part she was soon quite desperately devoted and she asked Dr Forman for an elixir which would alienate Lord Essex's affections and for a love philtre which would bind Lord Rochester. She was young and inexperienced. She had an almost religious faith in the effect. It must have been this that she discussed in the long days with her "sweet Turner". It was not a subject that she could have talked over with the rich young girls of her acquaintance. It may have been this that made her lonely.

Was she Rochester's mistress? The court thought that she was. But this situation, whether it existed in fact or in possibility, was not of a kind to suit the house of Howard. Lady Essex drew away from the king's favourite and a suit of nullity was set on foot. Overbury had been very coarse and crude about the countess. As his patron's wife his own position would be gone and Rochester would lean upon the Howard grouping. Northampton was ready to accept Rochester, but without this particular encumbrance. Overbury was offered by the king a post abroad, the most likely seems to be the embassy to Muscovy. He had never had the royal favour for both the king and queen disliked him. In consequence of his intractability it was decided by Northampton and Rochester that Sir Thomas Overbury should be imprisoned in the Tower for a few months. There we may leave him.

The proceedings for a declaration of nullity in regard to the Essex marriage were now begun. From the first the king had taken a great interest in the whole question. It was part of the difficulty of the case that he had come to his own solution. Witchcraft seemed to him to be the answer. This was a burden to the archbishop of Canterbury, who had been appointed to head the commission to hear the case, because much as he revered his sovereign he had a more prosaic mind.

There was thus a curious link between the king and Lady Essex. She belonged to a category of whom he had no close experience, the ladies of the court. She believed in sympathetic powders and he believed in the real old-time devil, a proud defeated prince. The courtiers, all around them both, considered that neither of these concepts were concerned with day-to-day reality. The king was no traveller and could therefore more easily give credit to far-flung voyages. Speaking in the gallery at Whitehall to the archbishop of Canterbury about the question of this marriage, His Majesty had said that "the Earl [of Essex] had once purposed to have gone to Poland to be unwitched".[1] The commission was composed of the bishops of London, Ely and Lichfield and Coventry, the two chancellors of the Exchequer and the duchy of Lancaster and other laymen. To these were added later the bishops of Rochester and Winchester, all meeting at Lambeth Palace under the chairmanship of the archbishop.

The king was as ever sympathetic towards his friends. He wished for a decision which might free Lady Essex. The archbishop for his part was unconvinced. Dr Abbot spoke of *maleficium versus hanc*,[2] and quoted for confirmation of his views the testimony of Melancthon, Pezelius, Hemingius, Polanus, Arcularius, Bèza and Zanchius. The king made a detailed reply, saying, "You know the old proverb *ex malis moribus bonae leges*: and it is not unlikely that the time of darkness gave the Devil occasion to devise such new tricks (look my Daemonology)".[3] He had other thoughts on this same point. "For though it be apparent that God made king Abimelech and his servants unable to abuse Sarah, Abraham's wife, and so was he made by God himself *eunuchus versus hanc*, and that it be not improbable that the Devil being God's ape, should imitate God's work by his filthy witchcraft . . . howbeit, it is very probable that it was long after that time the Devil put that trick upon the earth."[4]

Whatever the reasons for granting a nullity of Lady Essex's marriage, the fact that the king desired this outcome was inevitably not without its influence on members of the commission. The archbishop's own account of the developments in this case has an especial value for its

[1] *State Trials*, II, 814. [2] *Ibid.*, II, 795–6. [3] *Ibid.*, II, 800. [4] *Ibid.*, II, 799.

side-lights; thus we are given a glimpse of the strains within the Established Church between the primates and their principal lay officers. Among the members of the commission was Sir Daniel Dunn, by origin one of the Dwnns of Radnorshire, who since 1598 had held both the offices of master of Requests and dean of the Arches, the latter post coming within the archbishop's province. He was very vexing as the principal spokesman in favour of the decree of nullity. "I much suspected," wrote the archbishop, "the conscience of the man, knowing him reasonably well before, both out of mine own estimation of him, and out of the judgment of my two predecessors, the lords Whitgift and Bancroft, who held him for a man most corrupt."[1] This throws a clear light on a situation in which successive primates had not the power to move a royal appointee to their own courts. In the matter under dispute the bishops themselves were now divided, Winchester, Rochester, Lichfield and Ely supporting the decree.

At this point I must touch briefly on a matter that I find confusing. It had been decided, apparently by her Howard relatives, that Lady Frances must appear at her marriage with Rochester as a virgin bride. In consequence the commission agreed to appoint four matrons joined with two midwives to examine her. "Seven noble women of her consanguinity" led by her mother Lady Suffolk associated themselves with this committee.[2] Both groups declared that it appeared by the inspectors' report that Lady Frances remained *virgo incorrupta*, a phrase with the same meaning as the more usual *virgo intacta*. The problem is this. The judgment just given was that of a body selected and appointed by the commission. Surely if this evidence was correct the Essex marriage could never have been consummated and could at once be set aside as *matrimonium ratum sed non consummatum*. Did the archbishop disbelieve the evidence of those whom he had chosen? If so, this would explain his subsequent refusal to vote in favour of the decree. But in that case why did the Howards press forward with the matter? The only suggestion that I can offer is that the king was a strange man. There is reason to suppose that he disliked extra-marital intercourse on the part of his own favourites. The decree of nullity was passed, the archbishop of Canterbury and the bishop of London voting against it in the minority. Popular opinion is described as favouring Lord Essex and praising Archbishop Abbot. What was its value?

[1] In an account printed in *State Trials*, II, 712.   [2] The names of the members of these two groups and of the midwives are given in *ibid.*, II, 803.

As the year drew to its close three events occurred that were of importance to Viscount Rochester. On November 3, 1613, he was created earl of Somerset. It was still the custom to attach this historic title to a county and the name of Somerset was chosen for him, although he had no lands within that western shire. On the morning of September 15, Sir Thomas Overbury was found dead in the Tower of London. He had been vomiting for several days. On December 26, the earl of Somerset was married in the king's presence to Lady Frances Howard, who was dressed as a virgin bride. He had thus reached to the peak of his brief triumph.

Chapter 13

THE OVERBURY TRIAL

THE chief impression left by the earl of Somerset, even at the peak of his authority, is that of loneliness and isolation. This is reflected at the very moment of his marriage ceremonies. The number of those who gave him gifts was quite restricted. Sir Fulk Greville gave him a cup of gold. Sir Arthur Ingram, who was in no sense accepted by the more substantial courtiers, gave a set of kitchen utensils in silver and two pearls for the bride. Lord Northampton gave gold plate to the value of £1,500. The earl of Somerset took Sir Baptist Hicks's house at Kensington and settled there for a time. All that the new favourite had to support him was the interested favour of the great capitalists, Ingram and Hicks. As far as his personal life was concerned, the great peers stood aloof from him.

As long as he retained the king's favour the official world was his, and Bacon, as an example, prepared a masque to celebrate the marriage. The city, too, would place its favours where the king required. One important figure stood quite remote from the new favourite: the archbishop of Canterbury did not forgive him. It seems that Somerset never saw the dangers which would lie in the king's unslaked taste for theology.

Northampton, who had guided Somerset in politics, was soon to vanish. He was seventy-four, a great age in that century, and had suffered for some time from a "wennish tumour" in the thigh. He was brought to London and after some months of suffering he died in June 1614 in Northampton House in the Strand. He desired to be buried in the chapel at Dover Castle, the headquarters of his lord wardenship of the Cinque Ports. He had established hospitals according to the then practised forms of charity. His funeral inventory sets down his riches; he had an unusual taste for eastern wares, for carpets, porcelain, and the finer silks. As a politician he was "secret" in the Elizabethan sense of that expression. His death removed, with the exception of Raleigh, the last statesman who had come down from the old queen's days. It also foreshadowed the destruction of the influence of the house of Howard.

The office of lord treasurer, which had been in commission since Salisbury's death, was given to the earl of Suffolk, who would hold it until
his own disaster. Somerset took the post of lord chamberlain, which was
thus vacated. The favourite was singularly unprotected; but for some
time he went forward in peace. It was, however, one of his defects that
the presence of danger made him irritable.

These were the years when Thomas Sutton's will led to the foundation at the London Charterhouse both of a hospital for old and decayed gentlemen and of a school. The New River was completed by
Myddelton with the king's assistance and the water supply for London
was assured. There was a visit from King Christian of Denmark in
the summer after Northampton died. Both Suffolk and Somerset gave
£300 to the king, as an example to others, in a benevolence.

In the field of foreign policy there were difficulties in western Germany and the Low Countries and James I seems to have thought that
the remedy might lie in a Spanish alliance, a plan which throughout his
reign in England had a varying attraction for the Scottish king. Carr
followed him; it is unlikely that he had any ideas of his own upon this
subject. At the same time this line of action only served to separate the
Scottish favourite still further from the general body of the English lords
and gentry.

There were further difficulties with the two secretaries of state.
Neither gave a genuine support to their young superior. At first, after
Salisbury was dead, the king declared that he would be his own secretary and would train his new favourite in that work. But after a while
he became fatigued and two new secretaries of state were appointed.
It is worth considering both men a little. The senior was Sir Ralph
Winwood and the junior Sir Thomas Lake. Somerset gained no personal intimacy with either and between them they held him in a vice.
They were not only hostile and so much more experienced; but they
were also so much older. They had feared Northampton, but he was
dead. The favourite was not only ignorant but very young. It was almost like Susanna and the elders.

Lake was a civil servant, who slid carefully from one set of patrons to
another. He had begun as secretary for Latin letters and as a very dutiful dependant of the earl of Salisbury. He had later attached himself
through Northampton to the Howards and it need only be said that he
was the first person to conceive the project of advancing Sir George
Villiers. He was known favourably to the king as the persistent advo-

cate of Scottish courtiers. It was his misfortune that his wife, the daughter of Alderman Ryder, was a virago.

Sir Ralph Winwood was a very different and much stronger character. He was an example, rare in those times, of the self-made man. His father Richard Winwood of Aynhoe in Northamptonshire is described as *plebeius* and appears to have been a tenant of Magdalen College. He had had a distinguished career at Oxford and had married the step-daughter of Sir Thomas Bodley. He had held the post of agent at the Hague and had once been sent to Düsseldorf. He favoured, although not publicly, an aggressive anti-Spanish policy and had a strong belief in Sir Walter Raleigh. His outlook had a marked Puritan tinge. This last point was unfortunate for he was the first member of the official world to hear the accusations relating to the death of Sir Thomas Overbury.

During the early days of his rise to power Carr had received the great estate of Sherborne forfeited by Sir Walter Raleigh. In fact he made no new constructions on this land; but it was well situated for a country seat situated on the edge of his own county of Somerset. He was unfortunate that his marriage had no heir. In the later days of his full power his wife lived at Islington to be close to the ministrations of Dr Burgess.

In the political scene there was little to worry, if little to encourage him. Sir George Villiers was at court, but had not yet attained to influence. It seems likely that the complaints that the king now made to him were the result of the uneven temper of the young favourite lacerated by the still dangerous consequences which might emerge from the Overbury affair. It is as well to give almost in full the letter which the king addressed to him. This was in reply to what the favourite had written about court factions.

First, I take God [he wrote] the searcher of all hearts to record that in all the time past of idle talk, I never knew nor could out of any observation of mine, find any appearance of any such Court faction as you have apprehended, and so far was I ever from overseeing or indirectly feeling of it (if I had apprehended it) as, I protest to God, I would have run upon it with my feet as upon fire, to have extinguished it if I could have seen any sparkle of it. . . .

Next, I take God to record, that never man of any degree did directly or indirectly let fall unto me anything that might be interpreted for the lessening of your credit with me, or that one man should not rule all, and that no man's dependence should be put upon the King, or any such like phrases;

which, if I had ever found, then would I have behaved myself as became so great a King, and so infinitely loving a master.[1]

All this was encouraging if a trifle arid and the king went forward.

I did surely expect that the idle talk would wear out like the pope's cursing; especially seeing my own heart knew it to be without a ground. For I am far from thinking of any possibility of any man ever to come within many degrees of your trust with me, as I must ingenuously confess you have deserved more trust and confidence of me than ever man did, – in secrecy above all flesh, in feeling and impartial respect, as well to my honour in every degree as to my profit, and all this, without respect either to kin or ally, or your nearest and dearest friend whatsoever; nay unmoveable in one hair that might concern me against the whole world. And on those points I confess I never saw any come towards your merit; I mean on the points of an inwardly trusty friend and servant.

This is high praise, but a careful study shows that Somerset was praised for his loyal solitude. It may have been the fruit of his upbringing that he reported each offer that was made and each gift that was presented to him to the king. He was indeed strangely in isolation. His wife was attached to her sister Lady Wallingford, but the latter's husband was an old man of nearly seventy. Lord Hay, who had once been his master and who knew the ways of that court so well, had drawn away from him.

The letter now turned on the king's complaints of him.

But, as a piece of ground cannot be so fertile, but if either by its own natural rankness or evil manuring thereof it becomes also fertile of strong and noisome weeds, it then becomes useless and altogether unprofitable; even so, those before rehearsed rich and rare parts and merits of yours have been of long time, but especially of late, since the strange phrenzy took you, so powdered and mixed with strange streams of unquietness, passion, fury, and insolent pride, and (which is worst of all) with a settled kind of induced obstinacy, as it chokes and obscures all these excellent and good parts that God hath bestowed upon you.

The king wrote on for some time in the same vein. Certain phrases in the later part of this long letter sum up its core. "Consider that I am a free man, if I were not a king. Remember that all your being, except your breathing and soul, is from me. I told you twice or thrice, you might lead me by the heart and not by the nose. I cannot deal honestly, if I deal not plainly with you." This letter can be read in various ways,

[1] J. O. Halliwell, ed., *Letters of the Kings of England* (2 vols., 1846), I, 133.

but to my mind it seems to presage the end of the affair. Without the scandal of Sir Thomas Overbury, the favourite would have fallen. The king was at last fatigued with the Scottish gentleman, who had not responded very well to education. His home was on the Borders, not at the court. It had not helped that the king had isolated him from his companions. This was the end of Robert Carr with the long yellow hair.

In the course of 1615 the storm broke. Somerset had gone for a long visit to his brother-in-law Wallingford's house at Rotherfield Greys beneath the Chilterns. His wife, who was now *enceinte*, was with him. Among those in attendance on the countess was "sweet Turner". Already in July there had been whispers that Sir Thomas Overbury's death had been contrived. It was in the next month that there had been brought to England the death-bed confession made in Flushing by an English boy, who stated that while an assistant of the son of Dr Paul de Lobell, the French physician in attendance on the prisoner in the Tower, he had been bribed to supply a poisoned "clyster" to Sir Thomas Overbury.

This story reached Sir Ralph Winwood and he took it to Sir Gervase Elwes, the governor. Sir Gervase had been anxious for an official post and had paid £4,000 for the promotion to the lieutenancy of the Tower, which was procured for him by Lord Northampton. He was a solemn man and a gambler and had many children. At the same time he had accepted on the suggestion of Sir Thomas Monson, then in charge of the armoury at the Tower, the services of Richard Weston, then sixty years of age and with an undisclosed background. Weston had been assigned as personal attendant to Sir Thomas Overbury. At the end of his talk with Winwood, Elwes rashly decided to write to the king telling him all that he knew.

On September 10 he sent a letter with all the facts.[1] He declared that he had surprised Weston carrying a phial of poison and had been alarmed by the arrival of counterfeited tarts and jellies. Sir Thomas was in the care of Dr Mayerne, who on leaving London left behind him directions, and of his apothecary Dr Lobell, appointed by his physician, "an approved honest man, as I thought it, and still do". He then accused old Weston, with whom, he asserted, he had held religious conferences, to persuade him to a better course of action.

---

[1] For the most detailed modern survey of the evidence relating to Overbury's death, see Beatrice White, *Cast of Ravens* (1965).

But (as Weston hath since conferred with me) here was his, Sir Thomas's, overthrow and that which wrought it was (as he said) a clyster. The apothecary had a servant who was corrupted. Twenty pounds, Weston said, was given to him. Who gave it, who corrupted the servant, who told Weston these things, or what is become of the servant, I can give your Majesty no account, neither can I directly say that he ever named any as an actor in this business but Mrs Turner.

It was on the receipt of this letter that the king gave orders that the case should be put into the hands of Sir Edward Coke, the lord chief justice. The examinations began on September 17 and Weston was examined ten days later.[1]

Weston at first declared that Overbury's sudden death was caused by the "weakness and corrupt indisposition of his body", and that later "going into the Council Chamber of the Tower to see a friend that was in Sir Walter Raleigh's garden, he sat so long in a window that he was never well affected after". It was on October 1 that Weston first admitted visiting the countess of Essex on the introduction of Mrs Turner, whom he had known formerly. He further admitted that his son William had brought him from Lady Essex a little glass full of water of a yellowish and greenish colour. "I protest," said Weston, "that my son was not privy, or suspecting that it was poison, who dwelleth without Temple Bar at the *Beaver Hat*." This was the gist of the evidence, although what became of the little glass of poison is not quite clear.

Weston's statements contained some further details. It was stated that Sir Thomas Overbury had had an issue of his left arm before coming to the Tower and that he had "plaster for sores, [which] his own servant Davies brought unto him". He went on to give details of the time of Overbury's death. "He, being gone from him not above a quarter of an hour to my Lord Grey's for beer, at his return he found him dead, which was about seven o'clock in the morning."[2]

The next significant witness was Overbury's servant Lawrence Davies. He was the first to implicate the earl of Somerset. He stated that after his master's death he had seen in Weston's hands part of the white powder which he said that he would deliver back to my Lord of Rochester. Davies denied that he had ever received any white powder. Weston's version ran as follows: "A little before his death and as he taketh it two or three days he (the prisoner) received a clyster given him

---

[1] Cf. for the trial of Richard Weston, *State Trials*, II, 911–30.

[2] For one account of Overbury's death ,see Andrew Amos, *Great Oyer of Poisoning* (1846), *passim*.

by Paul de Lobell, then dwelling in Lime Street." About October 13 Lord Chancellor Ellesmere, the duke of Lennox and Lord Zouche were added to the panel of examiners. The earl of Somerset was placed in close restraint by Sir Oliver St John.

From the beginning of his troubles he had written letter after letter to the king and now he complained of being tried by his enemies. It is an eloquent comment on his isolated state that he should ask that no privy councillor be allowed to take part in the proceedings raised against him. He had also protested against the addition of Lord Chancellor Ellesmere to the list of judges. The king wrote to him in reply. "I need not," he said, "since Lennox hath long before this time told you my resolution on that point; whereupon you have bestowed so much scribbling and railing, covertly against me and avowedly against the Chancellor (Ellesmere)." The gist of his argument ran as follows.

I have nothing to look unto but, first, my conscience before God, and next my reputation in the eyes of the whole world. If I can find one man stricter than another in point of examination, I am bound to employ him in it; and when in my conscience I have set down a course, to change it at the influence of the party, without any other reason but because they will have it is very little for my honour. . . . And as my proceedings from the beginning of this business have been only governed by the rule of my conscience, as the Searcher of all hearts knows; so must I, to my great regret, confess and vow, that from the beginning of this business, both your father-in-law (Suffolk) and you have ever and at all times behaved yourselves quite contrary to the form that men that wish the trial of verity ever did in such a case.

The king's style was curiously soporific for it seems that he wrote as he spoke. Somerset had adverted to the fact that Ellesmere had been solicitor general at the time of the execution of the Queen of Scots. "But how far," he went on, "it is now out of time, after that the Chancellor hath serviced me more than thirteen years with all honour and faithfulness, having ever been a Regalist, to rake up from the bottomless pit the tragedy of my poor mother, I appeal to your judgment."

The letter wound on with many reflections of a general character, but contained two remarks that were revealing. The king was speaking of the accusation. If this "prove false, God so deal with my soul as no man among us shall rejoice at it as I. . . . If otherwise, as God forbid, none of you shall more heartily sorrow for it; and never King used that clemency that I shall do in such a case."

The trial of the less important prisoners was now begun. There was little doubt that most of them were guilty. They had clearly been instrumental in conveying poison. About Sir Gervase Elwes there were two opinions. If he was innocent, he was a fall guy and had been placed in an inextricable position. He could not be secure unless he left the Tower, but the moment that he resigned his office Overbury would be poisoned. And in course of time he would have been arrested as an accessory before the act. If he was a rogue he was at any rate a solemn one. To some extent his innocence and that of Lord Northampton hang together. If the latter had never intended Overbury's murder, all that he would require was a needy and not over-intelligent gentleman of sufficient social standing to be lieutenant of the Tower. Still, Northampton's intentions seem a matter that we have not sufficient evidence to penetrate.

Neither Weston nor Mrs Turner[1] had any contact with the king, and this likewise applies to Dr Franklin, who was accused of acting as the countess's agent. Mrs Turner declared that she "was ever brought up with the Countess of Somerset and have been for a long time her servant, and knew not that there was any poison in those things that were sent in to Sir Thomas Overbury". This was the last tribute that Lady Somerset was to receive in all these statements.

Franklin accused the Lieutenant roundly. Seven deadly poisons were "all given to Sir Thomas Overbury at different times and the Lieutenant knew of these poisons, for that appeared by many letters which he writ to the Countess, which I saw, and thereby knew that he knew of this matter. . . . [In one note] the Lieutenant used this speech, 'Madame the scab is like the fox, the more he is cursed the better he fareth' ". This does not sound like Sir Gervase's style, and perhaps the whole thing is a lie.

Franklin was nothing if not wholehearted. "Sir Thomas," he declared, "never ate white salt, but there was white arsenic put in it. Once he desired pig, and Mrs Turner put into it *lapis costitus*. At another time he had two partridges sent him from the Court, and water and onions being in the sauce, Mrs Turner put in cantharides instead of pepper. . . . For these poisons the Countess sent me rewards. . . . She was able to bewitch any man."

Sir Gervase Elwes told of the jellies which the countess sent him, how when they were placed in his pantry they turned colour and began to

---

[1] Cf. for the trial of Mrs Turner, *State Trials*, II, 930–5.

shake. "I saw them," he explained, "so black and foul and of such strange colours." During the trial of Dr Franklin there was a question of "*aqua fortis* being too violent a water." There was a discussion with the lady and powder of diamonds was substituted for it; so many poisons and so unavailing for in the end Sir Thomas Overbury died of the poison conveyed in the "clyster".

When Somerset was taken by Sir Oliver St John and placed first in the dean of Westminster's house, his wife was given the choice of confinement either in her own house in the Blackfriars or in Lord Wallingford's beside the tiltyard; she chose her own. All the accused were thus separated from one another. Overcome by the evidence brought against her, the countess admitted her guilt, but affirmed her husband's innocence. On December 1, she gave birth to the daughter, who was to be her only child, and in March both she and her husband were brought into the Tower.

There can be little doubt that she was guilty. She had a nervous temperament which caused her to send dose after dose. She was clearly careless about money. It was wonderful for Dr Franklin after a lifetime of iniquity to find a client who would discuss with him the use of powder of diamonds. Whether she had any secret reason for fearing what Overbury might say about her we cannot tell. She was certainly determined that he would never again see her rather simple husband.

Lady Somerset pleaded guilty and was treated at her trial with consideration.[1] She was charged with being accessory before the fact of the wilful poisoning and murder of Sir Thomas Overbury. In passing sentence Lord Chancellor Ellesmere declared that he did not doubt that the peers would signify to the king her humility and grief and would mediate that she might obtain the royal mercy. She was taken back to the Tower and the next day her husband's trial began.

The interesting element in this case is the question of the innocence or guilt of the earl of Somerset. At this period there was a presumption of the guilt of all those whom the royal officers had arrested. It was the practice of those in charge of state trials to endeavour to prove the guilt of those before them. In this particular trial much use was made of the unchallengeable evidence of the dead. To all the comments made by the lesser prisoners at their examinations and trials there was added the

[1] She was not denied visitors. "My Lord (Dorset) and I, my cousin Sackville and Lady Windsor went to the Tower to see my Lady Somerset", entry under April 28, 1617, V. Sackville-West, ed., *The Diary of Lady Anne Clifford*, 96.

statements that they made before their last journey when they were urged to free their consciences of all that they knew of any who had conspired against His Majesty; Sir Thomas Overbury had died in the king's charge in a state prison. A marmoreal weight was given to such statements made on the brink of eternity. The prisoners in question had been hanged the previous autumn. All of the peers now summoned would bear in mind that the king would not have consented to the prisoner's arrest but for grave reasons.

These points have their significance in this case as in the later matter of the charges against Sir Walter Raleigh. It is true Somerset had only been arrested, while Raleigh had already been condemned. Still, there was a sense in which both men would be regarded as outside that protection which would be given to a law-abiding citizen. In the case of both these men the king seems to have believed them guilty. As Somerset lay in the Tower, King James had written four letters to the new lieutenant, Sir George More, asking him to persuade the prisoner to plead in this sense at his trial.

There is little evidence as to the king's reactions at this time. Some impression may be obtained from the notes that King James made on various pieces of evidence that Bacon had received from Coke's examinations. The latter had been impressed by the countess's use of witchcraft and wondered whether Prince Henry had been poisoned. Here are a couple of statements with the king's comments. To the note that the viceroy of the Indies at Goa had reported to an English factor that Prince Henry had been poisoned by his mistress, the king added the comment: "No better than a gazetteer or passage of *Gallo Belgicus*." The statement that the countess had laboured Forman and Gresham, the conjurers, to enforce the queen by witchcraft to act with favour to her received the royal notation: "Nothing to Somerset."

It can be seen that the king was anxious to stop these rumours about Prince Henry, which were quite baseless, and that he was attached to his practice of assessing evidence. There seems however no sign that his affection was not dead. Somerset had very limited support from any quarter.

The court before which the earl and countess were summoned to appear was, as befitted their rank, composed of peers. These had all been especially invited and they did not represent the peerage in general but rather the peerage of the court. At first sight there appeared to be a certain balance among the ranks for six earls were present and fourteen barons, but in fact the earls of Worcester, Pembroke, Hertford,

Montgomery, Rutland and Sussex were accompanied by nine others[1] who would either by creation or succession receive earldoms in their time. Lords Gerard and Zouche held high official posts and Delaware was governor of Virginia. The youngest was Lord Dormer, who had just come of age and joined the court.[2] In fact only Monteagle, Dacre and Willoughby of Parham could be held to represent the country peerage. The exact religious position of Rutland at this date is not quite clear; but with this possible exception no Catholic peer was present. Not one of the Catholic country peers was summoned, nor was the earl of Essex or any of the Howards and their close relations. The few Scots with English peerages were also absent. It was a gathering of lords with all of whom Somerset had but a slight acquaintance. It must have been intimidating.

Sir Francis Bacon managed the prosecution. His speech had all those phrases which the king so relished. "As for the manner," he began, "the King, our master, who amongst other virtues excelleth in that virtue of the imperial throne which is justice, hath given us command that we shall . . . materially puruse the evidence, as it conduceth to the point of question."[3] It was part of the difficulty that so much of the chain of evidence was adduced to prove that Northampton and Essex between them had lodged Overbury in the Tower. The unsuccessful attempt to do away with Northampton's correspondence on this subject must have prejudiced the court against the prisoner; but it may have been that he had at one time hoped to escape even from this first charge.

Some evidence was supplied by a hostile witness, Laurence Davies, who had been Overbury's body servant. The rest was for the most part the evidence of the dead. Somerset spoke in some ways beside the point. Why pretend that he had not wished to keep Overbury in close confinement? "I had a care," he explained, "to his lodgings in the Tower that he might have the best air and windows both to the water and to the courtyard that he might have liberty to speak with whom he would."

The peers received full information about the poisons, the rosalgar, the arsenic, the mercury sublimate.

Then [said Bacon, with that warm oratory which was so persuasive] when they had this poor gentleman [Overbury] in the Tower close prisoner,

---

[1] These were the future earls of Bedford, Berkshire, Carnarvon, Cleveland, Devonshire, Dover, Leicester, Northampton of the Compton line, and Warwick.

[2] Lord Dormer had been the ward of the earl of Montgomery, whose daughter he married. They figure in the great Van Dyk family portrait in the double cube room at Wilton.

[3] Cf. for the trial of the earl of Somerset, *State Trials*, II, 966–1022.

where he could not escape nor stir; where he could not feed but by their hands; where he could not speak or write but through their trunks – then was the time to act the last day of his tragedy. Then must Franklin, the purveyor of poisons, procure five, six, seven, several poisons, to be sure to hit his complexion. Then must Mrs Turner, the lay-mistress of the poisons, advise what works at present and what at a distance. Then must Weston be the tormentor, and chase him with poison after poison, poison in salt-meats, poison in sweet-meats, poison in medicines and vomits, until at last his body was almost come by use of poisons to the state of Mithridates' body by the use of treacles and preservatives, that the force of the poisons was blunted upon him.

Of course these were the facts, but was Lord Somerset responsible? At the end of the trial he was found guilty and sentenced to death, but had he done it? It is difficult to challenge such a verdict, but it seems to me that Somerset was innocent. Overbury was Lady Somerset's enemy, but he was her husband's friend. There really does not seem to me to be sufficient motive. And with a shade more hesitation, I would suggest that Northampton, too, was innocent. Was Overbury of sufficient importance to that great peer that he should run the risk of murdering him? There is nothing very novel in my reading for it has the support of S. R. Gardiner.[1]

The situation of Lady Somerset was very different. She was a rich woman imbued with a profound belief in witchcraft. She was very simple to deceive; she had no one to talk to but her "sweet Turner". One of the curious elements in the case are the many poisons used without effect. There seems to me only one explanation. The chief purpose of her doctors and their associates was to bleed her for money. Perhaps she hardly knew the difference between magic and poison. In the case of the poisoners who were hanged the going had never been so good for them until they came to their last case. Somerset was taken back to the Tower; he and his wife were now together.

They stayed in the Tower for just over three years. In 1621 they were released with the choice of residing at either Rotherfield Greys or Caversham, Lord Wallingford's houses, and to being confined to a circuit of three miles about these places. Both of them lived on together for many years. Carr never returned to his native Scotland.[2]

The rise of Sir George Villiers was relatively gradual. Carr had been

[1] Cf. S. R. Gardiner, *History of England* (1864–6), II, 331–63.
[2] An impression of Somerset's tastes is given in the five volumes of *Civitates Orbis Terrarum* by Georg Braun published at Cologne between 1572 and 1618, the engravings being by Fr

raised by the king's own hand and he had had early at his side Sir Thomas Overbury. Villiers, on the other hand, was manoeuvred into position and he early earned the enmity of the new Prince of Wales. Many others besides his own supporters, Pembroke and the archbishop, looked on him favourably and thought that they might rise through him, and notably Sir Francis Bacon. There was also the fact that the queen supported him. In those early days before he came to his full power he seemed to have friends everywhere. He was in his youth so fresh and courteous and so *serviable*. In August 1616 he became Viscount Villiers, a minor rank for one who would become in time so great a favourite.

He was at this time twenty-four years of age, the portionless younger son of a Leicestershire knight now dead. Sir George Villiers the father, a substantial squire, had lived at the manor house of Brooksby near the turnpike road, nine miles from Leicester and six from Melton Mowbray. He had held the four manors of Brooksby, Howby, Goadby and Marwood, all in his native county and this compact property had passed to his eldest son. His widow, who would be important in the king's life, had the dower house of Goadby. She had been his second wife and there were many children from both beds. A will proved in 1559 gives the property of the Villiers of Brooksby at that date as rather more than three thousand five hundred acres. They had held for some generations the presentation to the advowsons of the churches of Brooksby and Howby; they were definitely Anglican and without any trace of recusancy in their male line.

The character of Villiers's training, a superficial knowledge of France based on a very ordinary English grounding, made him an excellent subject for the exercise of the king's wisdom. His rise was eminently tranquil; there was nothing that could not be assessed about him. On January 5, 1617, the new favourite was created earl of Buckingham; he was soon made lord lieutenant of that county. He had already received the Garter and the mastership of the horse; he was chief justice in Eyre north of Trent. From now on he would remain as long as the reign lasted the king's chief subject. With Buckingham now moving into his great position, it is time to examine what had been the king's relations with his second parliament.

Hogenberg and Simon van der Noevel. These contain full page views of Paris, Lyons, Cambrai, Hesdin, Béthune, St Omer, Calais and Rouen and other French cities. There is a double half-page map of Aden and one-third-half-page views of Mombasa, Quilon and Cefalu. The copy in the Newbattle Library is inscribed: "This booke the Earle of Somerset sent to the E. of Lothian, March 1636".

Chapter 14

THE SECOND PARLIAMENT

THE king had from time to time made his views known to parliament. The members of the house had grown accustomed to this. It is worth quoting his two brief comments on the common law and on the papists. In regard to the first matter he spoke as follows. "The other branch is anent the Common Law, which some had a conceit I disliked and (in respect that I was born where another form of law was established) that I would have wished the Civil Law to have been put in place of the Common Law for government of this people here."[1] As to the papists he gave this opinion. "As I have said in Parliament House I can love the person of a Papist being otherwise a good man and honestly bred, never having known any other religion; but the person of an Apostate Papist I hate."[2] The first section of this judgment gives the reason for his reaction to a letter sent him by the duke of Bavaria a little later in the reign. The duke wrote[3] from Munich in favour of George Talbot, a delicate elderly man who later succeeded as twelfth earl of Shrewsbury. He asked leave for him to return to England after having passed many years at the court of Bavaria. He explained that his health was in great need of recourse to medicinal waters. After his cure he had no desire save to devote himself to private studies. The duke begged that he might also have the free exercise of his religion in which he had been brought up since boyhood. This was an instance of the royal kindness; George Talbot had never known the Truth, as the king saw it. It is always interesting to note the strength of King James's own convictions.

Two other speeches had set out the king's ideas. The second was more sympathetic to the notions of his English subjects. The necessary quotations are perhaps rather lengthy; but they give a good reflection of King James's mind.

The state of Monarchy [he begins] is the supreme thing upon Earth, for Kings are not only God's Lieutenants upon Earth and sit upon God's throne,

---

[1] Delivered at Whitehall on March 27, 1610, printed in J. R. Tanner, *Constitutional Documents of the Reign of James I.*   [2] *Ibid.*, 22.
[3] Letter dated June 1618, Cal. Talbot MSS, Var. Coll., II, 312.

but by God himself they are called gods. There be three principal similitudes that illustrate the state of Monarchy, one is taken out of the Word of God and the others out of the grounds of policy and philosophy. In the Scripture Kings are called gods and so their power after a certain relation compares to the Divine power. Kings are also compared to the fathers of families for a King is truly *parens patriae*, the politic father of his people. And lastly, Kings are compared to the head of this microcosm of the body of man.[1]

In the second passage the emphasis is different.

The higher we are placed [he goes on] the greater shall our fall be *ut casus sicut dolor*: the taller the trees be, the more in danger of the wind; and the tempest bears sorest upon the highest mountains. Therefore Kings, that are not tyrants or perjured, will be glad to bind themselves within the limits of this law; and they that persuade them to the contrary are vipers and pests, both against them and the Commonwealth. For it is a great difference between a King's government in a settled State and what Kings in their original power might do in *individuo vago*.[2]

The first parliament of the reign had had an unsatisfactory ending, but it had lasted altogether for six years. In the course of time the judges had shown themselves as sympathetic to the king's claims and as early as 1606 had declared in favour of the legality of import duties or impositions levied by the crown. From the period of this decision there developed the project of the Great Contract. This was steered forward in Lord Salisbury's time; but it ultimately failed because while the king agreed to forgo the setting up of further duties, he would not recall those which he had already brought into play. The failure of the Great Contract was the occasion first of the adjournment of parliament in November 1610 and then of its dissolution in the following February.

This was followed by various efforts to raise funds by extra-parliamentary methods. The creation of the order of baronets in 1611 was a case in point. The next change was occasioned by Lord Salisbury's death. Sir Francis Bacon, at that time attorney general, approached the king with a private memorandum relating to the summoning of a parliament. It was his hope that the king would make him his manager in the house and the proposals contained two practical suggestions. These ran as follows.

12. What persons in particular in respect of their gravity, discretion,

---

[1] Printed in Tanner, *Constitutional Documents of James I*, 15.
[2] Printed in *ibid.*, 17.

temper and ability to persuade are fit to be brought in to be of the House, *bonis artibus*, without labouring or packing.

What persons in particular, as violent and turbulent, are fit to be kept back from being of this House, *bonis artibus*, without labouring or packing.

13. What use may be made of the boroughs of the Cinque Ports and of the Duchy of Lancaster and other boroughs at the devotion of the King's Counsellors for the placing persons well-affected and discreet.[1]

He also suggested that more privy councillors should find seats in the House of Commons.

The king accepted much of this advice, but did not appoint Bacon as manager. A rather unusual House of Commons was elected; but it is difficult to measure the extent of the king's responsibility. Two hundred and eighty-one members were elected for the first time on this occasion. It was the royal objective to obtain a large grant of supply. Four privy councillors took their seats including Sir Thomas Lake and Sir Ralph Winwood, the two secretaries of state. The government lawyers were there in force: Sir Francis Bacon, attorney general, Sir Henry Yelverton, solicitor general, Sir Robert Hitcham, attorney general to Queen Anne, and Sir James Ley, attorney to the court of Wards. There were eighteen holders of official posts about the court. These were on the whole small fry, the master of the Jewel House and the treasurers and secretaries to the two princes.

The new members included several men who would come into notice later in the reign, Sir Walter Cope, master of the Wards, Sir Thomas Monson, Sir Arthur Ingram and Giles Mompesson. One great man sat for the first time, Lionel Cranfield. He had been brought in for Hythe, one of the Cinque ports. Among the new members was Thomas Fanshawe, surveyor general and auditor of the duchy of Lancaster, who had looked after the filling of the many duchy seats. It is to be noted that only a proportion of these office-holders had been proposed by the court for candidature. Thus Richard Wynne, the heir of the great Gwydir family, had come in naturally as a representative for Carnarvonshire, which was almost an hereditary seat. The fact that the young man held the small post of groom of the chamber to Prince Charles was quite irrelevant.

Crown influence appeared in many Cornish boroughs and was reflected in the election of the Speaker, Sir Randolph Crewe, for Saltash. Sir Henry Vane the elder, then a very young man, was brought in for

[1] James Spedding, *The Letters and Life of Francis Bacon*, IV, 366–8.

Lostwithiel. There were also the duchy of Cornwall seats. The total number of lawyers elected to this parliament was forty-eight.

The influence of peers was not in the outcome of much importance. Two eldest sons had seats, the future earls of Warwick and Leicester, and Sir Henry Rich, who had a career in the next reign as earl of Holland. The number of seats actually controlled by the peerage was at this time small. Northampton had, curiously enough, the nomination for the tiny borough of Bishop's Castle in the Welsh marches. Lord Pembroke had great influence upon the three seats adjacent to his home, Wilton, Salisbury and Old Sarum. Lord Knollys controlled Abingdon and Wallingford and Reading; he was high steward of the last-named town. At Dorchester the duke of Lennox was high steward and at St Albans, Lord Chancellor Ellesmere. The almost empty borough of Corfe Castle in east Dorset was under the control of Lady Hatton. The influence of the great proprietor was now fading; it had depended upon his groups of client gentry. As an example the methods by which Lord Huntingdon had obtained seats for his brothers in the previous reign[1] were now outdated.

It is noticeable that a few constituencies, usually on account of their special seafaring or mercantile interests, insisted on electing a local resident. This was evident at Dartmouth and Totnes and King's Lynn. In other respects the control of constituencies was still imperfect.[2]

The total number of merchants in the house at this parliament was forty-two. But they were in no sense a group and there was not yet a vestige of the great lobbies, like that connected with the West Indian sugar trade, which grew up in the following century. Although Puritanism had its importance, it was not the common element of the opposition which it became in the succeeding generation. Further it can hardly be said that there was yet present a consistent opposition. Many of the lawyers had a line which varied upon occasion, and both the opposition leaders in this parliament, Sir Edwyn Sandys and Sir Dudley Digges, became later reconciled to the crown.

It is by no means clear that this parliament could have been divided into parties as we understand that term. The English squirearchy, on which the eighteenth-century House of Commons would be largely based, lay in the future. At this earlier time a House of Commons

[1] Cf. J. E. Neale, *The Elizabethan House of Commons* (1949), 171–3.
[2] As an example of this situation a little later, Sir Bevil Grenville wrote before the Long Parliament elections, "A town or two (in Cornwall) will choose me if I will serve myself, but will not give me leave to put in another", M. Coats, *Cornwall in the Civil War*, 25.

opinion did not exist. Rather was there present the aggregation of the opinions of the official world county by county. The body of the gentry in each county held together, those few who held the country seats, the medium number who had been sheriffs, the many who were in the commission of the peace. I am not speaking here of the Puritan minority. The climate of opinion was that of the great mass of the gentry who very rarely or never came to London.

There are two points to be made about Bacon's proposals. Whatever he might say about the necessity for choice, it did not seem that the court would have the power to deny a borough seat to a man of standing merely because he might be likely to express disagreeable opinions. Further, it was evident that however official influence was used, it could only bring into the house a relatively small proportion of the total membership.

Among the members there was a great variety in their knowledge of national affairs. The diarist Walter Yonge of Colyton is a case in point. He was the son and heir of a wealthy merchant of Lyme Regis and sat for Honiton. He was a Puritan mainly interested in local matters; still he had been at Magdalen and the Middle Temple.[1] He noted a report that papists should have a toleration here in England and that Protestant ministers should be permitted to preach only once a sabbath.[2] He gave a list of Catholics containing the names of the earl of Shaftesbury (who did not exist) and Lady Suffolk.[3] He repeated a story that Lord Bristol had poisoned himself and that all his hair and nails had fallen off.[4] In some ways this is not really a fair example.

The merchants were by no means a united body; there were jealousies against the city of London in the country towns. Outside the capital it was only in Bristol that a body of merchants existed who could exercise a certain pressure. Besides, at this time the great London merchants preferred to approach the court directly or through some privy councillor. The House of Commons was not an arena in which they had yet sought to exercise their influence.

In this session the rate of attendance at the House of Lords could not be considered high. The bishops were usually regarded as willing to

---

[1] Cf. an entry under July 12, 1622. "There was a great fish came ashore at Seaton, which was twenty three feet and three inches in length. His fins were like the leather which keeps the dirt from a coach wheel; his skin very smooth as an eel, but exceeding black; his teeth were big, round and sharp; his flesh was very white and felt like fat of pork", G. Roberts, ed., *Diary of Walter Yonge* (Camden Society, 1843), 63.

[2] Entry under August 19, 1622, *ibid.*, 63.   [3] Note under 1620, *ibid.*, 117.

[4] Entry under January 1627, *ibid.*, 99.

support the crown, but six of them never took their seats in the months that this parliament lasted. It is worth noting that these six bishops were all Elizabethan appointments.[1] During the ten years of his reign none of them had benefited from the king's promotions. Bishop Cotton of Salisbury was in weak health and died in the next year, but it seems reasonable to suggest that the other six saw no reason to come to London to support their sovereign's interests.

Twenty-seven of the lay peers were also absent.[2] These included the marquis of Winchester, who was a cipher and perhaps an invalid, and the earl of Arundel on a tour abroad. Among the other absentees were the earls of Oxford, who was then in Holland, Kent, an old and dying man, Lincoln, Bath and Bedford. It does not seem that any political approach can be revealed by this list. At that date Catholic peers could still take their seats; from this group Lords Vaux and Stourton were both away. The earl of Southampton could be regarded as the leader of the opposition. It is worth pausing upon this figure.

Henry Wriothesley, third earl of Southampton, stood at a certain distance from his sovereign throughout the reign. He had been one of Essex's chief supporters and so had forfeited the earl of Salisbury's confidence. He was still in prison at the king's accession and was immediately released and restored in blood; he received the captaincy of the Isle of Wight and the joint lord lieutenancy of Hampshire. He was also given the ribbon of the Garter. At this time he satisfied the king by becoming a communicating and ardent member of the Church of England in its Protestant expression. Until the old queen died, he had been nominally a Catholic, but real practising Catholicism was impracticable for so close a courtier. His tone of mind was Elizabethan and he had the personal vanity of that age. As many as eight different portraits of him still survive. Attention has been cast on him as Shakespeare's patron.

King James was attracted by the hunting in the New Forest and was accustomed to stay with him at Beaulieu.[3] But it seems that they were never intimate. Southampton was already thirty-nine when Salisbury died. He had strong independent interests in the colonisation of Virginia and in aggressive Protestant foreign policy upon the continent.

---

[1] The bishops of Carlisle, Hereford, Norwich and Salisbury and the holders of the Welsh sees of Bangor and St Davids.

[2] These figures and those throughout this chapter are taken from the careful study, by Thomas L. Moir, *The Addled Parliament of 1614* (1958).

[3] "The King was so pleased with his hunting at Beaulieu and he seems to have a purpose to visit it often", Cal. Salisbury MSS, XVIII, 270.

One of his closest intimates was Sir Edwyn Sandys. With the exception of a cousinship with the earl of Sussex, he had no blood relationship with the older peerage; his relations were the Catholics, Montagu and Arundell of Wardour.[1]

The king asked him to bring to England squirrels from Virginia.[2] He was markedly independent under Buckingham. The king knew that he could not be disloyal and he had a great practice of the use of courts. It seems that he distrusted the royal judgment and had no respect for the king's mind.[3]

The second parliament of the reign opened at eleven in the morning of Tuesday April 5, 1614. The king had gone from Whitehall to West-minster Abbey and there the procession formed. He rode the short distance on a fine horse, wearing his crown through the spring weather. In the House of Lords a silk curtain had been hung across a small recess in which sat the Spanish ambassador and his chosen guests the ambassador from Denmark and the envoy from the court of the archdukes.

The king spoke with that hyperbole which must have sounded so strange to his English subjects and, to the Puritans, repellent. He explained that those who looked on him with unpolluted eyes might see that his integrity resembled the whiteness of his robe, his purity the gold in his crown, his firmness and clearness the precious stones he wore, and his affection the redness of his heart. After this beginning the king's speech was divided into three parts, the first being *Bona animi*, the hope of religion. He made the rather unexpected statement that no religion ever gained by persecuting its enemies. *Bona corporis* included the matter of the security of the dynasty and *bona fortunae* dealt with his great need of money. He ended by saying that he hoped for a Parliament of Love.

As usual there was a storm at the opening of the session. Sir Thomas Parry of Hampstead Marshall, a former ambassador to France, sat as a county representative for Berkshire. The members moved against him on the charge that he had interfered in the Stockbridge election. He was suspended from the chancellorship of the duchy of Lancaster and from the privy council; he was also expelled from the house.

On May 4 the king addressed the commons in defence of his right to levy impositions. He regarded such a right as a great flower of his pre-

---

[1] Cf. Chart pedigree 11, indicating this relationship.
[2] Cal. S. P. Colonial, 1577–1660, p. 8.
[3] Cf. an excellent study by Dr A. L. Rowse, *Shakespeare's Southampton*.

rogative, the judges had assured him of their legality. Thomas Wentworth, recorder of Oxford and member for that city, had already vexed the king by his sharp speeches. On this occasion he declared that impositions were sinful and that they called down the Divine wrath on those who levied them. For this sin the Spaniards had been punished by the loss of the Low Countries and Henry IV of France had died like a calf under the butcher's knife. He cited from the Geneva version Daniel xi, 20. "Then shall stand up in his place in the glorie of the kingdom, one that shall raise taxes, but after fewe dayes he shall be destroyed, neither in wrath nor in battell. And in his place shall stand up a vile person, to whom they shall not give the honour of the kingdome: but hee shall come in peaceably, and obtain the kingdom by flatterie." These words had an effect on his sovereign and as soon as the session ended he was cast into prison.

An attack with a better intellectual foundation was made by Sir Edwyn Sandys, but the reports of his speech are now fragmentary.[1] Sir Henry Wotton and Sir Ralph Winwood supported the right to levy impositions, which they stated to be among the rights of hereditary but not elective monarchies. Sir Dudley Digges speaking for the opposition rested the claim of the House of Commons in this matter on an ancestral right: *Nolumus leges Angliae mutare*.[2]

It was at this point that the House of Commons sent up a message to the lords asking them to confer about this question. After some consideration the House of Lords refused to meet the commons about this matter. This decision was carried by a majority of thirty-nine to thirty. Although the king would desire a refusal of the request made by the House of Commons, one should not lay too much stress upon this voting. The majority included sixteen bishops and the only prelate who voted for a conference with the lower house was Archbishop Mathew of York, who was an old-fashioned Elizabethan.

We now come to the intervention of Bishop Neile, the step which led to that train of events which resulted in the ending of this short parliament. This deserves a fresh examination. It is one of those well-known episodes in the history of the kings and queens of England which needs a new evaluation. Unless in fact one can throw some fresh light upon the scene it hardly seems worth recounting the shop-soiled story of the bishop of Lincoln.

---

[1] The fragments are reported in *Commons Journals*, I, 493.
[2] 'We are unwilling to change the laws of England.'

Richard Neile was at this time fifty-two years of age and is interesting as one of the king's episcopal supporters, who did not receive his friendship. He came from the established middle class, the son of a tallow chandler and educated at Westminster. Thereafter he was sent by that rather Puritan lady the second wife of Lord Burghley to St John's College, Cambridge; he became a *protégé* of her great family. It seems reasonable to suggest that if the earl of Salisbury had been still alive he would not have made his one mistake.

As the years went on he had developed High Church views. He was Laud's consistent patron and finally his loyal supporter, when they held side by side the sees of York and Canterbury. In an intermediate stage when he had Durham House in the Strand, he made this the headquarters of bishops Laud and Buckeridge when they came to London. None of these prelates was in close touch with King James, although they all held high doctrinal judgments about the royal prerogative. He was separated from them by the Catholic character of their sacramental views. Unlike Laud, Neile was warm towards all clergymen. It is probably true to say that the ecclesiastical mind did not appeal to the old sovereign.

This being said, it is worth giving the *Noli me tangere* speech by which he warned the commons not to touch the royal prerogative in a little detail.

My Lords [said Bishop Neile] I thinke it a dangerous thing for us to conferre with them about this point of impositions. For it is a *Noli me tangere*, and none that have taken either the Oath of Supremacy or Allegiance may doe it with a good conscience, for in the Oath of Allegiance we are sworne to maintayne the privileges of the Crown, and at this conference we shall not conferre about a flower, but strike at the roote of the Imperial Crown, and therefore in my opinion it is neither fitte to conferre with them, nor give them a meeting.[1]

It seems to me that these were the most dangerous words used in the reign by any English politician. They make one feel that Laud, whose thought they reflect, was an originator of the coming conflict; they suggest that explosive situation which was one of the causes of the Civil War.

On the next day the House of Commons moved to the attack. They first decided to complain to the king about the words used of

[1] Cal. Hastings MSS, IV, 249.

them, but on consideration realised the damage that this course of action might do to their own cause; their own freedom of speech might be brought into question. In consequence they decided to bring their complaints against the House of Lords. Meanwhile they determined to attend to no other business until they had received some satisfaction. The king then intervened, writing to the commons to make it clear that it did not belong to them to call or to dissolve assemblies.

The lords sent back a temporising answer stating that the action against the bishop was grounded simply upon common fame. The complainants had not been present when the speech was made. The bishop of Lincoln expressed his regret with tears and declared that he had never meant to speak evil of the House of Commons. The lower house remained unsatisfied. On June 3 the king sent them a message that unless they proceeded to treat the question of supply he would dissolve parliament.

There was a further disturbance and Christopher Neville,[1] a former Catholic and one of the few members who had himself conformed to the Established Church, made an attack upon the courtiers as "spaniels to the King and wolves to the people". On June 7 parliament was dissolved. Four members, including Wentworth and Neville, were brought before the council, the king watching over the proceedings sitting concealed behind some hangings. All four were sent to the Tower. The house had sat for just over two months. No single bill received the royal assent.

[1] He was a brother to Lord Abergavenny.

Chapter 15

COURT MASQUES AND PLAYS

In 1620 during one of his accustomed visits to Wilton, King James went to inspect the ancient ruins of Stonehenge, riding northward through that rolling downland country which is so curiously known as Salisbury Plain. On his return with the earl of Pembroke to Wilton he instructed Inigo Jones, then at the height of his celebrity, who had since boyhood been a *protégé* of that great house, to investigate the ruins' history. The notes printed after his death set out his firm conclusions.[1] He held that Stonehenge was a Roman temple, which was dedicated to Coelus and had been founded either under the governorship of Agricola or a little later. He observed in the monument a mixture of proportions proper to Corinthian and Tuscan work, together with the plainness and solidity of the latter order.

In those days there was little consideration of archaeology, so that even Stonehenge was seen within the cocoon of the Roman past. There was an interesting contrast between the continental influences which played upon the successive courts around King James. In Scotland there was the long contact with France, the fruit of the "auld alliance". French was the only foreign language known to an influential group among the courtiers. The classics of the time, Machiavelli as an example, had come through France. A French edition of *The Prince* had been dedicated to the duke of Châtelhèrault. In England, from back in Elizabethan times, the foreign drift had come from Italy. This did not affect at all the English nation; it was the intermingling of two court cultures. Various matters had assisted in this development, the foreign travel of the nobility and greater gentry which had now begun and the establishment of permanent legations at each end of the Lombard plain at Venice and at Turin, which was now the duke of Savoy's capital. The permanent presence of Savoyard and Venetian ambassadors in London was an inevitable consequence. It was a result of these contacts that the masque in its Italian form became the staple of the royal en-

[1] Cf. Notes printed by John Webb in 1655 in *The most notable Antiquity of Great Britain, vulgarly called Stonehenge, on Salisbury Plaine.*

tertainment throughout the reign. It is worth examining in some detail the background from which it came.

Four sovereign duchies lay across the Lombard plain. Beginning at Piacenza in the territory of Parma, some fifty miles eastward from the Savoyard frontier, they spread out across the low rich lands along the Po until that river emptied into the Adriatic in those wide coastal marshes lying to the north-east of Ferrara. It was in the chief towns of the duchies and, perhaps above all, in the little foundered capitals like Sabbioneta, Guastalla and Mirandola in the Emilian plain that those settings for the masque were to be found, where the traffic drifted to and fro between Savoy and Venice, through Mantua and Padua. The high country which ran southwards to the summit of the Apennines in both the duchies of Modena and Parma lay quite aloof from these urban concerns.

All of these states were past their prime: their period of influence had belonged to the last years of the fifteenth century when the Este and Gonzaga chiefs had been *condottiere* leaders. They were now yielding to that fatigue which in the seventeenth century was invading Italy. They were all more or less bound, with certain shiftings of allegiance, to the Spanish power, which was now somnolent. Still, as far as entertainment was concerned the Spanish world, whether in Milan or in the south in Naples, was quite separate. It was not for any form of entertainment that King James valued the count of Gondomar. Akin to the four duchies and like them declining in an economic sense, but not so rapidly, were the mainland cities which were held in fee by the Venetian Most Serene Republic, Vicenza and Padua.

Parma, the westernmost of these states, had the least contact with England. The reigning duke, Ranuccio I, was the son of that Alexander of Parma who, when he was viceroy of the Spanish Netherlands, had corresponded with King James in Scotland. The close contact with Spain and with the *Milanese* still continued. The great ducal Palazzo della Pilotta was now in process of construction and the large Teatro Farnese was built in wood on the upper floor in 1618.

The neighbouring dukedom, that of Modena, was in a state of reorientation. The great days of the house of Este had ended with the death of the last duke of Ferrara in 1597. The papal forces, then holding the Romagna, had now occupied the duchy. Cesare d'Este, who was of illegitimate descent, had held the western territories of Reggio and Modena, which stood like Parma across the Via Emilia. This town had not previously been a capital and the vast ducal palace, one of the largest in Italy, was not yet begun in King James's reign. Modena was in poor shape during these years: it was the only Lombard capital which Lord Arundel does not seem to have visited. Both Parma and Modena would be formed in time to the dulled likeness of baroque Italy.

On the other hand these years saw the last period of glory of the court of Mantua. This little city, which the spirit of the baroque never touched, lay on the western edges of the Paduan plain half-surrounded by three freshwater lakes through which the Mincio ran. It had the evanescent perfect form of an old Renaissance principality. The Gonzaga dukedom had branched out into cadet lines who held Guastalla and Sabbioneta. They were all of them essentially a town nobility. At Sabbioneta, which was even then after the extravagances of Vespasian Gonzaga falling into ruin, there was a palace, an academy, a court library and a court theatre.

In Mantua the old palace stood, surrounded on three sides by houses with the church of Santa Barbara at its side. Flat roads ran out into the countryside westwards to Cremona and eastwards to Venetian territory. A canal wound slowly through the town joining the lakes; out in the fields there lay the summer villa.

Pageants had been traditional in the Gonzaga capital and there is a detailed account in the *Dialogi* of Leone di Somi of the settings arranged to celebrate the marriage of the duke of Mantua with the archduchess Eleanor in 1561. The principal constructions were of lath and plaster and set within the palace. These were, we are told, "enriched with so many reliefs, embellished by such admirable architecture (and) with such a variety of lovely inventions".[1] It was at this court that a pastoral banquet was added after a drama had been presented. For this purpose the duke had

built in a great hall two orders of square rustic columns, evenly spaced and bearing vaulted arches. Within the columns (which were hollow) there had been concealed many lamps, which, shining forth from shades made of coloured glass and skilfully placed, illuminated the whole room; still greater splendour was provided by several great globes filled with water, set in the middle of each archway. Above these, lamps had been placed in such number that each arch seemed lit up by a blazing sun. Between the two loggias was a space of about ten cubits; it was entirely roofed with a blue sky set with stars and having a magnificent great moon in the middle. The rays from this

[1] Translations given in Allardyce Nicoll, *The Development of the Theatre* (1927).

moon fell on a deliciously set table which stretched the whole length of the open space, and on which was spread a rich supper of diverse fruits – mostly artificial sugar fruits or else real fruits preserved in sugar.[1]

Later in 1608 there were various *intermezzi* and a performance of Guarini's *L'Idropica* to celebrate the marriage of Duke Francis IV. It is worth noting that the masques in England frequently centred round the marriages at court.

In Mantua many citizens were brought in to act as stage hands and an impression of the physical toil involved is given by Federico Zuccaro, who was travelling through Lombardy on this occasion.

Not less pleasure did I get [he explains] from seeing the huge engines, the windlasses, the stout cables, the ropes, and the cords by which the machines are manipulated; and the enormous number of men necessary for working them . . . more than three hundred of these stage hands are employed. One spark from a lamp, be it remembered, might bring all to ruin. Truly it was extraordinary that no disaster occurred, even although care was taken to provide huge jars, vessels, tubs, and pails of water ready for any emergency.[2]

The glass workers of Venice were employed in the construction of globes which were filled with coloured liquid and illuminated from behind by candle light. Just forty miles across the level plain lay Palladio's city of Vicenza. The Teatro Olimpico had been that master's last great work, completed in 1583. It was the first of the modern covered theatres.

How these Italian elements were brought to the English stage is not yet clear. While Inigo Jones's second visit to Italy can be dated quite elaborately, there is very little information as to his first. This is common form in the early lives of artists and of architects. In the case in question we depend to a great extent on an eighteenth-century brief biography[3] which states that he travelled in Lombardy and Venice at Lord Pembroke's expense. He was back in England from his first journey before Twelfth Night 1605, when the *Masque of Blackness* was presented.

One sharp distinction separated the English masques from those produced before Italian courts. Following a French example the leading personalities of the court took part in them by invitation. In consequence the words, which were by Ben Jonson, had less importance;

---

[1] Leone di Somi, *Dialogi*.   [2] Federico Zuccaro, *Il Passagio per Italia* (Bologna, 1608).
[3] Cf. the *Life*, printed as a preface to the 1725 edition of *Stonehenge Restored*.

attention was concentrated on the dresses of the ladies and on the ingenious contrivance of the scenes and settings. There was a background of
processions and of dancing. It was the presentation of the masque
which fell to Inigo Jones's responsibility. There was a masque each
year and sometimes two, from the time of the *Masque of Blackness* until
the end of the reign. The banqueting house at Whitehall was the favourite setting. It is worth giving two examples of the active participa-
tion of the court. In the *Masque of Hymen* in 1606 there emerged out of a
microcosm or orb eight men, namely, Lord Willoughby, Lord Howard
de Walden, Sir James Hay, the earl of Montgomery, Sir Thomas
Howard, Sir Thomas Somerset, the earl of Arundel and Sir John Ashley, in that order.[1] In 1609 the *Masque of Queens* was offered representing the queens of Caria and Palmyra. Queen Anne herself took part
supported by six countesses and five other ladies of her court.

The colours were composed most carefully. Gold was used to signify
both wealth and perfection, "while in the blue mantle was enshrined
the idea that dreams came in the serenity of the night".[2] Certain changes came about in English practice. Thus Francis Bacon suggests that
the colours which "shew best by candle light are white, carnation and a
kinde of sea-water greene, and that spangles as they are of no great cost,
so they are of most glory".[3] The robes worn by Queen Anne naturally
depended on her own preference. "The collors," wrote Inigo Jones on
one occasion, "are att her majesty's choice, but my opinion is that sever-
all fresh greenes mixt with gold and silver will bee most propper."[4]
Behind the scenes a crew of a hundred skilled men were labouring.

The king was on his own high seat surrounded at a lower level by
chairs for the ambassadors. There was a difference between these
masques and the entertainments which had marked his journey south.
The latter had been concerned, as had those shown before Elizabeth,
with more direct praise for the reigning sovereign.

As far as plays were concerned, the coming in of the new king made
little difference. Shakespeare, who had for so long worked for the
Elizabethan stage, had his accustomed share of royal favour. Both
Othello and *King Lear* were played at Whitehall before the king and
Macbeth was meant to signalise the opening of a Scottish reign. One
wonders how far the playwright captured the king's attention with

---

[1] John Nichols, *The Progresses . . . of King James*, etc. (4 vols., 1828), III, 5.
[2] Allardyce Nicoll, *Stuart Masques and the Renaissance Stage*, 160.
[3] Edward Arber, ed., *A Harmony of the Essays* (1871), 539.   [4] *Designs*, No. 97.

these presentations of barbarian sovereigns. The whole Shakespearean ethos seems to me to be essentially Elizabethan.

Two new plays, both produced in the middle period of King James's reign, are to my mind characteristic of the spirit of the epoch. They were both by John Webster and the first, and much the less significant, *The White Devil*, was printed in 1612 and acted by the Queen's Servants. It was based on a modern story, the account of the duke of Bracciano and his two wives. Paolo-Giordano Orsini had died as recently as 1585 and his first duchess was the aunt of the queen of France and of those princesses of Tuscany who had been considered as brides for the king of Scotland in James's youth. It was, however, the second duchess, "the famous Venetian courtizan", who was the White Devil. The cardinal of Montalto, later Pope Sixtus V, appeared in the action, but under the name of Monticelso. The central scene is the trial of the second wife Vittoria Corombona (*vere* Accoramboni) in a hall in Monticelso's mansion and in the presence of six lieger ambassadors. In Victorian times the light-hearted approach to the White Devil herself was reprobated. A few lines from the trial scene will indicate the general spirit of the work. They are spoken by Vittoria Accoramboni:

> "Condemn you me for that the duke did love me.
> So may you blame some fair and crystal river
> For that some melancholic distracted man
> Hath drowned himself in't. . . .
>
> Sum up my faults, I pray, and you shall find,
> That beauty, and gay clothes, a merry heart,
> And a good stomach to a feast, are all,
> All the poor crimes that you can charge me with."[1]

This was a little carefree, but so was King James's court.

The Duchess of Malfi was for the most part written in 1613 and its first performance must have taken place before December 16, 1614, the day on which William Ostler, who first acted the part of Antonio, died. When *The Duchess of Malfi* was published in 1623, the title page announced that it had been "presented privately at the Blackfriars, and publicly at the Globe, by the King's Majesty's servants".[2] This change from the Queen's Men to the King's represented a real gain in prestige for the playwright.

The sources for *The Duchess of Malfi* belong to an earlier period than

---

[1] John Webster, *The White Devil*, act iii, scene i.
[2] Cf. Webster, *The Duchess of Malfi*, ed. John Russell Brown (1964), Introduction, xviii-xx.

those of *The White Devil*. The former came directly from William Painter's *Palace of Pleasure*, which was almost a translation of a section of the second volume of Belleforest's *Histoires Tragiques*. This was in turn a very greatly expanded account of the story of the Duchess of Malfi in the twenty-sixth *novella* by Matteo Bandella. *Romeo and Juliet* is traced to another *novella* in this same source.

The actual original of the whole tragedy is found described in Notar' Giacomo's *Chronica di Napoli*, which was only printed two centuries later. It is worth quoting this commentary to show how very little Webster departed from this text.

It was common talk throughout the city of Naples that the illustrious Signora Joanna of Aragon, daughter of the late illustrious Don Enrico of Aragon and sister of the Most Reverend Monsignor the Cardinal of Aragon, having given out that she wished to make a pilgrimage to Santa Maria di Loreto, had gone thither with a retinue of many carriages and thence (from Loreto) departed with Antonio da Bologna, son of Messer Antonio da Bologna, and (had) gone with the aforesaid, saying that he was her husband to Ragusa, leaving behind her own male child of ten, who was Duke of Amalfi.[1]

From this it will be seen that one of the few new characters introduced in Webster's play is the duchess's brother Ferdinand, Duke of Calabria. It is stated by Notar' Giacomo that the duchess disappeared. In actual fact her father, the marquis of Gerace, was a natural son of the king of Naples. In Webster's play the duchess's descent is fully legitimate and the action turns on her sin against the glory of the house of Aragon.

Still an attempt to trace the origins of the story should not conceal from us the essentially Jacobean character of this careful study. The duchess of Malfi is the only one of Webster's figures who really comes to life. We are made to see her ruling in her palace at Amalfi, with its presence chamber, its apartments and courts and galleries, the hanging arras behind which the maid conceals herself, the courtyard where the carriages set out to take the guests down through the narrow streets to the Tyrrhenian sea. It is all imagined. There was no palace and no sovereign duchy. But Webster, of whom we know so little, appears not to have been a traveller. It was thus natural to envisage Malfi and also Bracciano as independent dukedoms such as Queen Anne's cousins held in Germany.

The character of the duchess was represented according to the custom of the time by a boy actor. The duke of Calabria and the cardinal

[1] On p. 331 of the ed. printed in 1845. Cf. *The Duchess of Malfi* (ed. F. L. Lucas, 1938).

are anxious for the honour of their house. The duchess is killed because since her husband's death she has borne children, the fruit of her union with the great master of her household. From the palace one looked down on the wide forests and green fields of the duchy, another example of a Germanic setting. Still, the action in no way concerns the people. The players are all members of the court, except for those who appear towards the end in the masque of madmen. The duchess makes her one visit to Loreto, but nearly all the words that are quoted here were spoken in her palace at Malfi, where she reigned and died.

A brief *catena* of quotations follows, although some are almost too well known for repetition. The lines spoken in the audience in the presence chamber suggests the duchesss of Malfi's lack of freedom beneath her brother's yoke.

> "This is flesh and blood, sir;
> 'Tis not the figure cut in alabaster
> Kneels at my husband's tomb."[1]

Later her brothers come to offer her a marriage with "the great Count Malateste". At this the duchess speaks.

> "A count, he's a mere stick of sugar-candy."[2]

And then there comes the celebrated passage.

> "Why should only I
> Of all the other princes of the world
> Be cas'd up, like a holy relic? I have youth
> And a little beauty."[3]

As the situation grew more difficult,

> "Methought I wore my coronet of state,
> And on a sudden all the diamonds
> Were chang'd to pearls."[4]

And then the rejection of the brothers' offer,

> "Their league is like that of some politic kings,
> Only to make themselves of strength and power
> To be our after-ruin: tell them so."[5]

The situation then develops quickly.

> "I will have none:
> Pray thee, why dost thou wrap thy poison'd pills
> in gold and sugar?"

[1] *The Duchess of Malfi* (ed. John Russell Brown), 34. [2] *Ibid.*, 71. [3] *Ibid.*, 81. [4] *Ibid.*, 99.
[5] *Ibid.*, 100.

"I account this world a tedious theatre
For I do play a part in't 'gainst my will."

"I am Duchess of Malfi still."[1]

And then when the executioners enter carrying a coffin, cords and a
bell, there come the duchess of Malfi's famous words.

"Who would be afraid on't?
Knowing to meet such excellent company
In th'other world."[2]

The last words were with the murderers. The cardinal of Aragon:
"Shall I die like a leveret?" And finally duke Ferdinand's:

"My sister, O, my sister, there's the cause on't
Whether we fall by ambition, blood, or lust,
Like diamonds, we are cut with our own dust."[3]

The fact that the story is supposed to have been set at the beginning
of the previous century and in the reign of Pope Julius II had little
relevance. It is rare among the plays of the period, other than chronicles, to have a date, in this case 1504, embedded in the script. The text,
however, has references to Paracelsus and even to Galileo. There are
also some allusions to the Bourbon court, and a comment on Calvinism.
It is curious that these tragedies of blood, as they are called, should
reach their climax in King James's reign. It is noticeable, as far as *The
Duchess of Malfi* is concerned, that the victims were strangled, for the
most part off stage, and in one instance poisoned.

There is no evidence of the king's reactions to these plays except
what can be gathered by Webster's promotion from writing a play for
the Queen's Men to one for his sovereign's. As a purely personal
opinion it seems to me that in *The Duchess of Malfi,* and in particular in
the character of that name, we come close to the very essence of the
Jacobean world in its court angle. There is none of that over-stressing
of the moral issues which was to characterise the taste of Charles I.
There is a sense of grandeur, in fact a quite unreal invented grandeur,
and with this goes a consciousness of jewellery. Every aspect of this play
is filled with a sense of the solitary condition of the royal state. This
chimed very well with the king of England's outlook. On one side of
their rather complex characters, both of the first two Stuart kings were
"cased up like a holy relic".

[1] *The Duchess of Malfi* (ed. John Russell Brown), 108, 112 and 124.   [2] *Ibid.*, 128.   [3] *Ibid.*, 170.

Chapter 16

THE JACOBEAN PALACE

THIS is the point at which we can best consider the great houses built during the reign. With an occasional rare exception, they were built by the wealthiest group among the courtiers and envisaged certain visits by the king and his attendants. Until this period of the reign the king was mobile, though he cut swathes only through a group of counties. We can also at this stage see the parts of England that he left unvisited. The old queen's progresses were an act of state and carefully considered; there was always in King James's journeys a certain element of royal caprice. As he grew older he moved less frequently and especially after his return from his solitary visit to his northern kingdom. In his deep middle age he accustomed himself to the domesticities of the Villiers family and moved less often. At this time, too, the new great houses were already taking shape.

The years of peace of the king's reign are seen reflected in the great Jacobean country palace, for this seems the only suitable expression for such a complex of building as Hatfield House. These vast houses were built for splendour and for peace. The old feudal families had been destroyed or transformed throughout the course of the Tudor century. The final dates had been 1569 and 1601, the years of the northern rebellion and the Essex rising. The rebellion can be considered under various aspects, but from one point of view it was the final manifestation of the spirit of the Wars of the Roses when the squires and lesser gentry, the farmers and their hands would take up arms at the call of a traditional leader, a Percy or a Neville, a Clifford or a Dacres. Its destruction can be seen as the final achievement of the victory of Bosworth Field. The Essex rising had of course a lesser consequence, but it was nevertheless the last occasion on which a political movement took place under the leadership of allied peers, Essex, Rutland and Southampton, supported by knights and other young men of possessions with a following of swordsmen. It was likewise a movement with a territorial basis, those sections of mid-Wales where Sir Gelli Meyrick had kept in being and worked up a Devereux faction. The Essex support could hardly have been either recruited or maintained without the presence of armed conflict, war in Ireland and war in the Netherlands.

It was a consequence of these two events that the households which maintained the great establishments were in the reign of James I wholly civilian. The big new houses were invariably in the south of England and for the most part in the home counties. They were in general closely linked with the court and built from the profits of court offices and windfalls. Their buildings had dynastic implications; they were to be the central homes of the great English families.

Those that had been built within the reign included Hatfield and Wimbledon, for the different branches of the house of Cecil, and Audley End which was intended to sustain the Suffolk Howards. Bramshill, built by Lord Zouche, lay on the eastern edge of Berkshire. Blickling, although of this exact period, hardly comes in the same category. It was placed away in the northern parts of Norfolk and had been constructed by Sir Henry Hobart from his legal fortune.

It is important to stress the unique quality of such a palace as Hatfield, lying in the tempered northern sunlight with its plants from the Low Countries and the great setting of its lawns such as were found in no other country. The largest palaces of Italy were in the future. The palaces in Italy in the *settecento* were mainly urban, limited in their extent by the surrounding quarters of the city, or, as in the cases of the papal families, dominating some township in the Alban Hills. Compared to Hatfield, even the more modern of the palaces built in the Loire valley would appear constricted. There was nothing to compare with this in Spain or in the impoverished architecture of the Germanies. Among private palaces it had the largest ground-plan in the whole world.

It was naturally to the great houses that the king returned and not to the smaller manors where he had put up in the earlier stages of the reign. The richest families had all established the great Jacobean household. Some officers who would dominate the interiors of the eighteenth-century houses now appear for the first time, the groom of the chambers is an instance.[1] There can also be traced in this reign those indoor servants of consequence, the groom of the great chamber and the groom of the bedrooms. There had now come into being that large civilian household which among the richest strata of the population would last in England for two hundred years.

[1] Cf. *Household Papers of Henry, ninth Earl of Northumberland*, appendix iii, 150, 154–5, 159.

There is some reason to believe that in many cases, except for the gentlewomen in attendance, these large civilian staffs were wholly male. At least that is the scheme set forth in the *Book of Household Rules* drawn up in 1595 for the guidance of the staff at Cowdray House by the young Lord Montagu. A list is given of thirty-six servants under the control of the steward of the household. The yeomen of the chamber appear to have done the work which was later reserved for women servants. According to the system here laid down Lord and Lady Montagu dined in the parlour, with the gentlewomen-in-waiting at a separate table in the same room. The household officers dined at four tables in the great hall and this was followed by a second service for the junior staff. It was suggested that dinner might be served at 10 am and supper at five in the afternoon, but these figures surely meant very little. There was no allowance made for change of season.

It appears likely that many of the servants slept on a palliasse in the long galleries which at Cowdray, as at so many of the largest houses, had come down from Tudor times. "I will," so runs one of the instructions in this book, "that he (the yeoman of my wardrobe) see the galleries and all lodgings reserved for strangers cleanly and sweetly kepte, with herbes, flowers and bowes in their seasons and the beddes . . . taken off, and Yrish rugges layd in their places."[1]

Similar arrangements were in force at Knole, according to the catalogue of the household of Richard, earl of Dorset. There, too, there was a table in the parlour set for Lord and Lady Dorset and also accommodation for the chaplain and four other gentlemen including Mr Matthew Coldreath, who is described somewhat equivocally as "my Lord's favourite". In the hall there was a clerks' table and another to accommodate the other menservants. There were also places set for the laundry maids, where sat among the rest, Grace Robinson, a blackamoor.[2] The resemblance between the practice in these houses may be due, at any rate in part, to the fact that the viscountess Montagu was by birth a Sackville and had lived at Knole throughout her childhood.

There was a good deal of gambling in these large mansions; the king enjoyed it. Lady Dorset played glecko or gleek as a relaxation after her gentlemen had read to her from Montaigne and the *Arcadia*. She notes in her diary that she lost £27 and some odd money, while playing in her chamber at this game with Lady Gray.[3] The game was fashionable for

[1] Cf. St John Hope, *Cowdray*, 129. [2] *The Diary of Lady Anne Clifford*, lvii and lx.
[3] Entry under 28 (December) 1616, *ibid.*, 45.

there is a comment in Lord Rutland's personal account that he had called for £6 and 20/- to meet his losses at gleek and chess.[1]

The funerals of the peers, at which from a long tradition the king was never present, were in a sense rehearsals for a royal visit. The cook was among the most skilled of the servants in the houses of men of rank. Thus for the funeral bake meats which were needed at the burial of the fifth earl of Rutland in 1612 it was noted that "Lord Willoughby's cook, Lord Exeter's cook, Mr Feilding's cook and Sir William Pelham's cook"[2] all came to Belvoir.

We have from the Rutland papers considerable evidence as to the preparations made for the king's visits. Thus in 1612 Lord Willoughby's wardrobe man arrived "with hangings for Belvoir brought against the King's Majesty's coming".[3] Lord Willoughby also sent two stags, while one each was provided by lords Huntingdon and Lincoln. For the next royal visit a Turkey carpet was brought from London and another set of hangings; there was also a long piece of crimson Mantua velvet. Sack, muscadine and Rhenish wine came from the capital, as did the glasses, but for some reason white and claret wine was bought at Boston. It seems that it was shipped direct from Bordeaux to that port. Soap and white starch both came from Stourbridge fair.

The fifth earl of Rutland does not appear to have been fond of reading, but his library contained a set of three books bound together, a volume of the king's speeches, a copy of *Basilikon Doron* and another of *The True Law for Free Monarchies*.[4] One entry in the accounts is rather fetching. "For seeking and fetching home a hound that was lost 8d., to the bellman of Newark for crying the hound that was lost 2d., and for crying him about the town 2d., and for crying him at the market cross on a market day 2d."[5] There was already play in the drawing chamber at Belvoir. The imports from abroad were quite considerable. Beside the Venice glasses, these included gilt plate of Nuremberg work and dried neats' tongues and bacon from Westphalia. My lord kept swans upon the Trent. Charcoal was made in Rapsley Woods and pit coal was dug locally. Twenty-two pounds in gold was set aside for betting on the Lincoln races.[6] One can appreciate why the king was very much at ease at Belvoir Castle.

From these and other evidences we know that the households were on a lavish scale, although the house itself had come down from earlier

---

[1] Cal. Rutland MSS., IV, 506. [2] *Ibid.*, 478. [3] *Ibid.*, 479. [4] *Ibid.*, 465. [5] *Ibid.*, 496.
[6] *Ibid.*, 513. All the other details about Belvoir come from these papers.

times; the earl of Northumberland's mansion at Petworth is a case in point. It is difficult to reconstruct the actual building as it was in King James's day and this applied to the family houses owned by the late earl of Essex's companions at Belvoir Castle and to a lesser extent at Beaulieu Abbey on Southampton Water.

In all these houses there was an atmosphere of luxury and, save for Lord Southampton's, an impression of extravagance. To these houses should be added Wilton and Cobham, on the uplands of the Isle of Grain beyond the Medway, which had been the king's gift to the duke of Lennox. These were the frontiers of the king's normal travelling. King James became increasingly a creature of habit; time and again he is found upon the road to Newmarket. Some of his short journeys began at Hampton Court, where he was accustomed to go to breathe the fresher air. In contrast to the old queen's practice the journeys which King James made, save for the solitary journey to his native country, were never acts of policy. There was nothing to resemble the progress through Norfolk and Suffolk which his predecessor had undertaken in 1578. Curiously enough he never seems to have gone to the eastern counties, that is to say the countryside which lay beyond Newmarket and Saffron Walden. The west of England was unknown to him. He went deep into Wiltshire, to Wilton and to Littlecote and to Tottenham Park to stay with the old earl of Hertford; but he seldom crossed the borders of East Dorset. One journey to Lulworth, that new white castle of Portland stone, which had come rather unexpectedly to the Suffolk Howards, is recorded and he stayed, one of his rare later visits to a small house, at Cranborne Manor, which the earl of Salisbury had just constructed. Longleat he did not visit and there seems no evidence that he ever crossed the borders of eastern Somerset. It was not that there were not great houses to receive him there; Barrington Court and Long Ashton and Montacute were large even by the standards of the home counties. It seems, however, that the king was not tempted to seek hospitality from those rich squires who were already connected with the opposition. It was probably for a similar reason that the king was not drawn to visit an Elizabethan manor house like Combe Sydenham with all its memories of Francis Drake. Beyond Somerset he did not think of going. In any case the small west country manor houses were not built to provide accommodation for a royal visit. For one reason or another he never went into the west of England.

Wiltshire and Hampshire the king knew well. He seems to have used

R 243

inns when travelling with the court to Wilton by the western road with nights at Basingstoke, Andover and Salisbury, although he may have had private accommodation in the cathedral city. On the way down to Beaulieu he broke the journey at Tichborne and at Winchester. The king was accustomed to repeat his visits to the great houses or perhaps it is more accurate to state the great households of his predilection. There were three visits to Lord Southampton at Beaulieu, whence he once rode through the New Forest to Wilton, perhaps the house that he visited most frequently until the development of Buckingham's ascendancy. He went three times to the marquess of Winchester's house at Basing, where his hostess was Lord Salisbury's niece. He was twice with the bishop of Winchester at Farnham Castle.

There seems no record of a visit by the king to Knole, that great palace which had been completed in the first years of his reign. He went once to Lord Lisle's seat at Penshurst. Sussex he does not seem to have ever entered. It is of interest to speculate on that omission. That county does not appear to have offered him his form of sport and a journey there led nowhere, a serious consideration for one whose journeys were always so purposeful and busy. No one would think of visiting that stretch of barren coast; going eastwards from the entrance to the Arun there were no harbours, just an empty stretch of water at Newhaven and then nothing till you came to the Cinque Ports.

The western borders of the county contained two groups of manors which had belonged to great families for four hundred years, the Percy holdings around Petworth and the Fitzalan complex about Arundel. But Northumberland was in prison and Arundel Castle was in disrepair. It seems that much of the furniture and hangings had been removed either to Arundel House in the Strand or to the new house in the healthy air of Highgate village. In western Sussex there was one great house, Cowdray, the home of Viscount Montagu; a house which Queen Elizabeth had visited in 1591. Still, except when a house lay on some line of route, the king did not visit the Roman Catholics. The same reason would apply to a ride through the Weald with its iron foundries to the small houses of those substantial squires whose homes lay sheltered by the south downs, the Shelleys at Michelgrove to the eastwards across the downs from Arundel, the Carylls at Warnham and their cousins at Harting and the Gages at Firle. All four were Catholic houses.

The king's preference was always for the northern and north-western roads from London. He would spend a night at the inn at Ware as he hastened towards Newmarket. He went to Sir Francis Fortescue at Salden and to Sir Edmund Hampden at Great Hampden. He criss-crossed Oxfordshire. He stayed at Stonor and in the immediate neighbourhood at Mapledurham. In the northern part of the county he was with Sir Anthony Cope at Hanwell Castle and with Sir William Pope at Wroxham in the next parish. In the first part of his reign it was the stag hunting that appealed to him. The palace at Woodstock provided a convenient centre for this exercise. Six stags' heads were preserved at Ditchley, each with a brass tablet which described the run. Three examples[1] will give a clear impression. "August 26th (1604). King James made to run for life to Dead man's Riding: I ran to Goreil Gate, where death for me was biding." The next two inscriptions come from six years later when the king was accompanied by his elder son. "August 22nd (1610). To Henly Knap to hunt me, King James, Prince Henry found me, Cornebury Park river to end their hunting drown'd me." And two days later. "The King and Prince from Grange made me to make my race, but death neare the Queen's Parke, gave me a resting place."

Repeated visits might prove, of course, a burden. Speaking of the summer's journey in 1608 Chamberlain wrote to Carleton. "The Progress holds on towards Northamptonshire as unwelcome in those parts as rain in harvest."[2] As an example the earl of Cumberland, who had rented a house in the county Grafton Lodge, was now to receive his third royal visit. In the summer of 1612 the journey continued for seven weeks. It went up through Northamptonshire to Belvoir, which proved a welcoming house, and turned southwards after reaching Sir George Savile's seat at Rufford Abbey. The return journey crossed Sherwood Forest and included a stay with Sir John Byron at Newstead. The king would go to Belvoir again in later life. He never seems to have visited Lincolnshire.[3] The great houses in that county belonged, like Grimthorpe Castle, to the later Vanbrugh period in English life.

In this connection it is interesting to note that King James appears to have shown no concern for old-fashioned ecclesiastical architecture. He never seems to have been to Exeter and Wells, or Chichester or Norwich or Lincoln. I do not think he visited Gloucester or Worcester,

---

[1] Cf. E. K. Chambers, *Sir Henry Lee* (1936), 210 and 213.
[2] Letter dated July 8, 1608, printed in John Nichols, *The Progresses . . . of King James the First*, etc., 200–1.   [3] He made one visit early in the reign to the city of Lincoln.

the cathedrals of the Severn valley. He certainly was not led to them by his Scottish training. In fact his knowledge of English history itself seems very sketchy. This was not a subject which Buchanan taught him. In his speeches and writings there are references to his Scottish ancestors, but very seldom to the English. There was one rather fumbling comment on William the Conqueror.

In the intervals between his journeys the king was for the most part at Whitehall, that rather ill-constructed and rambling palace which he had inherited at his accession. It was a great contrast to his Scottish palaces. There were so many rooms and some of them were spacious. There was ample opportunity for the reception of ambassadors. The stone gallery was one of the more enduring elements in this palace system. The southern range of buildings looked out upon the river with the various landing stages, the privy stairs and Whitehall stairs and Scotland dock. Unlike Henry VIII, King James did not care for unnecessary journeys on the river. The grey waters went sliding by. The king had a distaste for the great "wen" of London. It was at Royston and at Newmarket that he felt at home.

Chapter 17

THE COUNT OF GONDOMAR

INTO this world of new big houses and court masques there came the count of Gondomar. As an ambassador he was at home there and he did not go beyond it. Don Diego Sarmiento de Acuña was a year younger than the king of England and was the head of one of the richer families among the court nobility of old Castile. He had been born at Gondomar in the diocese of Tuy. During his early life he was employed in the coastguard service in Galicia, his native province. As a consequence he never underestimated the danger of English naval power to his own country. Like most members of his class he never left Spain except on duty and his first foreign embassy was to the English court. From the point of view of the sovereign to whom he was accredited, he possessed certain advantages. He was small and slight and he had that traditional approach of subdued and intimate courtesy which the grandees in Spain would use with their own sovereign. He was also a man of learning building up a choice collection of printed books and manuscripts, in all essentials a civilian, as was the king to whose court he came. He spoke fluent Latin and King James responded. As they walked together in the stone gallery of Whitehall or in the country palaces the king would set the subjects of the conversation and the count of Gondomar (for he obtained this title during his embassy and it is best to call him so) would reply with measured courtesy. King James had never heard anything like this before since the earlier ambassadors had belonged to the Spanish military tradition. He was enchanted.

As an ambassador Gondomar was on his mettle, faced with a situation in which the Anglo-Spanish relationship was continually disintegrating. He and his predecessors had spent heavily on building up what it was hoped would emerge as a peace party. I do not think that the courtiers should be blamed for accepting these gifts; most of those who accepted them seem to have been quite sincere in preferring peace. It was the climate best suited to their own advancement. But of course Gondomar's own circle was restricted. At the Spanish court the entrance had been confined to office-holders and to those who bore the necessary quarterings. There was no group in Spain to correspond to the great London merchant companies and to the independent-minded country gentry.

He had only one card to play, a Spanish marriage. Prince Henry was already dead before the time of his arrival. The new Prince of Wales was only fourteen years of age; there was no hurry for such preparations. Meanwhile the situation was difficult for the Princess Elizabeth had married the Elector Palatine, and there were hesitant negotiations now in progress for the eventual marriage of the young prince to the Princess Christine of France and Navarre, the eldest unmarried daughter of Henry IV. The idea of a Spanish match was naturally not novel. It was as old as the peace treaty; but the long experienced views of the earl of Salisbury and the hot-tempered and vivacious Protestantism of Prince Henry had prevented the project from becoming active. Now both were dead.

King James was a peace-making sovereign and Gondomar was the envoy of a king who needed peace. The ambassador had no experience outside the Spanish monarchy. The Anglican episcopate was wholly novel to him; he does not seem to have appreciated the solid block of opposition that they would offer to a Catholic Spanish marriage. It was a further drawback for Gondomar's relations with the king that he could not share with him in discussing the different aspects of the Reformed religion. Here the duke of Bouillon as a Calvinist had the advantage.

At the same time in all political matters there was a great difference between King James's approach and that of his own passive sovereign. The relations of Philip III with his minister the duke of Lerma and also to a great extent those of his son and successor with the count-duke of Olivares were informed by a spirit of dependence partly a result of the thin exhausted blood of the later Spanish Hapsburgs. But King James's attitude, first to Somerset and then to Buckingham, was totally different; these favourites were young men, they were his scholars.

King James in these days, now that Salisbury was dead, had that regal solitude that he had brought from Scotland. It was not in the tradition of a royal sovereign to reveal all his mind to those who came to him. He seems mostly to have seen Gondomar alone and to have allowed him a portion of his thought. The Spanish ambassador was charged with certain local duties and also with examining the position of England in the international situation.

The most pressing of the local duties was the continually reviving projects about Guiana. This was a matter which went back to the years of war in the last reign. The expedition of Sir Walter Raleigh and Laurence Keymeys had taken place then and the further project for a heavy expedition in which Sir Walter would serve the duke of Suder-manland belonged to the same period. But even in the present reign, with Sir Walter Raleigh in the Tower, there had been expeditions. In 1604 Charles Leigh, with a tiny company in the *Olive Plant*, sailed for the mouth of the Amazon and established himself for some time on the banks of the Wiapoco. This did not prosper and within two years the survivors had returned to England. A larger expedition under Robert Harcourt sailed in 1609 with the king's permission to establish a colony in Guiana, a favour which was due to the intervention of Henry, Prince of Wales. Harcourt then declared that "he tooke posses-sion of the land . . . in behalfe of our Sovereigne Lord King James . . . lying betwixt the Rivers of Amazone and Orenoque, not being actually possessed and inhabited by any other Christian Prince or State". This colony apparently expired about 1613.

Meanwhile there had been a third new expedition. An entry in the commonplace book of Sir Stephen Powle runs as follows. "Guiana, 13th 1610 being Tuesday Sir Tho. Roe our commander for the dis-covery of Guiana: and Sir George Brooke (as I heare since) departed for Dartmough where oure two shippes, and provision for two pinnaces bestowed in them, lay at roade for his comminge. Partners: the Earle of Southampton £800, Sir Walter Rawley £600, Sir Thomas Roe him-selfe with his partners £1100 and my self £20: which voyage God blesse."[1] There were complicated elements in the situation. The Spaniards had failed to occupy the hot lands which stretched away to the south-eastwards beyond the mouths of the Orinoco. A long march to the southwards from those coasts would reach in time to the banks of the Amazon, which was occupied at distant intervals by the settlements established by the soldiers of the king of Portugal. In the years follow-ing the union of the two Iberian crowns in 1580 little coordination had been established. Finally these distant coasts were far away from the sailing tracks of the Spanish treasure fleets homeward bound from the Caribbean. Various nations had their attention drawn to these empty

[1] Bodleian, Tanner MSS, 168, f. 2, printed in V. T. Harlow, *Ralegh's Last Voyage* (1932), 13.

lands. Thus the three Guianas, the British, the Dutch at Surinam and a little later the French at Cayenne, all came into being in these years.

It is only necessary to say that Roe's expedition did not prosper. At the end of the winter of 1611 Sir Thomas is found writing to the earl of Salisbury from the harbour of Port of Spain in Trinidad. Around him lay English, Dutch and French ships, loading with tobacco. "I may," he wrote, "with an humble bouldness presume to say I have seene more of this coast rivers and inland from the great river of the Amazones under the line [of the Equator] to Orenoque . . . than any Englishman now alive. I am now past the Wild Coast."[1] There was, however, no chance for Raleigh's release as long as Salisbury lived. This at least is my own impression. It is sometimes alleged that the minister was considering some support for Raleigh's Guiana expedition in the months before his death; but it is by his actions and not by his words that the intentions of the earl of Salisbury can best be judged.

These facts give the background to Olivares's problem, but the idea that Sir Walter Raleigh himself might be released had made no headway. The European situation on the other hand was very difficult and had become increasingly complicated since King James's only daughter had married the Elector Palatine. The murder of Henry IV by Ravaillac as he was driving along the rue de la Ferronnerie in May 1610 had prevented France from engaging in a German war and this particular danger would not arise again until the Cardinal de Richelieu became first minister; that war would not eventuate until King James was dead. The occasion for foreign intervention had been the complicated matter of the Cleves succession.

The duchy of Cleves has long since disappeared and its frontiers are forgotten. The reigning family has vanished. It belonged, as did *La Princesse de Clèves*, to the world of the sixteenth and seventeenth centuries. Kleve lies on a little hill in a flat rich country watered by the Maas and Rhine right up against the borders of the United Provinces. It looked westward across the *plattelande* of the Low Countries. The great river which had run so strongly through the Rhineland turned sluggish here. The name but not the place was known in England for the last duke of Cleves was a nephew of the Princess Anne, who had been the fourth wife of Henry VIII. Other territories had come to the ducal line by marriage, the duchies of Julich and Berg and the county

[1] Letter dated February 28, 1611, printed in J. A. Williamson, *The English in Guiana*, 55–7.

of Mark; these lay to the south and south-east of the old duchy.

The ducal family had a vague and wavering Catholicism, while the princesses had for the most part married into the Protestant ruling houses. Religions had long been mixed here. The two last dukes, father and son, had each been for many years insane. Julich and the neighbourhood was the principal Catholic area; but in both duchies as in the territory of the spiritual electorate, which intermingled with them, there had been for many years an influx of Protestants from the Spanish Netherlands.

There had been a Spanish and imperialist policy in regard to this long-foreseen succession to the duke of Cleves, who was on his mother's side a first cousin of the emperor. King James had also his associations with this family for the last duke had been married for the second time in a lucid interval to a princess of Lorraine. On the death of Duke John William in March 1609 the two senior heirs, the elector of Brandenburg and the count of Pfalz-Neuburg, representing the late ruler's eldest and second sisters, put forward their claims. Julich was immediately occupied by a garrison of imperial troops under the Archduke Leopold. Before the emperor made any decision as to the future of the territories, the two claimants came to an agreement. They decided jointly to occupy the whole under the title of "Possessing Princes". The opportunity for King James to mediate thus passed away, while the murder of Henry IV prevented the outbreak of a conflagration. Still the situation seemed to pre-figure the great war which was soon upon them. The count of Pfalz-Neuburg became a Catholic and married a Bavarian princess. The beginning of the Thirty Years' War was now in sight.

There was one minor aspect of the position which seems to have had its effect on Gondomar's appreciations. It was in 1614 that there began the slow piecemeal conversion of small individual princes, which was one of the effects of Jesuit policy. In that year the heads of two tiny principalities at the south-eastern edge of the Cleves complex joined the Roman Church, Count John III of Nassau-Siegen and his brother the first prince of Nassau-Hadamar. It may have been these changes which led the count of Gondomar to envisage a parallel conversion for the Prince of Wales.

This was certainly the key to his outlook in the marriage proposals which were soon revived. The king wanted a vast amount of money. The then Pope was opposed to a mixed marriage and the Spaniards wanted internal changes favourable to the English Catholics. The

proposed conditions looked at calmly appear as an intolerable inter-
ference in the domestic affairs of another country. Only one factor
could make them sensible; if the minority so favoured was in reality the
religion of the Prince of Wales.

It is worth considering why Gondomar and the other ministers of the
king of Spain should have spent so much effort on what appeared
superficially to be religious motives. To me it seems to be because in
this century of the wars of religion it was impossible to divorce the
religious from the political. What was most feared upon the Spanish
Main were Dutch and French Huguenot privateers and English expeditions. The whole outlook of the Spanish government ran in terms of
courts and not of nations. The security of Spain required that her trade
should not be endangered by English naval attack. With the situation
in Germany so incalculable, it appeared that the cause of Spain
required that the English court should be immune from French infidelity and Dutch and German Protestantism. To Gondomar the
solution would appear to be a Catholic sovereign. He knew only a tiny
segment of English life.

Chapter 18

THE SCOTTISH JOURNEY

TOWARDS the end of 1616 the king began to make plans for a journey
to Scotland in the next year in the warm weather. Somerset and his
wife were in the Tower and the new favourite Sir George Villiers was
making his way quietly. He was still under the influence of his original
promoters Archbishop Abbot and the earl of Pembroke. The king was
being pressed towards an anti-Spanish policy. It was true that he was
also influenced by the Spanish ambassador the count of Gondomar,
whose general effect has been considered. Still, the project for a marriage treaty for Prince Charles was for the moment in abeyance.

In this time the king gave weight to the judgment of his secretary of
state, Sir Ralph Winwood. It is worth noting that he had received this
appointment for life in the course of the Somerset administration. He
had held the post of minister at the Hague and had had much to do
with the arrangements for the Palatine marriage. It was Winwood,
above all, who persuaded the king to release Sir Walter Raleigh. In all
this strange project of the voyage to Guiana it was the prospect of the
moneys from the rich gold mine which would have influence with the
king. A sentence bearing on this point and found in one of Raleigh's
letters of prospectus will make this plain. He was insistent that the gold
lay only nine inches under grass. The metal, he explained, "did rise
up in a broad slate, and not in small veines, there was never a mine of
gold in the world promising so great abundance".[1] The king had never
shown any interest in maps or in the Indies, his interests were fixed upon
the continent of Europe. He had neither liking for nor interest in Sir
Walter Raleigh. It was an unusual permission for the king to grant,
possibly he was tired.

An interesting problem is what did the king expect from Raleigh's
voyage. Professor Harlow has suggested that he was aware of the negotiations with the French and that he expected that the French would

[1] In a document preserved in the Folger Shakespeare Library, Washington, D.C. Cf.
Ernest A. Strathmann, "Ralegh plans his last voyage", printed in *The Mariner's Mirror*
(1964), 261–70.

attack San Thomé, while the English removed the gold from the mine.[1] This seems to me to go against the king's profound lack of sympathy with any military adventure. Professor Harlow's second suggestion seems to me to get closer to the probable explanation. According to this variant the king had no knowledge of the situation of San Thomé. The concept of the forays on the Spanish Main was uncongenial. The one thing that he really needed was the gold. For the last active period of the reign this mass of treasure had a deep attraction for him. His needs were great. Once Raleigh had been unsuccessful, he moved across to another means of gaining a really astronomic sum of gold by involving his son in a Spanish marriage.

The king was solitary. His own family was now broken down. His only daughter was in Heidelberg. His wife was to all intents separated from him. In public they were united by a rather fatigued courtesy. His only surviving child in England was his younger son. At a later stage his favourite Villiers would provide a family for him; but that young man was still picking his way. Before the Scottish journey he would be created earl of Buckingham. In the reign this time was in some respects slack water.

Old Lord Ellesmere had died and Bacon had been made lord keeper. The king had been manoeuvred by Bacon into a quarrel with Sir Edward Coke; but there was no sense that this was final. The period of his personal association with the house of Howard was now drawing to a close. Northampton was dead and his nephew Suffolk was just part of the king's official world. Arundel for the moment was nearer to him, for on Christmas Day 1616 he received the Anglican Communion in the Chapel Royal. Although apparently at heart either a vaguely latitudinarian Christian or perhaps even an agnostic, he had been moving in this direction for some years. In 1607 the king's offer to stand godfather to his heir Lord Maltravers had involved the Anglican christening of his eldest son. In the course of 1616 a second secretary of state had been appointed, Sir Thomas Lake. He had been at court since the beginning of the reign. After the late queen's death the council had sent him to inform the king of Scots. He was named among those who were to accompany the king on his northern journey.

The king left Theobalds on his way northward on March 15, 1617. It was then rather early in the year, but he would spend two months before he reached the Scottish border. Those invited to Scotland in-

---

[1] Cf. V. T. Harlow, *Ralegh's Last Voyage*, ch. 1, "An Interpretation".

cluded, besides the duke of Lennox and other Scottish peers, two of the great lords through whose lands he would pass and at whose houses he would stay; the earl of Rutland who held Belvoir Castle and the earl of Arundel to whom Worksop had come as part of Lady Alathea's marriage portion. The earl of Buckingham was of the party. The other English peers were the brothers Pembroke and Montgomery and the earl of Southampton and Lord Mordaunt. The last named was a boy of eighteen, almost a page, a nominal Roman Catholic, who had been educated by Archbishop Abbot. He was one of those who soon adopted the king's religion. There were also three English bishops, Lancelot Andrewes of Ely, James Montague of Winchester and Neile of Durham. They travelled slowly, not more than sixteen miles a day.

The king had with him a vast retinue of household servants, grooms, ushers, yeomen, harbingers, purveyors, clerks. Where did they sleep? Were they accommodated in all the farms and ale-houses for miles around or did they sleep in tents in the parks and meadows of those who entertained their royal master? We read, for instance, of the great procession which wound out from York to Bishopthorpe when the king stayed with old Archbishop Mathew. It is worth noting that, except for one of his secretaries of state, he had none of his great English officials with him upon this journey.

In a letter to the Scottish privy council the king set out the purpose of his coming. "First," he wrote, "we are not aschamed to confesse that we have had these many yeirs a great and naturall longing to see our native soyle and place of our birth and breeding, and this salmon-lyke instinct of ours has restleslie . . . so stirred up our thoughts and bended our desires to make a Jornay."[1] He was leaving his great southern country and coming back to one which he could manage. His main difficulties were ecclesiastical and this may have been why he took so few Scottish peers with him. What he had learned in England in the religious sphere had passed them by, all except Lennox who had for so long been the king's reflection. The bishops had increased in number and in authority since he was last in Scotland and nearly all of them had now been consecrated through Archbishop Abbot. Moreover, as the years went by he had found at last a "manager", Archbishop Spottiswoode. In some respects he resembled those English bishops of good family, who had settled their stock among the landed interest. His brother had been at court in Scotland and had now become an

[1] Nichols, *The Progresses . . . of King James*, III, 309.

Anglican vicar; he would die as bishop of Clogher. His elder son, Sir John, inherited the property of Dairsie in Fife that he had bought for him and his younger son Robert was later Lord Newabbey, a Scottish judge. John Spottiswoode had been chaplain to the second duke of Lennox and had been nominated to the archbishopric of Glasgow when the king came to England. Since 1615 he had been archbishop of St Andrews. Such changes as the king now required went naturally with an episcopal constitution. Spottiswoode has often been described as an Erastian, but it seems to me that he was tactful and amenable and had the merits of sincerity.

It was always the king's intention to build up the kingdom of Great Britain. There was now no danger that any failure of the succession would ever divide England from Scotland. This was why he was now ready to grant Scotsmen English peerages and to make on this journey Arundel and Pembroke, and also Sir Thomas Lake, members of the Scottish privy council. He appears to have had thoughts of uniting the churches of England and Scotland. In this he was much assisted by Dr Abbot. The archbishop of Canterbury was a man of no concealments and it was from the first clear that he was wedded to that semi-Calvinist interpretation of Augustinian thought from which the king himself had never broken free. Before his promotion to the episcopate he had been domestic chaplain to Lord Dunbar, whom he had accompanied in 1608 to the general assembly at Linlithgow. On this occasion even Calderwood praised him. "The English doctors," he wrote, "had no other direction than to persuade the Scots there was no substantial difference in religion between the two realms, but only in things indifferent concerning government and ceremonies."[1] Under these circumstances it is curious that among those present on this journey was the newly-appointed dean of Gloucester, Dr Laud.

There was all the difference between the attitude of King James to his bishops, whether English or Scottish, and that later adopted by his son when he had succeeded as King Charles I. The latter sovereign had, whatever his personal reactions, a sense of dependence upon the judgment in all religious matters of his fathers-in-God. This was the High Church approach in germ. For James I the consecrated and anointed king was God's shadow in his kingdom. He was also, unlike his son, a learned man and could appreciate and value a learned prelate. For the rest it seems he took them as they came, noting that the Scots had

[1] Calderwood, *History of the Kirk of Scotland*, VI, 735.

this disadvantage that they had all been ministers of the Kirk. Still, nothing could break through the calm respect with which all bishops treated him. In a tract written before this time Dr Abbot had expressed his own outlook upon the king. His life was declared to be "so immaculate and unspotted from the world . . . that even malice itself could never find true blemish in it".[1] The king went forward quietly to his northern kingdom.

The weather freshened into spring. There was some hunting on the way, but not so much as when the king was younger. On May 13 he crossed the Tweed and entered Berwick. He would be gone again before the cold came down on him. There lay before him that period of short calm nights of summer in the Lothians.

The Scottish administration had been long-established. It was in the hands of those who had always had their master's confidence. The king was closer to the great lay lords, who were his friends, than he ever was to an ecclesiastic. The chancellor was Alexander Seton, now earl of Dunfermline; the treasurer was the king's old intimate the earl of Mar, who had come to the office once held by Dunbar and then by Somerset; the secretary Thomas Hamilton, now Lord Binning, Tam o'the Cowgate, also held the office of lord president of the court of Session. They were all regalians and except Mar they were without hereditary supporters. The king must have been grateful for their long-continued service, nor were they grasping. James I had never understood the value of money and this made it difficult for him to check or indeed to detect corruption. Many high English officials were ready to take this opportunity, but not the Scots.

The holders of high office in Scotland had long known the king and were in general in sympathy with his ideas. All of these now reflected his desires for a united kingdom. In the parliament which met on June 17 he put forward a proposal that the great lords should surrender to the crown their heritable jurisdictions. Old feudal rights were exercised in Scotland that had long since been swept away in England. In this measure he was unsuccessful; but he succeeded in an effort to provide a better basic salary for the Presbyterian ministers. His five proposals with a view to religious uniformity were wisely left in Dr Spottiswoode's hands to be brought up at a general assembly over which he would preside when the king was gone.

It has always seemed to me rather surprising that he should have

[1] Printed in *Harleian Miscellany*, IX, 560, *et seq.*

decided to modify the fittings of the royal chapel at Holyrood. After all he had come for a brief visit. The introduction of an organ, sent round by sea to Leith, appears particularly ill-judged. The king came with his English bishops to set up an English service. John Row sets out the view of the Presbyterian opposition. "And therefore (he) caused repair the Chapel Royall, in Halyruidhous, wherein was a glorious altar sett up, with two closed Bibles, two unlighted candles, and two basins without water sett thereon, organs put up, and His Majestie's Choristers appoynted to sing and say the English Service daily."[1] There were wooden figures of the patriarchs and apostles brought in from England. The king likewise introduced the practice of kneeling at the reception of Communion. This was natural if he was to have unity of practice between the state religions of his two countries; but this custom of kneeling suggested to the more earnest Scots either the Roman doctrine of transubstantiation or perhaps the consubstantiation which was accepted by the Lutheran churches on the continent. The king had been long away from Scotland; in England he was losing his sense of touch.

He visited St Andrews and went for quiet expeditions to Falkland and Linlithgow. Dundee was his farthest northern point. Then he came back again to Edinburgh and when he left on his homeward journey he went by Stirling, to Glasgow, Paisley and Hamilton. He continued to Drumlanrig and Dumfries, where it seems that he had never been before in his reign in Scotland. He reached Carlisle on August 4, but why did he take with him on this visit his English bishops?

At Carlisle the king was rejoined by his great train, which had come down from Edinburgh by the shortest way. He set off through that wild northern country, which no other English sovereign had passed for centuries. More often than on his outward journey he stayed in towns, Carlisle, Appleby, Kendal. The countess of Dorset was in the south, there was no one to receive him in the Clifford country. He was far from the line of Queen Elizabeth's progresses. He went to houses where he would be the only royal visitor, to Wharton Hall and Hornby Castle, which belonged to Monteagle's father old Lord Morley, and Hoghton Tower. He passed through the country of the Pendle witches, who had been tried five years earlier; he came at length to the earl of Derby's great house at Lathom.

Now he was back again in all the complex political life of his rich

[1] Row, *History of the Kirk of Scotland*, I, 113.

southern kingdom. He went south by no very direct route selecting the houses which he wished to visit. Thus he came to Gerard's Bromley where Lord Gerard was just about to set out for Ludlow to take over the lord presidency of Wales. The rain fell heavily in Staffordshire. He came at last to Stafford with Arundel sitting beside him in his travelling coach. Here he got out and mounted his "horse of state". He was met by the lord lieutenant of the county, the earl of Essex, who had come in from Chartley. Essex's friend Southampton was with the royal party and the king had changed his outlook since the trial of Lady Somerset.

The same day he set out for Sir Walter Aston's home at Tixall. This great house has now completely disappeared. All that remains is the large gaunt brick gatehouse, stranded in the fields. Tixall belonged, together with its estate and manors in three other midland counties, to young Aston, whom James had knighted at his coronation and who had since held the posts of groom and gentleman of his privy chamber. He had married before he came of age Gertrude Sadleir, the heiress of Standon Lordship in Hertfordshire, and had paid his guardian Sir Edward Coke £4,000 for marrying without his approval. His children were the authors of the verses printed in later years as *Tixall Poetry*.[1]

It is worth quoting a succinct account of Sir Walter's appearance: "He went very upright and straite: his skin very pure, all but his face, which was of a browne rudy complexion, with a little wen upon his cheeke his hayre a yellow red his beard a little sadde. He had something a high nose & a rough voyce, but would have spoken very well, noe drinker noe swearer, of an affable courteous behaviour free from all disease but a stone."[2] He would appear again in the king's life.

The king drifted down through the home counties into more familiar territory, to Ashby de la Zouche to stay with the earl of Huntingdon, to Warwick, where Sir Fulke Greville, the chancellor of the exchequer, had rebuilt the ruined castle which the king had given him, and then to Compton Winyates. This house then belonged to one of his wealthiest subjects, Lord Compton, to whom he gave in the next year the earldom of Northampton. He went on by way of his own palace of Woodstock, to Lord Norris's house at Ryecote where the free-standing private

[1] *Tixall Poetry*, printed by Arthur Clifford in 1823, containing poems by Gertrude Aston and the commonplace book of Constantia Fowler.
[2] Printed from B.M. Add. MS. 36542, in Bernard Newdigate, *Michael Drayton and his Circle* (Oxford, 1941), 148.

chapel dates from this time, across the Thames to Bisham to the Hoby family and so at last to Windsor Castle. The king was tired.

The count of Gondomar was awaiting the sovereign to whose court he was accredited. There was disquieting news about Sir Walter Raleigh. Where was the *Destiny*?

Chapter 19

THE HOWARDS' FALL

THE *Destiny* was lying in the harbour of St John's, Newfoundland. Her useless voyage was now almost over. She had only to return across the empty sea, back by what in later centuries would be the summer track of Anchor liners, home by the shortest of Atlantic crossings between Newfoundland and the Firth of Clyde. The Straits of Belle Isle were now free from ice. Sir Walter took his ship to Killybegs in Donegal and then down past the west of Ireland in the summer seas. Rounding Cape Clear, he made for the entrance of the open channel. He was approaching soundings coming in from the Atlantic over those steep shelving ledges to the shallow waters. He sat in his great cabin with the June sunlight pouring through the open windows in the stern considering to which port he should take the *Destiny*, to Brest or Plymouth.

It seems that he had had two plans, to bring back the gold ore from the Guiana field and, if this failed, to plunder the home-bound Spanish treasure fleet. If he had followed this second course of action he might well have gone home to a French port. Even Raleigh must have felt a certain doubt as to what King James might have done had he reached Plymouth with his holds full of bullion stolen from the king of Spain; but in France there would have been a welcome. He could have given the crew their share before they went ashore. The Huguenots had still their influence, he could have passed his later years in the French king's service. But now the position was very different.

The attempt made for the gold had proved a failure, Spaniards had been slain, and Raleigh's son Walter had also fallen. Among the older men Kemeys had been his one assured supporter, but Kemeys had killed himself. He had gone to his cabin as the *Destiny* lay at anchor in the Caribbean and had stabbed himself with his sword after he had fired his pistol. He was violently disturbed in mind; he could not bear the blistering words that Sir Walter had spoken to him after he had returned with the disastrous news of the failure and young Walter's death.

Neither his officers nor his men had been much use to him. His officers had been either too bad or too good, the former had abandoned him and gone off with their ship's companies and turned pirate, the latter did not forget that they were in the royal service. Some of his officers were men of birth who had joined for plunder, but they were not prepared to attack the Spanish treasure fleet in time of peace. His vice-admiral, who was in the *Star* during this voyage and eventually became Sir John Penington, the well-known flag officer under Charles I, adopted this line. As a result his holds were empty.

At the same time his ship's company would not take the *Destiny* to a French port; they would be put ashore penniless in a foreign country and perhaps imprisoned. There was really no alternative. He steered for England through the calm June weather. He landed at Plymouth and was soon arrested and after a time brought up to London. There he learned that his chief supporter in official life, the secretary Sir Ralph Winwood, had died of fever during his absence.

It is strange that the first problem which faced the king once Buckingham was a favourite should have been the disposal of Sir Walter Raleigh. This matter should be considered in some detail, for his treatment of Sir Walter Raleigh is probably the gravest stain that rests upon King James's character.

From the time that Raleigh was arrested at Ashburton by Sir Lewis Stukeley and brought back to Plymouth the king seems to have worried very little about his fate. The prisoner was strangely reluctant to escape. An opportunity offered to join a French ship at Plymouth, but he refused it. When he reached Brentford in Stukeley's charge he was met by La Chesnée, the interpreter at the French embassy, and later saw the French agent Le Clerc at his own house in Bread Street. This time he appears to have agreed and embarked on a boat making her way down river towards a French vessel. He was arrested off Woolwich and placed in the Tower of London; his fate was sealed.

It was on August 10, 1618, that he was sent to the Tower and eight days later he was brought before a commission, which had been especially appointed to investigate his case. It is worth pausing upon the names the king selected. They were Sir Francis Bacon, the lord keeper, Archbishop Abbot, the earl of Worcester, who was now growing old, and three officials of lesser rank, Sir Edward Coke, who had been dismissed from the chief justiceship, Sir Julius Caesar, the master of the rolls and Sir Robert Naunton, who was Winwood's successor. The archbishop was among the leaders of the anti-Spanish party and Bacon was remote from all foreign countries. Between them they represented the Protestant royalism of the English law.

Gardiner lays stress on the effect that Raleigh's lying must have produced upon his judges;[1] but this seems a Victorian point of view. The Jacobeans were not so naïve as to expect that a man in a predicament would speak the truth. Much of the explanation of his execution lies in the fact that he was already under sentence of death. The difficulty of his situation depended upon his explicit condemnation in his first trial. Further there were now charges of his dealings with the agents of the king of France. It might have been imagined that contacts with the Huguenots and with the Rochellois privateers would have aroused some sympathy, but these points seem to have been neglected. His case in fact was seen as the question of a condemned man who had been caught dealing with a foreign power. He had also attacked a Spanish town in time of peace.

In addition to the influence of the royal will which was hostile to him, there was also the distrust which Raleigh had aroused for so long among the courtiers. And then in the eyes of the great lords he was in no sense an equal, but just a simple gentleman, although a very thrusting one. We have to think back to the relations between Sir Philip Sidney and the earl of Oxford at the old queen's court. It is hard for us to envisage the gulf between rich earls, like his patrons Pembroke and Arundel, and Sir Walter Raleigh. Whatever the reason was, the great officials of the reign all let him die.

In the end he was executed under his former sentence. As for the king it seems that he was quite at ease. After all he could have allowed him to escape to France in the hours before he was lodged in the Tower. But he never seems to have felt any embarrassment. He even proposed that Raleigh should be handed over to the Spanish ambassador to be taken to Madrid and hanged there in the public square. It was the king of Spain, whose hope was always for peace with England, who turned down this proposition. The English form of patriotism, as we know it now, developed in its fullest form within the eighteenth century. Neither James I nor Charles II shared this relatively modern notion. King James was too much inclined to think about the kings his equals. The best that can be said for him is that Raleigh was the greatest enemy of that world peace which was the king's true aim. In that case he should never have let him sail.

[1] S. R. Gardiner, *History of England*, III, 142.

While Sir Walter Raleigh was still in the Tower there were two attacks developing upon the chief officials, the earl of Suffolk and Sir Thomas Lake. It was not so much the fall of the house of Howard that was remarkable, as its survival. For the first ten years of the reign this group had been retained in office by the favour of Lord Salisbury, who had married his only son to Suffolk's youngest daughter. Northampton's death in 1614 had deprived them of their working brain. They had survived the fall of their ally Somerset and now they were face to face with a new favourite. It is said that they made a half-hearted attempt to advance young William Monson to a favourite's place. Whatever the effort, it hardly survived its first beginning.[1] The two great office-holders of the Howard family were the earl of Suffolk, who had been lord treasurer since 1614 and had held the post of lord chamberlain from the opening of the reign, and the old earl of Nottingham, who had been lord admiral since 1585. It would have been hard enough for them to keep their places even if the administration of their offices had been impeccable.

The king had had a somewhat inexplicable affection for Northampton, but from the rest of that stock he stood aloof. He seems to have often had a certain warmth for those whose fortunes he had created, but as far as Lord Thomas Howard was concerned he had done little but set the seal of his approval on an ancient house. Lord Thomas had had his part in Elizabethan legend for he had been Sir Richard Grenville's last commander. He had received the Garter from the queen and the lord lieutenancy of Cambridgeshire and the high stewardship of that university. He was already acting lord chamberlain at the queen's death. There was little for King James to do except to accept Salisbury's recommendation that he should employ him.

There was, however, another factor. He was also the only member of the main line of the Howards who had all his life possessed the manoeuvring power of money. Through his wife he had obtained the estates of Charlton in Wiltshire and Escrick in Yorkshire. He had received as a child the property that had come to him as the elder son of the fourth duke's second wife. When he was only three, the duchess of Norfolk had left him the town of Saffron Walden and the estate of Audley End, which had been accumulated by her father Lord Chancellor Audley. And lately trouble had come upon him. It could not be pleasant for the king that he was so closely related to Lady Somerset.

[1] Cf. for an account, *Chamberlain Letters*, II, 144.

From another angle the fall of Suffolk and that of Sir Thomas Lake can be considered as examples of what happened when two of the great families ran into heavy weather, the Suffolk branch of the Howards and the elder Exeter line of the house of Cecil. For it is to be noted that the disaster to the Suffolks was purely political, it was not economic. It was simply a question of arranging the removal of a great house from the seats of power. It also serves to show how very strong was the position of the richest peers provided that the word treason was not brought into a charge.

As the years went by Lord Suffolk had increased his large possessions. He inherited the Dorset manors around Lulworth, which had belonged to his cousin the last Viscount Howard of Bindon. He had obtained the Charterhouse in the old queen's reign, but in 1614 he had moved to Northampton House in the Strand, which he had inherited on his uncle's death. It was rumoured that his relations had become strained with Lord Northampton towards the end.[1] He was a great builder at Lulworth, apparently, at Charlton on his wife's estate and above all at the seat that he erected at Audley End. John Evelyn visiting it some forty years from its completion describes[2] it as a "palace, to which is an avenue of trees but all this is much diminished by its being placed in an obscure bottom. For the rest it is a perfectly modern structure, and shows without like a diadem by the decorations of the cupolas and other ornaments in the pavilions." This suffices to indicate that when he came upon his troubles the earl of Suffolk was one of the richest of the greater peers.

His life seems to have been tranquil until he took over the treasury at a time when his wife was determined to build up his fortune, now seriously compromised by his extravagance. There were, however, special difficulties in obtaining money from the treasury, for this great office was responsible for the payment of the envoys abroad and any delay in the distribution of these sums would be speedily known about the court. It was not that Suffolk was insensitive to the weaknesses of his position. Even before he came to his last appointment he had attempted to relinquish to the king his patents for currants and Venice glass

---

[1] A letter written by Sir Henry Wotton to Sir Edmund Bacon and dated June 16, 1614 states: "To my lord of Suffolk he (Northampton) hath left his house, but hath disposed of all the movables and furniture from him. And it is conceived that he died in some distasteful impression, which he had taken against him upon the voices that ran of my lord of Suffolk's likelihood to be Lord Treasurer". Printed in Logan Pearsall Smith, *Life and Letters of Sir Henry Wotton* (2 vols, Oxford, 1907), II, 39.

[2] William Bray, ed., *Diary of John Evelyn* (1819), 209.

and silks lest they become grievances complained of in the parliament.

He had, besides, other matters to disturb him, his responsibilities as an undertaker for the plantation of Ulster and a dispute with Lord Dunbar's executors about Lady Howard de Walden's marriage portion. There had been trouble, too, in acquiring Lord Northampton's minor places and redistributing them among the family.[1] In connection with the treasury itself there were factors complicating the situation. Northampton had written to the king alleging that "the two last Treasurers pared down the robe imperial for their own profit",[2] an unwise accusation calculated to cause enemies to examine the Howards' own imperfect practice.

Established at the Exchequer and in control of the machinery sat Mr Bingley. From the very beginning of Suffolk's treasurership, Mr, later Sir John, Bingley pursued his superior with his quick invention. What was required from Suffolk was not planning but consent. He was not molested and was permitted to take this profit in his cautious way. Even as early as 1614 the agents of the diplomatic envoys had found the sub-treasurer hard of access. The ambassadors themselves had found that interviews with him proved both heavy and fruitless. It is very understandable that whatever men might say of the sub-treasurer, there were few who would attack his great bland lord.

This may in part account for the extreme slowness of the proceedings. It was not until October 14, 1619 that Lord Suffolk appeared before the Star Chamber court. Meanwhile the charges had been piling up. There had been difficulties in regard to the Alum contract and the Ordnance Office finance. Lord Salisbury had come forward to support his father-in-law and a clear view of the state of the case can be obtained by the letters sent down to Hatfield by Sir John Finett to report upon the progress of the treasurer's matter. A brief note will convey the nature of the charges.[3]

There was question of £3,000 taken out of the Receipt of Exchequer, part of the moneys paid in to His Majesty for the Dutch cautionary towns. Again there were the moneys charged upon the old debt of Ireland "for which Sir J. Bingley had a privy seal in 8 Jas I & which

---

[1] The reversion of the keepership of the tower of Greenwich and the moiety of the manor of Clun, Cal. S.P.Dom, 1611–18, 52 and 137, and the manor of Bishop's Castle.

[2] Letter from Northampton to James I, dated October 8, 1612, *ibid.*, 150.

[3] Cecil MSS 129, f. 162. For a fuller account of this case, cf. Mathew, *The Jacobean Age*, 159–77. The Finett correspondence with Lord Salisbury dated between October 22 and November 14, 1619 is printed in an appendix to that volume, 319–31.

as an *abissus* or gulf swallowed score of treasure never in danger to be accounted for", and there were the tiresome sums of £100 and £40 said to be taken by my lord "out of the Exchequer and paid to Mr Carter, the first for his building at Newmarket and the latter for his stable at Charing Cross". Further matters emerged very rapidly. There was reference to the £3,000 demanded from Courteen by Sir John Townshend on the lord treasurer's behalf, to the £1,500 *per annum* contributed by the farmers of the leases of Oswestry, the three thousand pieces taken from the Merchant Adventurers for confirming or renewing their charter, Sir David Murray's composition and Sir Miles Fleetwood's gifts. There were many other cases of this description. The actual affairs had all been operated by Sir John Bingley, who had contacted Lady Suffolk about each case. Historians have been unanimous in their condemnation of her, but this question has perhaps another side.

Lord Suffolk was a heavy man, solemn and extravagant; his money poured like water on his constructions. The great house at Audley End was most expensive and so was its interior, the oak screens overlaid with carvings, the dolphins on the ceilings and the elaborate stucco pendants. Perhaps the countess tampered with the state finances in order to retrieve her husband's cold extravagance? We cannot tell.

The Star Chamber proceedings went forward. The attorney general conducted the prosecution. He spoke of the moderation of the lords, who grieved rather than desired the punishment of offenders, such as was the earl of Suffolk, "a great star fallen out of their own firmament". With the countess he was curiously less respectful. He said that "if she yielded in anything brought against her, it was but as the mouse would do being in the lion's mouth".

The judges then gave their verdict. My lord of Canterbury "made a discourse suitable to his profession". Understandably he had never liked the couple. "The close," wrote Finett to Lord Salisbury, "was for my Lord Chancellor, which he seldom or never makes, as Your Lordship knows, without great applause. He fell to discourse how completely the King were saved if the Treasury and state of means were settled, what honour he had obtained above any of his predecessors as to have deserved the title of Uniter of Britain and the Planter of Ireland: how glorious the Church here was like a firmament of stars." Thus did Lord Verulam extend himself.

Amid a careful dignity, unhurried and with pomp the trial drew to a close. After a verdict of guilty, the earl and countess of Suffolk were sentenced to be detained in the Tower of London during the king's pleasure; the earl was condemned to pay a fine of £30,000. They acknowledged themselves guilty and surrendered to serve their sentence. Within a week they were released and retired to Audley End. Here they spent the winter exploring the possibility of the king's mercy. Lord Howard de Walden lost his court appointment. Through the ensuing months the great weight of the fine was pared away; by the summer their indebtedness was computed at only £7,000. The whole process carried forward the political elimination of a ruling family. At this time no great lord was ever taken away from his place among the peers of England. One wonders that the king did not receive more gratitude from those to whom he was so generous; but perhaps there is not much gratitude among the rich.

Suffolk's fall had been preceded in the same year by the elimination of his cousin, the earl of Nottingham. He was now aged and had held the office of lord admiral for over thirty years and he did not leave office as the result of a sharp attack. His power had slowly crumbled in his later years and he was ready to resign as soon as a royal commission reported the malpractices that had grown up under his rule. In this case it was arranged quite gracefully. He was exonerated from any direct responsibility and received £3,000 in exchange for the surrender of his office; an additional pension of £1,000 was then bestowed upon him.

The earl of Nottingham, or to give him his better-known title of Lord Howard of Effingham, had been in command at the defeat of the Armada. He remains a shadowy figure; there has been no biography. It appears that he maintained a great calm dignity unmarred by much intelligence. He was, perhaps, seen at his best with the embassy that he led into Spain in the early years of King James's reign. There his high port won appreciation from grandees who for centuries had regarded the admirals of Castile as among the greatest of their order.

He was the last survivor of the courtiers of Queen Mary's reign; his religious outlook was Elizabethan. He was just on eighty when he resigned. At this period it was not the practice for peers to resign the great court offices, but this was masked by the fact that men very rarely reached old age except among the country gentry and the farmers. In later life Nottingham fell into financial embarrassment and both his name and that of his eldest son appear among the lists of Cranfield's creditors, that great man Sir Lionel Cranfield who was now coming into power. It was probably for this reason that he left no mark on Jacobean building. Horsley, where he was to die, and his houses at Reigate and Effingham have disappeared. His whole estate has vanished in the built-up areas of central Surrey.

Meanwhile, Sir Thomas Lake had run into a storm which could not fail to overwhelm him. He had married his daughter to young Lord Roos and had unluckily accepted a mortgage on his lands at Waltham-stow on that occasion. It was the dispute about these lands which led Lake's wife to launch her wild attack upon Roos's grandmother, the countess of Exeter, and thus brought him into conflict with a great court family. The result of the ensuing trial, when contrasted with the Suffolk case, is quite instructive. The friendship of the young favourite for the Exeters was probably the factor that awakened the direct interest of the king. In this case, unlike the two others that have been discussed, King James came immediately upon the scene.

The earl of Exeter was at this time seventy-five years old and lived at Wimbledon House, a new great mansion now destroyed, with his young wife. He suffered from gout, an aged stupid peer. He had come south from Burghley for the more clement weather and had settled on this manor, which had been the first-fruits of Sir William Cecil's service of the crown. It lay along a southward-facing slope within an easy coach ride of the capital. The house looked down across the open countryside to Epsom and to the boundaries of Lord Nottingham's estate. Lord Exeter was like Lord Durrisdeer "an old retired house keeper".

It is necessary to give a brief account of this elder line of the Cecils to explain the situation which developed. This then consisted, besides some younger sons who were not involved, of Lord Exeter and his son and grandson and their three wives. One of Exeter's children was the redoubtable Lady Hatton, and there was also her niece Lady Diana for whose hand it was hoped that the young favourite Buckingham would be a *prétendant*.

Lord Burghley, the son and heir, a colourless figure in his fifties, lived in London with his second wife, a sister of Sir Robert Drury, whose history will be considered later. Lord Roos, the grandson, had inherited this peerage at eleven months from his mother who had died in childbirth at fifteen; he was always delicate. He grew up a youth of fantastic tastes with little stamina. He went to Italy and made a collection of pictures which he later handed over to Lord Arundel; he went to Paris and sought to marry the ageing duchess of La Trèmouille and he asked Lord Salisbury's aid in this affair.[1] Later he became incurably extravagant. It was thought by the Lakes that Lady Exeter had influenced her husband against their requests about the land at Walthamstow. The Roos marriage was childless and broke down. Young Lord Roos went to Italy and became a Catholic. He stayed at Rome and then moved on to Naples. He died in that city in 1618 in the heats of June. In all this matter he was just a cipher.

Meanwhile, Lady Lake had brought two accusations. She said in regard to her daughter's marriage that Lord Roos had been impotent *versus hanc*, a possibility. But it was the countess whom she wished to injure and she also said that Roos had had a *liaison* with his step-grand-mother.[2] This statement she bolstered up with ridiculous false evidence. It was not until February 1619 that the case between the families came on in Star Chamber. The king, interested in the case, presided for the first time in his reign at a Star Chamber hearing. In his opening speech he compared himself to Solomon "that was to judge between two women . . . and to finde out the true mother of the childe, (that is veritie)". The Lakes, for the husband supported his wife, stood by a forged confession in which the countess was alleged to have admitted her guilt.

The king adjourned the hearing to Wimbledon House to examine the scene of the composition of this confession. It was supposed to have been written in the great chamber there. The arras behind which Lady Lake's servant claimed to have concealed herself stopped well short of the ground and would have been useless for this purpose. The case broke down. When the king delivered judgment, he compared the crime of the Lakes "to the first plot of the first sin in Paradise, the Lady to the serpent, her daughter to Eve, and Sir Thomas to poor Adam, whose love of his wife (the old sin of Our Father) had beguiled him". Throughout his reign the king appears to have betrayed a lack of confidence in the virtue of the wives of his friends and servants.

What is interesting are the consequences. Sir Thomas was deprived of the secretaryship of state. He and his wife were each fined £5,000 and the other members of his family mulcted in smaller sums. £1,000 was to be paid immediately to Lady Exeter. When released from the

---

[1] Cf. Cecil MSS., 116, f. 84.
[2] The countess was the widow of Sir Thomas Smyth and a daughter of the fourth Lord Chandos; she was about eleven years Lord Roos' senior.

Tower the final sum that they were forced to pay amounted to £10,500. There was no paring away of their indebtedness. It was a contrast to the Suffolk trial with "its firmament of stars". Men suffered when they attacked the great.

A couple of months earlier in the same winter the king required Lord Wallingford to resign the mastership of the Court of Wards. He was now an old man and the king had taken a distaste to his wife; she was of dubious morals and a Catholic convert. It was she who had supported her sister Lady Somerset; the slate was now wiped clean.

Chapter 20

ECCLESIASTICS

MARCO ANTONIO DE DOMINIS was a corpulent Venetian prelate, a learned man but ignorant of the world. He must have had some initial influence behind him for he was appointed bishop of Segni in the papal states.[1] From there he was promoted to the archdiocese of Spalato in Venetian territory. Like Spalato, his birthplace the island of Arbe was in the Dalmatian territory of the republic. He entered into the views of the Venetian government and turned against the Jesuits, by whom he had been educated. At this time he was a man of about fifty, born in the same year as King James, and was engaged in writing his *De Republica Ecclesiastica*. He seems to have felt that this work had best be published in some foreign country. He was a celibate, who gave too much value to his own writings. He shared his government's coldness to the Holy See and was angered that he had been ordered to pay an annual pension of five hundred crowns to his successor at Segni. It was in 1616 that on the proposals of Sir Henry Wotton he came to England.

He seems to have felt that he would be recognised as an archbishop and would receive some comparable preferment. What he did not realise was that no foreign convert could ever reach the Anglican bench of bishops any more than a foreign convert could become a member of the episcopate of the Church of France. The year after his arrival the king conferred on him the deanery of Windsor and the mastership of the Savoy. He never really learned English, nor can his host Archbishop Abbot be considered as the type of Anglican who might perhaps like an Italian prelate. Further, he never understood the crucial importance of flattering the king. He was getting old and was lonely and very greedy. It is difficult to make money in a country in which one does not know the language; the efforts that he made repelled his hosts.

Towards the end of the winter in 1621 Pope Paul V died and was succeeded by Alessandro Ludovisi, cardinal of Santa Maria in Trastevere and Archbishop of Bologna, who took the name of Gregory XV.

---

[1] Described in *DNB.* as Segni in the state of Venice.

There had been some contacts, not precisely revealed, between De Dominis and the new pontiff. The Spanish ambassador held out to him the probability of his appointment to the archbishopric of Salerno in Campania, all the more possible since it lay in the Spanish viceroyalty of Naples. He does not seem to have considered what claim he had to such preferment. The whole episode shows how versatile was the count of Gondomar.

The Pope received the prodigal and then died. De Dominis was arrested and therefore never reached the Gulf of Salerno, that sparkling sea, and the sleepy city under the granite hills. Within a few months he died in the prison of the Inquisition. It was a misfortune that he had listened to the two ambassadors.

The sands of the archbishop's influence were running out. The king had not forgotten the opposition shown by the archbishop to his judgment at the time of the Essex divorce. He did not relish that his own patient arguments should be countered by any churchman. Dr Abbot and others had had influence when George Villiers was first introduced to court; but he had been very difficult in his opposition to a Spanish marriage. Besides, the ageing king was now turning towards a younger prelate.

In the morning of July 24, 1621 an unfortunate accident befell the primate. He was staying with Lord Zouche, a minor member of the administration, in his great house at Bramshill in Hampshire, which had been completed only recently. One day during his visit, when standing "in the presence of forty or fifty persons",[1] he shot at a deer with his cross-bow and mortally wounded Peter Hawkins, the park keeper.

An Apology for Archbishop Abbot was at once launched with quotations at large from Soto, Covarrubias and Suarez "who are great canonists and schoolmen".[2] The recent history of the two primatial sees in England was then examined. Instances were given[3] of the practice of Archbishop Whitgift, who used to hunt in Hartlebury Park while he lived at Worcester, at Ford Park in Kent and in the park of Lord Cobham near Canterbury where by the favour of that peer he killed twenty bucks in one journey, using hounds, greyhounds or his bow at his pleasure, although he never shot well. And the same practice was credibly reported of Archbishop Sandys. The subsequent rustication of Archbishop Abbot to his house at Foord was altogether unconnected with this

---

[1] *State Trials*, II, 67. [2] *Ibid.*, II, 67. [3] *Ibid.*, II, 68–9.

misfortune and resulted from his refusal to licence Dr Sibthorpe's sermon.

At the moment four bishops-elect were awaiting consecration: Dr Williams for Lincoln, Dr John Davenant for Salisbury, Dr Valentine Cary for Exeter and Dr Laud for St David's. The last-named had been promoted against Abbot's will and with his high notions it is no surprise that he scrupled the archbishop's capacity to lay hands on him until he received a dispensation for irregularity for shedding blood. Dr Davenant expressed his willingness and Dr Cary refused. It is rather surprising that Dr Williams refused likewise. Behind most of this new prelate's public actions there seems to lie some clear line of policy. He was at this time quickly gaining the king's confidence; perhaps it might be useful to attack the primate now that he was down.

Dr John Williams had long been known to his sovereign; his name at any rate had been familiar since the very beginning of the reign. His star had risen slowly in the night sky. As early as 1605, when he was twenty-three years old and a Fellow of St John's College, Cambridge, he had received his first living, Honington in Suffolk, from the king. Six years later he had exchanged this for Grafton Underwood, another royal presentation. Archbishop Bancroft smiled on him. As far back as 1610 he had preached before the king and two years later had been appointed as private chaplain to Lord Chancellor Ellesmere. In 1617 he had become chaplain to the king and had gone to Scotland with him.

He had much for which the king was very grateful. He had above all a swift understanding of his mental processes; he knew the areas of the king's knowledge. It seems that he never strayed beyond them. What a contrast this was to Francis Bacon who carelessly displayed before the king the areas of his recondite thought and imagined that his sovereign would be contented with the sugar plums he dropped as compliments. Dr Williams on the other hand always gave to him the thought of a learned equal who was just a shade discipular.

The main fault of English courtiers is laziness; they will not follow their sovereign's interests when these extend beyond the United Kingdom. There are plenty of examples of this trait in Hanoverian and Victorian times. Thus Williams, almost alone among the members of the Jacobean court, entered into King James's concern with anti-Arminian controversy. He had a quick Welsh courtesy. King James had never visited the principality and indeed he was his sole Welsh intimate. It is worth making a brief comment upon his background.

Dr Williams had that self-confidence which is natural in a Welshman who is sure of his long line of high descent.[1] He also had a sweeping Celtic imagination. Until he reached his own great eminence he never lacked supporters. Dr Vaughan was his first patron. "For by the time his bud began to blow," so explains his biographer, "it fortuned that Dr Vaughan afterward the Reverend Lord Bishop of London, came into Wales and took the school of Ruthyn in his way, where he found his young kinsman John Williams to be the bell-weather of this little flock."[2] It was Dr Vaughan who brought him to St John's College, where he was "much welcom'd to Cambridge by the Old Britains of North Wales".[3]

There were two years between Lord Ellesmere's death and Dr Williams's appointment to the deanery of Salisbury on September 10, 1619. He had also acquired another benefice and now he emerged as the king's friend. He was a sybaritic bachelor and he had some tastes which the king did not share; he designed gardens. His theological position somewhat resembled what would, in the nineteenth century, be called that of a broad churchman. He came in time to exercise power which was in effect episcopal. At the same time he had a warm feeling for the non-episcopal churches of the continent and he had a distaste for Laud's conception of a monarchical episcopate. Vestments were not within his range of interests. This brought him close to his own sovereign, who was at heart a Scotsman and anti-sacerdotalist.

His taste was seemly as can be seen from the Communion table, pulpit and "the faire screene" all of cedar, which he placed in the chapel at Lincoln College. He was generous to "the worthies of the Transmarine Churches". He had indeed a tolerance beyond his master's. "Is there," he used to say, "but one Tree of Knowledge in all the Paradise of the Church of God?"[4] He would follow his master, as few bishops were prepared to follow among all the various churches of the Calvinist obedience.

He accepted the king's judgment with deference and with submission. He really shared the king's dislike for the Arminian propositions. The king was at ease with him and produced his jovial railleries. He was sixteen years younger than his sovereign. There is no evidence that he

[1] Cf. The account by Bishop Hacket in *Scrinia Reserata*, 6. "The pedigree of the House of Williams of Cogwillanne hath as many brave strings in the root and spreads as wide in the branches, as I have seen produced from the store-house of their Cambrian Antiquities. It grows up in top boughs to the Princes of North Wales in King Stephen's days."
[2] *Ibid.*, 7.   [3] *Ibid.*, 7.   [4] *Ibid.*, II, 34.

ever controverted the king's opinion on any matter either in church or state. This was something which old Archbishop Abbot had also failed to do.

There was little of the Puritan about Bishop Williams; his mind ran on state maxims. He advised the duke of Buckingham to head an attack in parliament on the monopolists in order to disorganise the opposition. He was a great political churchman and his thought went back to "Splendian Wolsey",[1] as he called him. It was this that led the king to appoint him as lord keeper on Bacon's fall, and, as the profits of the office had been pruned, he gave him the rich bishopric of Lincoln. The deanery of Salisbury had been exchanged for that of Westminster, which he retained.

It was important for the king to keep about his person this able prelate who supported all his notions and never offered anything except a courteous encouragement. Still, one thing was now necessary: he had to be integrated into the Villiers family. So far as it was practicable the king achieved this.

It has been said that Dr Williams was sensitive to the king's reactions. This can be seen in the matter of King James's decision that Lady Catherine Manners should become an Anglican before her marriage to the marquess of Buckingham. Dr Williams had neither sympathy for nor experience of Roman Catholics. They were rare in the North Wales of his youth and absent from the Cambridge of his early manhood. Still he was successful with this girl, a Catholic from childhood. It cannot exactly be said that he converted her for she returned to Rome after Buckingham was murdered. But with his dulcet skill he reconciled her conscience with her opportunity, he showed how these two should go hand in hand. He was likewise successful with her father the earl of Rutland, a strong royalist. He convinced this not very intelligent Catholic nobleman that he should allow his daughter to accept the king's religion.

There was a certain parallel with the king's hopes for a Spanish marriage for the Prince of Wales. No more than any other bishop did he wish to see a Spanish queen, but he encouraged his sovereign to look with favour on demands made by Madrid. He never stood in the way of the king's wishes.

At this time there lay dying a great person who had subordinated her-

[1] Cf. *Scrinia Reserata*, II, 29.

self continually to the king's wishes. The queen had had dropsy for some years and the disease was now gaining fast upon her. She had established herself as King James desired at the centre of his great court functions and in the middle distance of his personal life. She had her brother, the king of Denmark, to protect her interests and he had made two visits to the English court. After she came to England she was almost unconsciously extravagant and was rescued from her debts by her husband's generosity. She was given as secondary residences old Greenwich Palace and Pontefract in Yorkshire and Havering-atte-Bower. In the end her total jointure amounted to £24,000 a year, to which was added £13,000 from the sugar and cloth duties. It is significant that when Somerset House was given to her she renamed her new headquarters Denmark House.

She seems to have had few intimates beyond Lady Jane Drummond, but she had a quality of mercy. She wrote to the king in an attempt to save Sir Walter Raleigh from execution and she was kind to Lady Arabella during her imprisonment in the Tower. Quite unlike her husband she had a carefree and fluid attitude to foreign states.

She was a great patron of the masque and liked to take her part in those fine and very costly shows which marked the middle period of the reign. She shared in the king's recreations when these were held within reach of London. She followed the fate of the young lions and leopards which were placed in the Tower of London; she had notice of their whelping.[1] She saw the two young crocodiles and the wild boar brought from Hispaniola by Captain Newport and she went to the Tower with her husband and the royal children to see the trial of the large lion's single valour "against a great fierce bear, which had killed a child that was negligently left in the Beare House".[2]

She was very fond of dogs. We know that she was attached to the small Italian greyhounds, which are seen in the Van Somers portrait. She was averse to reading and liked in every way an outdoor life. In this portrait she has a great farthingale of green velvet, buff leather gloves with gauntlet tops, deep cuffs of Brussels lace, three tiers in height, and that strange shovel-shaped grey beaver hat with a gold band and a setting of fire-coloured plumes. All this was serviceable in the English weather.

[1] Cal. S. P. Dom., 1603–10, 250. This may have given rise to the name *Lion's Whelp*, from *first* to *tenth*, small square-rigged vessels, which joined the Royal Navy a little later.
[2] Nichols, *Itineraries*, 259.

Before her health began to break she was a great figure at the court of England in some ways in counterpoint to the king. What she saw of Villiers she approved; her interests were limited to personal relationships; she was probably as popular as a queen consort could be. She had made a journey to the west country, to Bath and then to Bristol. She had entered the latter city in a chariot drawn by four milk-white horses, her maids of honour following the carriage, riding on palfreys two by two.

It seems that her religious interests were less than they had once been. In her last years priests from overseas came to her at Oatlands, her country palace. As she lay dying the archbishop of Canterbury and the bishop of London made her a visit on a point of duty, but not invited. The archbishop did not mention the Church of Rome, but spoke as follows. "Madame, we hope your majesty does not trust to your own merits, nor to the merits of the saints, but only to the blood and merits of our Saviour." The queen appears to have replied as they desired. "I renounce the mediation of saints and my own merits, and only rely on my saviour Christ, who has redeemed my soul by his blood."[1] What interests were truly close to her heart?

In a real sense she was a Scandinavian queen. She was careful to protect her morally frail husband, a strange task which she can hardly have expected in her northern court. We can see her best standing on the short turf holding her Italian greyhounds by a crimson lead.

[1] The actual account comes from a paper entitled "Madam the Queen's death and Maner theirof" among Sir James Balfour's MSS printed in *Abbotsford Miscellany*, 81. For an account from the Catholic side of her conversion, life and death, cf. the article by J. de la Servière in *Dictionnaire d'Histoire et de Géographie Ecclésiastiques* (1924), III, cols 337-9.

Chapter 21

BOHEMIA AND VIRGINIA

THE early years of Buckingham's ascendancy coincided with Bacon's tenure of the lord keepership. Sir Francis Bacon, who at that time held the post of attorney general, had become lord keeper on the death of Lord Chancellor Ellesmere in March 1617. Sir Edward Coke had been deprived of the chief justiceship of the King's Bench in the previous year, and his attempt to recover the royal favour by agreeing to the marriage of his daughter Frances with Buckingham's brother Sir John Villiers had had a very transient success. This last matter is principally notable as the first occasion on which a rift appeared between Bacon on the one hand and on the other the king and his new favourite. Nevertheless the promotion of Villiers, as marquess of Buckingham, and Bacon, as Lord Verulam, took place on the same day.

The lines of the last years of King James's reign began to form. Lionel Cranfield entered the royal service and became surveyor general of the customs. Lord Hay married Lady Lucy Percy and the release of the latter's father, the earl of Northumberland, from the Tower of London could be foreseen. Most significant of these various changes, the king's surviving son, now Prince of Wales, changed abruptly from a sharp dislike to a devoted friendship for the new favourite. The idea of a Spanish marriage for the prince, which had pursued the king's heir for many years, revived again. Buckingham became lord admiral; his power was growing.

In these days the king built his only royal memorial which now remains to him, the banqueting house which Inigo Jones added to the palace of Whitehall[1] to replace a building which had been burned. It gives an impression of the character of the new palace which King James did not live to construct. A resemblance to the Palazzo Madama at Turin suggests the royal buildings of the *seicento*. Inigo Jones had been appointed to the surveyorship of the king's Works in 1615; but beyond the banqueting house he built but little during this reign. At the queen's

[1] For an excellent and detailed account of the palace, see G. P. V. Akrigg, *Jacobean Pageant*, 279–86.

house at Greenwich the plan was made in 1616 and the ground floor probably constructed in the same year. The queen's death, which then took place, and the king's lassitude alike combined to limit the work of the great architect.

The field of foreign affairs was very difficult and, as far as the king's own conduct was concerned, the problem was in no way lightened by the presence of the count of Gondomar, who had now returned to London on his second embassy. The rebellion in Bohemia had led to the offer of that crown to the Elector Palatine and his acceptance was a clear affront to the king of England. He had in fact asked for his opinion and had then proceeded straight to Prague before the king could give a judgment. At the same time the king's attachment to the doctrine of hereditary right led him to desire to protect the territories of the Palatinate.

He constantly urged Spain to assist him in this cause; but the Upper Palatinate was in effect already lost. The Archduke Ferdinand of Styria, who had been elected Roman emperor on his cousin's death, had called the duke of Bavaria to his aid in reconquering Bohemia. This prince had had a certain claim upon these lands since the outcome of the Landshut war; but he also asked for the whole of Frederick's territory and the transfer of the electorate to his branch of the Wittelsbachs. This was a secret treaty, but a secret all the easier to maintain since the king of England had no envoy at the court of Munich.

Buckingham and the prince swayed from a pro-Spanish feeling to an enthusiasm for the project of saving the Palatinate. Throughout his life the prince would manifest a staid protective attitude towards his only sister. The various private efforts to raise funds for this purpose were ineffective; the king determined on his third parliament. This met on January 30, 1621, and sat for rather over a year. It was the last called during his effective reign.

The actual warlike efforts were very slight. The king loved peace and it was hard to convince him that he would not make the ideal peacemaker between the emperor and his son-in-law. Further the future of Bohemia was not long in doubt. On November 23, 1620 the Bohemian forces and their allies were scattered at the battle of the White Hill. King Frederick and his queen then fled from Prague, taking refuge in the territory of Brandenburg. Bohemia was henceforth in the possession of the Hapsburgs. The difficulty now solely turned upon Frederick's rights to his hereditary territories. The Bavarians occupied the Upper

Palatinate, while the lands round Heidelberg were threatened by an army under Spinola, which had marched in from the Spanish Netherlands.

For once King James and English public opinion, by which one means the opinion of the influential classes, were in agreement on a point of foreign policy. It was the fall of Prague which had brought them together. On June 9, 1620 Sir Horace Vere had gone to Theobalds to take leave of the king and a fortnight later had set sail from Gravesend with a regiment of just over two thousand men for Holland; they were then to move south-eastward to occupy the towns of the lower Palatinate. On reaching the territory Vere divided his forces, which had received some reinforcements from the Dutch. He himself occupied Mannheim, Sir Gerard Herbert took over the defence of Heidelberg Castle and Sir John Burroughs placed himself at Frankenthal. It was in fact a token force; but it was a body of English soldiers on the continent, a fact sufficient to persuade the parliament that England might be about to move into a general war.

The movement of the Spanish force into the Palatinate is curious, although disguised by Gondomar as a temporary measure to persuade the Elector Palatine to surrender Bohemia. It seems that in these days there were two strands of policy among the councillors at the Spanish court, those who held that peace with England was all-important and those who wished to follow the old-established policy of close alliance with the house of Austria. The situation was further modified by the death on March 21, 1621 of the King of Spain. Philip III was succeeded by his son Philip IV, a boy of sixteen. It was not at first clear who controlled him. Against the background of the parliamentary situation there stood the fact of these three English garrisons. In early 1622 the Elector Palatine made a brief visit to Mannheim, but apart from this he never again re-entered his own dominions. On September 16 the town of Heidelberg was taken by storm and Sir Gerard Herbert received a mortal wound in the attack. At the end of the same month Vere was forced to surrender and marching out with the honours of war took his soldiers back to the Hague. Burroughs held out until April 14, 1623, when he surrendered on direct orders from home. The king was henceforth free from any involvement in the great war upon the continent.

Still, this is to anticipate. When the house assembled the members were still convinced that the Palatine marriage would bring the king into a warlike Protestant (or in fact Calvinist) alliance with Holland

281

and in Germany. There was a similar divergence between the king's ideas and those of the men who were now building up Virginia. Both these contrasts are seen in action in the new parliament. The king abhorred warfare and it also seems that he did not understand the commercial world as it was now developing. Problems of trade had hardly occupied the king of Scotland. In these it was clear that he was losing touch.

It was as the reign progressed, with Raleigh dead, that the new commercial values became apparent. The voyage across the Atlantic is at last seen tranquilly as a trading venture. The break with the carefree Elizabethan projects becomes very evident. A novel sobriety overtook the management of overseas adventures. Certainly it is clear that the actual builders of Virginia moved on a plane of ideas which was very far distant from the world of their sovereign's clouded and theocratic rhetoric. By considering first the background of parliament, the king's speech and the standpoint reflected in the House of Commons, and then the workings of the headquarters of the Virginia Plantation, we can gain some impression of the two outlooks and their profound interior divergence.

In the study of this question all students owe a heavy debt to the late Professor Notestein and his assistants. The seven volumes dealing with the Commons' debates for 1621, which this historian has assembled, provide a singularly complete ground plan of the speeches and resolutions of that year. The third general election of the reign had just been held and, with the exception of the brief parliament of 1614, the government had been carried on without the support and embarrassment of the two houses since the dissolution in February 1611. Then Lord Salisbury had been still alive, and in all five sessions of his first parliament the sovereign had had the benefit of that statesman's unique experience.

Now the king needed money. His son-in-law had accepted the crown of Bohemia and had been driven from his new kingdom, and his own hereditary states were in grave danger. There was the security of the Palatinate to be considered. The speech from the throne, made under these circumstances, well indicates the king's approach. He had just come from the sermon which Bishop Andrewes of Winchester had preached before both houses, and the royal words were carefully pondered. The king's sentences could never lack assurance, and his utterance was hardly lightened by his strange and arid pleasantry.

It is true [he began] that in many sessions of divers Parliaments before this I have made many long discourses, especially to the gentlemen of the House of Commons, and to them have I delivered as I myself have said, a true mirror of my mind and free thoughts of my heart. But as no man's action, be he never so good, are free from sin, being a mortal, sinful creature, so some, through a spice of envy have made all my speeches heretofore turn like spittle against the wind upon mine own face and contrary to my expectations, so that I may truely say with our Saviour, I have often piped unto and you have not danced, I have warned and you have not lamented.[1]

The theocratic mood lay on him heavily.

All the world [he declared] cannot so much as create the least vermin, no more than Pharaoh's magicians could; nor can all the men on the earth create faith, but it is God that must give that[2] .... I will not say [the king continued in reference to his own achievements] I have governed as well as she (Queen Elizabeth) did, but I may say we have had as much peace in our time as in hers. I have laboured as a woman in travail, not ten months but ten years, for within that time I have not had a Parliament nor subsidy. And I dare say I have been as sparing to trouble you not with monopolies or in subsidies as ever King before me, considering the greatness of my occasions and charges.[3]

Then, turning to foreign relations, he explained that he had been reluctant in the matter of the Palatinate. "First," he declared, "for cause of religion for I leave that ground to the Jesuits and devil, from whence it came, to cast down crowns for cause of religion, and learn of my Saviour, who came into the world to stablish crowns and not to destroy them and to teach men how to obey." It came naturally to him to drop now into the vein of admonition. He described that "strange kind of beasts called undertakers" which had troubled him in 1614, and he spoke of the ills of his first House of Commons.

I have had [he began] two kinds of parliaments, the one when I came first into England when I was an apprentice and so inexperienced, governors in the *quondam* time being more skilful by long experience, and so many things might then be amiss which I have endeavoured to amend, considering there are two sorts of speakers which I would inhibit, first, lion-like speakers that dare speak of anything that appertains to princes, secondly, fox-like that seem to speak one thing and intend another, as to bring the King in dislike with his subjects.[4]

[1] *Commons' Debates*, Anonymous Journal (ed. W. Notestein), II, 2.
[2] *Ibid.*, 6.   [3] *Ibid.*, 8.   [4] *Ibid.*, 12.

The sentences become more complex, but the thought behind them is lucidly clear.

Then Sergeant Richardson was elected Speaker and the notes describe the conclusion of that day's ceremony. "The Speaker", so they run, "replied in a long continued oration, repeating what the King had spoken, and (declaring) that he desired that the dutiful liberty of the House should be given, and that kings were invisible gods and God an invisible king."

In the parish chest in the church at Hatfield Broad Oak, on the edge of that lonely stretch of Essex towards High Easter and the Roothings, there was discovered the notes of speeches in this parliament made by Sir Thomas Barrington, the local squire. Here we find the frame of the orations in the commons set down with a vivid turn of phrase, which the other contemporary annotators lacked. In quality and in manner the speakers varied greatly and it is possible to sense the fatigue induced by an array of facts even when sustained by the customary majestic periods. They are of especial interest since they all reveal the gulf between the king's outlook on foreign policy and that of the greater squires among his subjects.

In this connection it is worth quoting a speech made by Sir Edward Coke in the November of that year. "The first plague," he insisted, "among our sheepe was brought by a Spanish sheepe to England and could hardly be cured; and so *Morbus Gallicus* by them from Naples."[1] He was followed on the same subject by Sir Robert Phelips, who owned the great house which his father had built at Montacute in Somerset. "The designes of Spain," began Sir Robert, "are ever accompanied by falsehood, being resting on that greate Roman monster. Theay are reciprocall, and at Rome his religion and in Spain Rome's honour and preservation. I pray God remove from us that pollituick blaseing starr that hath long hung over us, that we feele not as well the misery thereof as we did of that Celestiall."[2] The day before Mr Thomas Crew had spoken to the same point in plainer language. "It were excellent that we might crop the House of Austria, and top the Indies from him. Every one would give with a swift and open hand."[3] The value of such words lay in the fact that it was only in this way that such sentiments could reach the king. Expressions could be used in that privileged arena that would never be heard at the English court. It was also in

---

[1] *Commons' Debates*, Diary of Sir Thomas Barrington, III, 467.   [2] *Ibid.*, 469.
[3] *Ibid.*, Anonymous Journal, II, 451.

the house that the work of the new Virginia Company would be assessed.

This had, in fact, been established since the early days of the reign; but it was only now that it became a prime object for the courtiers' investment. The actual chartered company had been set up in April 1606 and Lord Salisbury had established its court in London. One aspect of the nature of the plantation had appeared quite early. A letter among the Cecil MSS brings out this point. It was from Sir Walter Cope, a wealthy man, financially adventurous, who owned the large estate of Kensington near London. "My Lord Chief Justice [Popham]," wrote Sir Walter, "foreseeing in the experience of his place the infinite numbers of cashiered captains and soldiers, of poor artizans that would and cannot work, and of idle vagrants that may and will not work, whose increase threatens the State, is affectionately bent to the plantation of Virginia."[1]

There had been great developments and it was now seven years since the first shipment of Virginian tobacco had arrived in England. A plan for a tobacco contract was now before the House of Commons, and the members were brought to consider the question of their sovereign's new possessions. "Explayne," runs a note made by John Smyth of Nibley which gives the framework of one of his own speeches, "the meaning of the word *Foreen*, for Virginia and the Somer Islands are freeholds holden of East Greenwich, etc. Know the care to avoyd the inordinate plantyng of tobacco. To banish all was the desire of Gondemar."[2] A comment, made by Sir Walter Cope a little earlier in the session, is equally illuminating. "When," he began, "we made title to certayne mynes in the West Indies, twelve millions brought in in one year in the Queen's tyme. This great spring is kept from our poole, no marvaile if we want water."[3] Here was the old conception of the Spanish king's jealousies; but there were no mines and no Spaniards within Virginia.

It is clear that by this time the name of Virginia and the Summer Islands awoke a wide familiarity. Under one aspect they had importance for they were the *locale* of chartered companies for the mainland and the Bermudas.

Investment in these undertakings had been canvassed for some dozen

---

[1] Letter from Sir Walter Cope to the earl of Salisbury dated March 1606, Cecil MSS, 191, f. 120.

[2] *Commons' Debates* (1621), Diary of Thomas Smyth, V, 334.

[3] *Ibid.*, Parliament Notes by Sir Nathaniel Rich, V, 516.

years as a patriotic and religious duty, which was calculated to show a profit. Now men's thoughts were turned to the solid income from the tobacco trade and the strengthening of the king's plantations. In the house both these matters were discussed with calmness. There was also another strand which would emerge. "I would move," declared Sir Edwin Sandys in a debate towards the end of April, "that the poore that cannot be sett on worke maye be sent to Virginia. Never was there a fairer gate opened to a nation to disburden itselfe nor better meanes by reason of the abundance of people to advance such a plantation."[1] The subject was taken up by Sir Peter Frescheville: "Now for the way to have it [tobacco] brought in," he explained, "we see the Spanish way hinders us both in marchandize and money & then this way of Virginia and the Summer Ilands is a good way for the advancinge of their plantation, so brave and necessary a business, a furtherance to the good and benefitt of our nation, and also a ridding of that *inutile pondus* of unprofitable members of the Commonwealth."[2] Men had now freed themselves from Sir Walter Raleigh's grand conceptions. Masts and tobacco had replaced the gold which they had been so often promised.

It was not, however, in the House of Commons that exact information about the colonies could be collected. Accurate detail was hard to discover; but such knowledge as anyone in London then possessed would be found among the officers of the Virginia Company as they assembled for the meeting of their court in the low-panelled rooms in Sir Thomas Smith's house in Philpott Lane, or at Mr John Ferrar's. For the benefit of investors the company would set out their declarations, the *Nova Britannia* and *Virginia richly valued* and *Good News from Virginia* and Lord Delawarr's quiet *Relation*. These were in the nature of annual reports and had been issued under the authority of the treasurer, Sir Thomas Smith "once and for all the Primus moter in the [Virginia] Company".[3] The minutes of the court meetings suggest the breadth of Smith's experience.

The atmosphere of the court of the Virginia Company seems almost a generation away from that of the royal palace. It was in some ways a dim foreshadowing of the opposition world, which would develop in the next king's reign. The principal officers of the company were influenced by ethical conceptions. An evangelical quality was apparent

---

[1] *Commons' Debates*, The Belasyse Diary, V, 113–14.
[2] *Ibid.*, Diary of Sir Thomas Barrington, III, 148.
[3] Cf. Letter of Lord Sackville, *Records of the Virginia Company of London*, II, 259.

in their outlook and a strong dislike for gaming. They understood, in a fashion that the lavish Tudor world could not appreciate, the sin of waste.

There was a religious note which looked still further forward. This is reflected in the instructions given to Sir Thomas Gates, the first governor of Virginia[1] and also in those furnished rather later to Lord Delawarr.[2] Such a standpoint was held in its completeness by Nicholas Ferrar the elder, then deputy treasurer of the company. Beyond his care for the commercial policy, his Virginian interests were concentrated on the projected college at Henrico, where Indian children were to be instructed in "the true knowledge of God and understanding of righteousness". The governors dispatched bibles, psalters and communion plate to Virginia and the Bermudas. It is not surprising that the funeral sermon preached for Mr Ferrar at St Benet Sherehog by Dr White should suggest a Christian assurance closer in its character to Wilberforce than Raleigh. The preacher chose a text in Job, v, "Thou shalt come to thy grave in a full age, like as a shock of corn cometh in his season".

On the edge of the ethical and economic considerations lay the problem of the children who would be sent out to the new colony. "The City of London," wrote Sandys to Secretary Naunton upon this subject, "have appointed one hundred children from their superfluous multitude to be transported to Virginia, there to be bound apprentices upon very beneficial conditions. Some of the ill-disposed children, who under severe masters in Virginia may be brought to goodness, and of whom the City is especially desirous to be disburdened, declare their unwillingness to go."[3] In this connection the coffer books of Winchester contain an entry under the date of December 30, 1625: "60 shillings for the apparelling of six poor boys that went to Virginia." In the Barnstaple account books there appears an item of "10s. 4d. paid for shoes for three boys sent to Virginia".[4]

It may be that these practical details helped to commend the Virginia Company as an investment to those who attended King James's court. The support of the episcopate, given the interest of Sir Maurice Abbot and Sir Edwyn Sandys, was not surprising, and the names of Archbishop Abbot and the bishops of Bath and Wells, London and

---

[1] Instructions dated May 1609, *ibid.*, III, 14. [2] *Ibid.*, 27.
[3] Letter from Sir Edwin Sandys to Sir Robert Naunton, dated January 28, 1620, Cal. S.P. Colonial, 1574–1660, 23. [4] *Barnstaple Records*, II, 136.

Worcester are found with Dr Donne, the new dean of St Paul's, among the undertakers. The whole-hearted support of the rich world of London was, perhaps, less expected.

There is no reason to suppose that the courtiers possessed any precise knowledge of the new colony or that their interest had advanced beyond a genuine desire for making easy money in polite company. It is, however, certain that the list of the adventurers and shareholders contains almost all those names which a visit to the court might make familiar, the leading Cecils, Howards, Sackvilles and Herberts, Bedford, Chandos, Carlisle and Lady Shrewsbury, Paget, Drury, Sir Anthony Ashley, Conway, Calvert, Sir Walter Cope, Cranfield and Sir Baptist Hicks, Bingley and Garraway, Sir John Digby, Sir Henry Carey, Sir John Doddridge, Sir Charles Wilmot, Sir Horace Vere, Sir Drue Drury, Sir Thomas Chaloner, Sir John Ogle, Sir John Townshend, Calisthenes Brooke and Sir Hatton Cheke, Sir Christopher Perkins and Phineas Pett, Monteagle of the Powder plot, Sir Thomas Beaumont, Goring, Fanshawe, Craven, Fleetwood, Finch and Ingram, Sir Thomas Roe, Sir Oliver Cromwell, Sir David Murray and Fulke Greville.

The list in its entirety provides an interesting cross-section of the circle which possessed financial privilege or opportunity. Its ramifications are confined to London and to those families which resided, at least intermittently, in the capital. Beyond the names of the courtiers there come those of the richer merchants and the city companies, the Bakers and Barber Surgeons, Clothworkers, Drapers, Dyers, Fishmongers, Grocers, Goldsmiths, Girdlers, Innholders, Embroiderers, Ironmongers, Leathersellers, Mercers, Merchant Taylors, Salters, Stationers and Skinners. There were the Lord Mayor, Sir Humphrey Weld, the Elder Brothers of Trinity House, and three progressive corporations, Chichester, King's Lynn and Dover. The country gentry, as opposed to the courtiers and the parliament men, were hardly represented. Such squires as Sir Valentine Knightley and Thomas Barrington sat in the Commons. There were very few women, the only names registered being those of Lady Shrewsbury and Lady Berkeley. Catholics also were very rare; among the peers Petre, Eure and Clanricarde, and among the commoners Robert Stourton, Calvert, who became a convert, and possibly two of the Shelleys. Science is represented only by the naturalist John Tradescant.

Yet here it becomes manifest how difficult it is to sift any list of names into its categories, for where should one place Lord St Alban[1] with his ranging interests? Viewed from another angle the investors in the Virginia Company seem linked and gathered by the solid prestige of Sir Thomas Smyth and the zeal and financial courage of Lords Warwick and Southampton. These peers had now little contact with the court and inspired confidence in their integrity as they sat devoted to this business at the meetings of the company. With them went Lord Cavendish and the uninterested courtiers followed the guarantee that they provided.

Viewed from some aspects 1621 may be seen as the watershed of the two periods, a date by which the Stuart character of the century had been purged of its immediate Elizabethan influences. The old men were dead or in retirement. This year saw the fall of Lord St Alban and his deprivation of the great seal. Nottingham, the last of the Elizabethan councillors, had vanished. Those parliamentary manoeuvres which would lead up to the Petition of Right had now begun. Raleigh's last journey to the Orinoco and his death on the scaffold on his return to England after the burning of San Thomé had closed an epoch. More characteristic of the new age were the sailing of the *Mayflower* and Courteen's West Indian adventures. The tobacco plantations yielded a new and settled trade. The king was ailing.

[1] For the spelling St Alban, *see Complete Peerage*, XI, 282–3.

Chapter 22

THE BUCKINGHAM ASCENDANCY

THERE is another aspect under which the third parliament should be examined for it had important consequences and brought about the fall of the lord chancellor. The king had begun by setting forth the situation as he saw it. On January 30, 1621, he described the actual position of affairs. On the financial side he had explained the expenditure of his own moneys, his borrowings from the king of Denmark, and his authorisation of voluntary subscriptions.

And I am now [he declared] to take care of a worse danger against the next summer. I will leave no travail untried to obtain a happy peace. But I have thought it good to be armed against a worse turn, it being best to treat of peace with a sword in my hand. Now I shall labour to preserve the rest; wherein I declare that, if by fair means I cannot get it, my crown, my blood, and all shall be spent, with my son's[1] blood also, but I will get it for him. And this is the cause of all, that the cause of religion is involved in it; for they will alter religion where they conquer, and so perhaps my grand-child also may suffer, who hath committed no fault at all.[2]

He explained refreshingly that he had been ignorant of the customs of England at his first parliament and that the second had suffered "from a strange kind of beast called undertakers". He asked for a suitable grant of money. "Then," he concluded, "I shall be even honoured of my neighbour princes, and peradventure my government made an example for posterity to follow."

After this auspicious opening the house grew stormy. Sir Edward Coke, who was back in his seat after many years, attacked the mismanagement of the patent of inns granted to Sir Giles Mompesson. The patent for alehouses was next examined. Then further charges were brought against Mompesson in regard to the patent for gold and silver thread and that for the discovery of crown estates. Sir Giles came from the established landed gentry and had a certain friendship

---

[1] Presumably 'son-in-law' is intended.　　[2] *Proceedings and Debates*, I, 2.

10 ?PRINCESS ELIZABETH, QUEEN OF BOHEMIA
by Paul van Somer (Hon. Mrs Clive Pearson)

II CHARLES, PRINCE OF WALES
by Daniel Mytens (Hon. Mrs Clive Pearson)

and indeed a family connection[1] with the new favourite. He fled the country and disappeared from view. He is remembered in the literature of the time by the character of Sir Giles Overreach in Massinger's *New Way to pay Old Debts*. He lies in the great family tomb at Lydiard Tregoze, which contains the monument of the Golden Boy.

It was now that Cranfield launched his attack upon the chancellor. Bacon had been promoted to that office in 1618 and he had likewise received a further peerage title as viscount St Alban. It is simpler to refer to this great man by the surname which he rendered famous. The charge, which was one of bribery, was built up on several cases brought forward by Christopher Aubrey and Edward Egerton and rather later by Lady Wharton and by Holman and Smethwick. When all the evidence was completed, Bacon acknowledged his fault and awaited judgment. There were now other cases. He was finally sentenced by the House of Lords. He was to pay a fine of £40,000, to be imprisoned in the Tower during the king's pleasure, and to be disabled from sitting in parliament or from accepting any office. Through the influence of Buckingham a proposal that he should lose his rank and titles, as viscount, baron and knight, was defeated. As in other cases the king made things easy for him.

I suggest that, like King James, he lacked an interest in money and in the workings of finance. It had never been indicated that the moneys he received affected his legal judgments; in that sense he kept himself immaculate upon the bench. Presents *after* judgment or after some political service were in those days common form; he carelessly accepted the money *first*. It seems to me that his mind was probably far away from the details of his daily life, thinking out the *Novum Organum*, arranging his just judgments. This supposition may seem far-fetched; but it leaves intact the integrity of the legal side of his great career, the *causes célèbres*, which he tried from his high seat and the cases in which as attorney general he was the advocate for the crown. Gardiner seems in fact to view matters from this angle.[2] Bacon now disappears from court and from the history of the reign. The king retained goodwill towards him; there was nothing now to unite or to sunder them. As for Buckingham it seems that he could hardly understand the convoluted

---

[1] Sir Giles Mompesson and Sir Edward Villiers had married Catherine and Barbara, the daughters of Sir John St John of Lydiard Tregoze.

[2] "He [Bacon] laid himself open to the criticism of the moralist, by fancying that integrity of heart might be left to its own guidance", *History of England, op. cit.*, IV, 105. This is not, however, a very clear expression.

approach which Bacon always made to him. No man had less capacity to form a common favourite. In his last will Bacon made this declaration. "For my name and memory I leave it to men's charitable speeches, to foreign nations, and to the next ages." He was wise.

His disappearance marked the end of the political characters who had served their apprenticeship under the old queen's government. The men who now came into office would be found more manageable. This was the heyday of Buckingham's ascendancy. He was aided by a certain feeling for the House of Commons and for the general ideas held by the English country gentlemen. He never shared the king's feeling for Spain and would detach himself from Prince Charles's naïve enthusiasm. In his heart he never favoured the Spanish marriage.

His innocence was confused by Bacon's verbiage; he much preferred the somewhat coarse approach which Lord Keeper Williams in time would manifest. He was also, unlike most favourites, capable of a progressive detachment from the king without in any way endangering his hold upon him. There may be various reasons for this situation.

It has always seemed to me that King James's relations with his last favourite were technically innocent. He was certainly the type which attracted the king; but the latter was now in weakening health. There are certain converging arguments. I do not think that it is to apply a Victorian standard of morality to suggest that Archbishop Abbot was not likely to try to supply the king with another lover. He had always been a Puritan and rather stern. Again there was the case of the favourite's mother. Lady Buckingham was an unpleasing woman with a sense of worldly values and in the charge of Jesuit confessors; it does not seem to me that she could have managed the cosy relationship which she worked up with the king if he had seduced her favourite son. But the third instance has much more weight with me. The Prince of Wales had a hard cold purity which verged on prudishness. He was linked with Buckingham by the strongest friendship of his whole life. Surely this development would have been impossible if the favourite had been his father's *mignon*?

This is, perhaps, the place to set out the account of King James left us by Sir Anthony Weldon. The author could hardly be more prejudiced. He had inherited the office of clerk of the Green Cloth from his father and had been dismissed in the last years of King James's reign. He became a parliamentarian during the Civil Wars and his account was printed in 1650. Two reasons give it interest. Although hostile, it gives certain details which are of interest, in particular a list of the king's favourite wines, and it is also the basis from which Sir Walter Scott constructed his verbal portrait.[1]

He was [wrote Sir Anthony Weldon] of a middle stature, more corpulent though in his clothes than in his body, yet fat enough, his cloathes being ever made large and easie, the doublets quilted for stiletto proofe, his breeches in great pleites and full stuffed. He was naturally of a timorous disposition, which was the reason of his quilted doublets: his eyes large were rowling after any stranger come into his presence. His beard was very thin. His tongue too large for his mouth, which ever made him speak full in the mouth, and made him drink very uncomely, as if eating his drink, which came out into the cup at each side of his mouth.

His skin was as soft as Taffeta Sarsenet, which felt so, because he never washt his hands, only rubbed his fingers, and slightly with the wet end of a napkin. It is true, he drank very often, which was rather out of a custom than any delight, and his drink was of that kind of strength as Frontinack, Canary, High Country wine, Tent wine and Scottish ale, that had he not had a very strong brain, might have daily been overtaken, although he seldom drank at one time, above four spoonfuls, many times not above one or two.

Thus did he sit in his later days. There was little movement as his courtiers went to and fro before him at St James's Palace.

[1] It is evident that he must have used Weldon's account, *The Court and Character of King James*, reprinted in his *Secret History of the Court of James the First*, issued in 1811.

Chapter 23

THE VILLIERS FAMILY

THE king's life had been changed by the queen's death. He did not re-marry; he had done his duty by the married state. And it is a comment on the way in which his temperament was understood in the courts of Europe that there was no suggestion that he might do so. For most of the reign the queen and her own solitary court had provided a sort of equipoise. He had had his own rather attenuated family life; now all were gone except the Prince of Wales. These may have been factors leading to the way in which the king now threw himself upon the Villiers family.

In the long succession of his favourites it was only the youngest and the last whose family was brought into the royal circle. This was partly the consequence of George Villiers's affection for his brothers and still more the result of the influence that the countess of Buckingham gradually gained upon the king. The mother of George Villiers is a figure whom we see in silhouette. There is very little written evidence. We can only be sure that she was deeply unpopular in court and country; her favourite son always retained for her a deep affection.

Mary Villiers, by birth a Beaumont of Glenfield, belonged to a younger branch of the great mediaeval family of that name, which was now long past its prime. She had been a waiting-gentlewoman in the service of her cousin Lady Beaumont of Cole Orton and Sir George Villiers had married her when he needed a second wife to bring up his already numerous family. She would hardly have come into the king's life had the queen been still alive; as it was she fulfilled a double func-tion as a middle-aged gossip and as a nurse. This rather *bourgeois* life with the Villiers family had the effect of cosseting and also at times of bullying the failing king.

The Villiers family had their place in the middle rank of the landed gentry in prosperous Leicestershire. But they had had many sons and many daughters and the landed property had all passed to Sir William Villiers, the eldest step-son of whom no one has ever heard; he became a baronet in 1619 when that title was being offered to those of his standing in his own county. As a consequence it became Lady Buckingham's preoccupation to arrange marriages for her nieces and grandchildren, who had no dowry save the favourite's kinship.

The most remarkable of the alliances that she created was that between her niece Anne Brett and Sir Lionel Cranfield, who was soon to become Lord Treasurer Middlesex; but this marriage, which took place in 1620, failed to create a lasting tie with the duke of Buckingham. The marriages of the children of her own step-daughter Elizabeth Villiers, the wife of Sir John Boteler of Bramfield beside the palings of Hatfield Park, were arranged adequately.[1] Her grand-daughter Lady Margaret Feilding was married at the age of seven in 1620 to the marquess of Hamilton, but this marriage was the king's own doing.

It is curious, and also rather unusual at that period, that there was a strain of insanity in the Villiers family. It showed itself in Sir John Boteler's only son and in Lady Buckingham's eldest child John, viscount Purbeck.

Mary Villiers had been created countess of Buckingham for life in 1618 and was always a devout woman, for much of her life an Anglican. After her first husband's death she was twice married, to Sir Thomas Rayner of Orton Longueville and to Sir William Compton. The latter drank.

Her life was centred on the marquess and then on her two other sons. The elder had collapsed into insanity before this time at the end of his disastrous marriage to the only daughter of Sir Edward Coke and Lady Hatton. The younger was Christopher or Kit, a simple fellow, friendly in disposition and addicted to the bottle. Sir Robert Naunton, the childless secretary of state, had made him his heir. Sir Sebastian Harvey, the very wealthy merchant who was lord mayor of London, had, however, refused his offer for his only child. He could not hold a post more responsible than that of gentleman of the bedchamber. Through affection for the family he was granted, without payment, the earldom of Anglesey. Robert Carr and George Villiers had been King James's scholars, but Kit Villiers he could not teach. These points are made to stress the homeliness of the king's later years.

The other families, like the Cecils and the Howards, who had come

---

[1] Three of them became the countesses of Chichester, Marlborough and Newport. Helen Boteler became the wife of Sir John Drake of Ash and grandmother of the duke of Marlborough. Olivia Boteler married Endymion Porter.

to great fortune, had had experience of expenditure. In this sense Buckingham was a *nouveau riche*. It was marriage which set him up as a purchaser and builder. Lady Catherine was a great heiress; her mother had been a sister of Lady Suffolk and co-heiress of the Knyvet fortune. She was herself also the heiress to the barony of Roos which had come to the earl of Rutland when Lord Roos had died. The Manners lands would go to the heir male. Buckingham's first purchase was the estate of Burley-on-the-Hill in Rutland, where he had plans drawn up for a large mansion.

Two years later he acquired Wallingford House in Whitehall, and in the summer of 1622 purchased Newhall from Lord Sussex. Here he designed to transform the Elizabethan palace in accordance with prevailing standards. Buckingham's work at Newhall has every mark of haste. It stands in contrast with the relatively slowly accumulated building which had long been the practice of the great English families. There is a personal touch which seems to indicate what he and the king could do together.

Newhall, for which Buckingham was said to have given £20,000,[1] was already an immense building lying out in the fields beyond Chelmsford; a mass of Tudor brickwork with a great hall and high Elizabethan windows. The house had been built by Henry VIII and known as Beaulieu. The lofty gatehouse above the confined entrance-way into the forecourt, the chapel so much too considerable for private needs and the plain early Tudor gables all dated from this outmoded period. The earl of Sussex had reconstructed the mansion in those mid-Elizabethan years when the centre of interest in the house had shifted away from the chapel with its large old-fashioned windows showing the Crucifixion and St George and St Catherine with white heraldic roses and pomegranates. Over the entrance Sussex had placed an inscription in honour of his royal mistress. The present generation of Radcliffes were too poor to maintain this palace.

The favourite's energy of temperament desired an ostentation, which should be expensive and above all rapidly achieved. Here was little of that solid and calm magnificence which went to the planning of Hatfield and Audley End and to Lord Arundel's wide projects. And this was natural for Buckingham reflected King James's warm immediate favour. Thus the marquess showed a certain carefree haste as he

---

[1] Letter from Chamberlain to Carleton, dated July 13, 1622, Cal. S.P. Dom, 1619–25, p. 424.

planned his lime avenues, constructed the bowling greens and tennis courts and devised the gardens and their statuary. The house was carved open for the new wide staircase which led up to a sea-piece representing Sir Francis Drake in action. A picture of Hymen with a chaplet of roses was painted for the state bedchamber; the grounds were strewn with statues of Harpocrates and Nemesis and the Muses; a labyrinth was laid out and embellished with a figure of Minos. All was set up in those long Essex flats almost by accident.

The same spirit marked Buckingham's construction of his new town residence, York House, of which the watergate alone remains. Wallingford House was now left behind; he was never a man who would enter quietly into another courtier's unchanged possessions. Two letters will give an impression of this ordered rush. "York House," wrote Sir Thomas Wentworth to his friend Wandesford, "goes on passing fast, another corner symmetrical now appearing answerable to that other raised before you went hence, besides a goodly statue of stone, set up in the garden before the new building, bigger than the life of a Sampson with a Philistine between his legs."[1] Meanwhile, Buckingham's collections increased apace, tapestries of the Graces from Mortlake, "a most beautiful piece of Tintoret, another head of Titian, a St Francis from the hand of Cavalier Bellion, a picture of Our Lady by Raphael".[2]

By this time it was already the final year of the king's life. He had entered into his last fatigue. Buckingham in these matters was in the hands of his agents. He does not seem to have had much taste except for splendour. A letter from Balthasar Gerbier brings this out.

To conclude [this agent is found writing to his great patron] if your Excellency will only give me time to mine quietly, I will fill Newhall with paintings, so that foreigners will come there in procession; but we must proceed very quietly. Tuesday the paving of the cabinet with marble begins, which will be the grandest thing in the kingdom. . . . Madame has not given orders about the furniture of Persian cloth of gold.[3]

The unexpected purchasing power at his command appears to have entranced the favourite. Pictures, not all appropriate, came in from Holland and from Italy; groups of statuary were brought up on the tide by the Thames barges; away in Constantinople Sir Thomas Roe

[1] Letter from Sir Thomas Wentworth to Christopher Wandesford, dated June 17, 1624, William Knowler, ed., *Strafford Letters*, I, 21.

[2] Letter from Balthasar Gerbier to the duke of Buckingham, dated November 17, 1624.

[3] Dated February 1625, printed from Goodman's papers in J. S. Brewer, ed., *Court of James I*, II, 373.

offered to send a brig to the Aegean to bring back "pillars and tables of marble".

The marquess of Buckingham seems partly passive beneath this expenditure. He retained through life a certain simplicity, rather engaging. He never became absorbed into the mould of the great English families. With the exception of the earls of Rutland, an isolated stock, he made no marriage alliances with them. As he rose in the peerage to a marquessate and then to a dukedom, their sensibilities became affronted. It was, however, a service to the king that in the journey to Spain which he took with the Prince of Wales his reactions to that court and country were those of a proud and regal minister whose values were those of an English squire.

Chapter 24

THE SPANISH PRINCESS

THE best method of approach to the problem of the Spanish marriage is to study *Las Meninas*, the great picture by Velasquez in the Prado. In this the central figure is the Infanta Margarida Teresa as a child. She stands with a pink ribbon in the rather lustreless pale yellow hair which came from the Austrian side of the family; she is dressed in a heavy brocade which spreads into a half-crinoline until it stands on the flooring like a bell. The brocade is off-white with thick black stripes. There is an impression of the granite protection which surrounded Spanish princesses until they went out to their great marriages. The French were despised at the Spanish court; there was to be no repetition of the example of Marguerite de Navarre. The infanta here depicted was the daughter of Philip IV by his second marriage with his niece the Archduchess Marianna; she was therefore both grand-daughter and niece of the princess for whom Charles I was a *prétendant*. Like her she, too, became a Roman empress. There was, perhaps, something Moorish in the way that she was kept separate with her dwarfs and dressers. All the few Spanish princesses were delivered immaculate to their Catholic bridegrooms; there was not a great deal of education.

This picture represented a period rather over thirty years later than Prince Charles's visit, but there was not much change in that most static court. It was a world which King James never knew. Meanwhile, one portrait of the Infanta Maria Anna exists, painted at the time when Prince Charles was paying court to her. It was a panel by Bartolomé Gonzalez and the princess is shown wearing the Prince of Wales's feathers above her pale yellow hair. Compared to the pearl-hung satin in the Pourbus portrait of her sister the queen of France, she is dressed very simply. A dark jewelled cross hung from beneath her ruff. Her very smooth pale skin has touches of red upon the cheeks; she looks as if she might prove consumptive. Charles was a simple boy and there is something markedly virginal about the portrait. One can see[1] that it might well appeal to him.

The details of the journey of Prince Charles and Lord Buckingham to Madrid, which began incognito and ended in blazing publicity, are outside the scope of a study of his father the king. Besides, in this question of a Spanish marriage, the final decisions rested with the king of England and his council and on the advice tendered to the king of Spain. It does not seem that the pensions distributed by Gondomar had any influence upon this question. They seem to have been offered in the hope that a certain number of men of influence might favour peace with Spain. An element in the council who preferred a peace policy would also sympathise with an approach to Spain if this might help the situation of the Elector Palatine. It is difficult to believe that any English Protestant in his heart ever really wished for a Spanish queen. Some of the council realised the value of the great dowry to help to meet the king's expenses. The prince and Buckingham were young and were still to some extent their master's pupils.

Still, whatever might be thought about the marriage, there was one field in which the king of England and the Spanish advisers, such as the favourite, the count-duke of Olivares, were in a real agreement. They all desired wholeheartedly to preserve the peace. There is an aspect under which each manoeuvre can be better seen as a peace negotiation than as a marriage treaty and, when everything was over, the peace was broken.

It was not that the king had wished for the prince's journey; he reasonably had confidence in Lord Bristol, the resident ambassador, who was charged with these negotiations. But he had his old high dreams of what he and the king of Spain could do together. He wished, too, for peace in Europe and for the restitution of his lands to his son-in-law the Elector Palatine. He seems to have exaggerated the power of peaceful persuasion that the king of Spain possessed; he had no knowledge of his character. In that sense the statement of Olivares is likely to have appealed to him. "We have a maxim of state that the King of Spain must never fight against the Emperor. We cannot employ our forces against the House of Austria."[2] He shared the English ignorance of

---

[1] The portrait was brought back to England by the prince and Buckingham. It belonged to the latter's sister, Lady Denbigh, and remained at Newnham Paddox until the sale in 1938. It now hangs at Parham Park in Sussex.

[2] Cf. S. R. Gardiner, *History of England*, V, 106, *et seq.*, where the actual facts of this negotiation are set out carefully.

Spain, but he never seems to have understood the deep English hostility.

For various reasons there was in England less contact with Spain than with most of the other European nations. It lay quite apart from that by now accustomed highway which ran through France and the Low Countries to Geneva and thence to Italy. The ill-judged Armada had left a deep impression on the English mind. The rare Englishmen who found their way to Spain or to the Spanish viceroyalty of Naples were almost always converts to Catholicism, like the young Lord Roos. The real contact had been limited to old Lord Nottingham's solemn embassy. The Eaton-Wellingham correspondence[1] suggests that it was very rare to find an English factor in northern Spain even in 1631.

It was a consequence of this isolation and the long wars which preceded it that relationships with Spaniards were rare indeed. I can only think of two, the Spanish blood which Dona Maria de Salinas brought to her daughter the duchess of Suffolk and through her to the Bertie family and the English blood which Jane Dormer, duchess of Feria, brought to her husband's stock. This is considering families of the two courts; but there were a few associations at a different level. Thus Endymion Porter, who was Buckingham's secretary for Spanish correspondence, was a grandson of Gyles Porter who had married Juana de Figueroa y Mont Salve when attached to the embassy at Madrid in the first portion of the old queen's reign.

King James's early government in the days when Salisbury was still alive was concerned with Spain only as a menace, for war still continued between that nation and England's allies the United Provinces. Throughout his life the king never met a member of the house of Austria. It would seem that there was no one in this country who appreciated the movements of thought among the higher *échelons* of the Spanish state on such intimate matters as the marriages of the royal princesses. In fact there was during these generations the closest association between the two branches of the house of Hapsburg. The daughters of Spain, the infantas, made in the seventeenth century only the most glorious marriages with the king of France and with the Roman emperor. Further the princesses of that house and all the innumerable archduchesses of Austria had never married outside the circle of the Roman fold. The nearest to an exception in all the stock was the

[1] These letters were written between 1631 and 1642 and calendared in the State Papers, Domestic.

marriage of the duchess of Cleves, the mother of the last duke of that family, with a prince only half-redeemed from earlier Lutheran heresies. And quite apart from this the likelihood of a princess being in fact available had faded with the death of the Infanta Margarida who had been destined as the bride of the Archduke John, the heir of the Styrian branch of the house of Austria. The elder daughter was already queen of France and this left the Infanta Maria as the only princess available to make an Austrian marriage. The archduke died in 1619 and his next brother, the future Emperor Ferdinand III, was then only eleven years of age. He would have to wait some years for his young cousin.

This is not to say that the count of Gondomar, even after the Infanta Margarida's death, did not desire an English marriage; but he knew something of England and it seems that in his view the conversion of the Prince of Wales was essential to its success. That is presumably why he first suggested the unusual step that Prince Charles should visit Madrid. There is very little evidence that his ideas were reflected at his own court.

A brief description will make clear the stranglehold of Austrian influence. Philip III had been the son of Philip II by his fourth wife, who was also his niece, the Archduchess Anne of the senior line of the Austrian house. Philip III had been betrothed to the Archduchess Gregoria Maximiliana of the Styrian branch of the same house. On her death he had married her younger sister the Archduchess Margarethe. When he died his brother-in-law the Emperor Ferdinand II was uncle to Philip IV of Spain. It was soon evident in Madrid that the young English prince had not come to be converted. It must have been evident to all parties of advisers at the Spanish court that the new king's only sister in the course of time would marry the archduke who was to become king of the Romans.

Quite apart from the marriage, there was a desire to keep the peace with England unbroken. A ten years' truce was now operating in the Netherlands; but the Spanish statesmen saw it was desirable that England should not attack their exhausted country. This was the more necessary as the double royal marriages with France had not preserved them from danger in that quarter.

The actual entourage which built itself around the prince's journey was composed of two elements which were quite distinct. There was the prince's own household, which hurried after him with Sir Richard Vaughan of Golden Grove, the comptroller, at its head. This included

men like Sir Edmund Verney and had in general an Elizabethan distaste for all things Spanish. But there were with them four minor
characters, who were supporters of the Spanish match. All were men of
Catholic sympathies. Endymion Porter, who acted as interpreter, and
Francis Cottington had travelled out with the prince; the other two
came later. Sir Tobie Mathew was already a convert and Cottington
and Sir Walter Aston, with whom the king had stayed at Tixall, were
to die in that communion. Endymion Porter was all his life the patient
husband of a convert wife. Still, none of the prince's grouping whatever
their views could penetrate the private mind of the king of Spain.

As has been said, there were two factors which had helped to reconcile
a section of the English council to the unwelcome prospect of a Spanish
marriage; the immense dowry which it was hoped that the princess
would bring based on the gold and silver imports from America, and the
aid that it was thought that Spain might give to retrieve the Elector
Palatine's position. The second question was dealt with upon traditional
lines. It was at first suggested in Madrid that the Elector Palatine must
abdicate the throne of Bohemia, from which he had already been cast
out, and also surrender his electorate. Attention was then turned upon
the Elector Palatine's eldest son Prince Frederick Henry, who was at
this time nine years of age. It was proposed that he should go to Vienna
for his education and should eventually marry an archduchess. It
was at any rate implied that he should, during his stay in the Austrian
capital, become a Catholic. Then after the marriage the Upper and the
Lower Palatinate should be restored to him and the electorate also
would come back on the death of the duke of Bavaria on whom it had
been conferred. Already this involved something that the Emperor
Ferdinand might not be in a position to exact.

The king of England asked through his ambassador that his nephew
might have Protestant tutors with him so that his faith might be preserved. The Spaniards began to give way on other matters. They suggested that the Elector Palatine should administer his former territories
in his son's name. Later they proposed that he should take them over
and finally that he and not his son should become Elector Palatine when
the Bavarian elector died. But was there in fact even an archduchess
available? The new emperor was at this time a widower with one unmarried daughter, the Archduchess Cecilia Renata, who was now
twelve years old and already engaged in negotiations which would lead
her to become the queen of Poland.

It was at this point in the affair that Lord Bristol made his error. He assumed that the king's desire was to re-establish his sister's family, and imagined that for this object a change of religion might prove acceptable. He would get into trouble over this matter in the next reign. The king and queen of Bohemia refused all overtures, nor would the Spanish government agree to make any recommendation except a Hapsburg marriage for the young and presumably converted prince.

Before coming to the proposed conditions for the Spanish marriage it should be remembered that royal marriages between a Catholic and a Protestant were at that date almost unknown. There had been two examples, the second marriage of the Prince of Orange, not then a Calvinist, with the Princess of Saxony and that of the Duke of Lorraine with the Princess of Navarre. The two French princesses, who adopted the Reformed faith, had both still been Catholics when they married.

Nevertheless on April 24, 1623 a dispensation reached Madrid from Rome; but it was hedged round by conditions not only relating to the arrangements for the infanta's worship and for her education of the children until they reached twelve years of age, but also calling for the repeal of the penal statutes. It is worth considering with some care the provisions now put forward by the king of Spain. The infanta's household were to be nominated by Philip IV and the religious needs of the new queen and her attendants were to be served by a bishop and twenty-four priests all resident at the court and none of them amenable to English law. Wherever the new queen fixed her dwelling there was to be erected a public church to which English Catholics should have access. At the privy council, under the king's pressure, these conditions were accepted.[1] There were also certain private articles. The king was asked to undertake to give a perpetual toleration in England, Scotland and Ireland and to assure that in each country the Catholics would be free to exercise their own religious worship in private houses. No law relating to the Catholics, without affecting their fellow-subjects, should ever be put into force against them. The king was to agree to ask parliament to repeal the penal laws and likewise to undertake never to give the royal assent to any fresh laws which might be proposed against the Catholic body.

One wonders what was intended by these extraordinary conditions. They fall into two sections, the first deals with the married life of the

[1] Certain councillors were absent. These included the earls of Arundel, Pembroke and Southampton, Lords Brooke and Zouche, and Sir Robert Naunton.

princess and the second with the provisions for religion in England. The Spaniards, it is a truism, are a proud people. The household and the bishop and the priests were to build up requirements for grandeur; these were not what the Spaniards accepted from other nations. It is worth examining for a moment the conditions exacted from the queens from France, although there was in these cases no difference in religion. In every case the French household was to be left behind on the French side of the frontier, the river Bidassoa. The built-in Spanish household met them there. This, of course, created certain strains. These occurred in the case of the queens in the third marriage of Philip II and the first marriage of Philip IV. They were to become most evident in the case of the Princess of Orléans, who would be the first wife of Charles II. The idea that the French queens might be surrounded by a household appointed by the king of France was totally unacceptable.

The religious clause relating to the Catholic populations of the three kingdoms do not make sense except upon the supposition that the Prince of Wales had decided to become a Roman Catholic. Then it would be possible to imagine that the Anglican king might be expected to agree that relief should be offered to his son's co-religionists. Whatever might be supposed to be the religious ardour of Olivares and his circle, they could never have imagined that a foreign king would change his policy on religious questions and above all change it for ever.

If these ideas should be correct, it follows that once it was clear that the prince would remain an Anglican the conditions were piled up so that they would not be accepted. The king and Olivares would then turn quietly to the Austrian marriage. Two circumstances prevented this development which Buckingham foresaw as reasonable and inevitable. The Prince of Wales was twenty-three, but young for his age, retarded in development. Contacts with the ladies of the royal family had been few. For him the charm of the infanta may have lain in her inaccessibility. He lingered in Spain unwilling to return without her. The conditions therefore were made more onerous. It was said that after the marriage she must remain in Spain for a further year until it was manifest that James I had made the required changes. Buckingham was ready to return and the king became alarmed lest Prince Charles should find himself in a position near captivity.

Both Prince Charles and his father therefore signed the required marriage articles, both public and private. All that can be said about King James's action is that he seems always to have been turning over maxims of statecraft. It is not suggested that among his virtues he had the character of a truthful man.

Meanwhile, the earl of Rutland had been sent in command of the *Royal Prince*, in which gold leaf had been expended in a special cabin for the infanta. Workmen in London were constructing what was to be her Catholic private chapel. Both Lennox and Buckingham had been advanced to English dukedoms. On August 30, 1623 the prince left Madrid in the hot weather and moved to the Escorial. Three days later his coach drove out towards the north. He was accompanied by Cardinal Zapata and a royal escort. He had been in Spain just six months for he had entered Irun on March 2. On the morning of September 12 he was met six leagues from Santander by Sir Thomas Somerset and Sir John Finett with the news that the *Royal Prince* was riding in the harbour there. The bells were ringing in Santander as he approached. His barge had some difficulty in making the flagship after nightfall and he went on board Sir Sackville Trevor's ship *Defiance*. The next morning he was rowed across to the *Royal Prince*.

When the prince reached London without his bride the city was illuminated. There were one hundred and eight bonfires between St Paul's and London Bridge. Lighted candles were placed in every window. The same evening Prince Charles and the duke of Buckingham reached the king at Royston. James I went on struggling for a little, making fresh demands on the king of Spain on behalf of the Elector Palatine, raising difficulties about the infanta's dowry and then postponing any question of the marriage. On December 30, Lord Bristol was instructed to return to England. Two days earlier, at the urgent request of Buckingham and Charles, the king agreed to summon parliament. This, as Olivares had long foreseen, would lead to war with Spain. King James's Spanish policy was now in ruins. This was the effective end of the king's rule.

12 INFANTA MARIA ANNA OF SPAIN
by Bartolome Gonzalez (Hon. Mrs Clive Pearson)

13 JAMES I
by Daniel Mytens (National Portrait Gallery)

Chapter 25

THE MIDDLE DISTANCE

WE have now come almost to the end of the king's life. So far I have concentrated on his own close personal contacts. Now I propose to discuss three men, who can fall into the category of courtiers, who had been disabused of any feeling for the court. Sir John Holles, Sir Robert Drury and Sir George More were all of them considerable figures; the first and second were among the richest commoners in the country, while the third man belonged to a court and London family which had taken to the land. Various reasons can be brought forward for their failure: they had all a strong Elizabethan background and the old queen had stayed both at Loseley and at Hawstead. King James, who was himself so improvident, perhaps did not take to men who like Sir Robert and even more Sir John had such a lucid love of money. There is the further interest that John Donne, who was for at least much of the reign a failure, was swung in his private life between Sir George More, who was his father-in-law, and Drury, who was his greatest patron. These three knights all nourished an anti-Spanish feeling which was common form among the English gentry, and coupled with an Elizabethan mood there went a clear attachment to the queen's religion. Associated with these gentlemen there went another landowner of medium fortune, Sir John Oglander, who has left a detailed account of the king's character by one who had some contacts at the court but mainly saw him in the middle distance.

Sir John Holles stood somewhat apart from the others. He was an admirer and a lifelong friend of Sir Walter Raleigh. He had a constant feud with Gilbert, earl of Shrewsbury. He had also an enemy in Sir Edward Coke for in youth he was said to have been the lover of Lady Elizabeth Hatton. These details are given to set his place in the Jacobean world. He was, perhaps, too quick with his rapier to please the king. His chief seat was at Houghton in Nottinghamshire and he also had the house which he later called Clare Palace in the county town. Houghton, "a seat both pleasant and commodious lying between the

x

forest and the clay",[1] had been built in two stages, the tower and the south front in the early sixteenth century and the hall and the north court towards the end of King Henry's reign. He proposed to pull down Houghton and rebuild it on higher ground above the barns, but this project never got beyond the planning stage.

His cousin Gervase Holles has left a description of Sir John.

He was [he wrote] a personage of a gallant presence. He was full six feet high, straight and of a strong limbe. In his youth he was somewhat leane, but in his later days he grew well in flesh, but not corpulent. His hayre was of a light browne, somthing towardes an auburn; his eyes were grey, he had a white skin, and his cheekes were rosy. He carried a majesty in his countenance, and in his face there was a strange mixture of severity and sweetnes. His motion was stately, befitting so great a person. I heard a lady once say that he came when he was a young man to the Earl of Huntingdon's, where he found divers persons of quality in dauncing, and he fell into the daunce with them with his cloake and rapier on, which he performed with the best grace that ever shee see anything done in hir life. Accordingly he had a most becomming seat on horsebacke, and was an excellent horseman; in his youth he had a very active body, nor was it at all unserviceable in his olde age; for I have seen him walk often from Chaloner House in Clerkenwell (where he then lived) to the Parliament of Westminster, his coach passing after him.[2]

Another aspect of his character is set out carefully. "He was naturally just, but nothing liberall, no man living more ready to oblige by his interest and endeavours, but not at all by his purse."[3]

He was much occupied in developing his London property. This included, besides numerous cottages and sixty gardens, one hundred and seventy acres in St Clement Danes with outlying lands in St Giles and St Pancras in the fields and in Kentish Town. "By theis . . . improvements he advanced his estate before his death to neare eight thousand poundes *per annum*."[4]

He had withdrawn from court after the queen's death. He took offence at the number of the Scottish courtiers. "King James brought along with him a crew of necessitous and hungry Scots, and filled every corner of the Court with these beggarly blew caps."[5] Sir John occupied the county seat for Nottinghamshire in the House of Commons; he was comptroller of the household to Prince Henry and had a friendship

[1] Gervase Holles, *Memorials of the Holles Family* (Camden Society), LV, 39.
[2] *Ibid.*, 111.   [3] *Ibid.*, 114.   [4] *Ibid.*, 95.   [5] *Ibid.*, 94.

for the earl of Somerset. During the Buckingham ascendancy he paid £10,000 for the Houghton peerage and a further £5,000 for the earldom of Clare; but, as in other cases, these payments seared him. He felt that he had been tricked by the court of Wards in the case of Robert Sutton. "The loss of Mr Sutton's wardship", wrote Gervase Holles, "made him much averse to K. James for whome living he had little kindness, nor indeed was he a friend to his memory. I have heard him say 'that he came to governe a people that he knew he was not worthy of, and then he was ruled himselfe by two beggars and a base fellow, Suffolke, Northampton and Salisbury'."[1] In connection with this judgment it must be remembered that he had quarrelled with Lord Burghley and had a distaste for popery and for the Spaniards. It was after the king was dead that he was accustomed to conclude his many strictures on his late sovereign with the rather stern expression "which now he feels". His younger son was Denzil Holles and his daughter married Sir Thomas Wentworth, later earl of Strafford. He was the true type of the disobliged nobleman. His only memorial is Claremarket, the site of the London School of Economics.

In the course of the development of his London properties in 1607 Sir John Holles leased two pieces of land at the north and east side of the wall at the back of Drury House to Sir Robert Drury, who was then building up a much smaller but still valuable property in the western portion of the parish of St Clement Danes. Apart from this business transaction there is little evidence of much contact between the parties. Sir Robert Drury had associations with the world of government which Sir John Holles lacked. He had married the daughter of his guardian Sir Nicholas Bacon. His own two sisters were the wives of Lord Burghley, the earl of Exeter's eldest son, and of Sir Edward Cecil, later viscount Wimbledon. Sir Robert was the head of a family of substantial Suffolk landowners; his estate extended for several miles to the southward from the verge of Bury St Edmunds. A description of his house will help to indicate his status.

The building of Hawstead Place had begun just over a hundred years before in 1502; but there had been changes throughout the century especially in anticipation of Queen Elizabeth's visit in 1578. Hawstead Place was entered from the south through a gatehouse and across a triple arched bridge over the moat which enclosed the house and the terraced gardens round it. Beyond this bridge stood a gateway which

[1] *Memorials of the Holles Family*, 97.

led into a square courtyard faced on the north side by a house built of brick and timber.[1] This was an old-fashioned ceremonial approach to quite a smallish residence. On the west side of the house was the hall and buttery and on the east the chapel and the parlour. Bedrooms occupied the whole of the first floor.

Sir Robert had been knighted by Essex; his career was influenced by this first master. In the last years of the queen's reign he had seen much service, especially in the Low Countries. His "lamed arm" dated from this time. The family consisted of the Drurys and their only daughter. Lady Drury was to some extent a patroness of the Puritan clergy of the neighbourhood and the living of Hawstead, where the presentation belonged to her husband, was regularly filled in their time by men from Emmanuel. Sir Robert was among those who accompanied the earl of Nottingham on his visit to Spain as envoy extraordinary and on his return was elected to parliament for Suffolk as a county member. This and a certain attendance at court were the limits of his public service.

Sir Robert's mind was set upon an embassy and he made attempts in 1609 to obtain an appointment to Madrid. Throughout the succeeding years he envisaged being sent to various capitals. A choleric temper and a tendency to get involved in Chancery suits perhaps stood in his way. At any rate King James never indicated any wish to promote him.

It was at this time that he came in contact with John Donne. In another fashion Dr Donne desired and at this time did not obtain a position in the public service. The failure to appreciate this great man throws light upon the nature and the limitations of the king's interests. He was now thirty-eight, three years Sir Robert Drury's senior and miserably poor. He had been private secretary to Lord Chancellor Ellesmere and had been dismissed from that position when he made a secret marriage with Anne More, a girl of sixteen, the niece of his patron's second wife. At this time Donne, who had been brought up a Catholic, had been an Anglican at least since he had entered Ellesmere's service.

In the course of December 1610 the Drurys lost their child at Hawstead. Elizabeth Drury was just over fourteen years of age. It is possible that Donne knew the family through his brother-in-law William Lyly.[2] At any rate he undertook to commemorate her by writing *An Anatomie*

---

[1] The house was demolished in 1829. This description is reprinted in R. C. Bald, *Donne and the Drurys* (Cambridge, 1959), 16, from the account in Cullum's *History of Hawstead*.

[2] Cf. *Ibid.*, 69–83.

of the World and *Of the Progres of the Soule*, which were the first published of all his poems, coming out in 1611 and in the following year. In 1611 he accompanied the Drurys on their visit to France and the Low Countries and on their return moved with his wife and children into a small free-standing house opening on to the west side of Drury Court, which stood within the enclosure of Sir Robert's properties and at the entrance to Drury House. The gatehouse opened out into the street still known as Drury Lane.

For the years to come he and the Drurys were equally cut off from court preferment. It is worth examining this matter for it shows something of the nature of the reign. Donne came from a well-established city family, impoverished by his father's early death. He had travelled and knew French, Spanish and Italian. It was his dismissal from Ellesmere's household that initially had barred his progress. Curiously enough his object was the same as his patron's, some foreign embassy. It does not seem to be fanciful to give as one of the reasons of his failure his absorption in the Elizabethan age. In this he resembled both Drury and Holles. He, too, had gone on foreign service; he had sailed as a secretary on Essex's voyage to sack Cadiz. His poems, which are often not easy to date, have something of the flavour of this period reflecting his own concern for the cognate subjects of geography and astrology. As an example some lines for Elizabeth Drury show his temporal preoccupations which in their character belonged wholly to the earlier reign:

> She whose rich eyes, and brest
> Guilt the West Indies. . . .[1]

There seems to have been likewise a tendency to concentrate upon Guiana. In addition to the epigram *Cales and Guyana* there are other references.[2] The Spanish notices were more in keeping with the new king's reign as "And Midas joyes our Spanish journeys give"[3] and "Though every inch were ten Escurialls".[4] But all the same the atmosphere remained Elizabethan.

> O thou O Elephant or Ape will doe,
> When any names the King of Spaine to you.[5]

---

[1] From *An Anatomie of the World, The first anniversary*, printed in H. J. C. Grierson, ed., *The Poems of John Donne* (1929), 214.
[2] Cf. "Eclipse the light which Guyana would give", and "Guianaes rarities", *ibid.*, 186 and 141.   [3] *Ibid.*, 109.   [4] *Ibid.*, 221, and cf. "you th'Escuriall", 169.   [5] *Ibid.*, 131.

This was the old world and to the court no more congenial. Still the way of life, which ultimately developed with Donne's undertaking Anglican orders, kept him dissociated from the king's ideas. His attitude will be considered once again when we come to the last phase of the reign. He was not ordained until 1615 and in that same year Sir Robert Drury died.

Donne's father-in-law, Sir George More of Loseley beyond Guildford, also belonged to those who were disappointed in King James's reign. He was older than Holles and Drury and unlike them not a soldier. He had business interests and had bought the wardship of Edward Herbert, later Lord Herbert of Cherbury. He held various local offices and was master of the swans for Surrey. He had entertained the old queen and been knighted by her. King James came to him twice after doubting whether his house was large enough for a state visit. He had been appointed receiver to the Prince of Wales; he was one of those disappointed by Prince Henry's death. He sat in parliament throughout the reign either for Guildford or for his county. Sir George was for a time chancellor of the Order of the Garter and for fifteen months he held the lieutenancy of the Tower. After this he had no more employments. The Loseley archives contain drafts of memorials[1] to the king which were unanswered. Sir John Holles, Sir Robert Drury and Sir George More were united as courtiers who had failed to gain the king's attention. In fact all their houses, Houghton, Hawstead and Loseley, were really centres where the values of the old reign still survived.

An interesting account of how King James was seen not by the courtiers but by the country gentry was found among the papers of another of Sir George More's sons-in-law, Sir John Oglander. He had been born in 1585 and was a considerable landowner, his property centred on Nunwell in the Isle of Wight. This was another house in which the old queen's memory was reverenced. They had after all seen the topsails of the Armada as they beat slowly up the Channel past St Catherine's Point. The account, headed "a note on King James", is long and rambling; I think it best to extract the marrow from it.

King James the First of England [he begins] was the most cowardly man that ever I knew. He could not endure a soldier or to see men drilled, to hear of war was death to him, and how he tormented himself with fear of some sudden mischief may be proved by his great quilted doublets, pistol-

---

[1] Cf. A. J. Kempe, ed., *The Loseley Manuscripts* (1838), a disappointing source.

proof, as also his strange eyeing of strangers with a continual fearful observation.[1]

And then he goes into a long-winded jest.

This [Sir John continues] is but to give you a taste of his fearful nature. Otherwise he was abundantly the best scholar and wisest prince for general knowledge that ever England had, very merciful and passionate, liberal and honest. He was wondrous just between parties and had a very tender conscience, witness the difficulty to draw him to pardon murder or any notorious crime. . . . He was the chastest prince for women that ever was, for he would often swear that he had never known any other woman than his wife. A virtuous, modest woman, he would both highly grace and commend. He loved to be accounted good. . . .

For the present delivery of his mind he was the best of that age: he hated all men that spoke ill of others, saying no man need fear damnation if Sir Richard Weston was gone to Heaven, as having a tongue that spoke ill of all men. He had many witty jests and also, in his passion, many profane. A great politician and very sound in the reformed religion. He spoke much and as well as any man, or rather better, but for bodily action—put riding aside—he did not, or could not, use much: his body for want of use growing that way defective. If he had had but the power, spirit and resolution to have acted that which he spoke, or done as well as he knew how to do, Solomon had been short of him.

A passage follows on "his facile good nature", and a reference to the many hungry Scots, who were really outside Sir John's experience.

He was [he goes on] excessively taken with hunting, although in his latter time, by reason he could not ride fast, he had little pleasure in the chase: his delight was to come in at the death of the deer and to hear the commendations of his hounds. He was an infinite lover of fruit, as grapes, melons and the like, and as free a drinker of sweet wines and Scotch ale. As he would swear much, so his ordinary oath was 'God's wounds'.

His only faults were that he was infinitely impatient, in which humour he would not forbear profanity. . . . Secondly, he loved young men, his favourites, better than women, loving them beyond the love of men to women. I never yet saw any fond husband make so much or so great dalliance over his beautiful spouse as I have seen King James over his favourites, especially the Duke of Buckingham. . . . He was not popular nor plausible to his subjects that desired to see him. He could not endure to be seen of the commons, especially at his sports.

[1] Francis Bamford, ed., *A Royalist's Notebook. The commonplace book of Sir John Oglander* (1936), 193–8.

Sir John Oglander closes his account by describing his own contacts with his sovereign.

King James came twice into the Island and hunted in the Park, where once he dined, and the other time in the Castle [Carisbrooke]. . . . When he first came into the Island, he was much taken with seeing the little boys skirmish, whom he loved to see better and more willingly than men. In the first year of the reign, when he came to Beaulieu, all our companies for a grace and honour to my Lord of Southampton came out of the Island and trained before him.

There are certain comments to be made upon this piece of portraiture. It is sharply in black and white, for over twenty years the views had crystallised in the English country. The timorousness is insisted on again and again as is the Solomon-like quality. Actual expressions of the king's are unlikely to have reached Sir John Oglander. Again the widespread knowledge of the king's weakness is in this case centred on his relationship with the duke of Buckingham. This was not seen in these explicit terms in the court circle.

I am not aware of any views about the character of King James preserved in the correspondence of the Catholic country gentry. The references to the king in the different letters of the Trevelyan family sent back to Nettlecombe in Somerset are uniformly favourable.[1] One point seems common to all the Anglican landed circle, they were not prepared to welcome a Spanish bride. In the circles closer in than this towards the court criticism was muted.

To conclude the chapter I should like to examine the last promotion of Sir Henry Wotton. In 1623 he was coming towards the end of his third period as ambassador in Venice. He was fifty-five years of age, a little younger than his royal master. The days were past when the king had given lavishly to his young companions. Sir Henry was the younger and portionless son of a great court family, the Wottons of Boughton Malherbe in Kent; but his general situation was unpropitious. His elder half-brother Lord Wotton had become in recent years a Roman Catholic and he himself had been denounced by Scioppius, the German controversialist; nor in his heart did he agree with King James's policy. He was a careful man, a trifle idle.

As he sat in his embassy he contemplated the future. The house was furnished in the modern style with pictures and armour and gilded

---

[1] Cf. *Trevelyan Papers* (Camden Society), III, 68–97.

leather on the walls, a ground carpet in the dining-room and appropriate arras, the whole acquired at a low rate from Venetian Jews. Within the house he diverted himself with an ape upon a chain. In the summer he retired to his villa on the Brenta, staying through the vintage and playing at bowls in the cool evenings. He was interested in the florists' gardens at Chioggia, and sent to the king both rose cuttings and melon seed. In questions of architecture he had a solid appreciation of the Palladian manner. Pictures he knew and loved and turned to profit. In some ways it must have been a strain as he sat in his green velvet armchair looking out on the canal and discussing the "extraordinary greatness" of the dolphins in the Giudecca.

At this time Sir Henry Savile was sinking quietly at a great age. He was Provost of Eton, where he had printed his great edition of St Chrysostom, and also held the wardenship of Merton. He had been appointed although a layman, which meant that one obstacle had been removed. Sir Henry Wotton had a sharp desire to obtain the first of these two places. As Savile's illness grew more serious, the different candidates for the succession gathered round. These included, besides Wotton, his colleague Sir Dudley Carleton (who had married Lady Savile's daughter), Dr John Hammond and Sir William Beecher, who held the clerkship of the privy council. The king, to the disappointment of the candidates, appointed a Scottish layman, Thomas Murray.

Within a year, however, the new provost was himself in failing health and the matter was agitated once again. In March 1623 the former lord chancellor wrote to the secretary of state with a direct request. "Mr Thomas Murray, Provost of Eton (whom I love very well)," began Lord St Alban, "is like to dye. It were a preety cell for my fortune. The College and Schole I dare not dout but I shall make to flourysh."[1] To this letter Sir Edward Conway replied with courtesy stating that to his regret the place had been already promised to Sir William Beecher.

For a fortnight Dr Murray lingered on and the day following his death the Visitor of the college, the bishop of Lincoln, went down to Eton. It was a complication in the situation that the duke of Buckingham was out of England and that nothing could be done till his return. Already the candidates had assembled in some force and Dr Williams reported that Sir William Beecher, Sir Dudley Carleton, Sir Albertus Morton (Wotton's nephew) and Sir Robert Eaton, secretary to the late

[1] Letter from Lord St Alban to Secretary Conway, dated March 25, 1623. S.P. Dom. Jas I, CXL, No. 32.

queen, were among the number. The names of Sir Robert Naunton, Sir Ralph Freeman, the master of Requests, and Sir Henry Wotton were shortly added. At this point the ambassador was recalled from Venice.

The situation now became entangled for, while some sort of promise had been made to Sir William Beecher presumably in return for money payments, Wotton was pressing for his substantial arrears of salary and allowances. It was fortunate for him that these had been permitted to accumulate until the government had removed him from his post. The governing factors seem to have been the reversions in Wotton's possession which he could now dispose of to advantage. As far as the government was concerned he surrendered the claims which arose from his expenditure in Venice. To Buckingham himself he offered the reversion which he had purchased to the mastership of the Rolls, while he satisfied Sir William Beecher's claims by the gift of the reversion to half a Six Clerks' place in Chancery. In the summer of 1624 the late ambassador to Venice was rewarded by the appointment to the provostship of Eton. In the last years of the reign these purchases and surrenders had been worked out as a fairly perfect system. They did not affect the king's expenditure.

Chapter 26

THE FINAL MONTHS

THE last eighteen months of the reign may almost be said to have taken
place in the presence of an abdicated king. James I had little belief in
parliaments and knew their limitations. In his earlier years of rule in
England he had kept discussion of foreign affairs away from the debates
of the House of Commons and there had been wisdom in this action.
The expert knowledge of these questions was shared between the secretaries of state and the present, and to a lesser degree the past, ambassadors. Now Buckingham and the prince decided that they would work
with parliament because for the moment their opinions coincided with
the general notions of the landed gentry. These were simplified indeed
and mainly consisted of the idea that England was confronted by two
important "popish" nations, Spain and France. The empire was little
known about in London; there was small understanding of its curious
and amorphous power. It was widely held that the king of Spain could
secure the restoration of the Elector Palatine if he should wish to do so.
On February 12, 1624 King James for the fourth and last time opened
a parliament. In May this parliament was to be prorogued, but not until
it had carried through the impeachment of Lord Middlesex.

This was a consequence of his breach with Buckingham following on
his support for the Spanish marriage as a result of the need that he felt
for the Spanish dowry. He seems always to have been curiously aloof
from the normal English short-sighted interest in foreign policy. He
appears to have been a solid man, valued rather than liked by the old
king. It seems that this impeachment was not based on the gross and
varied exactions which had brought down Lord St Alban and Suffolk,
who had been his predecessor as lord treasurer. It was rather a question
of Middlesex having perpetuated the rather loose practice of the city
merchants, when he took over the reins of power. But the king appears
to have been too broken to go much into details. He made a speech in
his favour in the House of Lords. Two comments on the attack may be
repeated. In a letter of April 15 Sir Dudley Carleton wrote that the
offences with which he was charged were "not very heinous or inexcus-

able in these days, but he must be sacrificed unless the King interferes".[1] Thomas Fuller giving a rather later tradition states: "*Perdidit Fides* (Middlesex's motto carved on his new house Copt Hall); he was lost at Court for his fidelity to King James in sparing his treasure, and not answering the expensiveness of a great favourite."[2]

One of the pathetic elements in this case is the useless effort made by the king to gain some support for Middlesex among the peers. It is stated by Hacket in his life of Williams that the king "courted many to take side with the Treasurer and prevailed little".[3] He, who had been so generous with grants of money, had not cultivated friendship to the same degree, and what could he do with his heir against him? This prosecution of Middlesex had been started by the new duke of Buckingham, but it had also been stoked up by the Prince of Wales. It always seems to me that this was the most displeasing year of Prince Charles's life. His attitude to his father was the worst of his many failures in personal relationships. He suffered from a gentle and shy insensitivity.

The Princess Elizabeth was now in Germany and the king was thus isolated from his own family. The appointments of this year were not his work. Sir George Calvert, who had been secretary of state for some six years, resigned his office and his seat in parliament and was raised to the Irish peerage as Lord Baltimore. He had at first been a *protégé* of Sir Robert Cecil and had gradually passed over to the pro-Spanish wing of Buckingham's adherents. Perhaps the king vaguely knew that he had become a Catholic, this is not certain. His successor Sir Albertus Morton, who is less well known because of his early death, had received through Buckingham both the Paris embassy and then the secretaryship. He was entirely wedded to the favourite's new ideas on foreign policy; he had but little to do with his own sovereign.

As the king grew weak his taste for fruit increased. He loved Barbary melons[4] and there is an account by Bishop Goodman which is worth recording.

I think that King James every autumn (of his last years) did feed a little more than moderately upon fruits; he had his grapes, his nectarines and other fruits in his own keeping, besides, we did see that he fed very plentifully on them from abroad. I remember that Mr French of the Spicery, who sometimes did present him with the first strawberries, cherries and other fruits

---

[1] Letter dated April 15, 1624, *Cal. State Papers, Dom.*
[2] Thomas Fuller, *The Church History of Britain* (1845), III, 188-9.
[3] *Scrinia Reserata*, 189-90.   [4] Goodman, *Memoirs*, II, 383.

and kneeling to the King had some speech to use to him . . . but the King never had patience to hear him one word, but his hand was in the basket.[1]

This liking for fruit suggests to me that the king had lost his teeth. The bishop has another comment. "Going to Theobalds, to New-market and stirring abroad when the coldness of the year was not yet past, it could not be prevented but (that) he must fall into a quartan ague."

There is another comment.[2] It seems that the king was quieter now, "contrary to his former hasty and passionate custom, which often in his distemper would bid a pox or a plague on such as flocked to see him." No prince had greater claims upon his bishops. No more steadfast protector of the Protestant Church of England by law established ever wore the English crown. Queen Elizabeth had had a political element mixed with her churchmanship and Charles I, although a devoted Anglican, was uxorious and had a Catholic wife. King James was not uxorious and his aims were theological. The idea of conversion warmed him; it was surely this that drew him to Dr Donne, not his sermons, for these were hardly sympathetic to the royal taste.

He was always concerned that the eldest sons of Catholic peers should be taken from their parents and brought up in the state religion. He was responsible for the Protestantism of their descendants, the dukes of Ormonde and the earls of Barrymore.[3] Again, his mind here had a narrow swing; he never thought about the greater gentry. The two most notable church appointments of his later years were Williams to the diocese of Lincoln and Donne to the deanery of St Paul's. But it seems that the latter had little contact with his sovereign. He lived in his own private circle with Magdalen Herbert and the young Lord Falkland. He held a second living, St Dunstan's in the West; he had insomnia and was disturbed by the sound of the cathedral bells. He studied Spanish. There was a kind of refinement in Donne's world, which seems to me inimical to James I.

Bishop Williams's approach was another matter altogether. He would attend the ailing king and the royal death-bed, and he was fitted for this task. He had those deep Protestant sympathies which the king from his childhood days had never lost. He appreciated, as few others did, the

---

[1] *Memoirs*, I, 409–10.   [2] Halliwell, ed., *Autobiography of Sir Simonds D'Ewes*, I, 160.

[3] There is a list, dating from June 1613, of the noblemen's heirs to be brought to England for education as Protestants, the sons and heirs of viscount Gormanston and lords Delvin and Trimlestown, the grandsons of lords Barry and Dunboyne, and Lord Power, already a peer aged fifteen years. Cal. S.P. Ireland, 1615–25, p. 83.

king's strictly channelled erudition. Coming from old north Welsh stock, he retained much of the layman in his disposition. He understood quite well the old king's wit, both the simplicity and the strain of bawdy. He had a certain flexibility. He understood, although he did not share, what the king felt about the Spanish marriage. It seems that he was at home with the old man in a way that he could never be with his stiff young successor.

The broken relations with Spain, the plans for the prince's marriage with Henriette-Marie of France, hardly seemed to touch the king. On March 5 he was attacked by a tertian ague. The long winter was slowly ending; at Theobalds the king lay dying. Through life he had been remarkably consistent, though his pawky wit was better understood in his northern kingdom. He had gone on writing verses, the last was on his visit to Burley-on-the-Hill. He was now leaving his realms to his humourless only surviving son. He had always *given*. It was not so much the king as his needy courtiers who benefited from the sale of titles. He had always strived, sometimes by strange means, to pay his debts. Thus Phineas Pett, the great shipwright, had received the money[1] for a baronetcy from a wealthy north-country recusant, who founded the family of the earls of Derwentwater. There was perhaps little to be said for the viscounties, a curious form of title, which the king created on what would later be known as the Irish Establishment; but his new earldoms in the English peerage were very different. They cost a great deal of money, normally about £10,000. They went to families of the landed gentry of impeccable financial standing. None of these stocks dishonoured the peerage by their bankruptcy. This was in fact the heyday of the wealthy English county families. Especially since coming south the king had had but little dealings with the middle classes. He suffered in this from a narrowed horizon. The old queen had played her part before the nation; the crowds along the roadside all could hear her calculated, loud asides. But King James was domestic; perhaps his outdoor-servants, his huntsmen and the keepers of his hunting lodges, were the only members of the working class that he was near to.

His illness grew upon him; he would not live to see the break of spring. Abroad Maurice of Nassau, now Prince of Orange, lay dying at the Huis dem Bosch outside the Hague. The king's intimate Scottish

[1] "His Majesty in his princely care of me by the means of the honourable the Lord High Admiral, had before my coming bestowed on me for the supply of my present relief the making of a knight baronet." W. G. Perrin, ed., *The Autobiography of Phineas Pett* (Navy Records Society), vol. LI, 121.

family was departing, the two brother dukes of Lennox died, the younger at Kirby in this last winter. While the king himself was very ill, his young *protégé* the marquess of Hamilton died in London. In these years he had come to value him; he had made him lord steward and had given him an English earldom, Cambridge. Now, there were rumours, absurd and baseless, that Hamilton had died a Catholic.[1] He could not bear this happening to "a graceful gentleman". The king had now but a fortnight to live. He was losing those who had come from Scotland with him. It was just a year since Bothwell, the terror of his youth, had died in Naples. Death came to the king at Theobalds on March 27, 1625.

His body lay in state with three new silver candlesticks from Spain on either side.[2] The burial took place on the May 5 at Westminster Abbey in summer weather. The bishop of Lincoln, as was right, was chosen to preach the funeral sermon. His words would go forward with their broken baroque imagery, the gilt was cracking. At last he reached his peroration with this sentence. *Dormivit Salamon.* Solomon slept.

---

[1] John Southcote, *Diary* (Catholic Record Society), 104.
[2] *Correspondence* of Amerigo Salvetti, envoy of the court of Tuscany, p. 16 in Skrine MSS, Historical Manuscripts Commission's XIth Report.

Appendices

SELECT CHART PEDIGREES

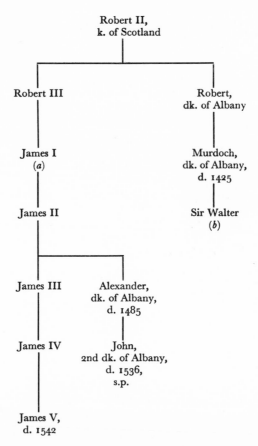

(a) The Stewarts of Atholl (ext 1625) and the Stewarts of Buchan (ext 1580) were descended from the two uterine half-brothers of James II, the sons of Joanna Beaufort, widow of James I, by her second husband, Sir James Stewart, the Black Knight of Lorne. The Stewarts of Traquair were descended from a natural son of the first earl of Buchan.

(b) Andrew, first lord Avandale, was the legitimated son of Sir Walter and from him descended the Stewarts of Ochiltree and Avandale, and the Stewarts of Methven.

The Stewarts of Darnley, later earls of Lennox, were descended in the male line from the same stock as Robert II. The Stewarts of Blantyre were cadets of the Garlies family, later earls of Galloway, but the ancestry of their progenitor, Sir William Stewart of Jedworth (d. 1402) is uncertain.

Table 1. The Stewart main lines

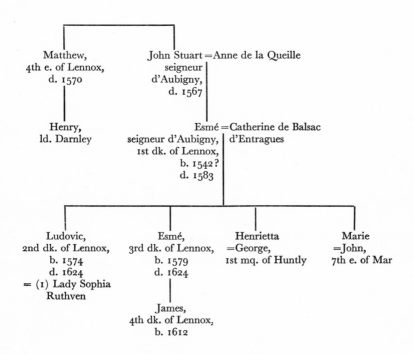

Table 2. The Stuarts of Aubigny

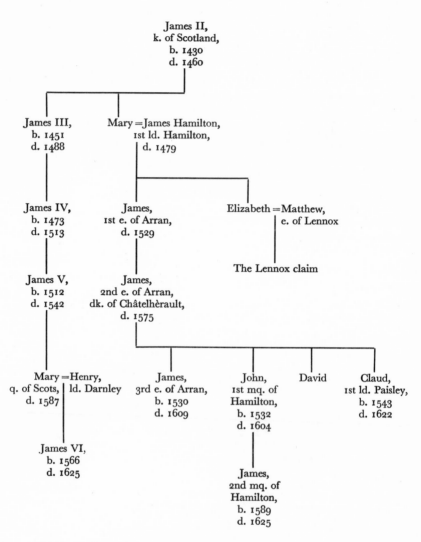

Table 3. Succession to the Scottish crown. The house of Hamilton

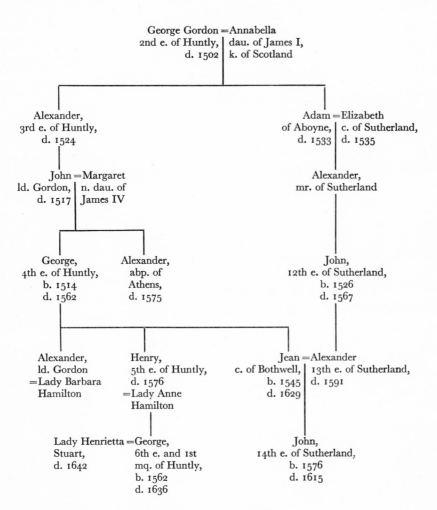

Table 4. The Gordons

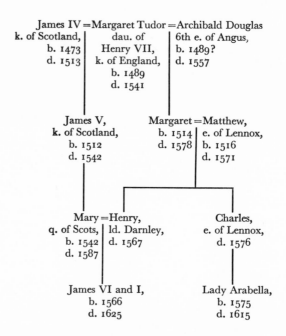

Table 5. Lady Arabella's claim

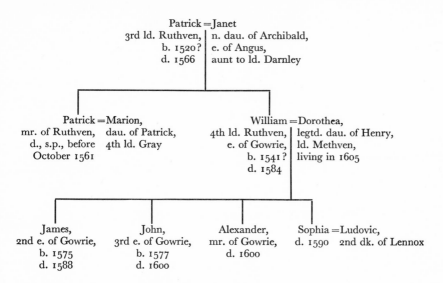

Patrick = Janet
3rd ld. Ruthven, | n. dau. of Archibald,
b. 1520? | e. of Angus,
d. 1566 | aunt to ld. Darnley

Patrick = Marion,   William = Dorothea,
mr. of Ruthven, dau. of Patrick,   4th ld. Ruthven, | legtd. dau. of Henry,
d., s.p., before 4th ld. Gray   e. of Gowrie, | ld. Methven,
October 1561   b. 1541? | living in 1605
                                     d. 1584

James,   John,   Alexander,   Sophia = Ludovic,
2nd e. of Gowrie,   3rd e. of Gowrie,   mr. of Gowrie,   d. 1590   2nd dk. of Lennox
b. 1575   b. 1577   d. 1600
d. 1588   d. 1600

Table 6. The house of Gowrie

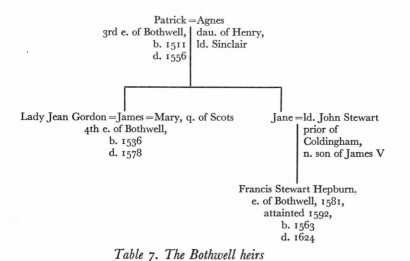

Patrick = Agnes
3rd e. of Bothwell, | dau. of Henry,
b. 1511 | ld. Sinclair
d. 1556

Lady Jean Gordon = James = Mary, q. of Scots   Jane = ld. John Stewart
4th e. of Bothwell, | prior of
b. 1536 | Coldingham,
d. 1578 | n. son of James V

Francis Stewart Hepburn,
e. of Bothwell, 1581,
attainted 1592,
b. 1563
d. 1624

Table 7. The Bothwell heirs

331

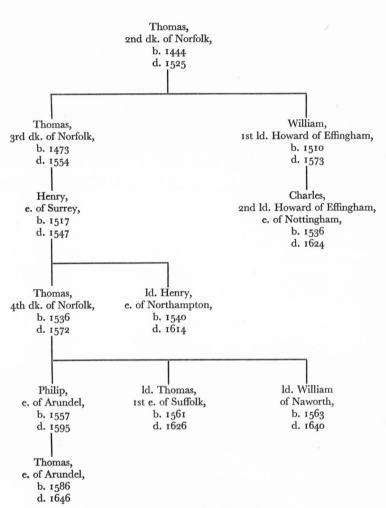

Thomas,
2nd dk. of Norfolk,
b. 1444
d. 1525

Thomas,
3rd dk. of Norfolk,
b. 1473
d. 1554

William,
1st ld. Howard of Effingham,
b. 1510
d. 1573

Henry,
e. of Surrey,
b. 1517
d. 1547

Charles,
2nd ld. Howard of Effingham,
e. of Nottingham,
b. 1536
d. 1624

Thomas,
4th dk. of Norfolk,
b. 1536
d. 1572

ld. Henry,
e. of Northampton,
b. 1540
d. 1614

Philip,
e. of Arundel,
b. 1557
d. 1595

ld. Thomas,
1st e. of Suffolk,
b. 1561
d. 1626

ld. William
of Naworth,
b. 1563
d. 1640

Thomas,
e. of Arundel,
b. 1586
d. 1646

Table 8. The Howards. Chart diagram

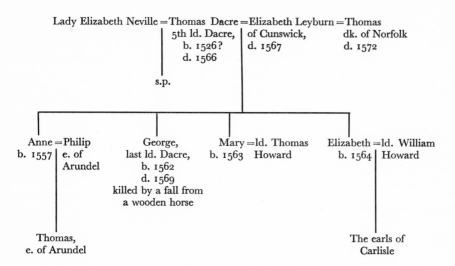

Table 9. *The Howards. The Dacre inheritance*

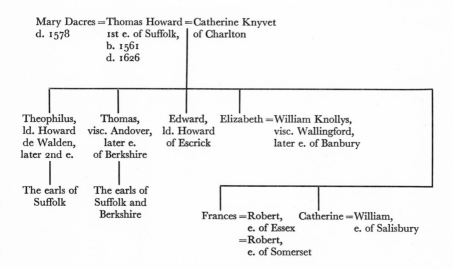

Table 10. *The Howards. The Suffolk line*

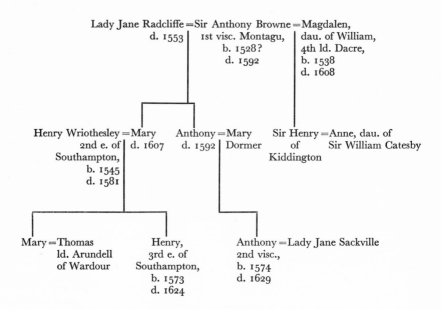

Lady Jane Radcliffe = Sir Anthony Browne = Magdalen,
d. 1553   1st visc. Montagu,   dau. of William,
b. 1528?   4th ld. Dacre,
d. 1592   b. 1538
d. 1608

Henry Wriothesley = Mary   Anthony = Mary   Sir Henry = Anne, dau. of
2nd e. of   d. 1607   d. 1592   Dormer   of   Sir William Catesby
Southampton,   Kiddington
b. 1545
d. 1581

Mary = Thomas   Henry,   Anthony = Lady Jane Sackville
ld. Arundell   3rd e. of   2nd visc.,
of Wardour   Southampton,   b. 1574
b. 1573   d. 1629
d. 1624

Table 11. Southampton's connections

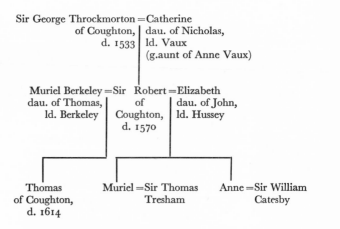

Sir George Throckmorton = Catherine
of Coughton,   dau. of Nicholas,
d. 1533   ld. Vaux
(g.aunt of Anne Vaux)

Muriel Berkeley = Sir   Robert = Elizabeth
dau. of Thomas,   of   dau. of John,
ld. Berkeley   Coughton,   ld. Hussey
d. 1570

Thomas   Muriel = Sir Thomas   Anne = Sir William
of Coughton,   Tresham   Catesby
d. 1614

Table 12. The Throckmorton stem

334

SELECT BIBLIOGRAPHY

The Reign in Scotland

I · HISTORICAL MANUSCRIPTS COMMISSION REPORTS

Calendar of Breadalbane MSS
—— *Forbes Leith MSS*
—— *Gordon Castle (Huntly) MSS*
—— *Mar and Kellie MSS*
—— *Maxwell Witham MSS*
—— *Moray MSS*
—— *Murray of Ochtertyre MSS*
—— *Sutherland MSS*

II · COLLECTIONS OF STATE PAPERS

Acts of the Parliament of Scotland
Border Papers, 1560–1603
Calendar of State Papers, Scotland
Exchequer Rolls of Scotland
Hamilton Papers, 1532–90
Register of the Great Seal of Scotland
—— *Privy Council of Scotland*

III · LETTERS, DIARIES AND CORRESPONDENCE

Arniston Memoirs (1571–1838), ed. George W. T. Ormond (1887).
Black Book of Taymouth, ed. Cosmo Innes (Bannatyne Club, 1855).
Blairs Papers, ed. M. V. Hay (1929).
*Book of Caerlaverock, ed. Sir William Fraser (2 vols, 1873).
*Douglas Book, ed. Sir William Fraser (4 vols, 1885).
*House of Gordon, ed. J. M. Bulloch (New Spalding Club, 1907).
*Memorials of the Earls of Eglinton, ed. Sir William Fraser (1859).
*Memorials of the Earls of Haddington, ed. Sir William Fraser (1889).
*Scotts of Buccleugh, ed. Sir William Fraser (1878).

*Commissioned by the heads of the respective families, these six books are valuable only for the documents and correspondence which they contain.

Book of Dunvegan, ed. Rev. R. C. McLeod (Third Spalding Club, 1938).

†Calderwood, David, *History of the Kirk of Scotland* (1524–1625), ed. Thomas Thomson and David Laing (8 vols, Wodrow Society, 1842–9).

†Gordon, Sir Robert, *The Genealogical History of the Earldom of Sutherland* (1813).

†Hume of Godscroft, David, *History of House and Race of Douglas of Angus* (1644).

†Kingston, Alexander, viscount, *Continuation of the House of Seytoun* (Bannatyne Club, 1829).

† *These four authors were only contemporary with a portion of the events described, Calderwood being born in 1575, Sir Robert Gordon in 1580 and Lord Kingston in 1621. Hume of Godscroft was born about 1560, but his work has the note of eulogy.*

Correspondence of King James VI of Scotland with Sir Robert Cecil and Others in England, ed. John Bruce (Camden Society, 1861).

Correspondence of Robert Bowes (Surtees Society, 1842).

Correspondence of the Earl of Ancram, ed. D. Laing (1875), first vol. These letters begin in 1616.

Historie and Life of King James the Sext (1566–96), ed. Thomas Thomson (Bannatyne Club, 1825).

House of Forbes, ed. Alistair and Henrietta Tayler (Third Spalding Club, 1937).

Letters of Queen Elizabeth and King James VI of Scotland, ed. John Bruce (Camden Society, 1861).

Letters to the Argyll Family (Maitland Club, 1839).

Melville, James (d. 1614), *The Autobiography and Diary of Mr James Melvill*, ed. Robert Pitcairn (Wodrow Society, 1842).

Melville of Halhill, Sir James (d. 1617), *Memoirs of his Own Life*, ed. Thomas Thomson (Bannatyne and Maitland Clubs, 1827).

——, *Memoirs of Sir James Melville*, ed. A. Francis Steuart (1929).

Moysie, David, *Memoirs of the Affairs of Scotland* (1577–1603), ed. James Dennistoun (Bannatyne and Maitland Clubs, 1830).

Narratives of Scottish Catholics under Mary Stuart and James VI, ed. William Forbes-Leith, S.J. (Edinburgh, 1885).

Papers relative to the Marriage of King James the Sixth of Scotland with the Princess Anne of Denmark (Bannatyne Club, 1828).

Relation of the Master of Gray (Bannatyne Club, 1836).

Row, John, *History of the Kirk of Scotland* (1558–1637) (Wodrow Society, 1842).

State Papers and Letters of Sir Ralph Sadler, ed. Arthur Clifford (2 vols, Edinburgh, 1809).

State Papers of Thomas Earl of Melros (Abbotsford Club, 1837).

Stirling's Register of Royal Letters, ed. C. Rogers (1835).

IV · LATER AND RECENT WORKS

Bellesheim, A., *History of the Catholic Church in Scotland*, trans. D. O. Hunter Blair (1887–8), I, II.

Brown, Peter Hume, *History of Scotland* (1911).

——, *Early Travellers in Scotland* (1891).

Burton, John Hill, *History of Scotland* (1873).

Davidson, John, and Gray, Alexander, *The Scottish Staple at Veere* (1909).

Dickinson, William Croft, *Scotland from the earliest times to 1603* (1961).

Donaldson, Gordon, *The Reformation in Scotland* (1960).

Grant, I. F., *The Social and Economic Development of Scotland before 1603* (1930).

Inventory of Monuments in East Lothian (1924).

Inventory of Monuments in Mid-Lothian and West Lothian (1929).

Lang, Andrew, *History of Scotland* (1903), first 2 vols.

Lee, Maurice, *James Stewart, Earl of Moray* (1953).

——, *John Maitland of Thirlestane* (1959).

McCrie, Thomas, *Life of Andrew Melville* (1899).

McGibbon, David, and Ross, Thomas, *The Castellated and Domestic Architecture of Scotland* (5 vols, 1887–92).

Mathieson, William Law, *Politics and Religion* (1902).

Nobbs, Douglas, *England and Scotland 1560–1707* (1952).

Pagan, Theodore, *The Convention of Royal Burghs of Scotland* (1926).

Rait, Robert S., *The Parliaments of Scotland* (Glasgow, 1924).

Terry, Charles Sanford, *The Scottish Parliament, its Constitution and Procedure* (1905).

Warrack, John, *Domestic Life in Scotland* (1920).

V · WORKS BY KING JAMES, COMPOSED IN BOTH HIS KINGDOMS

1. *The essayes of a prentise in the diuine art of poesie* (1584).
2. *Ane fruitfull meditatioun*, etc. (exposition of the 7, 8, 9 and 10 verses of ch. XX of Revelation) (1588).
3. *Ane meditatioun vpon the first buke of the Chronicles of the Kings* (XV, 25-9) (1589).
4. *His Maiesties poeticall exercises* (1591).
5. *Daemonologie, in forme of a dialogue*, etc. (1597).
6. *Basilikon Doron* (1599).
7. *The true lawe of free monarchies* (1598).
8. *A counter blaste to tobacco* (1604).
9. *Triplici nodo, triplex cuneus : or an Apologie for the oath of allegiance*, etc. (1607).
10. *Declaration du Roy Jacques I pour le droit des rois* (1615).

These collected works were published by Bishop Montague (*The workes of James, King of Great Britaine, France, and Ireland, published by James, bishop of Winton*) in 1616. After this date the king wrote:

11. *A meditation upon the Lords prayer* (1619).
12. *A meditation upon the 27, 28, 29 verses of the xxvii chapter of S. Matthew. Or a paterne for a Kings inauguration* (1620).

The Poems of James VI of Scotland were edited by J. Craigie for the Scottish Texts Society, 1948, and *The Works of James I* were edited by C. H. McIlwain, beginning in 1918.

The Reign in England

I · HISTORICAL MANUSCRIPTS COMMISSION REPORTS

Calendar of Ancaster MSS
—— *Bouverie MSS*
—— *Buccleugh and Queensberry MSS*, III.
—— *Coke MSS*, containing the correspondence and memoranda of Secretary Coke.
—— *De L'Isle and Dudley MSS*
—— *Denbigh MSS*, for personal detail of the Villiers family grouping.
—— *Drummond Moray MSS*, including a correspondence between Winwood and Buckingham in 1617.
—— *Eglinton MSS*, including a list of expenses at the English court in 1603.
—— *Gawdy MSS*
—— *Hastings MSS*, II.
—— *Hothfield MSS*, containing notes left by Anne Countess of Dorset.
—— *Kenyon MSS*
—— *Kilmorey MSS*
—— *Manchester MSS*, including letters dealing with the Summer Islands.
—— *Mar and Kellie MSS* including the Kellie-Mar correspondence.
—— *Middleton MSS*
—— *Muncaster MSS*, including letters from Lord William Howard.
—— *Portland MSS*, III, including the Conway correspondence.
—— *Powys MSS*, including a short correspondence between Sir Edward Herbert and Secretary Calvert.
—— *Rutland MSS*, I, II, containing elaborate details of the life at Belvoir.
—— *Sackville MSS*, pt. I, *Cranfield Papers, 1534–1612*.
—— *Salisbury (Cecil) MSS*, containing the official correspondence of the first earl of Salisbury.

Calendar of Stafford MSS, including a detailed inventory of Costessey Hall in 1622.
—— *Stewart of Alltyrodyn MSS*
—— *Talbot MSS*
—— *Wells Chapter MSS*
—— *Westmorland MSS*, containing an account of Lord Salisbury's last days.
—— *Wingfield Digby MSS*, including the correspondence of Sir John Digby in 1610–12.

II · COLLECTIONS OF STATE PAPERS

Acts of the Privy Council.
Calendar of State Papers, Colonial.
——, *Domestic.*
——, *Venetian.*
Clarendon State Papers.
Journals of the House of Lords.
Lords Debates in 1621, (Camden Society).
Parliament Notes by Sir Nathaniel Rich, Belasyse Diary, Barrington Diary and other accounts of the transactions of the Parliament of 1621, ed. Wallace Notestein, F. H. Relf and H. Simpson.
Register of the Privy Council of Scotland.
State Trials.
Strafford Letters, ed. William Knowler (1739).
Winwood, Sir Ralph, *Memorials of Affairs of State* (3 vols, 1725).

III · LETTERS, DIARIES AND CORRESPONDENCE

Carew-Roe Correspondence (Camden Society, 1860).
Correspondence in G. Goodman, *The Court of King James the First* (2 vols, 1839).
—— Thomas Birch, *Court and Times of James I*, ed. R. F. Williams (2 vols, 1849).
Correspondence of Jane Lady Cornwallis (1842).
Diary of John Rous, ed. Mrs Everett Green (Camden Society, 1856).
Diary of John Southcote, C.R.S., I.
Diary of Thomas Crosfield, ed. F. S. Boas (1935).
Diary of Walter Yonge (Camden Society, 1848).
Egerton Papers (Camden Society, 1840).
Fortescue Papers, ed. S. R. Gardiner (Camden Society, 1871).
Journal of Sir Roger Wilbraham (Camden Miscellany, 1902).
Knyvett Letters, ed. Bertram Schofield (1949).
Letters in James Spedding, *The Letters and Life of Francis Bacon* (7 vols, 1861–74).

z   339

Letters in John Nichols, *The Progresses . . . of King James the First* (4 vols., 1828).
—— M. F. S. Hervey, *Life and Correspondence of Thomas Earl of Arundel* (1921)
Letters of Lady Brilliana Harley, ed. T. T. Lewis (Camden Society, 1854).
Letters to several persons of honour written by John Donne, ed. John Donne, D.C.L. (1651).
Lismore Papers, ed. Rev. A. B. Grosart (1886–8), II, III.
Original Letters Illustrative of English History, ed. Sir Henry Ellis (2nd series, 4 vols, Camden Society, 1827).
Oxinden Letters 1607–1642, ed. D. Gardiner (1933), I.
Tixall Papers, ed. Arthur Clifford (1815).
Trevelyan Papers (Camden Society, 1872–3), II, III.

IV · AUTOBIOGRAPHIES, MEMOIRS, MEMORANDA, ETC.

Autobiography of Edward Lord Herbert of Cherbury, ed. Sidney Lee.
Autobiography of Sir Simonds D'Ewes, ed. J. O. Halliwell (2 vols, 1845), I.
Brief Lives (notes by John Aubrey), ed. A. Clark.
Commonplace Book of Sir John Oglander (A Royalist's Notebook), ed. Francis Bamford (1936).
Conversion of Sir Tobie Mathew, ed. A. H. Mathew.
Diary of Lady Anne Clifford, ed. V. Sackville-West (1923).
Hacket, John, bishop of Lichfield, *Scrinia Reserata: a Memorial of John Williams* (2 pts, 1693).
Historical Collections, ed. John Rushworth (8 vols, 1721–2).
Holles, Gervase, *Memorials of the Holles Family 1493–1656*, ed. A. C. Wood (1937)
Letter Book of Sir John Holles (*Calendar of Portland MSS*).
Life and Works of Sir Henry Mainwaring (Navy Records Society, 1920–2).
Life of Anne Countess of Arundel and Surrey, ed. Henry Duke of Norfolk.
Life of Lady Anne Clifford (Roxburgh Club, 1916).
Life of the Lady Falkland, ed. M. F. Howard (1908).
Loseley Manuscripts, ed. A. J. Kempe (1838).
Memoir of Robert Cary, Earl of Monmouth, ed. G. H. Powell (1905).
Memoirs of Anne Lady Fanshawe, ed. H. C. Fanshawe (1905).
Memoirs of Sir George Courthop (Camden Miscellany), XI.
Memoirs of the Verney Family, ed. Frances Lady Verney (1892), I.
Montagu Musters Book, ed. Joan Wake (Northamptonshire Records Society, 1935).
Observations by the Rev. John Bowle, chaplain to the Earl of Salisbury, printed in *Desiderata Curiosa*.
Poems of Ben Jonson, ed. Bernard H. Newdigate (1936).
Poems of John Donne, ed. H. J. C. Grierson (1929).
Poems of Richard Corbett, ed. J. A. W. Bennett and H. R. Trevor-Roper (1952).

Relation of the death of Prince Henry, ed. John More, bishop of Ely, printed in *Desiderata Curiosa*.

Robert Loder's Farm Accounts, 1610–20 (Camden Society, 1936).

Walker, Sir Edward, *Historical Discourses* (1705).

Weldon, Sir Anthony, *The Court and Character of James I* (1650), reprinted in *Secret History of the Court of James the First* (1811).

Works of William Drummond of Hawthornden, ed. L. E. Kastner.

Wotton, Sir Henry, *The Life and Death of George Duke of Buckingham* (1685).

V · LATER AND RECENT WORKS

Akrigg, G. P. V., *Jacobean Pageant* (1962).

Allen, J. W., *English Political Thought 1603–60* (1938).

Amos, A., *The great oyer of Poisoning* (1846).

Brett-James, Norman G., *The growth of Stuart London* (1935).

Caraman, Philip, S.J., *Henry Garnet* (1964).

Chambers, E. K., *Sir Henry Lee* (1936).

Coke, D., *Sir John Coke* (1937).

Corbett, Sir Julian, *England in the Mediterranean 1603–1713* (1904), first vol. only.

Davies, Godfrey, *The Early Stuarts 1603–60* (1937).

Devereux, W. B., *Lives and Letters of the Devereux 1540–1646* (1853).

Edwards, E., *Sir Walter Ralegh* (1868).

Evans, F. M. G., *The Principal Secretary of State* (a survey from 1558 until 1680) (1923).

Friedrich, Carl J., *The Age of the Baroque 1610–60* (1952).

Gardiner, S. R., "Britain under James I" (*Cambridge Modern History* (1906), III).

——, *History of England 1603–42* (1864–86), first 5 vols.

Harrison, G. B. (ed.), *A Jacobean Journal 1603–6* (1941).

Hill, Christopher, *The Century of Revolution 1603–1714* (1961).

Huxley, Gervas, *Endymion Porter* (1959).

Jourdain, Margaret, *English Interior Decoration* (1950).

Longueville, T., *Curious Case of Lady Purbeck* (1909).

McElwee, W. L., *England's Precedence* (1956).

Mathew, David, *Sir Tobie Mathew* (1950).

——, *The Jacobean Age* (1938).

Moir, Thomas L., *The Addled Parliament of 1614* (1958).

Morris, J., S.J., *The condition of Catholics under James I* (1871).

Nicoll, Allardyce, *Stuart Masques and the Renaissance Stage* (1937).

Owen, C. L'Estrange, *Witchcraft and Demonianism* (accounts of arraignments in England between 1605 and 1622) (1933).

Pellegrin, A. G., *John Florio and Basilikon Doron of James I* (1961).

Prestwich, Menna, *Cranfield, politics and profits under the early Stuarts* (1966).

Reid, R. R., *The King's Council of the North* (1921).

Rowse, A. L., *Ralegh and the Throckmortons* (1962).

——, *Shakespeare's Southampton* (1964).

Seventeenth Century Studies presented to Sir Herbert Grierson (1937).

Sisson, C. J., "King James the First of England as poet and political writer" (*Seventeenth Century Studies*, etc. (1937), see above).

Smith, Logan Pearsall, *Life and Letters of Sir Henry Wotton* (1907).

Statham, E. P. (ed.), *A Jacobean Letter Writer* (J. Chamberlain) (1920).

Stebbing, W., *Sir Walter Ralegh* (1899).

Stone, Lawrence, *The Crisis of the Aristocracy 1558–1641* (1963).

Summerson, Sir John, *Architecture in Britain 1530–1830* (1953).

Tawney, R. H., *Business and Politics under James I* (1958).

Thirsk, Joan, *Agrarian History of England and Wales, IV, 1506–1640* (1966).

Townshend, Dorothea, *Life and Letters of Endymion Porter* (1897).

Trevelyan, G. M., *England under the Stuarts* (1904).

Wake, Joan, *The Brudenells of Deane* (1953).

Waterhouse, E. K., *Painting in Britain 1530–1790* (1953).

Wedgwood, C. V., *The Thirty Years War* (1938), introductory chapters.

Williams, Charles, *James I* (1934).

Williamson, H. R., *King James I* (1935).

Willson, D. H., *King James VI and I* (1956).

MAIN EVENTS IN THE LIFE OF JAMES I

1566   Birth at Edinburgh Castle.
1567   Coronation as King James VI of Scotland.
1578   Comes to power as king.
1579   Esmé Stuart reaches Scotland.
1581   Execution of the regent Morton.
1582   The Raid of Ruthven.
1583   Esmé duke of Lennox dies in France.
1584   Execution of the earl of Gowrie.
      James Stewart made chancellor.
1585   James Stewart driven out of public life.
1587   Execution at Fotheringhay of the queen of Scots.
1589   Marriage with Princess Anne of Denmark.
1591–4 The Bothwell frays.
1594   Prince Henry born.
1596   The Octavians appointed.
      Princess Elizabeth born.
1598   *Basilikon Doron* written.
1600   Prince Charles born.
      The Gowrie conspiracy.
1603   Death of Queen Elizabeth I and accession as King James I to the
        English throne.
      Main and Bye plots.
      Imprisonment of Sir Walter Raleigh.
1604   Hampton Court conference.
      Peace with Spain.
1605   Robert Cecil created earl of Salisbury
      The Gunpowder Plot.
1612   Death of Robert earl of Salisbury.
      Death of Henry prince of Wales.
1613   Robert Carr created earl of Somerset.
      Marriage of Princess Elizabeth to Elector Palatine.
1616   Trial of earl and countess of Somerset.
1617   George Villiers created earl of Buckingham.
1618   Execution of Sir Walter Raleigh.
1619   Outbreak of war in Bohemia.
      Death of Queen Anne (of Denmark).
1621   Fall of the lord chancellor, Francis Bacon.
1623   Prince Charles and Villiers make a journey to Madrid.
      Villiers created duke of Buckingham.
1625   James I dies at Theobalds.

INDEX